INSIDERS' GUIDE® SERIES

INSIDERS' GUIDE® TO

KANSAS CITY

FOURTH EDITION

KATIE VAN LUCHENE

INSIDERS' GUIDE

GUILFORD, CONNECTICUT
AN IMPRINT OF GLOBE PEQUOT PRESS

All the information in this guidebook is subject to change. We recommend that you call ahead to obtain current information before traveling.

INSIDERS' GUIDE ®

Editor: Amy Lyons
Project Editor: Lynn Zelem
Layout Artist: Kevin Mak
Text Design: Sheryl Kober
Maps by XNR Productions, Inc. © Morris Book Publishing, LLC

ISSN 1542-7404
ISBN 978-0-7627-5343-7

Printed in the United States of America
10 9 8 7 6 5 4 3 2 1

CONTENTS

Directory of Maps

ABOUT THE AUTHOR

Katie Van Luchene is a Kansas City native who is often asked where to find the best local food, little-known shopping venues, and favorite hot spots. A natural-born storyteller, she shares her enthusiasm for the town she loves through her roles as the editor of *KC Magazine* and author of this book.

ACKNOWLEDGMENTS

We're tweaking a famous phrase to say that behind every great city is a great woman. In the case of Kansas City's renaissance, there are actually several female leaders to thank. When Kay Barnes was mayor of Kansas City, Missouri, she made good on her political promise to create a vibrant urban core filled with residences and commerce, new attractions and arts venues.

Kudos as well to Carol Marinovich, Kay's mayoral counterpart in Kansas City, Kansas, who brought us the Kansas Speedway. Today the entertainment district surrounding the racetrack is the state's most popular tourist destination. Best of all, it gave new pride to a city that had taken a backseat to its more glamorous sister for decades.

Meanwhile, Mayor Peggy Dunn (the only one of the trio still in office) has turned suburban Leawood, Kansas, into an exhilarating display of shopping and entertainment venues. There's even an old-fashioned town square complete with an outdoor skating rink surrounded by condos and unique shops.

And while Brenda Tinnen doesn't hold a political office, she's the Queen of Kansas City in our book. As the general manager of our new Sprint Center arena, this hometown girl parlayed her previous roles at the STAPLES Center and Kodak Theatre into bringing a dazzling list of headliners to Kansas City. Less than two years after opening, Sprint Center was herealded as one of the best concert venues—number 5 in the U.S. and number 16 in the world.

To these four fierce and fabulous women, we are forever in your debt.

Hats off as well to the artists, musicians, chefs, historians, and innkeepers on both sides of the state line whose passions and talents make this city so enticing for visitors and residents alike. And to the thousands of mentors, teachers, caregivers, philanthropists, and volunteers: You're the reason we're known as the Heartland.

I'm saving my most personal thank-you note for my husband, the handsome guy by my side as I explore this marvelous city. Jerry Foulds, you continue to be my best friend and my hero.

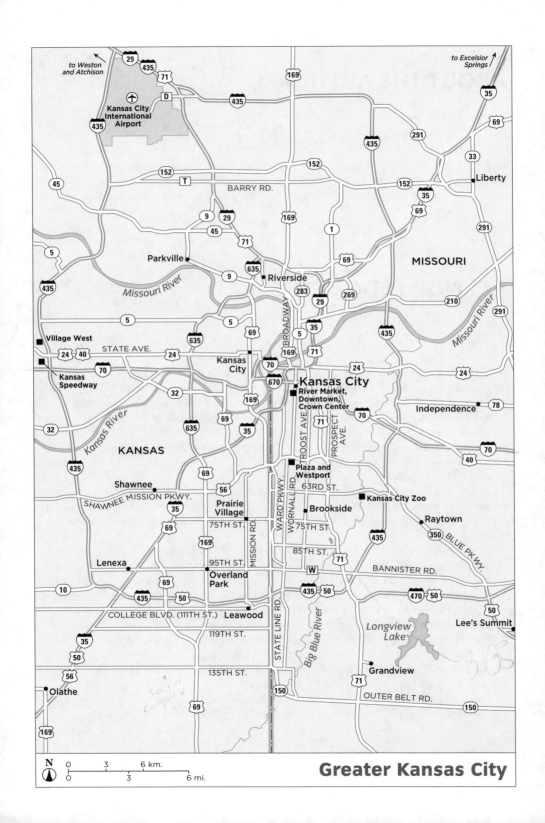

Greater Kansas City

to Weston and Atchison

to Excelsior Springs!

Kansas City International Airport

BARRY RD.

Parkville

Riverside

MISSOURI

Liberty

Missouri River

Missouri River

Village West

STATE AVE.

Kansas City

Kansas Speedway

Kansas City

River Market, Downtown, Crown Center

Independence

Kansas River

KANSAS

Shawnee

SHAWNEE MISSION PKWY.

Plaza and Westport

63RD ST.

Kansas City Zoo

Prairie Village

Brookside

Raytown

75TH ST.

75TH ST.

BLUE PKWY.

Lenexa

85TH ST.

BANNISTER RD.

Overland Park

95TH ST.

COLLEGE BLVD. (111TH ST.) Leawood

119TH ST.

Lee's Summit

Longview Lake

Big Blue River

135TH ST.

Olathe

OUTER BELT RD.

Grandview

WARD PKWY.

WORNALL RD.

MISSION RD.

STATE LINE RD.

ROOST AVE.

PROSPECT AVE.

BROADWAY

N

0   3   6 km.

0   3   6 mi.

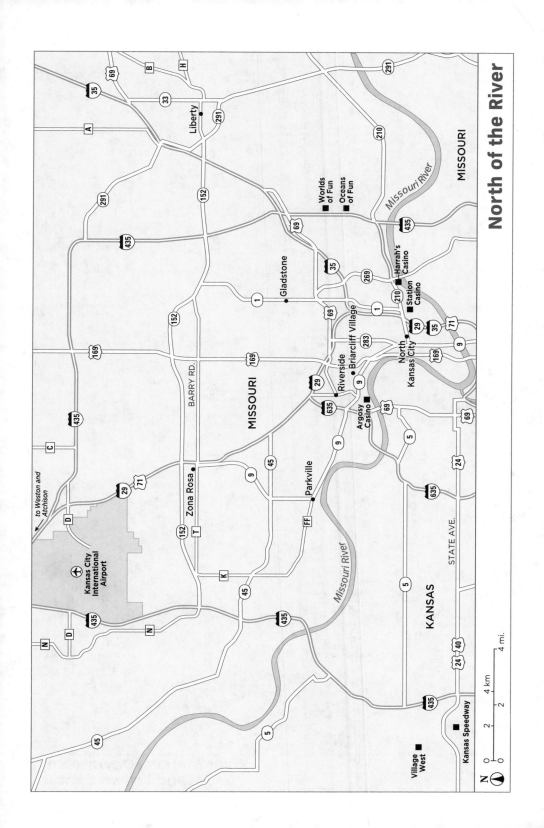

North of the River

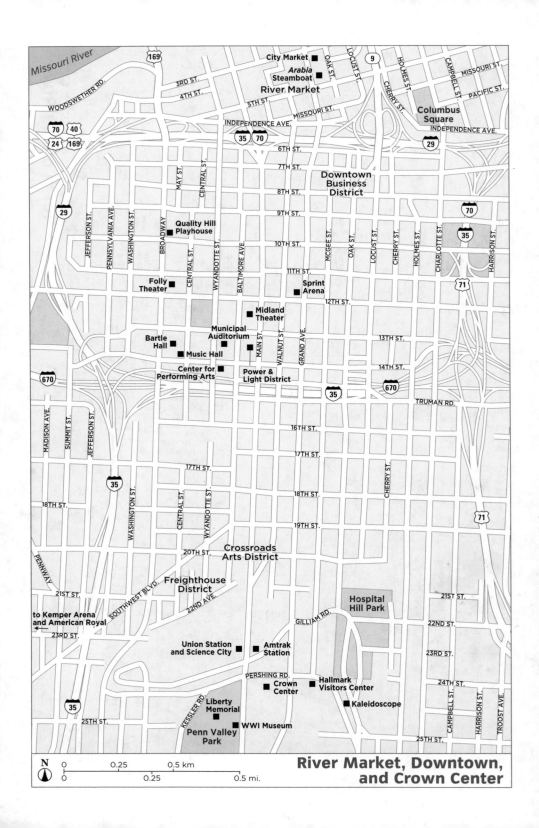

River Market, Downtown, and Crown Center

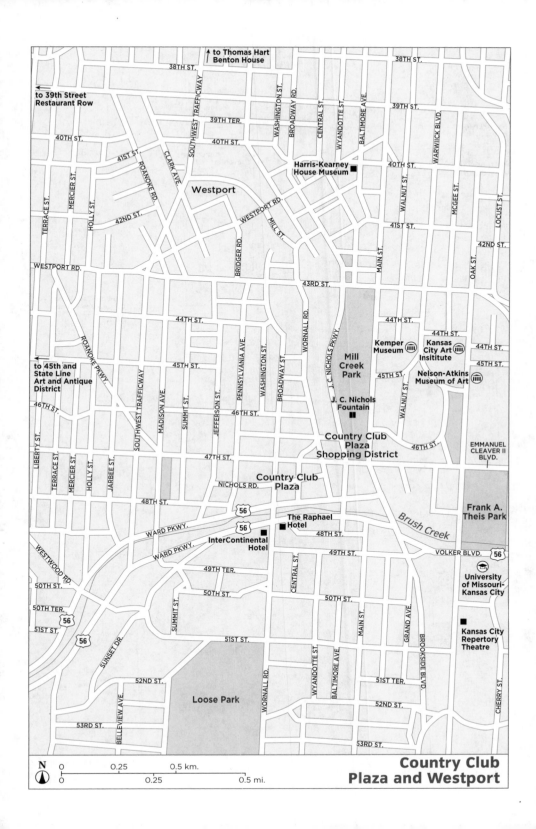

Country Club Plaza and Westport

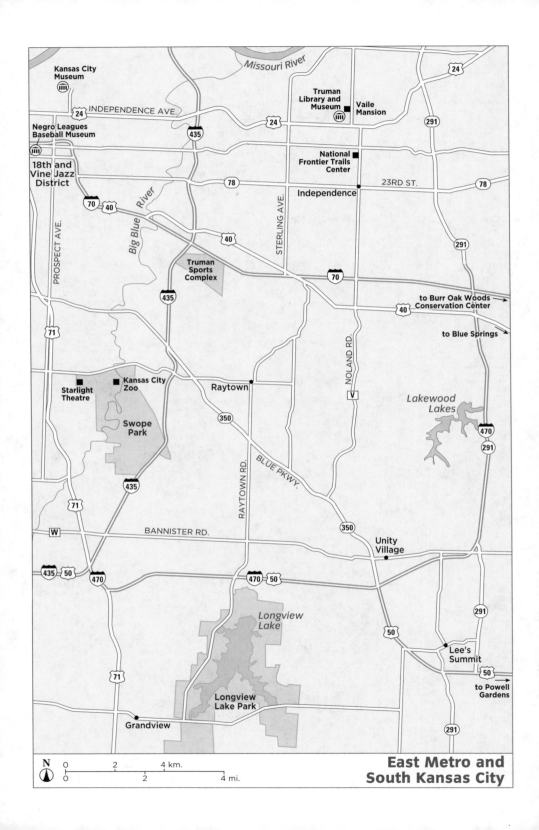

Missouri River

Kansas City Museum

INDEPENDENCE AVE.

Truman Library and Museum

Vaile Mansion

Negro Leagues Baseball Museum

18th and Vine Jazz District

National Frontier Trails Center

Independence

23RD ST.

Big Blue River

STERLING AVE.

PROSPECT AVE.

Truman Sports Complex

to Burr Oak Woods Conservation Center

to Blue Springs

NOLAND RD.

Starlight Theatre

Kansas City Zoo

Swope Park

Raytown

Lakewood Lakes

BLUE PKWY.

RAYTOWN RD.

BANNISTER RD.

Unity Village

Longview Lake

Lee's Summit

to Powell Gardens

Longview Lake Park

Grandview

N

0   2   4 km.
0   2   4 mi.

**East Metro and
South Kansas City**

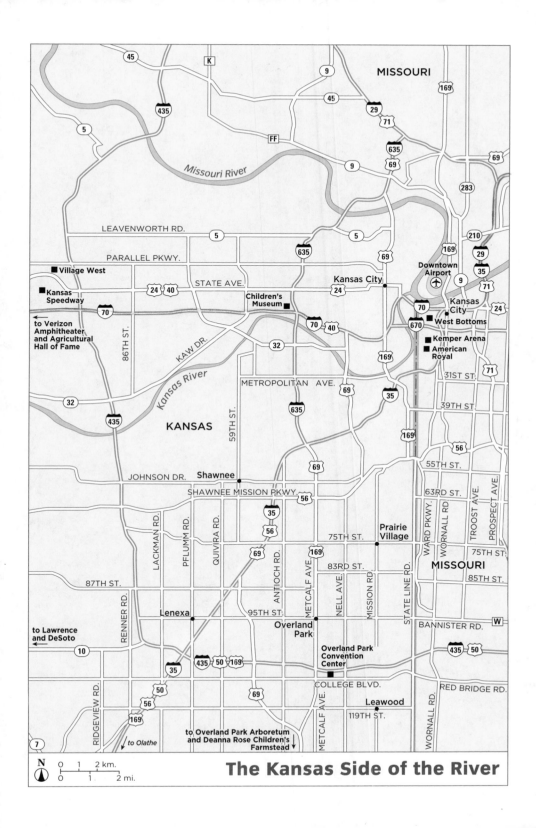

The Kansas Side of the River

HOW TO USE THIS BOOK

Naturally, as a travel guide, this book is ideal for anyone planning a visit to Kansas City, whether it's a vacation, as home base for a series of day trips, or a few days before or after a business meeting. Consider this your VIP pass to the best Kansas City has to offer in attractions, dining, nightlife, and shopping. As a mover and a shaker, you won't want to miss a thing.

We've also put together a helpful guide just for the *movers*. Are you considering a move to the Kansas City area or do you already live here? Be sure to check out the blue-tabbed pages at the back of the book, where you will find the **Living Here** appendix that offers sections on relocation, real estate, education, health care, and media. The relocation section also includes a listing of service providers, such as gas companies and new-neighbor groups, to help you quickly feel at home in your new town.

Traveler or transplant: Welcome! But perhaps the optimum use for this book is for the reader who lives in Kansas City but hasn't really lived it up yet. You'll tap your foot at jam sessions, talk to natives and newcomers, meet historians and artists and gardeners and zookeepers. And we guarantee you'll read about restaurants you didn't know existed, find hidden retail gems, meet some fascinating people, and discover new reasons to be proud of your hometown.

For pioneers headed to Santa Fe, Oregon, and California, Kansas City was the gateway to the future. But for you it might be the gateway to your past. Independence, Missouri, is home to not one but two vast genealogical libraries. Family-history seekers come by the busloads to the Mid-Continent Public Library's Genealogy and Local History branch and the Jackson County Historical Society Archives and Research Library in the Independence Square Courthouse. The National Archives for the seven central states is now open, housing more than 60 million pages of historical records.

So whatever your reason for purchasing this book, we sincerely thank you and hope you'll enjoy it—and Kansas City—to its fullest. *NOTE:* Unless otherwise indicated all listings in this book are located in Kansas City, Missouri; other cities and towns will be designated MO (Missouri) or KS (Kansas).

HOW THIS BOOK IS ORGANIZED

Travelers familiar with the Insiders' Guide series will recognize the book's easy-to-use format. Those friendly features you appreciate are all here, including Insiders' Tips—designated with an 🛈 —that let you in on local secrets and Close-ups that provide an in-depth look at some of our top attributes.

Like all Insiders' Guides, this one has been organized to help make the most of your trip to the City of Surprises, from how to navigate our streets to where to find the culinary dish you crave. Lucky for you, no matter what food you fancy—whether it's a luscious risotto studded with truffles (even this carnivorous city has a strong vegetarian contingency!), the Kansas City strip that made our town famous, or a garlicky chicken spiedini—it's never more than 20 or so minutes away.

If, however, your passion is dashing for a dressing room at a chichi boutique, you're in luck. In Shopping you'll discover the inside scoop on where to find fashions, antiques, decor, and discount shoes.

In The Arts you'll discover our world-class museums, symphony, ballet, live theater, and opera. Next we suggest you head to Annual Events and Festivals. Chances are there's a music festival, street fair, tour of a historical area, or neighborhood block party going on right now. Looking for more outdoor fun? Spend an afternoon at the Kansas City Zoo, one of our beautiful arboretums and lakes, or one of three exciting waterparks, and you won't miss the mountains or beach. Grab a towel and open the book to Parks, Lakes, and Recreation. If you'd rather watch sports than participate, you won't go wanting here: With Royals and T-Bones baseball, Chiefs football, and professional hockey and soccer teams, there's a game in town nearly every week. And our Kansas Speedway offers NASCAR fans an exciting day at the races. Start your engines in Sports.

Whew! That should get you started!

AREA OVERVIEW

Kansas City has always been known as a vibrant mix of urban sophistication and small-town friendliness. But now there are five billion more reasons to love us. That's the price tag for our downtown makover alone.

There's also more of us to love. When you say "Kansas City," you're really talking about one diverse, exciting region that encompasses two states and 50 unique communities. Thanks to recent expansions, Greater Kansas City spans 18 counties in more than 9,100 square miles filled with 2.4 million happy, friendly folks.

Our unified advantage—along with our central location, well-educated and productive workforce, and low cost of running a business or buying a home—makes us a magnet for corporations to build headquarters here. Our attributes made it easy for Forbes.com to name us one of the "Best Cities to Get Ahead."

Although Kansas City is a vast metroplex, locals think of home as separate neighborhoods (such as Brookside), destinations (Country Club Plaza), or geographical areas (the Northland). Before your eyes glaze over, we've divided the region into five handy little areas, described below. Maps of each are found in the front of this book. We'll refer to these areas throughout the book. And remember, just about any destination in the metro is 20 minutes away or less.

METROPOLITAN AREAS

North of the River

What was once considered just a pretty area to build a home near a golf course or a bluff overlooking Downtown Kansas City has become an exciting destination filled with shopping and entertainment districts. Leading the pack is the historic city of Parkville, with storefronts filled with art galleries and festive eateries. Adding to the mix are new shopping and dining centers, Briarcliff Village and Zona Rosa.

River Market, Downtown, Crown Center

Here's where it all began 160 years ago. And despite the mass exodus to the suburbs during the 1950s and 1960s, the central core remains the heart of our city. Fortunately it's coming back into its own, thanks to entertainment venues such as the River Market, newly refurbished urban lofts that draw upscale professionals, and the vibrant Power & Light District. The 18th and Vine Historic Jazz District, which gave the world the jazz jam, is the still the place to hear some of the region's most talented musicians.

The Crossroads Arts District has attracted artist studios and some of the area's most dynamic restaurants, while just south, Crown Center offers a stay-and-play mecca for travelers.

Country Club Plaza and Westport

Any trip to Kansas City must include a day of shopping on the Country Club Plaza, a 14-city-block potpourri of more than 180 stores, boutiques, and dining establishments set among 40 fountains and 50 public works of art. If the Rodeo Drive of the Midwest is a little too upscale for you, Historic Westport offers a more laid-back social scene, along with casual dining options.

Nearby is the popular 39th Street corridor, with a number of home-grown restaurants that range from upscale to friendly dives, and the 45th and State Line Art and Antiques district will thrill the collectibles hunter. This is also where to get your fill of breathtaking art collections at the Nelson-Atkins Museum of Art and the Kemper Contemporary Museum of Art. Take a short drive south past neighborhoods filled with stately mansions to find Brookside, an old-fashioned Main Street USA enclave with a collection of cafes, unique shops and galleries, and even a five-and-dime store complete with creaking wooden floors and penny candy.

East Metro and South Kansas City

Independence, Missouri, is still Harry's town, with the Truman Presidential Museum and Library all spiffed up and ready to tour along with his home. Local do-gooders Kenneth and Cindy McClain have lovingly restored the historic Independence Square into a vibrant neighborhood featuring dozens of shops, eateries, and attractions. Nearby is the sports complex that also bears the 33rd president's name and is home to the Royals baseball and Chiefs football teams. South Kansas City's other claim to fame is the Kansas City Zoo, set within the Swope Park, second only to New York City's Central Park in acreage. This majestic green space also holds Starlight Theatre where Broadway shows and headliners perform under the heavens.

The Kansas Side of the River

Wyandotte County is where NASCAR fans get their fill of racing action. Bring your earplugs to the Kansas Speedway, and your credit cards to the shopping havens sprinkled throughout nearby Prairie Village, Overland Park, and Leawood. Don't forget your water bottle. Scattered throughout these suburban ZIP codes are acres of hiking and biking trails and bucolic parks and lakes.

OUTLYING AREAS

You can learn more about each county's many charms by logging onto their Web sites, listed in "Community Profiles" found elsewhere in this chapter. But for now, here are snapshots of some of our favorite new neighbors.

Atchison, Atchison County, KS

Located 50 miles northwest of downtown Kansas City, the town of Atchison is known for its picturesque setting on the Missouri River and its favorite daughter, Amelia Earhart. Another claim to fame is Nell Hill's, a home decor emporium that draws busloads of shoppers from surrounding states. Discover details about this proud little community in Day Trips and Weekend Getaways.

St. Joseph, Buchanan County, MO

Draw, partner! St. Joseph provides a wealth of attractions that celebrate our Wild West roots, such as the Jesse James home and the Pony Express Museum.

Excelsior Springs, Clay County, MO

This area was once dubbed the "Health Center of the Nation" thanks to its therapeutic waters. Resorts like the Elms Hotel catered to President Harry S. Truman and Al Capone (but never on the same weekend).

Lawrence, Douglas County, KS

To University of Kansas alumni, Lawrence has always seemed like part of Kansas City as Kansas Highway 10 becomes bumper-to-bumper Jayhawkers going back and forth on game day. With an exciting arts community and thriving downtown, it's no wonder Lawrence is one of the fastest growing areas in the region.

THE CENTER OF IT ALL

Although it's true that Kansas City is just 250 miles from the geographical center of the United States, we like to think that the term "heartland" refers more to our lovable people than the logistics. After all, we're home to Hallmark Cards, Helzberg Diamonds, and Russell Stover Candies—so you might say Cupid is a permanent resident.

We're all heart, too, when it comes to helping people in need and supporting the arts. Consider this: Among Kansas City households that donated, the average contribution was $3,375, or 50 percent above the U.S. average of $2,247 (estimated for 2007). When we're not giving, we're taking—taking

Vital Statistics

Mayors: Mark Funkhouser (Kansas City, MO) and Joe Reardon (Kansas City, KS)

Governors: Jay Nixon (Missouri) and Mark Parkinson (Kansas), who took office after Governor Kathleen Sebelius became Secretary to the Department of Health and Human Services in April 2009.

United States senators: Christopher Bond and Claire McCaskill (Missouri); Sam Brownback and Pat Roberts (Kansas)

Average maximum temperatures (degrees Fahrenheit): 38 (January); 65 (April); 89 (July); 69 (October)

Average minimum temperatures (degrees Fahrenheit): 21 (January); 45 (April); 70 (July); 48 (October)

Average precipitation (in inches): 1.30 (January); 3.37 (April); 4.02 (July); 2.98 (October)

Average annual snowfall (in inches): 21

Total population (as of July, 2007): 2,307,357 (29th largest U.S. city)

Kansas counties: Atchison, Leavenworth, Wyandotte, Johnson, Franklin, Miami, and Linn

Missouri counties: Caldwell, Clinton, Clay, Ray, Jackson, Lafayette, Cass, Johnson, and Bates

Total combined region: More than 9,100 square miles; 132 miles from the northwest tip of Atchison County to the southeast corner of Bates County. And this may surprise you; More than 103 square miles of our metroplex is water.

Median age: 35.4

Average household income: $66,700

Median price for house: $144,200 (vs. $197,100 nationally)

Major airports: Charles B. Wheeler Downtown Airport, Kansas City International Airport

Major interstates: I-435, I-35, I-70, I-29, I-635, I-670

Total consumer spending: $35.9 billion

Hotel and motel rooms in the area: More than 30,000

Nicknames: City of Fountains, City of Surprises, The City Beautiful, Number 1 "Kid-Friendly City" (Overland Park, KS)

Major colleges and universities: Avila University, Johnson County Community College, MidAmerica Nazarene University, Park University, Rockhurst University, University of Missouri–Kansas City, William Jewell College

Famous Kansas Citians: Harry S. Truman, Jean Harlow, Casey Stengel, Ginger Rogers, writer Calvin Trillin, Walter Cronkite, golfer Tom Watson, handbag designer Kate Spade, actors Chris Cooper and Paul Rudd, jazz musician Pat Metheny, and Maurice Greene, once the fastest man on Earth

Just passing through (important people who lived in Kansas City): Count Basie, Ernest Hemingway (journalist at *The Kansas City Star* for six months), and Walt Disney

Homegrown companies: Hallmark Cards, Sprint-Nextel, H&R Block, Helzberg Diamonds, Garmin International, AMC Theatres, Lee Jeans, Russell Stover Candies, American Century Investments, Applebee's, Black & Veatch, YRC Worldwide, and Three Dog Bakery

Products invented here: McDonald's Happy Meal, K.C. Masterpiece Barbecue Sauce, Teflon coating, Valomilk, Eskimo Pies, Hostess Twinkies, Rival Crock-Pot, the multiscreen movie theater, the outdoor shopping center, and the swing style of jazz

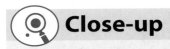 **Close-up**

Notable Events in Kansas City's History:

June 26, 1804: Lewis and Clark camp here during their first expedition to the Louisiana Territory.

1821: Francois Chouteau, a Frenchman from St. Louis, establishes a fur company at the Kaw River.

1821: Missouri is admitted to the Union.

1833: John Calvin McCoy opens a supply store 4 miles south of the river on the Santa Fe Trail.

June 1, 1850: Town of Kansas (in Missouri) is incorporated.

1854: Kansas-Nebraska Act; many historians consider this the beginning of the Civil War.

1859: Thriving town welcomes 1,500 steamboats.

July 3, 1869: Hannibal Bridge opens, first rail bridge to span the Missouri River and provide a direct rail link to Chicago.

1871: Stockyards expand, giving us the start as prime meatpacking center. That means steaks, folks.

1889: Town officially becomes Kansas City, Missouri.

1899: City's first convention hall is built.

1900: Convention hall burns to the ground. Three months later it's rebuilt in time to host Democratic Convention.

1903: Missouri River floods the West Bottoms, leaving 22,000 people homeless.

1905: William Strang Jr. builds an interurban railway to encourage residential area in what is now Overland Park, Kansas.

1910: Joyce Clyde Hall sells postcards out of his suitcase at the YMCA—the start of Hallmark Cards.

1914: Union Station is built; during its heyday, 271 trains passed through daily.

1915: Parks and boulevard system is built, earning us the title "City Beautiful."

1921: The Liberty Memorial site is dedicated; completion is on November 11, 1926.

1923: The Country Club Plaza opens for business.

1931: While the rest of the country sagged under the Depression, Kansas City thrived, thanks to the Ten-Year Plan, which created jobs and saw the construction of the City Hall, new courthouse, and miles of new roads.

1933: Nelson Gallery of Art opens.

1943: Kansas City Monarchs, the all-black baseball team, celebrates 43 straight wins.

October 15, 1949: WDAF, Kansas City's first television station, begins regular programming.

Friday the 13th, 1951: The Kansas River floods the West Bottoms again, leaving more than 20,000 homeless.

1960: The Chiefs football team plays its first season in Kansas City.

April 8, 1969: The Kansas City Royals play their first game.

January 12, 1970: Chiefs win Super Bowl IV, beating the Minnesota Vikings 23–7.

1972: River Quay, entertainment area near the River Market, takes off.

1972: Kansas City International Airport opens.

1973: Worlds of Fun opens, as does Crown Center's hotel and entertainment complex.

1976: Kansas City hosts the Republican National Convention.

1985: Royals win the World Series.

1988: City hosts the NCAA Final Four basketball tournament.

1991: Emanuel Cleaver II becomes the first African American mayor of Kansas City. He serves until 1999, when Kay Barnes is elected the city's first female mayor.

1996: Voters across five counties pass the Bi-state Cultural Tax, the first two-state effort of its kind in the country. Work begins to restore Union Station.

1997: The 18th & Vine district comes back to life with jazz venues, the Kansas City Jazz Museum, and the Negro Leagues Baseball Museum.

2000: Kansas City, Missouri's urban areas begin a revitalization period with warehouses being converted to lofts and art studios. The Crossroads Arts District is born.

2001: Kansas Speedway, home to NASCAR races, opens in Kansas City, Kansas.

2004: Groundbreaking takes place for the South Loop redevelopment area including the H&R Block Headquarters, the Power & Light District, the Sprint Center, and the renovated President Hotel. Filming starts on Mending the Heart of an American City, the documentary that will capture it all. Kansas City International Airport completes a three-year, $258 million renovation project.

2006: H&R Block's world headquarters opens downtown. The Kauffman Performing Arts Center breaks ground at 16th and Wyandotte.

2007: Kansas City welcomes the new Power & Light (P&L) District, Sprint Center, and Bartle Hall ballroom expansion. The city's cultural world expands with the Bloch Building at the Nelson-Atkins Museum of Art and the Nerman Gallery of Contemporary Art at Johnson County Community College.

2008: The P&L District continues to add new restaurants and nightspots. The Sprint Center draws more than 1.3 million people to Downtown. After a $28 million renovation, Midland Theatre reopens.

2009: A renovated AMC Mainstreet opens within the P&L District. Schlitterbahn Vacation Village's first phase opens near Village West in Kansas City, Kansas. The Sheraton Sports Complex Hotel shows off its Coco Key Water Resort, the largest indoor water park in Missouri. The Kansas City Royals unveils gorgeous updates to its Kauffman Stadium. Powell Gardens, the 915-acre botanical oasis, opens Heartland Harvest Garden, a 12-acre first-of-a-kind feature. The Kauffman Center for the Performing Arts, designed by famed architect Moshe Safdie, takes shape. When completed in 2011, the structure will host performances by the Kansas City Symphony, Ballet and Lyric Opera as well as world-class artists and entertainers.

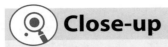 **Close-up**

Resources for More Information

Hungry for more? Although this book provides a portable entree into the City of Surprises, following are sources to enhance your visit.

MEDIA

Our daily newspaper, *The Kansas City Star*, publishes several photo-rich books on a variety of subjects from history to barbecue to the Flood of '51. See the entire library at www.thekansascitystore.com or call (816) 234-4636. To check on current news and weather reports, visit the paper's Web site, www.kcstar.com.

KC Magazine provides a well-rounded look at the town's most interesting people and places. Each monthly issue also includes a calendar of events, restaurant reviews, and a dining guide. It's a must-read for locals and welcome lifeline for expatriates. Call (913) 894-6923 for subscription information, or check out www.kcmag.com. Every city needs an "alternative" paper and ours is *The Pitch*. Read it for irreverent takes on culture, music, film, and politics; if nothing else read it for Charles Ferruzza's restaurant reviews. It's available free at kiosks all over town, or at www.pitch.com.

An online source, www.presentmagazine.com, gives an interesting view of the food, music, and art scene in town. Young hipsters get their news at *Ink*, a free paper available in kiosks and locations throughout the metro. Find it online at www.inkkc.com.

TOURISM SITES

Well before your trip, access these chamber of commerce and visitor center Web sites for up-to-the-minute information about festivals and events. Or call to receive brochures, maps, and special offers by mail.

CONVENTION AND VISITORS BUREAU OF GREATER KANSAS CITY

If you only have the time—or patience—to contact one visitor center, this should be it. Its quarterly magazine, *Visit KC*, lists a calendar of events, information about dining and nightlife, kid-friendly activities, and even area day trips. Call (816) 221-5242 or (800) 767-7700; or log on to www.visitkc.com. Satellite locations at Union Station and Crown Center offer a wide variety of brochures and maps.

CONTACT INFORMATION FOR OTHER AREA TOWNS

Atchison, KS
(913) 367-2427
www.atchisonkansas.net

Bonner Springs, KS
(913) 422-1020
www.bonnersprings.org

in the sights and smells of our town, that is. Some of the best aromas come from hickory smoke swirling around the barbecue restaurants that dot our city. We'll admit we didn't invent this method of slow cooking—we just perfected it.

Just ask the members of the Kansas City Barbecue Society, the largest organization devoted to the art form in the world. The group, whose motto is "Barbecue: not just for breakfast anymore," sanctions more than 140 national barbecue contests each year, including the granddaddy of 'em all, the American Royal, held next door to our celebrated stockyards each fall. But don't box us in as just a place to get barbecue—or world-famous steaks, for that matter. We offer the hungry visitor a variety of dining experiences that rival any other cosmo-

Clay County, MO
(816) 468-4989
www.clayedc.com
www.desotoks.org

Excelsior Springs, MO
(816) 630-6161
www.exspgschamber.com

Independence, MO
(816) 325-7111
www.visitindependence.com

Jackson County, MO
(816) 881-4440
www.jacksoncounty.gov

Johnson County, KS
(913) 715-8999
www.jocogov.org

Kearney, MO
(816) 628-4229
www.kearneychamber.org

Lawrence, KS
(785) 865-4411
www.lawrencechamber.com

Leawood, KS
(913) 339-6700
www.leawood.org

Lee's Summit, MO
(816) 525-2424
www.lschamber.com

Lenexa, KS
(913) 888-1414
www.lenexa.org

Miami County, KS
(913) 294-4045
www.miamicountyks.org

North Kansas City, MO
(816) 274-6000
www.nkc.org

Olathe, KS
(913) 764-1050
www.olathe.org

Overland Park, KS
(913) 491-0123
www.opcvb.org

Parkville, MO
(816) 741-7676
www.parkvillemo.com

Platte County, MO
(816) 270-2119
www.plattecountyedc.com

St. Joseph, MO
(816) 764-6566
www.saintjoseph.com

Weston, MO
(816) 640-2909
www.westonmo.com

Wyandotte County, KS
(913) 321-5800
www.visitthedot.com

politan city. You'll find plenty of James Beard award winners among our roster of chefs.

Have a hankering for Argentine chimichurri sauce or crawfish étouffée? How about authentic pollo mole, osso buco Milanese, sauerbraten, or spanikopita? Do you savor sushi or designer pizza? Brittany-style mussels or Moroccan lamb kabobs on your mind? Dim sum sound good? Or would an ice-cold beer and chili dog hit the spot?

Answer yes to any of these culinary cues and you've come to the right place. And make sure to visit locally owned restaurants for a true Kansas City experience. Some of the best are members of the KC Originals, a group of around 48 eateries listed at www.kcoriginals.com.

i See jaw-dropping views of Kansas City at the City Hall Observation Deck at 414 East 12th St., the top of the Liberty Memorial at Penn Valley Park, or two restaurants within the Crown Center area: Skies (our only revolving dining choice) and Benton's.

JAZZ AND BLUES

Our music came to us from cities such as New Orleans by way of the Mississippi and Missouri Rivers. And, like our barbecue that incorporates tomatoes for texture and molasses for sweetness, we created our own distinct recipe for jazz.

Musicians such as Count Basie took aspects of gospel, ragtime, and blues and turned them into swing, an infectious rhythm that got people out of their chairs to dance at the Reno Club in 1936. Charlie "Bird" Parker's alto sax propelled the art form even further with a new manic yet compelling sound called bebop.

The 12th Street nightspots where these geniuses jammed are long gone, but you can still hear live music in clubs, restaurants, and festivals all over town. In fact, you can experience a rousing jazz jam at 12 O'Clock Jump, held every Sat at midnight at the Mutual Musician's Foundation at 18th & Vine. A jazz museum and nightclub in this historic neighborhood celebrates the music and provides a forum for today's talented newcomers.

OUR CLIMATE, BOTH WEATHER-WISE AND CULTURALLY

You'll find Kansas City to be a casual, friendly place where shirtsleeves—even nice shorts and sandals in summer—are appropriate for most restaurants. When in doubt call to ask, but long gone are the days when diners were handed ill-fitting jackets in order to be seated.

As for the temperature, the old saw "if you don't like the weather, just wait a few minutes and it will change" is certainly true here. Situated in the temperate zone, Kansas City experiences an annual average temperature of a pleasant 55 degrees, with a few days in winter that drop below 20 and a few in summer that go above 90.

It's hard to pick a favorite time to visit. Spring comes early in the heartland, with our trees and flowers exploding in a display of fragrance and color. Summer means cornflower blue skies, emerald lawns, ripe red tomatoes at the farmers' markets, and enough outdoor festivals to keep you from noticing the humidity.

In fall the landscape becomes a jewelry-store window of crimson and gold as elms, maples, and giant oaks take on autumn's hues. In fact, many first-time visitors are amazed at the forest-like vistas throughout our city. During winter the colors—although man-made—are no less brilliant as 250,000 holiday lights outline the towers and spires of the Country Club Plaza, our spectacular Spanish-style outdoor shopping and entertainment district. The Zona Rosa entertainment district, in the Northland, also goes "bling" for the holidays with vintage lighting displays.

You'll be glad you brought a just-in-case umbrella any time of year. Here in the home of corn-fed beef, we rarely complain about the rain that grows that golden crop.

i Travelers on a budget should start at the Kansas City Convention and Visitors Bureau Web site, www.visitkc.com, for special offers and ready-to-print coupons for some of Kansas City's most popular attractions. Recent values included two-for tickets to attractions, discounted rates at hotels, and wine-and-dine offers at some of our city's most popular restaurants. And you can't beat free; check the list of places to visit that are priceless. One of our favorites? The thrilling view of Downtown from the 30-story Art Deco City Hall, the fourth-tallest city hall in the world. Check often, because selections change.

GETTING HERE, GETTING AROUND

Arriving in Kansas City is a snap. After all, we are nearly the center of the country, so just about any way you choose to come—plane, train, Volkswagen bus or limo—you're mere hours away. It's the *leaving* you might find difficult. Visitors are often hooked on our many charms and start dialing real estate offices. Until then, as you'll see in this chapter, finding your way around town is easy. And we're such a friendly bunch that if you so much as look lost while navigating the streets of Kansas City, chances are a kind native will offer to help.

GETTING TO KANSAS CITY

As you're driving in from the airport or on an interstate you might wonder, "Where's the city?" We assure you, it's here—and worth the trip. But before you see our skyline rising like the Emerald City out of limestone bluffs, you'll pass fields of corn and beautiful forested hillsides. Relax and enjoy the view as your vehicle becomes a decompression chamber: You're in Kansas City now, where the pace is carefree and the natives are so nice that you'll feel right at home.

Getting to the City from the Airport

Chances are if you're flying the friendly skies, you'll be coming into **Kansas City International Airport,** or KCI. When making travel plans, remember that the airport is listed as MCI.

The **KCI Shuttle** provides transportation between the airport and more than 90 metro-area hotels and runs from 4 a.m. to 11:55 p.m. daily. Ticket counters are located near each airline baggage claim area at Terminal A—gates 1, 15, 30; Terminal B—gates 31, 50, 60; or dial "5000" on a white airport courtesy phone. Expect to pay around $17 per person from the airport to the Plaza. Call (816) 243-5000 or (800) 243-6383 for more information, or log on to www.kctg.com. Nonstop travel to and from Johnson County is available for $45 for up to three passengers.

A private car service is a convenient way to go—and besides, isn't it an ego-booster to be greeted at the airport with your name printed on a sign? **Carey Limos** has courteous drivers and plush Lincoln Town Cars at your disposal. Call (816) 471-1234 or (800) 808-1131. Another quality service is **Leader Limo,** which offers luxury sedans, vans, minicoaches, and stretch limos. Call (866) 770-5323 or (816) 753-5323, or visit www.leaderlimo.com.

Other Area Airports

Although Kansas City International handles all scheduled commercial flights, several smaller fields support private pilots flying into town. The **Charles B. Wheeler Downtown Airport** serves corporate jets and charter flights. For more information call (816) 243-5248 or check www.flymkc.com. Other airports include the **New Century AirCenter** in Johnson County, (913) 782-5335; **Independence Memorial Airport,** (816) 795-8774; and **Lee's Summit Municipal Airport,** (816) 251-2492.

Private air charter companies serving the metropolitan area are **Air Charter Team,** (816) 283-3280 or (800) 205-6610, and **Executive Beechcraft Inc.,** (816) 842-8484 or its KCI location at (816) 243-6440.

GROUND TRANSPORTATION

Bus Services

The Kansas City Area Transportation Authority maintains the city bus system we call the Metro, which serves primarily the central corridor of Kansas City, Missouri. The **Metro Area Express** (MAX to his friends) is a rapid-transit service that runs from the River Market to the Plaza and all points in between including downtown and Crown Center, the trendy Crossroads Arts District, and Westport. Stylish MAX buses use dedicated lanes during rush hour. That means the average travel time from the Plaza to downtown is less than 17 minutes, with no fumbling for quarters to feed the meter once you get there.

MAX is rolling seven days a week, from 5 a.m. to 1 a.m., and transit times range from every 9 minutes during rush hour to every 30 minutes after 7 p.m. Even the price is right at $1.50, which includes free transfers to all other buses. MAX has an easily identified logo. Visit www.kcata.org for details and routes. Not many SUV-wielding sub-urbanites take the bus, but those who do have access to the Johnson County Transit, affection-ately called **"The Jo."** For schedules and fares, call (913) 362-3500 or visit www.thejo.com.

Taxis

You'll find taxis in Kansas City; just don't expect to find them queued up on every street corner as in Chicago. You will find them at most hotels in town and at the Power & Light District. Most taxi companies have direct-connection phones at the airport, but a cab ride to the Plaza will cost around $40. Most large hotels have taxi stands, or call **Yellow Cab** at (816) 471-5000 for round-the-clock service. The entire fleet is air-conditioned and drivers accept credit cards. Wheelchair-accessible vehicles are available.

Trains and Interstate Buses

The renovated **Union Station** is so spectacular you might miss your train because you can't help ogling the gorgeous architecuture, rich plaster work, and painted details on the ceiling. The waiting room features five of the original wooden benches and a large, historic wall clock.

Passengers enter at the northeast corner of the Grand Hall. Short-term parking is available in front of the station; long-term parking is provided in the covered parking structure in the back.

Two trains with daily departures serve Kansas City: the Southwest Chief, between Chicago and Los Angeles, and the Missouri River Runner, which travels between Kansas City and St. Louis. For station information only call (816) 421-3622. For reservations and schedules call (800) USA-RAIL or visit www.amtrak.com.

Greyhound and **Jefferson Bus Lines** share terminals at 1101 Troost Ave. in downtown Kansas City, Missouri. Call (800) 231-2222 or (816) 221-2835 for fare and schedule information. A word of caution here: This location is not the saf-est in town, especially at night.

Car Travel

Depending on where you're staying during your visit, you can certainly enjoy areas of Kansas City without a car. On the Country Club Plaza, for example, some of the city's best dining, shop-ping, and nightspots are just a lovely stroll away from several fine hotels. Stay at Crown Center and you have an entire world of attractions at your feet. Or choose a downtown hotel with easy access to the Power & Light District, the Sprint Center, and our cultural centers. However, if your lodging is in a suburb like Overland Park, you'll need a car to get around. There's nothing scarier than watching a group of conventioneers with name tags sprint across six busy lanes of Metcalf Avenue in search of burgers and beers.

Auto Rental Companies

Avis, (816) 243-5763, (800) 331-1212
Budget, (816) 243-5757, (800) 677-3681
Dollar, (816) 243-5600, (800) 800-4000
Enterprise, (816) 966-8188 or (913) 383-1515 in
  Kansas, (800) 736-8222
Thrifty Car Rental, (816) 842-8550

Freewheelin' Freeways and Roundabout Roads

Today the Kansas City area has far more freeway miles per person than any other major U.S. city. That means, wherever you want to go in the metropolitan area, you can get there if you have directions and about 20 minutes.

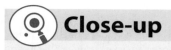

Welcome to the World's Friendliest Airport

When Kansas City International opened in 1972, it featured an innovative layout that connects three C-shaped terminals to a central loop. From the air it looks like Mickey Mouse's head sporting an extra ear. This configuration provides the shortest distance from curb to gate—75 feet—of any major U.S. airport. Check-in counters, baggage retrieval, and parking are also just steps away. One trip here and you'll see why *Travel Digest* named KCI the world's "Most People-Friendly Airport."

How friendly, you might ask? Well, we're spending $1.2 billion to renovate the place, including new parking spaces and spiffy artwork, such as designs embedded into the floors.

Facelifts are fine, but what you'll really enjoy are the expanded dining options throughout our three terminals. Now you can savor some of our famous barbecue while waiting for a flight, or enjoy a cold brewski from one of the Midwest's best microbreweries, Boulevard.

PARKING

Now, about that parking. The nearest parking lots to the terminals (A, B, and C) provide free parking for the first half hour. After that it's $2 for one-half to one hour, then $2 per hour up to a maximum of $18 per day. Circle parking is the same price, except the maximum is $12 per day. Economy parking is available at satellite lots for $5.50 per day. To reach these lots, take Paris Street off Cookingham Drive before you reach the terminal. Park in the lot (again, A, B, or C) that matches the terminal for your flight. For instance, if you're flying on Southwest Airlines, park in Lot B. The free shuttle will take you to your terminal.

AIRLINES SERVING KCI

	Phone	Terminal	Gate
Air Canada	(888) 247-2262	A	10–12
AirTran	(800) 247-8726	A	15
American	(800) 433-7300	C	76–79
Continental	(800) 523-3273	C	67–69
Delta Connection Comair	(800) 354-9822	B	56–60
Delta	(800) 221-1212	B	56–60
Frontier	(800) 432-1359	C	84–85
Midwest Airlines	(800) 452-2022	A	23–30
Northwest	(800) 225-2525	C	61–64
Skybus	www.skybus.com (Web site only)	C	87–88
Southwest	(800) 435-9792	B	31–39
United	(800) 241-6522	A	10–12
USAirways	(800) 428-4322	A	1–9

Numbered streets—those running east and west—follow a grid that starts at the river and are numbered sequentially both north and south. Main Street divides the town between east and west. Kansas City, Missouri, and most of Johnson County, Kansas, follow this pattern.

In both Missouri and Kansas you may turn right on a red light after stopping unless otherwise posted. And beware, hot-footed drivers: some areas have installed mounted cameras to catch lawbreakers who drive through red lights. The punishment is a hefty ticket. And we've also heard about tickets handed out to jaywalkers, especially on busy downtown streets and on the Plaza. As in all cities, you'll want to lock your car doors and place valuables such as cameras and suitcases in a locked trunk. And avoid walking alone at night.

If you're planning to drive here in the middle of winter, check out the road conditions posted by the departments of transportation. For Kansas it's (800) 585-7623 or **www.ksdot.org,** and in Missouri (800) 222-6400 or **www.modot.mo.gov.**

i When buying plane tickets online, enter KCI (for Kansas City International Airport) and you might wind up in Kono, Indonesia. (How's the weather?) You'll find us instead at MCI, a holdover from our Mid Continent International days. And because all the airport codes starting with "K" were taken, we'll remain MCI.

Tours

For the grooviest ride in town, catch the **Magic Bus,** decked out with love beads, lava lamp, and classic TV shows from the '70s. **The Gangster Tour** provides a look at mob houses and infamous crime scenes, year-round. Visit www.kctg .com or call (816) 243-5000.

View our town's diverse architecture on a Historic Kansas City Foundation walking tour. These popular excursions include downtown's art deco buildings; Union Cemetery, the final resting place for many of Kansas City's founders and Civil War casualties; 18th and Vine, with museums devoted to Kansas City jazz; the Country Club Plaza; and more. Call (816) 931-8448 or visit **www .historickansascity.org** to reserve a tour at least two to three weeks in advance. Some of the tours are adaptable for vans or buses.

Agenda Kansas City can plan sightseeing tours of your choice, including historic sites, a day of shopping, or a night on the town via vans, minicoaches, or limos. This full-service team can arrange group tours and events, or plan a delightful day for an individual. Call (913) 268-4466 or (888) AGENDAKC, or check out **www.agenda kansascity.com.**

For a late-night party on wheels, try the new **Kansas City Strip,** a trolley system that connects revelers to dozens of nightspots and dining options from 18th and Vine to Waldo, the Power & Light District to Westport. Catch it every Friday and Saturday night, 7 p.m. to 3 a.m.; details at **www.thekansascitystrip.com** or (816) 512-5555.

HISTORY

There's real drama in our town's 180-plus-year history, a story filled with fascinating heroes and colorful rascals. Yet, unlike an old-fashioned Western it's not always easy to tell if the central characters are wearing white hats or black.

In our struggle to change from mudville to metropolis, we've endured heartbreak such as cholera, fires, and a Civil War that left emerging towns on both sides of the state line bloodied and raw.

Yet our history is also filled with stories of pluck and perseverance. Our early trailblazers—men such as McCoy, Swope, Nelson, Van Horn, Vanderslice, and Volker—often came here looking to make a buck or build a reputation, fell in love with the town, and became our most staunch boosters. Today, a century and a half later, we honor the new pioneers who are taking us forward with vision and vitality. These are the leaders who keep Kansas City in the forefront in the world of the arts, commerce, and health care.

Our story starts where it all began: at the river.

WHERE THE RIVERS MEET

Our landscape—fertile valleys and tallgrass prairies, limestone bluffs and wide rivers—was formed when glaciers inched across the shallow seas covering the areas now known as Kansas and Missouri. Ages later other emigrants traveled here by way of the Missouri River. Indians came—the Hopewell, Shawnee, Delaware, and the Kanza who gave us our name—in wooden canoes. French traders arrived in pirogues and keelboats. These were followed by steamboats, often magnificently appointed, before railways and roads crisscrossed our lands.

On June 26, 1804, explorers Meriwether Lewis and William Clark camped on the confluence of the Kansas and Missouri Rivers during their first expedition to the Louisiana Territory. The view they saw from the bluff that would become Quality Hill is still a commanding one today. A handsome statue commemorating the expedition stands at Case Point near downtown. (See details in Attractions.)

It would be nearly two decades before the town really came into being. In 1821—the year Missouri was admitted to the Union—a French-

man from St. Louis, Francois Chouteau, established the American Fur Company at Kawsmouth to feed Europe's craving for beaver-felt hats. Five years later Chouteau's post was destroyed by flood. Would he leave this spot? *Mon dieu!* At the time his enterprise brought in what would now amount to $5 million a year. He moved to higher ground upriver near what is now Troost Avenue. It wouldn't be the last time the river (America's second longest after the Mississippi) would turn on the people who tried to tame her.

ℹ️ Trek to Clark's Point at Eighth and Jefferson to take in the view of the river below and imagine what it was like for the area's first visitors, such as Lewis and Clark. The overlook didn't get its name for half the famous expedition party, however. It was named to honor former city councilman Charles H. Clark in 1933.

By 1833 the area just east of Indian Territory had captured the attention of another early entrepreneur. John Calvin McCoy, a college-educated surveyor and son of a Baptist minister, opened a supply store 4 miles south of the river on the Santa Fe Trail. He called the place West Port. Today Westport is still a thriving center of commerce, filled with restaurants, shops, and bars. One of its most popular, Kelly's, started life as a tavern in 1836.

McCoy also founded Westport Landing on a rock ledge across the river from Chouteau's settlement. In 1838 McCoy and 13 other men formed a company and bought a 271-acre tract surrounding the river landing for $4,220. The growing town needed a name and, thankfully, the group rejected Possum Trot and Rabbitville for Town of Kansas. The name stuck, and the town was incorporated on June 1, 1850. We wouldn't become Kansas City until 1889.

The township thrived, thanks in part to the romanticized depictions of the frontier by writers such as Washington Irving. Yet travelers seeking the land of the quixotic passages in books and newspapers were disappointed by their first glimpse of our corrugated landscape. By 1840 the settlement was a square mile of land carved out of 130-foot limestone canyons so rugged its 500 residents called it Gully Town. Thick vines and dense forests of oak, hickory, elm, hackberry, and walnut awaited workers. The land was slashed with deep ravines plowed out by rushing streams. After a rain, Gully Town became Mudville.

Yet still they came.

CHOLERA STRIKES

In 1849 the burgeoning settlement met with its first serious setback when cholera killed nearly 30 percent of its residents and drove out hundreds more. There were scarcely enough people left to bury the dead.

Yet by March 1853 the port was thriving once more, driven in part by the Mexican trade over the Santa Fe Trail and the discovery of gold in California. In 1850, 600 wagons got their start at Kansas City. Just 10 years later the trade amounted to 16 million pounds of merchandise each year. In 1859, 1,500 steamboats landed at the site.

The city's first hotel—a two-story frame structure at Main Street and the levee—was established in 1846 by Thompson McDaniel to handle the travelers.

i Get a glimpse—actually an eyeful—of what our river town must have looked like around 1840. A mural that depicts riverboats and a tiny settlement on the bluffs has been painted on a brick building just east of the Broadway Bridge in the River Market area.

At the same time the Wyandot tribe owned and operated a ferry across the Kansas River, then known as the Kaw, which today's Lewis and Clark Viaduct spans. The name of the tribe has presented some debate: Wyandot is the correct Indian spelling. The English added another T, and the French tacked on an E. But that's nothing compared to the confusion created when the township was incorporated as Kansas City, a duplicate of the larger city across the water.

THE CIVIL WAR

But soon the division between Kansas and Missouri was deeper than the river that cut through the land. By 1850 one in five Jackson County residents was African American. Of these, nearly 3,000 were slaves. Communities, even families, were divided on the issue of slavery.

Many historians trace the beginning of the Civil War to May 1854, when the Kansas-Nebraska Act opened the former Indian Territory to settle-

i Civil War history buffs will want to pick up two brochures produced by the Civil War Round Table—a 25-stop driving tour that includes important battle sites throughout the Kansas City region and a walking tour that details important locations, including Loose Park and the John Wornall House. Call (888) 397-1236, or write to the Monnett Battle of Westport Fund, P.O. Box 22528, Kansas City, MO 64113-0528.

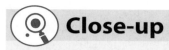

Close-up

Kansas City's Colorful History

- Artist Frederic Remington sold his first painting in Kansas City. The 23-year-old arrived here in 1884 and his commercial endeavors—a hardware store and a saloon—failed miserably. His paintings, however, were popular and he sold them through an art supply dealer before moving to New York.

- In 1904 Lyda Burton Conley studied law and became the first Native American female lawyer in the country. She used her new degree to petition Congress to pass a bill prohibiting the removal of the Huron Indian Cemetery in downtown Kansas City, Kansas. The resting place remains there today, a small plot of land surrounded by businesses between Sixth and Seventh Streets on Minnesota Avenue.

- The City Union Mission received a much-needed boost from a most unlikely patron when, in 1934, 92-year-old bordello owner Annie Chambers was moved to tears during a funeral sermon by Reverend David Bulkley. She deeded her opulent brothel to his cause, and her residence at Third and Wyandotte Streets was converted into a women's shelter.

- One of the world's most successful companies started at the YMCA. In 1910, 18-year-old Joyce Hall arrived in Kansas City from Norfolk, Nebraska, with a shoebox of postcards, which he kept under his bed at the Y. His room became the company's first address, and today the Shoebox line of cards honors that humble beginning.

- A mural in the Missouri Capitol in Jefferson City by Kansas City artist Thomas Hart Benton depicts our rambunctious town in the 1930s. The central character in the colorful painting was Boss Tom Pendergast—for which Pendergast himself posed—dealing with real estate developer J. C. Nichols and banker William T. Kemper.

- When John Calvin McCoy married Virginia Chick in 1838, he was late for the wedding. His future father-in-law sent out a search party and found him—in his wedding attire—feverishly finishing a neighbor's barn roof just minutes ahead of a thunderstorm.

- Mayor Milton McGee laid out Grand Avenue—the first road from the Missouri River to the town of Westport—just wide enough to get his horse and buggy turned around without having to back it up.

- The Muse of the Missouri fountain between Eighth and Ninth on Main celebrates the river's importance in Kansas City's history. Sculptor Wheeler Williams had planned to model the fish fountainheads after native Missouri River fish. But when he deemed our catfish too ugly he fashioned his own hybrid with a carp body and bluefish head.

- At one time Alexander Majors's Pony Express freight and stagecoach company employed 4,000 circuit riders, including 15-year-old wagonmaster Billy Cody. But by 1860 the telegraph and railroad spelled doom for the operation, and "The Great Bullwhacker" lost his fortune. In 1895 the entertainer, now known as Buffalo Bill Cody, made his former employer part of his Wild West show.

- Some of our city's liveliest history happened in nightspots along 18th and Vine during the Jazz Age. You can relive those days—to a more refined degree—at the district's American Jazz Museum; the Blue Room, which doubles as a museum and nightclub; and during 12 O'Clock Jump jazz jams on Sat night at the Mutual Musicians Foundation. Get event information on the 24-hour Kansas City Jazz Ambassadors' Hotline, (816) 753-5277.

- Where will you find the only monument and museum in the world dedicated solely to World War I? It's not Washington, D.C., or Normandy—it's the 217-foot-tall Liberty Memorial right here in Kansas City. Major renovations, started in 2002, have returned the site to its former glory and added a fascinating museum.

ment. The conflict between abolitionists and pro-slavery groups plunged the land, known as "Bleeding Kansas," into political and military strife. A year later a battle known as the "Gettysburg of the West" was waged across Westport and west into what is now Mission Hills.

A RETURN TO PEACE AND PROSPERITY

In 1863 the government sent troops to protect the Santa Fe traders and business began to boom once more.

Yet the city, after four years of neglect, was in deplorable shape. The streets were quagmires, making traffic almost impossible. In the spring of 1865 the city negotiated a loan of $60,000 to improve road conditions and open thoroughfares. Once again things began to hum, and soon the hotel on Main Street was registering 27,000 arrivals a year.

In the meantime the settlement across the Kansas River was also growing, although more slowly. Growth escalated when the settlement's first packing plant was built in the Central Industrial District in 1868, and it soon developed a solid base of railroads, stockyards, and industries. During this time Kansas Citians began riding to work, school, and the movies on a "bunch of bananas": yellow streetcars that numbered 700 at the height of their eight-decade run beginning in 1869. The influx of rubber-tired buses and personal vehicles retired the last of the streetcar bells in June 1957.

BRIDGE TO THE FUTURE

In those days, despite our growth, the towns of Leavenworth, Kansas, and St. Joseph, Missouri, were leaving Kansas City, Missouri, in their dust. They had populations of 15,400 and 15,000, respectively, to our 4,000. But what these lusty rivals didn't have were city boosters such as Robert Van Horn and Kersey Coates, who helped secure the first rail bridge to span the Mighty Mo and provide a direct rail link to Chicago. On July 3, 1869, the opening of the Hannibal Bridge was celebrated by a parade, barbecue, and fireworks. More than 20,000 people watched as the Hannibal, the pride of the Hannibal & St. Joseph Railroad, steamed across the bridge with 10 railcars in tow.

Within five years our population had soared to 32,000.

SIN CITY AND ITS SAVIORS

Yet not all of our growth was positive. In 1866 the James Gang began its crime spree by robbing a bank on Liberty, Missouri's town square. Along with 10 compatriots they made off with $62,500; one bystander was killed. During the 1870s the gang was linked to nearly two dozen heists.

There was plenty of money to go around. In those days we had more gambling houses than any other city in the nation. One of these, Marble Hall, was a favorite of Wyatt Earp, Bat Masterson, Buffalo Bill Cody, and Wild Bill Hickok.

This era also marked the start of our meatpacking industry. Two plants for slaughtering cattle and hogs were opened, and in 1871 the stockyards were expanded in the West Bottoms. By 1878 the freewheeling town's population had surged by 70 percent. There were 80 saloons, actually a lifesaver because the murky water supply made drinking whiskey a virtue. Annie Chambers's posh brothel at Third and Wyandotte Streets was doing brisk business as well, and if customers tired of her establishment, they had 40 other bordellos to sample.

Our prosperity also brought conveniences. In 1879 the Missouri and Kansas Telephone Company printed its first directory, listing 46 subscribers in Kansas City, Missouri, and 12 in Kansas City, Kansas. We had an opera house, Exposition Hall, a public waterworks system with 15 miles of water mains, and a two-man fire department.

i World leader and bank robber: We celebrate both our famous native sons, Harry S. Truman and Jesse James. The lives of both men are displayed in museums and homes dedicated to their importance in the Midwest and the world.

Yet when William Rockhill Nelson moved to Kansas City from Indiana in 1880, he was appalled to find unpaved roads and haphazard walking boards instead of sidewalks. Soon he was using his newspaper, the *Kansas City Evening Star*, to instigate change. After he won his crusade for better fire protection and street lamps, he focused on public recreation and parks. Read more about this benevolent bear of a man in the Media chapter.

Nelson also convinced others of the importance of green spaces and planned roadways. Colonel Thomas H. Swope donated the largest gift of land in the city's history, before or since: a 1,334-acre tract of land 4 miles from downtown. It became the park that bears his name: the second largest public green space in the United States after New York's Central Park.

In 1891 landscape designer George Kessler was hired to create boulevards and parks using classical architecture while celebrating our eccentric topography. He carved roadways out of gorges and around hills to create wonderful scenic drives and boulevards. Buildings were springing up as fast as the roses in one of the city's loveliest green spaces, Loose Park. By the late 1880s a building spree had given the town the nickname "Athens of the West," based on architecture with high ornamentation and neo-Gothic styling. We built the third largest train station in the world, Union Depot, in the West Bottoms and constructed the luxurious Coates House Hotel and Coates Opera House . . . never mind that the latter was next to a cow pasture.

Real estate developers were following Kessler's boulevards to the south. J. C. Nichols built Crestwood, a small shopping area, at 55th and Oak to serve his residences.

By 1890 we had 25 schoolhouses, 35 miles of cable car track, and nearly 6,000 new houses. Scottish immigrants laid out the city's first golf course in the Hyde Park neighborhood in 1894. The game was a hit: These days around 300,000 Kansas Citians—or 15 percent of our population—are golfers.

KANSAS CITY SPIRIT

In 1899 the city's first convention hall, designed by Frederick E. Hull, opened to the rousing music of John Philip Sousa's band. A year later, fire destroyed the building just three months before the Democratic Convention was to be held. But even as the fire blazed, people circulated through the crowd soliciting donations for the building's reconstruction. A frenzied 90 days later, the convention nominated William Jennings Bryan in one of the world's largest indoor arenas—certainly its newest. The phrase "Kansas City Spirit" was coined that day. Locals strutted around town wearing badges boasting, "I Live in Kansas City—Ask Me."

Six hundred visiting journalists picked up the story and soon newcomers were jamming the streets. One person drawn to the vivacious city was 18-year-old Joyce Clyde Hall, who in 1910 sold postcards from a suitcase under his bed at the YMCA—the start of Hallmark Cards.

The city's resolve would be tested again in 1903 when spring rains turned the Missouri River into an inland sea, flooding the West Bottoms. It destroyed bridges, swept away the stockyards, filled the Union Depot, and left 22,000 people homeless. Public relief money came pouring in, and the area began to rebuild within days.

The trauma of the flooding drove William B. Strang Jr. to develop a flood-free residential area in Johnson County, Kansas. To encourage development he built an interurban railway in 1905 to take residents from downtown to home and back. It extended to the small town of Olathe farther west. Another peril—this time man-made—soon took over the West Bottoms and eventually spread over the entire city. An infamous political machine started when Jim Pendergast opened a saloon in the area. Soon his younger brother, Tom (profiled in this chapter's Close-up), was named superintendent of streets.

By 1912 the city had 55,000 telephones, 221 churches, 72 public schools, 2,100 acres of parks, 70 miles of boulevards, and 260 miles of street railway. It also had 81 movie theaters with an average weekly attendance of nearly 450,000, almost twice the population of the city. General Hospital, an institution built to serve the city's 24,000 black residents, became the first hospital in the nation to be run and staffed completely by African Americans.

We had other reasons to be proud. Workers hung a 6-foot clock in the archway at Union Station in the fall of 1914. The Beaux Arts–style station replaced Union Depot in the flood-worried West Bottoms. The new $60 million station at Pershing Road and Grand featured a 95-foot ceiling in the Grand Hall, three 3,500-pound chandeliers, and a North Waiting Room that held 10,000 people. During its heyday, 271 trains passed through the depot daily. Read more about Union Station's sad decline and remarkable restoration in Attractions.

By 1914 the city had another important industry, this time in the service sector. The Federal Reserve Bank opened that year and by 1921 ranked fifth in bank-clearing volume nationwide. This attracted other federal agencies to the area, and by 1939 more than 100 federal offices were located in the metropolitan area.

Money was indeed flowing during the Gilded Age, just in time for Charles Tivol to open his jewelry store on Petticoat Lane, where a suitor could purchase a one-carat diamond for $175. The diamonds are a bit pricier these days, but the service is still unmatched at the family-owned business now on the Country Club Plaza and two other locations.

THE JAZZ AGE: GOOD TIMES AND BAD

On January 16, 1920, prohibition of liquor became part of the U.S. Constitution, yet here the Pendergast political machine kept the city wide open. It was the start of the Roaring Twenties, and no town bellowed louder. Nightclubs flourished thanks to police who were paid to ignore gambling, prostitution, and liquor. Tom Pendergast's own gambling hall had two windows, marked DONATIONS and REFUNDS.

Jazz musicians knew they could always get a gig in Kansas City. Duke Ellington, Cab Calloway, and other bandleaders stopped here on tours, and our local groups kept the beat with the best of them. Pianist William "Count" Basie got his start with Bennie Moten's Kansas City Orchestra. Music poured out of nightclubs along 12th Street and 18th and Vine. The Reno Club, Harlem Nite Club, and big dance halls such as the El Torreon kept swinging all night. One young player frequented the Reno Club to listen to his idol, saxophonist Lester Young. Eventually this young man, Charlie "Bird" Parker, would create a musical style all his own.

Kansas Citians had plenty of other amusements. Fairyland Park opened in 1923. That same year the first retail building on the Country Club Plaza made its first sale and the Pla-Mor Ballroom, billed as America's largest indoor amusement center, opened in 1927. It was soon attracting 4,000 dancers nightly. When they weren't shopping, dancing, or riding the Ferris wheel, residents could listen to four local radio stations.

We stopped moving long enough to salute when five prominent Allied commanders, including General John J. Pershing and French Marshal Ferdinand Foch, joined Vice President Calvin Coolidge to dedicate the site of the Liberty Memorial in 1921. It was the country's only monument to World War I. Coolidge, by now president, returned on November 11, 1926, to formally dedicate the completed memorial, with its majestic 200-foot shaft rising from a hill overlooking Union Station.

We had other heroes to celebrate as well. Formed in 1919, the all-black Kansas City Monarchs baseball team traveled the Midwest in the 1920s and 1930s, when baseball was segregated. The players thrilled fans with 43 straight wins in 1943. A team member, Jackie Robinson, was the first black player to sign with a major league team, the Brooklyn Dodgers, in 1947. Another Kansas Citian got his start during this decade. Harry S. Truman, unsuccessful as a haberdasher, was handpicked by Tom Pendergast to run for a post on the administrative court that governed Jackson County. He won, but Pendergast soon learned that Truman would not become one of his lackeys. Independence is still Harry's Town;

you can visit his museum and farmhouse. Find out more in Attractions.

HIGH TIMES

While the rest of the country was suffering during the Depression, Kansas City continued to thrive, thanks in part to Pendergast. In 1931 the Ten-Year Plan created jobs and and resulted in a new City Hall, a courthouse, miles of new roads, and art deco–style Kansas City Power & Light building. For years it was the tallest building in Missouri; it remains the most stunning, especially at night when its prismatic glass and automated lighting system change the tower's colors. Two years later the Nelson Gallery of Art and Atkins Museum opened on the property formerly occupied by newspaper publisher William Rockhill Nelson.

It was the end of a decade—and the end of an era—when in 1939 Pendergast pleaded guilty to income tax evasion and was sentenced to 15 months in Leavenworth Prison.

WAR AND RESURGENCE

When the United States went to war, Kansas Citians went to work. Defense jobs drew 40,000 workers to Kansas City between 1940 and 1943. Most of them clocked in at the Pratt & Whitney aircraft engine plant at Bannister Road and Troost Avenue, where former homemakers and farm-hands built the 2,000-horsepower engine used in Navy fighter planes.

On August 14, 1945, Missouri's favorite son, President Harry S. Truman, declared that the war was over. The troops came home, minus some 1,250 soldiers from Jackson County who died in action.

The jubilant country was dancing to Charlie Parker's bebop music. And here in the Midwest, we stared at our Philcos as the town's first television station, WDAF, began regular programming on October 16, 1949. By the fall of 1950 kids were watching *Whizzo the Clown* on KMBC–TV. His audience was growing fast; during the next decade 100,000 babies were born in Kansas City.

As we celebrated the centennial of the city's incorporation, things looked rosy. We had a new outdoor venue, Starlight Theatre. Mickey Mantle played outfield for the Kansas City Blues, a team in the American Association. And the Katz Drug store was selling Davy Crockett coonskin caps for 98 cents.

Then, on Friday the 13th, 1951, after 40 days of rain the Kansas River poured over its dikes to flood the Argentine district and the West Bottoms . . . again. By Saturday the Kaw had engulfed the stockyards and factories in the area and forced the evacuation of 15,000 people. Once again the city rallied. In memory of the city's mettle when it rebuilt the Convention Hall in three months in 1900, workers rebuilt the destroyed American Royal facilities in time for the livestock show weeks later. Illustrator Norman Rockwell painted "The American Spirit," showing a worker rolling up his sleeves while holding a blueprint.

THE TIMES ARE A-CHANGIN'

By 1962, when I-70 was replacing U.S. Highway 40 as the primary entry from the east and west, city commuters were already touting the new 55-mile I-35. Soon it would link folks who lived in Johnson County with their downtown jobs. The exodus from downtown began in earnest in 1947 when Sears Roebuck and Co. opened its first suburban store on the Country Club Plaza. Downtown stores became increasingly irrelevant. Emery, Bird, Thayer closed in 1968. Dillard's, which replaced the venerable Macy's store, moved to the suburbs in 1989. Only the Jones Store Co. was left, and it turned off the lights in 1998.

It was also a time when landmarks were destroyed to make room for expressways and parking lots. More than 125 buildings came tumbling down, including the former Lyric Theater at 622 Main St., Kansas City's first public school at Independence Avenue and Cherry Street, and Bob Potee's glittering gambling house at No. 3 Missouri Ave. in the area now known as the River Market.

But the '60s also brought plenty to cheer about. The Chiefs professional football team played its first season in Kansas City after owner Lamar Hunt transplanted the team from Dallas. Kansas City voters approved an ordinance that required taverns, amusement parks, and public pools to admit minorities. And on September 17, 1964, the Beatles played a half-hour concert to screaming fans at Municipal Stadium. The Fab Four eventually would record their own version of "Kansas City," the city's anthem.

Another crowd filled the stadium when the Kansas City Royals pitched the first ball on April 8, 1969. It was Ewing Marion Kauffman, the man who started Marion Labs, who brought the team to Kansas City after the A's moved to Oakland.

We crowded the streets on January 12, 1970, to welcome home the Chiefs, who had just won Super Bowl IV in New Orleans, beating the Minnesota Vikings 23–7. We continued our move to official sports town with the construction of a twin stadium. Arrowhead Stadium opened for the Chiefs in fall 1972; Royals Stadium housed the baseball team a year later. Today the baseball facility is called Kauffman Stadium—or simply "The K"—to honor the late baseball team owner.

When we hosted the Republican National Convention in 1976, Crown Center impressed delegates and media representatives, as did the elegant new Alameda Plaza Hotel, the first large luxury hotel to grace the Country Club Plaza. If anyone visited River Quay (pronounced *key*), an entertainment district near the City Market, it would be their last chance. The area opened in spring 1972 with 13 antiques shops, restaurants, and art studios taking over refurbished buildings, some dating back to the Civil War. Then organized crime took over and sleazy bars began to proliferate. Several buildings were leveled by suspicious explosions, and before the end of the decade River Quay was kaput.

But good things often come from disasters, and the demise of River Quay also helped signal the end of organized crime in Kansas City. While River Quay was folding, Westport was growing. By fall 1974 extensive sections of the old town were being revitalized for restaurants and shops.

HIGH INFLATION, HIGH EXPECTATIONS

Like every other American city, we were hit hard in the 1980s with skyrocketing inflation rates and high unemployment. But we momentarily forgot 17 percent mortgage rates when the Royals won the 1985 World Series. A champagne-soaked Ewing Kauffman celebrated with third baseman George Brett, pitcher Dan Quisenberry, the other players, and 41,628 screaming fans.

Kansas City continued its reputation as a sports town when we hosted 15,000 visitors for the NCAA Final Four basketball tournament in April 1988. We celebrated other sports heroes, for reasons that often went deeper than skills with a club or a bat. Golfer Tom Watson resigned from the Kansas City Country Club (where he learned to play golf) in 1990 because the club would not allow a Jewish businessman, Henry Bloch, to join. In 1992 George Brett made the 3,000th hit of his career at Royals Stadium. Two years later he retired, perhaps because his biggest fan, Ewing Kauffman, was no longer in the stands to watch him play. The philanthropist had died the year before.

WORKING TOGETHER

As we started looking toward our 150-year anniversary, city leaders began to push for a renewed interest in our central core. In 1996 voters across five counties passed the Bi-state Cultural Tax, the first two-state effort of its kind in the country. Work began to convert the grand old depot into a science museum and entertainment venue, a project that would cost more than $200 million. Soon voters were also saying "yes" to restoring the Liberty Memorial.

We maintained our interest in public art. Bartle Hall got its Sky Stations—some call them "hair curlers"—in 1994. Giant shuttlecocks dotted the lawn at Nelson-Atkins Museum of Art. We continued our love affair with fountains: Water displays define the entrances to business parks, government buildings, and neighborhoods.

We stopped razing and started restoring historic buildings from the River Market area to the

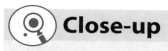 **Close-up**

Thomas J. Pendergast

Every great city has both demons and do-gooders in its roster of historical figures. In the case of Thomas Pendergast, we got both. The powerful Pendergast political machine began, fittingly enough, with a horse race. Jim Pendergast used his winnings to launch a saloon below the bluffs in the West Bottoms, an area filled with warehouses, rail lines, and livestock pens. His watering hole also served as a bank for the working class. He was elected alderman in 1892 and soon extended his influence to the north end of the city. Eighteen years later his younger brother, Tom, replaced him as alderman. The Pendergast tradition of finding jobs for the unemployed and feeding the poor during holidays continued, even after Tom moved out of the West Bottoms into a mansion at 5650 Ward Parkway.

Boss Tom parlayed 5 years on the city council into a 30-year reign over graft, prostitution, gambling, and rigged elections. And he determined that real power and wealth were tied to business. His Riverside Racetrack pulled in plenty of dough, his Jefferson Hotel was the place to buy liquor and a little action, and his Ready-Mix Concrete Company paved Brush Creek, which fronts the Country Club Plaza.

The Pendergast power reached its zenith (many would say its nadir) between 1925 and 1939. Hundreds of nightclubs operated around the clock. Operators, gamblers, and prostitutes didn't fear police raids; they knew they'd soon go free.

The rest of the nation was noticing. NBC Radio tagged Kansas City a "hot spot" for hoodlums. In 1938 the *Christian Science Monitor* called Kansas City "wider open than any place outside Reno" and blasted residents for being "astonishingly complacent about it all." Not everyone was. Missouri Governor Lloyd C. Stark—who had once sought Pendergast's support and was denied—called for a federal probe of Boss Tom. The crime? An insurance fix he set up through the statehouse, a place referred to as "Uncle Tom's Cabin."

Crime may have been high during this period, but so, too, was the city's growth. Some say Kansas City avoided the worst of the Depression because the Pendergast connections attracted federal funds to the area. Pendergast supported a $40 million public works project, a 10-year plan that changed the city's skyline. By 1930 the city had impressive new buildings, including the Federal Reserve Bank Building, Board of Trade, Kansas City Power & Light building, the 29-story City Hall, Jackson County Courthouse, and the Municipal Auditorium, these last two constructed with concrete from Pendergast's concrete company. Pendergast's company also provided the materials for the Nelson Art Gallery and the runways at the new Municipal Airport.

Pendergast handpicked politicians, including a Jackson County judge, Harry S. Truman, who became a candidate for the U.S. Senate in 1934. Truman, a celebrated straight shooter himself, admired Pendergast's ability to get things done but stood up to Boss Tom when it came to shady dealings. Was Pendergast a friend or foe? Most historians admit he was both. To workers, particularly immigrants who came to a new city without connections, he was a godsend. The city paid 400 Pendergast captains to stop by houses during the 1930s and 1940s to make sure there was enough coal for the winter, enough food for hard times, a job if you needed one. The grateful masses kept electing Pendergast's picks.

Ballots, in fact, would be Boss Tom's downfall. Over 60,000 of those votes were found to be cast by "ghosts" who were falsely registered. Vagrants were paid 25 cents for every vote. Eventually 259 Pendergast supporters were convicted by federal juries for conspiracy involving voting fraud.

Pendergast's own betting addiction ended his glory days. He was arraigned in 1939 for failure to pay taxes on a bribe he took to pay off gambling debts. After serving 15 months in prison, he lived quietly at his home at 5650 Ward Parkway until his death in 1945. His stronghold on city government was over, but he left another legacy: When the books were audited the city was $22 million in debt.

With a new reform group in control, what we lost in revenue and vibrancy—slot machines were trucked away and jazz clubs lost their crowds—we made up for with a renewed civic pride.

downtown Garment District, Hyde Park, and the Northeast area; Quality Hill and West Bottoms to the east side of town.

We also began to honor our history by paying tribute to the people, places, and events that formed our city. In 1997 we opened the Negro Leagues Baseball Museum and the Kansas City Jazz Museum at 18th and Vine Streets, once the heart of the African-American neighborhood. The driving force behind these redevelopments was Emanuel Cleaver II a Methodist minister who was mayor of Kansas City from 1991 to 1999. Cleaver made history as the first African-American mayor of the city. His replacement, Kay Waldo Barnes, was the first woman to hold the office.

Other cities within the metropolis began to thrive under fresh leadership. Even the sister city across the river awoke from more than a century of slumber. Carol Marinovich, the new mayor/chief executive of the Unified Government of Wyandotte County/Kansas City, Kansas, thrilled residents and surprised some neighboring cities when she announced plans for the new Kansas Speedway. The track, which opened in 2001, hosts three NASCAR-sponsored races each year to bring an estimated $170 million boost to the city's economy, the equivalent of a Super Bowl every year. Meanwhile, Ed Eilert, mayor of Overland Park, Kansas, for 20 of the city's 40 years, transformed the bedroom community into the state's fastest-growing city.

LOOKING FORWARD

Visitors and newcomers have always been surprised to find in Kansas City a town that's vibrant and varied, friendly yet sophisticated. The best is yet to be. There's a palpable new energy here, especially in the urban core that's been neglected for so long. Like many positive changes it started on two fronts. Corporate leaders stopped waiting for a master plan and slowly began to put their money and influence into opening offices, living spaces, and cultural venues downtown. Meanwhile young artists began to create lofts and studios out of abandoned buildings between downtown and Crown Center, creating an exciting avenue of arts that brought in patrons and encouraged restaurants and retail shops. Even the storied West Bottoms are coming back with new art galleries, cafes, and businesses.

It has paid off in one of the country's most spectacular downtown transformations, including an entertainment district, a new arena, and renovated hotels.

KANSAS CITY'S PROMINENT CITIZENS

Kansas City's leaders are continuing a tradition that began almost as soon as the town took hold: that of giving back to the community through endowments, expertise, and plenty of cash. For instance, 72 percent of households in Kansas City made charitable gifts in 2007. And of those, the average pay-out was $3,375—50 percent above the U.S. average. So cheer these modern-day heroes—named and unnamed—who continue to make this city a great place to live and work. As you'll see in the profiles below, their reach often extends beyond our borders to help millions through education and medical research.

Henry Bloch

The cofounder, with brother Richard, of H&R Block Inc., the national tax preparation firm, has enhanced the lives of many residents. The Henry W. and Marion H. Bloch Foundation has provided money to expand facilities at the University of Missouri–Kansas City business school, now called the Henry W. Bloch School of Business and Public Administration.

But this couple's most lasting legacy will always be the remarkable Bloch Building expansion to the Nelson-Atkins Museum of Art. Henry's brother, the late Richard Bloch, founded the R. A. Bloch Cancer Foundation with his wife, Annette. The foundation's cancer hotline offers support to those newly diagnosed and has established cancer survivor parks in dozens of cities across the United States, including a lovely sculpture garden on the west side of the Country Club Plaza. Annette recently granted $10 million to support the cancer center at the University of Kansas Hospital, which will bear her name.

Donald and Adele Hall

"When you care enough to give the very best" could be the slogan for this couple's generosity as well as that of Hallmark Cards, the company founded by Donald's father.

For more than five decades the Hall family has changed the landscape of the city for the better, with his Crown Center complex, the Henry Moore sculpture garden at the Nelson-Atkins Museum of Art, and countless other projects. The couple recently sent the city their "very best"—a $60 million check to the Nelson-Atkins Museum of Art. That brings to a total of $100 million the amount the Hall Family Foundation has contributed to the museum over the years.

Barnett and Shirley Helzberg

Shirley spent untold millions renovating an old schoolhouse south of downtown into a marvelous antiques store and restaurant called Webster House, and donates time and money to the arts and health care in her hometown. Her personal pet projects are the Kansas City Symphony and Starlight Theatre, but any time there's a need, people know they can find a soft heart here.

Barnett, who was mentored by Ewing Kauffman, made helping young entrepreneurs his second career after selling his jewelry business to Warren Buffett of Berkshire-Hathaway. He established the Helzberg Entrepreneurial Mentoring Program in 1995. And Rockhurst University, where he has been an adjunct professor for more than 10 years, recently renamed its business school the Helzberg School of Management to honor the couple.

R. Crosby Kemper Jr.

Kemper's banking empire, UMB Financial Corporation, spans several states, yet his generosity remains chiefly in his hometown. In 1973 he donated $3.2 million to construct Kemper Arena in the West Bottoms, and a $6 million gift in 1990

resulted in the Kemper Museum of Contemporary Art. Kemper has always been one to come through for a worthy cause, such as his $1 million gift to rebuild the city's bankrupt orchestra, now the Kansas City Symphony, and a $2 million donation to the Liberty Memorial restoration fund.

James and Virginia Stowers

As founder of the mutual fund empire American Century Investments, James Stowers has put his money where his heart is. Both cancer survivors, this couple has poured millions into the Stowers Institute for Medical Research, built along the thriving Brush Creek Corridor.

Ewing & Muriel Kauffman and Family

Everyone in Kansas City knows the story about how the man who built a multimillion-dollar company, Marion Labs, saved the Royals baseball team. Today, the Royals Stadium is often just referred to as The K, a nickname for the late great entrepreneur and philanthropist. The Ewing Marion Kauffman Foundation supports mentoring programs through the Kauffman Center for Entrepreneurial Leadership. Kauffman's vivacious wife helped get a 911 system in the Kansas City area, and the Muriel McBrien Kauffman Foundation has assets of about $300 million.

Muriel's daughter, Julia Irene Kauffman, now oversees the foundation's works. Its most generous gift to date is more than $100 million for the new Kauffman Center for the Performing Arts, a $330 million civic landmark due to open in 2011.

OTHER RESOURCES

We celebrate our rich history at dozens of museums and visitor centers throughout Kansas City. You'll find listings for interesting places such as the Grinter House, the first home built in Kansas City, Kansas; Missouri Town 1855; the Jesse James Farm and Museum; President Harry S. Truman's farm and museum; and the Gem Theater, which showcases our jazz heritage, in the Attractions chapter under History.

TRACE YOUR OWN FAMILY HISTORY

The Kansas City area—in particular Independence, Missouri—offers genealogists and family historians a wellspring of information. A good place to start your search is the **Jackson County Historical Society Archives and Research Library** (www.jchs.org), located in the Jackson County Courthouse at 112 West Lexington Ave., Room 103. It contains 20,000 photographic images and a 2,000-volume library of reference books, periodicals, letters, and more. The society's bookshop sells more than 600 titles, including maps and books relating to Jackson County, the westward expansion, and the Civil War. **The Mid-Continent Public Library** (www.mcpl.lib.mo.us) and its adjacent 12,000-foot Genealogy and Local History Department are wonderful resources for tracing ancestors. The collection includes the U.S. population censuses for 1790 to 1920 as well as family and county histories. The branch is located at 317 West 24 Highway, Independence;

call (816) 252-7228 for hours. A new genealogy center will open in spring 2008. The **National Archives at Kansas City,** near Union Station, houses more than 60 million pages of historical records for Kansas, Missouri, Iowa, Minnesota, Nebraska, North Dakota, and South Dakota. It recently hosted a 2010 Census Road Tour. Who says history is boring? Call (816) 268-8000 or visit www.archives.gov/central-plains/kansas-city.

The **Black Archives of Mid-America Inc.,** at 2033 Vine, Kansas City, Missouri, is one of the largest collections of African-American memorabilia, artifacts, and research materials in the Midwest. There is an admission fee. Call (816) 483-1300 or visit www.blackarchives.org for information.

At the **Johnson County Archives** (www.archives.jocogov.org) you'll find documents relating to the history of Kansas and the county, including marriage licenses, wills, and naturalization records from the late 1880s. The center is located in the County Administration Building, 111 South Cherry, Suite 500, Olathe, Kansas; call (913) 715-0400.

ACCOMMODATIONS

Our reputation as the Heartland extends to lodging choices travelers will find in Kansas City. It could be the *ahh*-inspiring decor of the Bridal Suite, a bird's eye view of our skyline, or just a heart-felt greeting when you check in. Good manners abound, yes, but you'll also find great accommodations. Your footsteps will echo across lobbies lined with enough marble to rebuild ancient Rome, and when one hotel boasts of running water, it's referring to the five-story waterfall to your left. Plenty of famous folks have registered at our front desks over the years, including movie stars and rock stars, glamour queens and gangsters—Al Capone used one area resort as his hideout—and more than our share of presidents. Harry S. Truman, in fact, showed the world he was still commander-in-chief, despite the headlines, at one of our downtown hotels. And if you think you saw Tina Turner, Sir Elton John, or Oprah just now in the lobby, you're probably right. Our new Sprint Center has been a magnet for the world's most celebrated entertainers and celebrities.

There are rooms to fit every taste and pocketbook, from ultraposh retreats and bed-and-breakfast inns to budget-pleasing motels and even campsites. And if you're traveling with Fido, you'll be pleased to know that several of the larger hotels offer special beds and other treats.

Naturally for a city our size, every hotel, motel, and extended-stay chain is represented—just right for ratcheting up your frequent-travel points. In addition to these national names, we offer some one-of-a-kind lodging choices. To see a complete roster of available accommodations, check out the Hotel and Motel Association of Greater Kansas City's Web site at www.kansascitylodging.org. There's also a handy link on www.visitkc.com.

WHERE TO STAY

Deciding where to stay all depends on what you desire during your visit. The downtown area is home to our financial, business, and convention services. It's also where you can see our city in stages—or "on" stages, as it were. Our grandest theaters—many of them turn-of-the-twentieth-century gems—are downtown. We have a treasure chest of other gems for you in the urban core: Our grand old hotels have been renovated into spectacular boutique accommodations. Here you can roam the hallways, ballrooms, and nightclubs, such as the Hilton President Hotel's Drum Room, which once hosted Frank Sinatra, the Marx Brothers, and Patsy Cline. It's also the official hotel for the new Power & Light District, an entertainment destination that includes restaurants, nightspots, and shopping. The Aladdin Hotel is the "newest" old lodging choice, which originally opened in 1936 and offers vintage-hip guest rooms and a Martini Loft. Hotel Phillips is a chic and popular historic hotel just steps away from downtown's many arts venues and attractions. And between downtown and Crown Center are dozens of art galleries and artists' studios in the Crossroads Arts District

Speaking of Crown Center, this sprawling complex combines two luxury hotels and dining, shopping, and attractions all in one neat package, along with an old-fashioned town square that sports an outdoor ice-skating rink, fountains, and live entertainment. And it's all in the shadow of our magnificent Liberty Memorial, the country's only museum and memorial dedicated solely to World War I.

Locations in and around Westport and our famous Country Club Plaza offer so many dining, shopping, and nighttime entertainment options you could book a room for a month and not see it all. This area also boasts two world-class art museums, lovely parks, and the reason we're called the City of Fountains. History buffs who are wild about Harry will find hotels and bed-and-breakfasts close to his museum and home in Independence.

But don't discount accommodations in out-lying areas. For instance, Overland Park offers some of the best shopping west of Fifth Avenue. And when we say take it outside, we're not being rude: Johnson County has miles of walking trails linking public parks and waterways. Dozens of private and public courses make this a golfer's paradise. Wyandotte County, Kansas, will tempt you with hotels in Village West, the 400-acre entertainment area surrounding the NASCAR race track. And you won't have to gamble on getting a good night's sleep, along with grand entertainment, at the spectacular Argosy Casino Hotel and Spa with a view of downtown. Not to be outdone, Kansas City's Harrah's Casino hit the jackpot with updates to its hotel. But the action at the tables and top-notch acts in the VooDoo Lounge may mean you'll never touch the king-size bed.

As for when to come, spring and fall are our most glorious times of year, when gardens and trees look particularly pretty, and during summer there's a festival or event every weekend. Every winter our entire city dresses for the holidays as 250,000 colored lights illuminate the Country Club Plaza on Thanksgiving night. Hotel rooms overlooking the magical ceremony—our ver-sion of Mardi Gras—often are booked a year in advance. Come anyway; the dazzling view con-tinues through mid-January.

So let's get you checked in. We've divided this chapter into four categories: Hotels and Motels, Extended Stays, Bed-and-Breakfasts and Inns, and RV Parks and Camping. The first two categories are listed by location. The others are listed alphabetically. All places to stay are located in Kansas City, Missouri, unless other-wise noted.

Price Code

Prices reflect the average rate for high season, double-occupancy accommodations.

$	Less than $60
$$	$60 to $110
$$$	$111 to $160
$$$$	$161 and up

HOTELS AND MOTELS

Country Club Plaza and Westport

EMBASSY SUITES HOTEL $$
220 W. 43rd St.
(816) 756-1720
www.embassysuites.com
The waterfall and mini-rainforest in this all-suite hotel's 12-story atrium are so gorgeous you might want to pitch a tent. But check out your room instead; the bedroom and separate living room make it ideal for families and business trav-elers. More pluses include a made-to-order com-plimentary breakfast and an afternoon manager's reception where you'll be treated to your favorite beverage. And the location, halfway between the Plaza and Westport, means you have 60 or so restaurants to choose from within minutes. Now aren't you glad you booked another day?

HAMPTON INN & SUITES $$
4600 Summit
(816) 448-4600, (877) 410-4600
www.hamptoninnkc.com
Here's how to have the Country Club Plaza practi-cally at your front door and still have enough cash left for a big-shot dinner out. This nine-story hotel has 203 oversized guest rooms, including two-room suites with fully equipped kitchens bigger than many apartments. A continental break-fast and evening reception are complimentary. There's also a fitness room and indoor pool to help you keep in shape for those days of nonstop shopping.

THE Q HOTEL & SPA–WESTPORT $$
560 Westport Rd.
(816) 931-0001, (800) 942-4233
www.theqhotel.com

When General Manager Doug Gamble turned the Quarterage into Kansas City's first "green" hotel, he looked for ways to care for the environment while still offering creature comforts. That means guests are asked to sort their trash, can borrow bicycles to tool around the area, and take advantage of regular yoga classes. And instead of a typical on-site fitness center with a lonely treadmill, stays include a free pass to a full-scale gym just a block away. With a free hot breakfast with made-to-order omelet along with an evening reception, the workout might be advised. Other pluses that earned it a "Best Hotel" rank from *The Pitch* newspaper include luxe bedding and a special rate that includes a $25 credit towards dinner at bluestem, one of Kansas City's most lauded restaurants just two blocks away.

THE RAPHAEL HOTEL $$$
325 Ward Pkwy.
(816) 756-3800, (800) 821-5343
www.raphaelkc.com

Thank goodness, some things get better with time. That's certainly the case with one of Kansas City's most beloved hotels, which just had a major facelift without losing any of its charm. Its location, just across Brush Creek from the famous Country Club Plaza and near stellar art museums, makes it a perennial favorite with travelers. The many amenities earned the Raphael a nod as one of the world's best places to stay by *Travel + Leisure* magazine in 2009, the same year readers of *KC Magazine* named it "Best Boutique Hotel." The Raphael has 35 rooms and 88 spacious suites filled with amenities as plush as the robes.

The makeover extended to the hotel's restaurant, renamed Chaz, with a new color scheme that's the equivalent of a Valentine's Day box of chocolates in red and gold. The romantic vibe continues with Executive Chef Peter Hahn's menu, which focuses on classic American fare with a continental twist. There have been countless marriage proposals at the sumptuous booths and tables here, with piano music filtering in from the bar lounge. You can read more about this Kansas City favorite in the Restaurants chapter.

Crown Center

HYATT REGENCY CROWN CENTER $$–$$$
2345 McGee St.
(816) 421-1234, (800) 233-1234
www.crowncenter.hyatt.com

The Hyatt's lobby lounge makes quite a first impression with a dazzling sculpture that drops from the two-story ceiling like golden raindrops. It's an elegant place to listen to piano music or the restful sounds of a fountain while you enjoy a cocktail. The hotel is connected to the 85-acre Crown Center complex via an elevated walkway, so you can stroll in climate-controlled comfort to shops, restaurants, live theater, and movie houses. Crown Center Square, called Kansas City's "Rockefeller Center" by *National Geographic Traveler*, is host to year-round entertainment and an outdoor ice-skating rink. Another skywalk takes you to Union Station, the city's historic train station that includes great restaurants and unique entertainment choices.

> **i** How many balls are suspended in the sculpture hanging in the lobby of the Hyatt Regency Crown Center? Give Up? The strking arwork designed by Vermont artist Irv Harper contains 1,965 small silver globes.

The Hyatt's 733 rooms and suites feature 24-hour room service, minibars, and movie channels. Other amenities include a complimentary health club, an all-weather pool, tennis courts (even a fitness concierge), and a dazzling downtown view.

And within the Hyatt are two dining choices so superb they'll forever change your concept of "hotel restaurants." You'll find detailed descriptions in the Restaurant chapter, but for now think about the Peppercorn Duck's rotisserie-roasted duck and buffet filled with every chocolate dessert imaginable. It's open for dinner only, Thurs through Sat. Or combine a little sightseeing with your grilled steak at Skies, the city's only revolving rooftop restaurant. The lounge provides a breathtaking view as well.

THE WESTIN CROWN CENTER $$$$
1 Pershing Rd.
(816) 474-4400, (800) 228-3000
www.westin.com/kansascity

Thank goodness for the Hall family, owners of Hallmark Cards, who converted an eyesore called Signboard Hill into one of the city's most exciting tourist areas. At its heart is the Westin, whose five-story lobby waterfall makes dramatic use of the original hill's natural limestone.

The 724-room hotel's location just keeps getting better and better with a $10 million renovation. Trust us, the Heavenly Bed® deserves its name. Even your pooch gets a special dog bed while a guest! The Westin's neighbor is Union Station, with several excellent restaurants, entertainment, and Science City, all accessible via an elevated walkway that looks like something out of Disneyland's Tomorrowland. But you can enjoy plenty of action without leaving Crown Center. Enjoy a burger in a converted streetcar, take in a movie, or shop dozens of unique boutiques. Kids can learn new artistic skills at Kaleidoscope or simply color a placemat at Crayola Cafe. As a guest of the Westin, you'll have a ringside seat for the activities at Crown Center Square, including summertime concerts, hunting for the Great Pumpkin, and lighting the mayor's Christmas tree. Even when there's nothing happening outside, the downtown skyline view from Benton's rooftop steakhouse is stunning.

Downtown

THE ALADDIN HOLIDAY
INN DOWNTOWN $$-$$$
1215 Wyandotte St.
(816) 421-8888
www.hialaddin.com

After an extensive renovation, this historic building, originally built in 1926, offers the kind of retro-chic that would make it popular in any major city. But the slender, brick 16-floor beauty is situated right in the heart of our downtown's convention and entertainment district with an architectural styling that echoes the more than 60 art deco buildings in the area. Today's Aladdin offers 193 guest rooms, including two suites, with exquisite bedding (including a menu of pillow choices) and such amenities as the CitiScape Day Spa. But what we enjoy most are the revamped restaurant, the Zebra Room, and the Martini Loft.

CROWNE PLAZA $$-$$$
1301 Wyandotte St.
(816) 474-6664, (800) 227-6963
www.crowneplaza.com/kansascity

This 28-story high-rise has had several names and personalities, beginning as the Americana in the 1970s. Today, as Crowne Plaza, it's more handsome than ever, graced with rich woods, mission-style furnishings, and a hint of the art deco architecture found in many of its surrounding buildings. The location puts Kansas City's cultural attractions and business services at its door. Choose a quick bite or elegant evening dinner at the City Bistro or City Grille. Or get your java fix at the on-site Starbuck's in the lobby.

HILTON PRESIDENT KANSAS CITY $$-$$$
1329 Baltimore
(816) 221-9490
www.hilton.com

If you like to say "They don't build 'em like they used to," you'll enjoy all the lush trappings from the 1920s when the President first arrived on the scene: gorgeous marble and intricate plasterwork decorate every inch of public space. Today the 213-guest-room palace is the official hotel to the exciting 24/7 area known as the Power & Light District. If you're in the market for an impressive corporate shindig or special event, the President's grand ballroom will wow your guests with an elegant space and unmatched views of downtown. All in all, we'd say the $45 million for the makeover was well spent.

The President also brought back its famous Drum Room from the 1940s. Luminaries such as Frank Sinatra, Tommy Dorsey, and Duke Ellington all performed here. Today guests can sit in the Rat Pack booth and enjoy live entertainment on Fri and Sat nights along with the Drum Room's tasty nine-ounce martinis. Alas, the Marx Brothers won't be on the stage, but some of Kansas City's best jazz talent will be. The restaurant side is also getting noticed with its laid-back atmosphere and menu choices that include a 10-spice roasted duck and all your favorite steaks and chops. The happy hour (and reverse happy hour that's perfect for a late-night bite) will make you just that: happy.

**KANSAS CITY MARRIOTT
DOWNTOWN** $$$–$$$$
200 W. 12th St.
(816) 421-6800, (800) 228-9290
www.marriotthotels.com
With an ideal downtown location, underground link to the convention center, and superb meeting facilities, the Marriott is convention central. It's also the place where Kansas Citians stop in for cocktails before heading across the street for a night at the Folly, Midland Theatre, Music Hall, Lyric Opera, or Kansas City Symphony. In 1997 the Marriott nearly doubled in size by merging with the historic Muehlebach Hotel at 1213 Wyandotte. Together, the two properties offer 983 rooms and suites. During its prime the Muehlebach was Kansas City's favored host for celebrities, presidents, and four musicians from Liverpool who held a news conference in the ballroom on September 17, 1964. Other news was made here as well: In the wee hours of November 3, 1948, Harry S. Truman chose the hotel to announce that he had been reelected.

The two hotel towers are now linked via a covered walkway. Together the properties offer 10,000 square feet of meeting space, including two ballrooms, 32 breakout rooms, and a 12,000-square-foot exhibit hall. The complex features a fully equipped health club and indoor pool, full-service business center including secretarial services if requested, and gift shop. There

are also plenty of places to dine, enjoy a cocktail, or simply relax. For breakfast, lunch, or dinner head to Lilly's or the Pam Pam Room, a Kansas City tradition for generations. The Muehlebach Lobby Lounge offers a refined cocktail hour, and the 12th Street Bar on the lobby level of the Marriott adds jazz to the mix on Fri and Sat nights.

East Metro
**COCO KEY WATER RESORT
AT THE HOLIDAY INN–SE** $$–$$$
9103 E. 39th St.
(816) 737-0200, (866) 754-6962
www.cocokeywaterresort.com
Missouri's newest and largest indoor water park made a splash when it opened with 55,000 square foot of liquid fun in 2009. No matter the weather, it's always a balmy 84 degrees, making the variety of body slides, tipping bucket, and adventure river a blast for the entire family. Little ones will enjoy the Dip-In Theater, where a movie or cartoon is always on the screen. Book one of the 374 guestrooms and the water park is free. Or you can reserve a day for a birthday party, scout outing, or just a day of play. Just be sure to bring your own towels, but leave the snacks and drinks at home: the resort has two fast-food restaurants to appease any hungry kids. And for the big-kid baseball fans, it's just a stroll across the walkway over eight lanes of I-70 to the Kauffman Stadium to see the Royals play.

North of the River
AMERISTAR CASINO HOTEL $$–$$$
3200 N. Ameristar Dr.
(816) 414-7000, (800) 499-4961
www.ameristar.com
If your interpretation of "a little R & R" is "I'm ready to roll the dice," the Ameristar is for you. The 184 guest rooms and suites are quite nice, but it's the entertainment outside that keeps the reservations phone ringing.

The casino's decor—with an arched, blue-sky ceiling and dancing water fountains—makes it one of the most beautiful in the Midwest. Guests can partake of more than 160 table games,

Kansas City's largest collection of slot and video poker games, 18 state-of-the-art movie theaters, or a stroll along the Victorian-era streetscape. And everyone gets lucky at the hotel's restaurants. Choose from a brew pub, steakhouse, oyster bar, or Arthur Bryant's, an offshoot of the famous barbecue joint downtown. And Ameristar makes sure children have fun while parents play; Kids Quest provides activities in a safe, supervised environment.

Ameristar's three live music venues pay off big as well. The Star Pavilion hosts top touring talent such as B. B. King, Tony Bennett, Aretha Franklin, and Willie Nelson, while Depot No. 9 brings down the house with rock 'n' roll and blues.

ARGOSY CASINO & SPA $$–$$$
777 Northwest Argosy Pkwy.
Riverside, MO
(816) 746-3100
www.argosycasinos.com/kansascity
You can bank on having a great time at the Argosy. The feeling is pure top-rate, from the minute you enter the Tuscan-style lobby to the moment you sink into the plush bedding in your suite. And do book a suite if you're feeling in the chips. Request one of these luxury palaces with a view of the twinkling downtown skyline off in the distance.

Opened in 2007, the Argosy offers 250 regular rooms and 8 suites with enormous bathrooms with rain showerheads (trust us, you'll want one for your home) and jetted tubs. Two 42-inch HD plasma-screen televisions add to your comfort. Although it's hard to pull yourself away from lounging in that plush robe, you have too much to do, such as treat yourself to a massage or facial in the elegant day spa, or try one of five dining venues—from fancy wood-fired steakhouse and Kobe beef burgers to a casual deli. Don't worry: You can work off those calories in the fitness center where each treadmill has its own TV.

And of course Argosy offers all the gaming action you could want, including a plush new poker room with seven tables dealing out Seven-Card Stud and Omaha and Texas Hold 'Em.

Any open seats are announced throughout the casino, so you can enjoy the slots until it's time to get your game face on.

THE ELMS RESORT & SPA $$
401 Regent
Excelsior Springs, MO
(816) 630-5500, (800) THE-ELMS (843-3567)
www.elmsresort.com
You never know whom you might meet at this retreat just 30 minutes from Kansas City; Presidents Harry S. Truman and FDR slept here. So did Al Capone. In fact, plenty of national celebrities and much of Kansas City society have stayed here. The Elms's history actually precedes its grand opening date of 1912: The property was originally built in 1888 as a luxury resort to take advantage of the area's mineral waters. When the building's wide wooden verandas and pine interiors twice were destroyed by fire, they were replaced by native Missouri limestone. The hotel is still a haven of serenity and style, with 153 guest rooms and suites. A world-class spa and wellness center includes Swiss and Vichy showers, massage treatments, facials, manicures, and pedicures. In 2009, readers of KC Magazine rated it "Best Day Spa." With its 16 acres of gently rolling hills, the Elms also provides plenty of opportunities for an afternoon stroll or jog.

When you're ready for cocktails you can unwind in the lobby lounge or the second-level library lounge. The Elms's Dining Room serves breakfast, lunch, and dinner or sumptuous weekend breakfast buffet in a graceful setting with a wall of windows overlooking the landscaped grounds.

If you can pull yourself away from that late-morning massage, there's plenty to do in Excelsior Springs. Along with golf courses and antiques shops, there's the fascinating Hall of Waters Spa and Mineral Baths, where you can choose your favorite bottled water from around the world or indulge in other spa treatments. And the Jesse James Farm and Museum in nearby Kearney, Missouri, provides a fascinating look at the area's favorite bandit hero.

HARRAH'S NORTH KANSAS CITY CASINO & HOTEL $$–$$$
One Riverboat Dr.
N. Kansas City, MO
(816) 472-7777, (800) HARRAHS
www.harrahsnkc.com

Harrah's hotel and convention center is so attractive that you might come here without so much as peeking in the gaming area. The 392 rooms and suites are luxurious and amenities abound, including 24-hour room service, an indoor swimming pool, and an exercise room. There's even an arcade to keep kids and teens happy for hours. But you'll be tempted to play once you see Harrah's 30,000-square-foot addition to its Mardi Gras Casino. With over 2,000 slot machines and plenty of tables, we're betting you'll find lots to keep you entertained.

When you're hungry head to one of four themed restaurants, including casual choices such as Toby Keith's I Love This Bar & Grill, and Moby's Fish Tales. Meanwhile, get a taste of primo Italian fare at Mike & Charlie's, where pastas are king. The Range rustles up sizzling steaks, seafood, and prime rib in an upscale Southwestern setting. And the smoking-hot nightclub, VooDoo Lounge, has put Harrah's on the map with live music or smokin' hot DJs. See details in Nightlife.

Overland Park, Kansas

THE DOUBLETREE $$–$$$
10100 College Blvd.
Overland Park, KS
(913) 451-6100, (800) 222-TREE
www.doubletree.com

This hotel's name is certainly appropriate: It's surrounded by a densely forested park that includes a 4-mile hiking and biking trail. In fact, guests have watched deer graze and families of ducks paddle along the streams that meander through the woods. Creature comforts are inside as well, starting with Doubletree's signature chocolate chip cookies. Each of the 356 rooms and 17 suites on 18 floors features a Sweet Dreams bed. The hotel's entertainment options include a lounge where you can relax over cocktails while watching the sun set over that parklike vista.

Trofi Restaurant, with its beautiful fountain and multitiered design, is a favorite with the Johnson County set. The menu will tempt you with pan seared trout, grilled steaks, or the most decadent mac and cheese you've ever encountered. If you're in town during a holiday, call to see if brunch is being served; it's a not-to-be-missed extravaganza.

THE MARRIOTT $$–$$$
10800 Metcalf
Overland Park, KS
(913) 451-8000, (800) 228-9290
www.overlandparkmarriott.com

With 391 rooms and 7 suites, this just-renovated hotel is an island of style in the heart of bustling Overland Park. The public areas are plush and inviting, and three distinct dining choices give you plenty of reasons to make this your home-away-from-home. At Epicure you can find all your favorite American fare, as well as "Fit for You" healthy entrees. The Marriott is also home to Nikko Japanese Steakhouse, which combines an evening's entertainment with fabulous food. Skilled chefs chop and prepare teppanyaki dinners in front of you on large stainless-steel grills. To work off your meal, do some laps in the indoor pool, head to the fitness center, or take advantage of nearby outdoor activities.

SHERATON OVERLAND PARK HOTEL AT THE CONVENTION CENTER $$–$$$
6100 College Blvd.
Overland Park, KS
(913) 234-2100, (888) 625-5144
www.sheraton.com

It's really the second half of this lodging's title—the Convention Center—that's its claim to fame. The space boasts the largest ballroom in Kansas and a 60,000-square-foot exhibit hall. We also consider it an art gallery thanks to more than 60 pieces of fine art, mostly by area artists. The Sheraton Hotel, which is connected to the convention center via landscaped courtyards and an all-weather walkway, offers 412 rooms and a fitness center. Get VIP treatment on the Club Lounge floors with complimentary breakfast, evening cocktails, and—if you simply must work—access to a complete business center.

Its restaurant, 1906 Bar and Grille, takes its name from the year in which William Strang Jr. developed the railroad that led to the development of Overland Park. The menu offers comfort food with a sounthern twist. Perhaps that's why readers of The Pitch bestowed it with a "Best Hotel Food" award.

WHITE HAVEN MOTOR LODGE $
8039 Metcalf
Overland Park, KS
(913) 649-8200, (800) 752-2892
www.whitehavenmotorlodge.com
Since 1957 the White family has been turning guests into friends at their pretty little motor lodge. Its charm comes from a blast-from-the-past design with a swimming pool out front, a groovy retro sign, and furniture that leans toward French provincial. It provides the kind of comfort, value, and friendliness that make you expect to see Ward and June Cleaver and the boys pull up in a station wagon. To encourage the extended-stay trade, every room has a refrigerator, and a continental breakfast is served each morning in the coffee lounge.

Wyandotte County, Kansas

CHATEAU AVALON $$$–$$$$
701 Village West Pkwy.
(I-435 and State Ave.)
Kansas City, KS
(913) 596-6000, (877) KC-AVALON
www.chateauavalonhotel.com
What's Cleopatra doing on the plains of Kansas? Relaxing in a jetted spa with Chroma therapy lighting, that's what.

This cross between a bed-and-breakfast and a high-end resort features custom-made mattresses and posh linens, 60-inch flat-screen TVs with DVD players and surround sound, a rose-petal turndown, and made-to-order in-room breakfast. Cleo, baby, you never had it so good. Chateau Avalon offers 62 luxurious themed suites, including six two-story accommodations, such as the Castaway Isle, a tropical island para-

dise. Or perhaps the Casablanca is more to your tune; here you'll slumber in a replica of 1940 Morocco, complete with piles of plush pillows and a DVD of the famous movie. It seems miles away from the rat race—but is actually just a few minutes away from the Kansas Speedway.

GREAT WOLF LODGE $$$–$$$$
10401 Cabela Dr.
Kansas City, KS
(913) 299-7001, (800) 608-WOLF (9653)
www.greatwolflodge.com
From its hand-carved totem poles to the rustic furniture you'd swear you were at a ski lodge on a snowcapped mountain peak. But the main draw is pure tropics: an indoor water park where an eye-popping assortment of fountains, pools, slides, and jets stay a pleasant 84 degrees year-round. Every few minutes a giant bucket atop the 12-story tree house tips and drenches the crowd below. Hold on to your swim trunks! The Triple Twist is a first-of-its-kind, five-story series of waterslides and funnels that becomes an LED-lighting experience at night. After dinner in the Bear Claw Cafe, it's story time in the lobby as children cuddle with parents by a massive stone fireplace. Sleepy eyes snap open when a menagerie of animated woodland creatures brings a giant clock tower to life. One of the most compelling attractions of Great Wolf, however, is its six different themed suites, including the Wolf Den with a decorated enclosure for tired little cubs. Momma bears will enjoy being pampered in the Elements Spa.

EXTENDED STAYS

With Kansas City's growing base of national and international corporations, extended-stay facilities give newly hired executives a homey place to board. Individuals and families relocating to our city will find temporary residences that truly feel like home. For options, contact **Extended Stay** (www.extendedstaydeluxe.com) or **Extended Stay America** (www.extendedstayamerica) to find fully furnished apartments, duplexes, and homes for specific needs. In the meantime, here's one of the most popular in town.

**RESIDENCE INN BY MARRIOTT–
UNION HILL** $$-$$$
2975 Main St.
(816) 561-3000, (800) 331-3131
www.residenceinn.com/mciuh

When Hallmark hires a new manager from out of town, they'll often treat the trainee to these deluxe townhomes overlooking the company's headquarters at Crown Center. The services are amazing, including complimentary grocery shopping, van transportation up to 5 miles, breakfast, local restaurant delivery, and an evening hospitality hour. Accommodations include studios, doubles, and a two-level penthouse that includes a queen-size bed on each floor, plus a pullout sofa bed.

BED-AND-BREAKFASTS AND INNS

Rocking chairs on wide verandas, breakfast sausages grilled on a tree-shaded patio, a grand piano in the parlor, and fresh flowers on your nightstand . . . for those who treasure the personal touches found only at a bed-and-breakfast, we have just the cozy spot for you. Several, in fact. This list includes urban settings, Plaza addresses, and a horse ranch in the tallgrass prairies of Kansas.

**CIRCLE S RANCH GUEST
RANCH & COUNTRY INN** $$
3325 Circle S Lane
Lawrence, KS
(785) 843-4124, (800) 625-2839
www.circlesranch.com

Nestled amid 1,200 acres of sprawling prairie and wooded glens, Circle S has won enough awards to turn a cowgirl's head. It has become a popular place for everything from business meetings to marriage proposals, but rarely in the same weekend.

In fact, owner Mary Cronemeyer has coordinated dozens of weddings, from sweet ceremonies in the wildflower meadow to blowout bashes at the Party Barn. Twelve spacious guest rooms feature decor ranging from pioneer quaintness to cowboy whimsy—witness the showerhead in a bucket—plus a private bath and breathtaking

view. An eight-person hot tub in the silo will give you something to talk about for months.

Mornings start with a ranch hand's breakfast of scrambled eggs, biscuits and gravy, crispy hash browns, and—if you're lucky—some golden preserves from Mary's grandmother's apricot tree. Spend the rest of the day browsing boutiques in nearby Lawrence, call dibs on a rocking chair on the wraparound porch, or stroll the trails until a hammock calls your name. Chances are you won't be alone: White-tailed deer, quail, and wild turkey share the ranch with 200 head of cattle and quite a few bison.

If you take along a picnic basket, ask for extra apples for the horses. Along with personal retreats and special occasions, Circle S has found a niche with girls' slumber parties—adult style. Mary greets guests with whirling blenders of margaritas while manicures, pedicures, and massages await. All-night videos and popcorn complete the theme.

HAWTHORN BED AND BREAKFAST $$-$$$
One Hawthorn Place
Independence, MO
(816) 252-2607
www.hawthornbb.com

Many guests arriving at this stately, 1900 stone mansion make the same announcement, usually accompanied by a sigh: "I could live here." Thankfully, Jim and Wendy Allen *do* live here, and have turned it into one of the Midwest's most welcoming inns. A few of the elements that set it apart are the lushly landscaped two-acre estate and the extra-large guestrooms and two-room suite. No frou-frou here; the rooms are handsomely appointed with antiques, beautiful fabrics, and art. The first floor is equally as elegant, with gleaming oak floors, antique rugs, and chandeliers. No wonder Hawthorn hosts so many weddings, showers, and family reunions. Guests are greeted with beverages and snacks upon arrival, and a lavish breakfast awaits in the sunny dining room the next morning. Borrow a book from the library and relax, or head to the historic Independence Square just 2 miles away for a day of shopping and sightseeing. There are five guest quarters, each with a private bath with plenty of modern amenities.

THE INN ON CRESCENT LAKE $$–$$$
1261 St. Louis Ave.
Excelsior Springs, MO
(816) 630-6745
www.crescentlake.com

Motor up the long curving drive to this majestic 1915 Georgian-Colonial with stately white columns and you might expect Scarlett O'Hara to sashay down the steps. That illusion will end as soon as you hear innkeeper Patrick Delugeau's French accent. He was born in the Loire Valley and his wife Beverly spent her teen years in Brittany. After a four-year search, the couple found this charming inn on 22 wooded acres with two crescent-shaped ponds that inspired the inn's name. You'll be just as enchanted by the sun-filled solarium and sweeping staircase, gorgeously decorated rooms and suites. There are 10 in all, each with a private bath and unique personality. The Garden Room's private deck comes complete with a hot tub for wishing on a star. It also affords a private entrance and is wheelchair-accessible. The two-story Cottage, separate from the main house, is a little love nest or ideal family get-away choice that offers a living room, half bath, and kitchen on the lower level and king-size bed, sitting area, whirlpool tub for two, and walk-in shower above. Or reserve the Pool House with an inspiring view of the pool and lakes. The water does, indeed, beckon guests during nice weather. Share a paddleboat, take a dip in the pool, or aim a fishing pole at the bass, sunnies, or catfish. Or take a walk around the estate's paths. Breakfasts are a delightful way to meet fellow travelers over such wake-me-ups as sour cream waffles with banana syrup or biscuits and sausage gravy. Once you're mesmerized by this enchanting place, you'll understand why so many couples say "I do" to holding their weddings and receptions here.

OPHELIA'S $$
201 N. Main
Independence, MO
(816) 461-4525
www.opheliasind.net

Cocktails, dinner, a little light jazz, and you're off to dreamland. It's all part of the package at Ken and Cindy McClain's stylish inn just upstairs from the restaurant of the same name. The couple even tossed in a little history: Ophelia's is across the street from Clinton's Soda Shop, where a young Harry Truman used to dish up ice cream. The seven rooms and one spacious suite each have a private bath. A continental breakfast is brought to your door in a basket. Ophelia's is on historic Independence Square with a plethora of restaurants and unique shopping choices—including a home decor store, fashion boutique, kitchenware emporium, haberdashery, movie theatre, and even a bowling alley. Cindy, you've been busy!

SOUTHMORELAND ON THE PLAZA $$–$$$
116 E. 46th St.
(816) 531-7979
www.southmoreland.com

Perhaps the Midwest's most celebrated inn, the Southmoreland is a magnificent 1913 colonial revival on a quiet residential street just 2 blocks from the Country Club Plaza. Inside you'll understand its long list of kudos, including being six-time winner of the Mobil Four-Star award, one of America's Top 25 Favorite Inns, and Inn of the Month from *Travel + Leisure*. Mark Reichle and Nancy Miller Reichle have added several improvements since taking ownership a decade ago, including a carriage house suite named for George Kessler, the landscape architect who designed the inn's namesake park. The suite is separated from the main building by a lovely brick courtyard and offers unmatched privacy and comfort. Guests can relax in front of the wood-burning stove or in a jetted tub for two.

Similar charming details appear in the inn's other 12 rooms, which are named for Kansas City celebrities. Guests in the pastel Clara and Russell Stover Room, for example, find a tiny box of chocolates on their pillows, and the Satchel Paige knotty pine sleeping porch re-creates the baseball legend's favorite fishing cabin. Each room has a private bath and such special treats as a fireplace or jetted tub. You'll also appreciate what's happening in the kitchen. Guests are treated to wine and hot hors d'oeuvres upon arrival. For dinner you'll have your choice of dozens of restaurants on the Plaza. In the morning awake to an incredible breakfast that may include the inn's famous French toast stuffed with Swiss cheese and brown-sugar ham, fresh fruit, and chocolate-zucchini bread. In warmer weather Mark often treats guests to grilled sausage or ham steaks on the patio. It's just one highlight of what makes staying in a bed-and-breakfast so special—you're treated like family.

RV CAMPSITES AND RESORTS

BASSWOOD COUNTRY INN AND
RV RESORT   **$$–$$$**
15880 Interurban Rd.
Platte City, MO
(816) 858-5556, (800) 242-2775 (reservations
only)
www.basswoodresort.com
Here's a campsite and fishing resort that hits all the right notes. At least that's what Bing Crosby and Rudy Vallee thought when they were guests of millionaire A. G. Stephens's Basswood Sportsmen's Club in the 1940s. Harry and Bess Truman also stayed here on vacations from the rigors of the presidency. A more recent guest was actor Matthew McConaughey, who has a suite named in his honor.

No doubt he agreed with *Peak* magazine, which called Basswood "perhaps the most beautiful wooded lakefront setting in the Kansas City area." It's without a doubt the fishiest: Four freshwater lakes are stocked with catfish, bass, crappie, and carp.

Basswood packs a summer's worth of activities into the site. There's a large selection of videos to rent at the store, where you'll also find basic groceries, RV and camping supplies, packaged liquor, and gifts—and even pizza baked fresh every day from 5:30 to 8 p.m.

Accommodations include the private Mother-in-Law Cottage with two bedrooms and full kitchen; the Celebrity House Suites and Country French Suites. There are full hook-up RV sites (30 and 50 amp) plus water/electric-only

sites for tents and pop-ups, including deluxe sites with patios. Guests can use the two picnic shelters, laundry facilities, and superclean bathhouses with shower stalls and vanities. Wireless Internet is available throughout the resort. Basswood Resort, open year-round, is just 5 miles from Kansas City International Airport and near the attraction-packed towns of Independence, Parkville, Weston, and St. Joseph.

JACKSON COUNTY PARKS AND
RECREATION CAMPGROUNDS
(816) 503-4805
www.jacksongov.org/parks
Jackson County, Missouri, offers three public campgrounds with a total of 250 camping sites, all about 15 minutes from Kansas City proper. They are available by reservation for stays up to 14 days, and at least one camper must be 21 or over. The camping facilities include showers, restrooms, attendants, picnic tables, and ice.

Longview Lake Campground is within nearly 5,000 acres of parkland and includes a 930-acre lake with full-service marina. Attractions include a 4-mile nature trail, horse park, launching ground where colorful hot air balloons take off and land, swimming beach, and 27-hole public golf course. The campground is open Apr 1 through Sept 30ad offers 113 sites (59 with full electricity). Lake Jacomo Campground is within beautiful Fleming Park, at 7,800 acres the largest parkland in Jackson County. At its heart is 970-acre Lake Jacomo, and there's the smaller Blue Springs Lake as well. More than 1.5 million visitors a year make the best of its many pleasures, including a nature preserve, an Audubon center, a marina that hosts sailboat regattas, a swimming beach, nature trails, and more. The campground, open from Apr 1 through Oct 31, has 57 large, tree-lined sites available. Blue Springs Lake Campground, also within Fleming Park, is open during the same period with 82 camping choices. Bring your swimsuits; this site is five minutes from the beach.

RESTAURANTS

Of all the things that surprise first-time visitors to Kansas City—from our cosmopolitan ambience to our far-from-flat topography—nothing seems to floor them more than our food. Not just how good it is, mind you, but how diverse it is.

Tourists already know about the superiority of our beef thanks to Calvin Trillin's 1974 book, *American Fried*, which begins, "The best restaurants in the world are, of course, in Kansas City. Not all of them; only the top four or five."

But you don't have to be a card-carrying carnivore to eat well here. Foodies can have a world tour of authentic cuisine from Mexico to Mongolia and cooking styles from Cajun to Catalan. Vegetarians can get their five-a-day at a number of excellent eateries in town, and fish lovers will get along swimmingly. Wine aficionados will want to raise a toast to this city. *Wine Spectator* hands out awards around here like party favors. Two of our restaurants have received the magazine's Grand Award, a distinction only 100 in the world can claim. But sometimes it's not what's on the menu that makes it worth your trip. Lots of dining rooms serve a side of blues or jazz with their burgers or beefsteaks. You'll find just about every national chain restaurant here, including the Capital Grille, P.F. Chang's China Bistro, Cheesecake Factory, and Houston's. These are all fine dining experiences, to be sure, but this book focuses on independent restaurants to introduce you to our regional cooking and original recipes.

All restaurants are in Kansas City, Missouri, unless otherwise noted.

Price Code

Our price code is based on dinner for two, without appetizers, dessert, alcoholic beverages, tax, or tip. Your own bill may be higher or lower depending on what you order and normal fluctuating prices. *Bon appétit.*

$.................. Less than $20
$$ .... $20 to $40
$$$ ....$41 and up

AMERICAN/CONTINENTAL

THE AMERICAN RESTAURANT $$$
25th and Grand Ave. (Crown Center)
(816) 545-8000
www.theamericankc.com
With a sparkling view of downtown and the city's only Mobil Four-Star rating, this American beauty is the place to woo a lover or wow a client. The soaring space was designed by Walter Platner two years before he did Manhattan's late,

great Windows on the World, and it is stunning, especially when shutters on the floor-to-ceiling windows are opened just at sunset. Don't be surprised when a room of delighted diners bursts into applause. The food easily matches the theatrics. The legendary James Beard was brought in as a consultant in 1974 to create refined yet soul-warming interpretations of classic American cooking.

Mr. Beard would be proud. In charge of the kitchen is James Beard award winner (for Best Chef in the Midwest 1999) Debbie Gold, who resumed her reign here several years after leaving the American with then husband, Michael Smith, to open 40 Sardines in Overland Park. Debbie's menu pays homage to the Midwest's bounty of meats, game, and produce. But before you think "meat, potatoes, and plenty of gravy," take a look at a recent midwinter menu: pumpkin ravioli, free-range pheasant, a meltingly tender sable fish, and artisanal cheese platter. And you've never had a Peppermint Patty quite like this. The service is stellar as well under general manager Jamie Jamison's sure hand. Watch for the special events like wine dinners Jamie hosts here; they are quite spectacular. And chances are if you ask for "the usual" at the bar, you'll get it. Willie Grandison, named Best Bartender in the Country by *Playboy* and *Cheers* magazine, has been holding court here for 30 years. A note on dress: although the American has eased its formal reputation—jackets at dinner are merely suggested now—it's still a refined restaurant where you might see black tie and ball gowns before opening night at the Lyric Opera. The American is open for dinner only.

i Save 40 percent on dinner? We'll bite! Sign up on www.kansascitymenus .com for discounted gift certificates to some of KC's top restaurants. The offer arrives via e-mail once every quarter, and the best ones are gone within minutes, so be quick or go hungry.

AVENUES BISTRO   **$–$$**
338 W. 63rd St. (Brookside)
(816) 333-5700
www.avenuesbistro.com
There was already plenty to like about this place: a location in the Brookside neighborhood (with a coveted parking lot), a friendly waitstaff, efficient bartenders, and a menu that covered global dishes. But when chef owner Joe Birch scaled back prices, Kansas City responded with a collective cheer. During happy hour, the 12 or so tapas are $4 and cocktails just $5. And at Avenues, the tapas aren't tiny portions; we often make a meal out of the lobster mac and cheese or Pork Morengo with a lusty tomato sauce. But it's more fun to share a variety of small plates with friends as a prelude to dinner. If that's the case, entrees to try (nothing over $20) include the braised shortrib stroganoff, pan seared halibut, or the award-winning steak frites.

But we beg you: leave room for the flourless chocolate cake. We know one socialite who takes an entire cake to parties, calling it her secret family recipe. We won't tell. Servers know how to read

the table, either providing polished assistance or jumping in to take a picture of the birthday party. Need some help choosing wine? You're in luck: Timothy O'Neal loves nothing better than sharing his latest discovery from Spain or a delicious bargain from Mendocino. Sunday brunch (sans the wine) is just as tempting (and crowded) thanks to a menu that includes six types of eggs Benedicts, bananas foster pancakes, and praline orange French toast. Reservations are a must for any visit.

BLUESTEM   **$$$**
900 Westport Rd. (Midtown)
(816) 561-1101
www.bluestemkc.com
When husband-and-wife chefs open a restaurant, it can't help but be high on the romance meter. That's the mantra at this 43-seat bistro that has been rocking the local foodie contingent since 2004. What makes it romantic is the pacing—don't expect to eat and run to catch an eight o'clock movie. Dinners start with amuse-bouche, a complimentary sampling of tastes. This is your first glimpse of Colby's attention to detail (and a reason he's been a James Beard Award contender several times): Each miniature canapé is presented like a gem at a jewelry counter.

Entrees might have you reaching for your camera before tucking into such masterpieces as wild salmon with crispy sweetbreads or a beautifully grilled strip steak next to mahogany-colored roasted onions. Like many fine establishments in town, diners can choose three- to five-course fixed-price repasts. But bluestem offers as many as 12 courses; this last one—described as a "spontaneous collection from the chef"—is only available Tues through Thurs and only if the entire table says yes, please. Megan's skill with pastries is evident in the dessert selection, which includes a citrus crème brûlée and silky malted-chocolate sponge pudding.

Sunday brunch is often a "Who's Who" of local chefs from other eateries, and the wine bar connected to the restaurant is a swanky place to spend an evening. Even here the cocktails are thoughtfully crafted and there are enough tempting appetizers to turn it into a light meal.

CAFE SEBASTIENNE $–$$
4420 Warwick Blvd. (Country Club Plaza)
(816) 561-7740
www.kemperart.org/cafe
No one would blame executive chef Jennifer Maloney if she skimped on food presentation; her restaurant's location within the Kemper Museum of Contemporary Art should be visual stimulus enough. Diners are surrounded by artwork; in fact in the main room every square inch of wall space is covered in paintings. But Jennifer's menu is more than up to the challenge. Salads—such as the ode to autumn, with seasonal greens, smoked Gouda, turkey, pears, honey-baked pecans, and curry-mustard dressing—are works of art. The foie gras–stuffed quail and risotto are simply dreamy, the roasted beef tenderloin with turnip-and-fig gratin divine. And for some fans, the meal isn't over until they've polished off a wedge of chocolate budino, a decadent flourless torte served with fresh fruit and whipped cream. Lunch is served Tues through Sat, and dinner is available Fri and Sat with a Sunday brunch.

CAFE TRIO $–$$
4558 Main
(816) 756-3227
www.cafetriokc.com
Fans of this popular restaurant worried when they learned Trio was moving from its mid-town location. "Things will never be the same," they moaned. That's true: things are better than ever. A larger space with room for private parties, a view of the Country Club Plaza from an expansive back deck, a talented chef who's put his own stamp on the menu, and service that's more polished yet still friendly. The only down side for regulars is that they can no longer just pop in; reservations are a must. The owners wisely kept favorites from the old menu, like the Mac Daddy (a gooey macaroni masterpiece with three gourmet cheeses, bacon, and red peppers), pistachio-crusted tilapia, and a 20-ounce KC strip. New entrees include a decadent osso bucco and New Zealand rack of lamb.

Cafe Trio shares space with the swanky Starlet Lounge, named for the Hollywood actresses whose photos loom overhead and inspire several of the martinis. There's live music five nights a week. Thankfully, as before, Trio attracts a wide variety of patrons, and they're all welcome: the city's most stylish gay men, straight couples from the suburbs on their way to or from the theatre, attractive young singles meeting friends after work. When not staring at your date (or flirting with that cutie across the room), you can admire the changing art provided by local talent.

i Although lots of restaurants and bars offer early-evening happy hour drink and appetizer specials, KC's young and beautiful crowd are more apt to venture out late at night. Voila! The reverse happy hour, usually from nine-ish to close. Grand Street Cafe, Avenues Bistro, re:Verse, and Kona Grill are just four. We feel an afternoon nap coming on.

CHAZ IN THE RAPHAEL HOTEL $$
325 Ward Pkwy. (Country Club Plaza)
(816) 756-3800
www.raphaelkc.com
For decades, Kansas Citians and tourists alike have have considered this space the most romantic restaurant in town. It could be the piano music coming from the lounge, the private booths, or the food that can make even the toughest customer starry-eyed. Or it could be that, unlike so many other eateries in town, you can actually hear your partner's sweet nothings whispered from across the table. A recent makeover may remind you of a red-velvet box of Valentine chocolates. Adding to its lovey-dovey ambience is the fact that the Raphael Hotel's lobby is just a few steps away. Executive chef Peter Hahn keeps the menu fresh with items borrowed from Asian, French, Italian, and even Southwest cuisines. One of his signature entrees is a New Zealand rack of lamb, but you can also try a flavorful bison ribeye or lighter diver scallops. Desserts can be decadent or whimsical, as with the Reese's Dream with peanut butter mousse enrobed in chocolate ganache. Or there's always that chocolate waiting on your pillow upstairs. The lounge offers tasty

appetizers along with some of the city's best musical performers from Tues through Sat. Lunch and dinner are served Mon through Sat. Breakfast is served daily.

CLASSIC CUP CAFÉ $$
301 W. 47th St. (Country Club Plaza)
(816) 753-1840
www.classiccup.com

This longtime Plaza favorite offers a running fashion show as bags tagged with Armani Exchange, Betsey Johnson, and Halls pass by its row of tables on the sidewalk. There's also a popular deck out back and the inside tables have wall-to-wall windows plus a fireplace for coolish weather.

The food is good from any vantage point. This is the place for a power breakfast with business leaders making deals over eggs Benedict or biscuits and gravy. At Sunday brunch, the pace is more relaxed, but the food is just as tempting. The pancakes are so famous you can now purchase the mix to go.

Lunch favorites include the spicy Thai pizza, salads, and pastas. Daily specials live up to the name. Dinners might start with gnocchi with a Gorgonzola-walnut sauce. Entrees include grilled rack of lamb and roasted chicken. And while other restaurants may close for a few hours between lunch and dinner service, Classic Cup offers an in-between menu with many of its favorites to tide you over or fuel the next round of shopping. To accompany your meal there are 40 wines by the glass as well as an 800-bottle wine cellar. You'll be glad you saved room for dessert once you taste the Classic Cup's legendary bread pudding with hot caramel sauce. The Classic Cup is open seven days a week, and reservations are a good idea.

EBT RESTAURANT $$–$$$$
1310 Carondelet
(I-435 and State Line, in the atrium of UMB Bank)
(816) 942-8870
www.ebtrestaurant.com

Don't be turned off by the nondescript bank building housing this popular restaurant. Step inside the big square edifice and you'll see why

it's one of our picks for a romantic anniversary or first date.

The name comes from Emery, Bird, Thayer, our town's first department store, founded in 1863 at 11th and Grand. The grand store closed in the '60s, and decades later its gorgeous mezzanine tearoom was reborn as EBT Restaurant using such artifacts as the massive sandstone column capitals and ornate brass elevator cages.

A major makeover in 2006 gave it sex appeal with rich colors and enormous lighting fixtures that look as if they've been borrowed from a Moroccan palace.

Dinners are just as compelling, such as the coriander grilled lamb chops served with shallot marmalade glacé and sweet potato puree, and parmesan-breaded Chilean sea bass. Lunch is popular as well when executives conduct business over peppered beef tenderloin, Caesar salad, or blackened pork tenderloin sandwich. Owner Ed Holland (who also grows the roses you see throughout the room) has been known to flambé a mean cherries jubilee. EBT also caters to music lovers. The lounge offers live jazz Mon through Sat and a delightful new small-plate menu to go with the wine selection. More hidden delights await in that big bank box: wine dinners and vodka tastings. Now that's rich!

> **i** We can't imagine you can get through this chapter and still be hungry. But if so, you'll find more menus listed in our Nightlife chapter. It's not all chicken fingers, either. Several of our lounges offer fine cuisine, but their claim to fame is a mean martini or wine selection.

GRAND STREET CAFE $$
4740 Grand (Country Club Plaza)
(816) 561-8000
www.grandstreetcafe.com

Like a diva who just can't give up her bee-hive hairdo, this popular restaurant was long overdue for a makeover. While some fans will miss the gargantuan botanical wallpaper—quite eyecatching in 1991—we can rest easy that many of our favorites remain on the menu. The melt-in-your

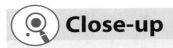

Close-up

Kansas City Originals

Kansas City Originals is an organization that supports the cause of restaurants with a few locations or less. At this writing, 40 individual dining spots make up the roster, with more coming on board every year. The Web site (www.kcoriginals.com) has links to individual restaurant sites that include menus, directions, and hours. And be sure to sign up for a KC Originals PowerCard. This free frequent-diner card accumulates points every time you dine at one of the member establishments. Join at any of the members' locations or online.

Aixois
2501 E. 55th St.
(816) 333-3305
www.aixois.com

The American Restaurant
2450 Grand Blvd.
(816) 545-8001
www.theamericanrestaurant.com

Anthony's Restaurant
701 Grand
(816) 221-4088
kcanthonysgrand.com

Blanc Burgers + Bottles (2 locations)
4710 Jefferson St.
(816) 931-6200

10583 Mission Rd.
(913) 381-4500
www.blancburgers.com

The Broadmoor Bistro
6701 W. 83rd St.
(913) 993-9700
www.broadmoorbistro.org

Cafe des Amis
112½ Main St., Parkville
(816) 587-6767
www.cafedesamiskc.com

Cafe Sebastienne
Kemper Museum of Contemporary Art
4420 Warwick Blvd.
(816) 561-7740
www.cafesebastienne.com

Cafe Trio
4558 Main St.
(816) 756-3227
www.cafetriokc.com

Cafe Verona
206 Lexington, Independence
(816) 833-0044
www.cafeveronarestaurant.com

Carlo's Copa Room
14944 W. 87th St.
(913) 825-5200
www.coparoomkc.com

Cascone's Restaurant
3737 N. Oak Trafficway
(816) 454-7977
www.cascones.com

Chaz on the Plaza
325 Ward Pkwy. (Raphael Hotel)
(816) 802-2152
www.raphaelkc.com

City Tavern
101 W. 22nd St.
(816) 421-3696
www.citytavern.net

Coach's Bar and Grill (2 locations)
414 W. 103rd St.
(816) 941-2286

14893 Metcalf Ave., Overland Park
(913) 897-7070
www.coach-s.com

Em Chamas Brazilian Grill
6101 N.W. 63rd Terrace
(816) 505-7100
www.emchamas.com

Extra Virgin
1900 Main
(816) 842-2205
www.extravirginkc.com

Garozzo's (4 locations)
528 Harrison
(816) 221-2455

9950 College Blvd.
Overland Park, KS
(913) 491-8300

1547 Northeast Rice Rd., Lee's Summit
(816) 554-2800

13505 S. Mur-Len Rd., Olathe
(913) 764-6969

www.garozzos.com

Gaslight Grill
5020 W. 137th St.
(913) 897-3540
www.gaslightgrill.com

Harry's Country Club
112 Missouri Ave.
(816) 421-3505
www.harryscountryclub.com

Hereford House (4 locations)
5001 Town Center Dr., Leawood
(913) 327-0800

17244 Midland Dr.
(913) 268-8000

19721 East Jackson Dr., Independence
(816) 795-9200

8661 North Stoddard Ave.
(816) 584-9000

JJ's
910 W. 48th St.
(816) 561-7136
www.jjs-restaurant.com

Johnny Cascone's
6863 W. 91st St.
(913) 381-6837
www.cascones.com

Kokopelli Mexican Cantina
5200 W. 95th St., Prairie Village
(913) 385-0300
www.kokopellimexicancantina.com

La Bodega
703 Southwest Blvd.
(816) 472-8272
www.labodegakc.com

Le Fou Frog French Bistro
400 E. 5th St.
(816) 474-6060
www.lefoufrog.com

Lulu's Thai Noodle Shop
333 Southwest Blvd.
(816) 474-8424

Marina Grog & Galley
22 A St., Gate 1 at Water's Edge,
Lake Lotawana
(816) 578-5511
www.marinagrogandgalley.com

Michael Smith Restaurant
1900 Main St.
(816) 842-2202
www.michaelsmithkc.com

Nara
1617 Main
(816) 221-6272

Ophelia's Restaurant
201 N. Main St., Independence
(816) 461-4525
www.opheliasind.com

Pierpont's at Union Station
30 W. Pershing Rd.
(816) 221-5111
www.pierponts.com

Piropos at Briarcliff Village
4141 N. Mulberry Dr.
(816) 741-3600
www.piroposkc.com

The Prime Rib Grill by Hereford House
100 E. 20th St.
(816) 842-1080
www.primeribgrill.com

re:Verse
618 Ward Pkwy.
(816) 931-7811
www.reversekc.com

The Shields Manor Bistro
121 Main St., Platte City
(816) 858-5557
www.shieldsmanorbistro.com

Starker's Restaurant
201 W. 47th St.
(816) 753-3565
www.starkersrestaurant.com

Tatsu's French Restaurant
4603 W. 90th St., Prairie Village
(913) 383-9801
www.tatsus.com

V's Italian Ristorante
10819 E. US Hwy. 40
(816) 353-1241
www.vsrestaurant.com

Webster House
1644 Wyandotte
(816) 221-4713
www.websterhouse.com

Westchase Grille
11942 Roe Ave.
(913) 663-5400
www.westchasegrille.com

Zest
10681 Mission Rd.
(913) 381-5678
www.zestkc.com

mouth double pork chop is one example. Forget your table manners for once and pick it up by the handles to devour every succulent morsel. It's available for lunch, dinner, and brunch. Rick and Kristi Ghilardi recently bought the place from the PB&J conglomerate, and along with changing the decor, they're working hard to reclaim its popularity. They're on the right track with chef Ian Hockenberger at the helm; his dry-aged KC strip and pan-seared snapper are first-rate. The prices rate first with us: lobster salad accompanied by zesty deviled eggs for lunch is just $10, most dinner entrees come in at less than $10, and the brunch deal is one of the best in town.

Happy hour gets you a cocktail for three bucks; we know some bon vivants that show up for a late brunch and hang out until happy hour starts at 3 p.m. until close. Never mind that it's a school night. On balmy afternoons or evenings, the patio overlooking the meandering Brush Creek is the place to hold court.

JJ'S $$
910 W. 48th St. (Country Club Plaza)
(816) 561-7136
www.jjs-restaurant.com

In 1996 JJ's was one of only six restaurants worldwide to receive the Grand Award by *Wine Spectator* magazine. Although the list has grown, some say that Jimmy Frantze's intimate bistro still offers the best wine list in town. It's certainly the largest at 40,000 bottles. Do what locals do when it comes to JJ's: look beyond the construction going on across the street because the food and wine collection are worth it. Dinner is served through the arched doorway where white linen–topped tables and tall plants divide the open space. Exuberant paintings by local artist Mike Savage add color to the walls. There's colorful food as well, starting with Paco's Shrimp, a savory appetizer of jumbo shrimp stuffed with a horseradish sauce, deep fried, and served with a mustard sauce and red-pepper coulis. The menu focuses on steaks, including a pan-seared filet medallion with a peppercorn and red wine cream sauce. JJ's is open for lunch on weekdays and for dinner seven days a week.

M&S GRILL $–$$
4646 JC Nichols Pkwy.
(816) 531-7799
www.mandsgrill.com

If Mom's no longer interested in making your favorite meatloaf or pot roast, head to M&S Grill for these classics along with dishes that are way out of your mama's league. Of course the food and ambience are terrific; they're by the team that brought you McCormick & Schmick's (see separate listing), one of the city's premier seafood emporiums. M&S is a bit more laid-back but the bar area is just as bustling come happy hour when the barkeeps are slinging cocktails featuring fresh-squeezed juices, and a juicy cheeseburger or crisp calamari will set you back only $1.95. The menu proclaims the T-bone the "greatest steak in the world," and with it weighing a hefty 24 ounces, we'll have to take their word for it. Just save room for the red velvet cake with cream cheese frosting. Lucky you, M&S Grill just added a Sunday brunch.

MICHAEL SMITH $$–$$$
1900 Main St.
(816) 842-2202
www.michaelsmithkc.com

Chef-owner Michael Smith first came on the Kansas City scene in 1994 as half of a talented team with then-wife Debbie Gold that wowed guests at the American Restaurant. In 1999 the couple shared the James Beard Best Chef in the Midwest award, a first for Kansas City. In 2002 they left the cozy confines of the American to open their own place, 40 Sardines, in Leawood, Kansas, and turned this urban location into a hot destination. Their breakup rocked the foodie world again in 2006. Michael opened his own self-named place in the Crossroads, adding a more casual tapas place next door called Extra Virgin a short time later. (Meanwhile, Debbie returned triumphantly to the American.) Are your eyes crossed yet? The more sophisticated space, Michael Smith, remains the place to be on First Fridays when the neighborhood becomes one big art gallery walk. Michael continues his focus on Mediterranean fare: a little Spanish, a soupçon of French, a dash of Italian. Tender braised rabbit is served with gnocchi, morels, and persillade; a Spanish serrano ham salad comes with avocado, frisee, and aged sherry vinegar and olive oil dressing; slow roasted pork is joined by a scallion risotto, blistered tomatoes, and marinated goat cheese. Meanwhile, Extra Virgin's small plates and decor reflect the happy colors, aromas, and tastes from Spain and Italy—burnt sienna, saffron, and red—with braised meats and fresh pastas. The restaurant has an open kitchen, wood-fired oven, good-sized bar, and patio out front that is a popular spot for the beautiful crowd.

OPHELIA'S $$
201 N. Main
Independence, MO
(816) 461-4525
www.opheliasind.com

When Ken and Cindy McClain created this hip, urban restaurant and inn, they gave after-hours life to historic Independence Square. The American regional menu is as artfully done as Cindy's paintings on the walls. Favorites include the brandy-laced crab soup and roasted rack of lamb. And at just under $18 the salmon and jumbo sea scallops in a saffron white wine beurre blanc isn't just a culinary standout, it's a bargain. Lunch is casual with a kick, such as chicken salad with port wine apples and candied walnuts and a smoked pork sandwich with pickled red cabbage. A low-fat spa menu is also available for lunch and dinner, a thoughtful touch for guests staying at the inn upstairs. Lunch and dinner are served every day but Mon, and brunch is available on Sun. On Fri and Sat evenings there's live jazz in the bar; the large open space makes it easy to listen and still enjoy a conversation. To turn a delightful evening into a good night, reserve a room at the inn upstairs, where Cindy has worked her creative magic with seven rooms and one luxurious suite. See Accommodations for more information.

PACHAMAMA'S $$–$$$
800 New Hampshire
Lawrence, KS
(785) 841-0990
www.pachamamas.com

Who in the world would drive 30 minutes to go to dinner? That's easy; anyone who's ever dined at Ken Baker's handsome restaurant. The food is distinctive and the atmosphere is romantic. Lush greenery creates a rainforest effect, a visual reference to the restaurant's Incan name, which means Mother Earth. That's where the maternal theme ends: Mom never cooked like this. Think comfort food with a twist with succulent dishes like osso bucco and slow-roasted pork shoulder with cheddar grits. With well-paired sides, it's a lot to enjoy. Smaller appetites may prefer the more casual Star Bar where most items are $10 or under, including a terrific burger and five-cheese pizza. Need another excuse for the half-hour trek? Pachamama's hosts a wine tasting every Friday night.

> **i** Some of our top restaurants make happy hour positively giddy by offering hors d'oeuvres and cocktails for pocket change. Avenues Bistro delights its patrons with $4 cocktails and $5 small plates (about half off), Pierpont's serves around half a dozen appetizers, and McCormick & Schmick's has shrimp cocktails and burgers with fries for $1.95.

PIERPONT'S $$
Union Station, Pershing and Grand (Crown Center)
(816) 221-5111
www.herefordhouse.com

We nominate Pierpont's as one of the most glamorous restaurants in town. The bar is particularly stunning with its dark woods and and mirrored shelves that bartenders reach by climbing a 14-step rolling ladder. It gives a whole new meaning to "I'll take that straight up."

Owner Rod Anderson has created a menu that earns wolf whistles as well. There's a regular menu that favors the steaks Kansas City is known for. But we're particularly fond of the three- or four-course small plate dinners for $28 or $33 respectively. The crab and corn bisque is usually on our check list, followed by beef filet, then one of the decadent desserts. The wait staff suggests you allow 90 minutes to enjoy it all. If you're rushing to one of the theaters or events within Union Station, you might consider happy hour in the bar where a variety of appetizers—including hamburgers, calamari, and skewered chicken—are available for less than two bucks. The expansive lunch menu ranges from light salads to lusty pastas and a lobster salad on brioche with its own fan club.

Rod has made a commitment to his wine cellar as well, with more than 300 labels on the menu and 3,000 more stored below. On Sun, bottles go on sale for up to 50 percent off. What a guy.

R BAR & RESTAURANT $$
1617 Gennessee (West Bottoms)
(816) 471-1777
www.rbarkc.com
Once the area known for Kansas City's famous stockyard trade, the West Bottoms is now a neighborhood coming into its own as a magnet for boutique eateries, art galleries, and unique shops. The cowboy influence—albeit in a cheeky way—is evident in the R Bar's decor. The long bar looks like it's seen its share of rodeos and if you visit the Web site you can't help but notice there's a horse in the center of the room.

But it's the food, conceived and prepared by up-and-comer chef Alex Pope you'll want to hitch your wagon to. He learned under two local James Beard Award winners, Debbie Gold and Celina Tio, at the American Restaurant before R Bar owner Joy Jacobs snapped him up. This is comfort food with a sophisticated wink. His foie gras is served on a cinnamon raisin bagel with whisky apple butter, and a meltingly tender pork belly nestles next to pickled cherries and smoked collard greens. The egg noodles with chunks of pumkin and walnuts in a sinfully rich brown butter sauce is what dreams are made of and diets are for.

But back to that bar, pardner. Two of Kansas City's stand-out mixologists keep things interesting. Shawn Moriarty (the dapper gentleman in the vest) has a following from his days at another local restaurant, and Arturo Vera-Felicie recently won top honors at Greater Kansas City Bartending Competition. Fittingly, he named his winning concoction the West Bottoms Social Club.

Within a few months of opening, the hip crowd soon discovered R Bar, turning the slender space into a sea of shoulders most weekends. Reservations are a must, especially Thurs through Sat when owner Joy Jacobs schedules a wide variety of musical talent including the popular duo of Kathleen and Frenchie, David Basse, or Angela Hagenbach.

ROOM 39 $–$$
1719 W. 39th St.
(816) 753-3933

ROOM 39 MISSION FARMS
10561 Mission Rd.
(913) 648-7639
www.rm39.com
Don't let the cute room with mismatched chairs fool you: chefs and co-owners Ted Habiger and Andy Sloan have created a sophisticated menu. Lunch could be a simple bowl of butternut squash soup or seared bass over roasted beet risotto. Dinner continues the love story with New Zealand king salmon with pureed cauliflower and a few ingredients we've never heard of. And, really, isn't that the point of dining out—to update our culinary dictionary? If you see Green Dirt Farm on the listing, don't worry: it's artisanal cheese and lamb from a small provider in nearby Weston. Ted and Andy insist on buying locally whenever possible. Good luck getting a table in the morning, when Kansas City's elite cool their heels to wait for the best brioche French toast around. Fans of Room 39 who live out south were thrilled when the owners opened a second location at the ritzy Mission Farms a few years ago. The decor may be a little more refined, but the food retains the same quality.

ROZZELLE COURT $
4525 Oak St. (Country Club Plaza)
(816) 751-1279
www.nelson-atkins.org
Dining here is like a short trip to Tuscany, where you're surrounded by carved stone, a ring of arched openings in the balcony above, a gurgling fountain, and the golden glow from skylights

three stories above. And where else can you fold your napkin, stand up, and say, "Now where do you suppose they keep the Rembrandt?"

Frankly, once you've tasted the food you won't mind pushing a brown plastic tray through the cafeteria line. First-timers are often surprised by the fare: a recent menu included olive oil poached salmon and stuffed quail breasts. Salads are works of art and desserts are delectable as well, ranging from Key lime pie to almond cheesecake. Wine is available by the glass or bottle.

Lunch is served Tues through Sun (the museum is closed Mon), and the live music that accompanies Fri dinners turns this enchanting room into one of the most popular in town. Admission to the museum is free, and the food is reasonably priced. Now that's art. Read more about the Nelson-Atkins Museum of Art in the Close-up in the Arts chapter.

SAVOY GRILL $$$
219 W. Ninth St. (Downtown)
(816) 842-3890
www.savoygrill.net

As the city's oldest restaurant, there simply isn't another place in town so imbued with history, romance, and gentility. If those accolades sound dated, so be it. The deeply carved wood paneling, stained glass, and cushy dark booths certainly worked for Harry S. Truman, who was such a regular customer they named Booth No. 4 in his honor.

Perfectly grilled steaks and steamed lobsters are the mainstays here, and dinner might start brilliantly with steamed mussels brought to the table in a big tin bucket. White-jacketed waiters provide service reflective of some of the steepest prices in town. Reservations are suggested for both lunch and dinner. Lunch is available Mon through Sat, dinner seven days a week.

SKIES $$–$$$
2345 McGee (Crown Center)
(816) 435-4199
www.crowncenterhyatt.com

Breathtaking panoramic views of the skyline are on the menu at this revolving restaurant on the 42nd floor of the Hyatt Regency. In fact, with 72 windows and 23 color murals gracing the walls, you're surrounded by the sights of Kansas City wherever you look. Although the menu offers nothing revolutionary (sorry, we couldn't resist) the mesquite-grilled steaks are expertly prepared. For dessert go for the Sky High Pie, three layers of homemade ice cream on a graham cracker crust. Or head to the lounge for an after-dinner drink and tell the bartender, "One more trip around the city, please." Skies is open for lunch and dinner, Tues through Sun. The lounge offers that stunning view until midnight on weekends.

STARKER'S RESTAURANT $$$
201 W. 47th St. (Country Club Plaza)
(816) 753-3565
www.starkersreserve.com

This Kansas City gem provides everything fine dining should be: beautifully prepared food served in a gorgeous setting. It was started by beloved, late restaurateur Cliff Bath, who named it for Harry Starker, a gregarious 15th-century British gourmand. Harry, it was said, often indulged in whiskey and wine before engaging in naked public jaunts, hence the phrase "stark naked." New owner John McClure has imbued his own culinary style to the place, bringing in his love of Creole cooking honed in New Orleans. To wit, a grilled foie gras with Creole beignets or fried green tomatoes for starters. Entrees range from succulent steaks to pan-seared sea scallops on a bed of braised collard greens. Wine dinners and themed menus—like the annual heirloom tomato dinner—are legendary; be sure to ask about the next scheduled event. Starker's wine cellar was one of the first in Missouri to earn a Grand Award from *Wine Spectator*. Lunch is more casual, with a swoon-worthy hamburger stuffed with cheese from a local farm. In fact, chef McClure is fastidious when it comes to supporting the Midwest's excellent produce and meats. Reservations are a must here, and although casual attire is welcome, Starker's is worth dressing for. Hear that, Harry?

12 BALTIMORE CAFÉ
HOTEL PHILLIPS $$
106 W. 12th St.
(816) 221-9292
www.hotelphillips.com

This corner restaurant within an historic hotel is just the place for a power breakfast, quick lunch, or casual dinner before strolling a few blocks to the Power & Light District or the theatre. And thanks to an expansive happy hour (three to seven every weekday), it's definitely the spot to commiserate or celebrate with friends after work. If you're lucky you'll be tapping your table to your favorite tunes; 12B hosts live music on Sat. Check the schedule online. Brunch is a steal here (especially for a hotel dining room); just under $15 for the buffet and menu choices. As a matter of fact, overall the prices here are remarkable. Ten bucks will get you the day's soup plus two sliders—mini burgers. We happen to favor the veggie version. Giant salads or decadent ravioli may be more to your liking. Steaks on the dinner menu tend to climb past the $30 range, but savvy diners know to order a burger for just 10 bucks, or share several appetizers with friends. The calamari may be the best in town.

YIAYIA'S EUROBISTRO $$
4701 W. 119th St.
Overland Park, KS
(913) 345-1111
www.yiayiaskc.com

There's something comforting about a restaurant named for the co-owner's beloved family member; *yia yia* means grandmother in Greek. Many of the recipes are ones she brought back from her travels around the world. We're grateful every time we taste appetizers like the duck confit over polenta with crimini mushrooms. No wonder the servers seem proud to bring the custom-designed charcoal-and-white plates to your table.The nightly specials—typically grilled fish and steaks with at least one signature pizza—are always winners. As a nice touch they offer the pasta servings in two sizes; order a half portion and you'll still be amazed at the number of noodles placed in front of you. Half of Johnson

County must have Styrofoam boxes in their fridges marked with "YY" and the date. But the double-cut pork chop is so savory you'll want to eat every morsel in one sitting. The lodgelike ambience is compelling as well, with limestone walls, slate floors, and a sunny patio. The place usually fills up fast for both lunch and dinner. A brunch is offered on Sun.

WEBSTER HOUSE RESTAURANT $–$$$
1644 Wyandotte (Downtown/Crossroads)
(816) 221-4713
www.websterhousekc.com

In this beautifully renovated schoolhouse-turned-antiques shop, it's the dining rooms that go to the head of the class. This is a popular place for the ladies who lunch, folks who work downtown, and shoppers who have discovered the nearby stores in the Crossroads Arts District. Handsome chef Charles D'Ablaing keeps the mix fresh with a menu that changes daily, but with any luck the lunch list will offer the goat cheese soufflé—a tender mound of baked cheese served with greens and sliced fruits of the season. It's a lovely way to spend an afternoon before searching the rooms for stunning 18th- and 19th-century European and American antiques and unique giftware (see Shopping). The chef shines as well in the evening, where a recent menu listed lemon verbena–braised chicken with green tomato fritters. Perhaps because the private rooms are popular for special events and wedding receptions, one of the most popular desserts is wedding cake with a delectable buttercream frosting. We'll say "I do" every time. Webster House has also become the place to gather with friends over wine and appetizers before heading out to the monthly First Friday gallery walk in the Crossroads Arts District.

ASIAN

SAIGON 39 $
1806½ W. 39th St. (Midtown)
(816) 531-4447

This family-owned Vietnamese cafe is often voted the best in Kansas City thanks to its award-winning dishes. Stir-fried dishes are very popular, and the spicy pineapple soup is a unique taste sensation you could easily learn to love. Think you can take the heat of the kitchen? Better watch how you order your dishes—mild, medium, or hot—because the cooks will comply. An extra-spicy version of the crabmeat-and-squid soup has become an ad hoc prescription during cold and flu season; it's guaranteed to knock the germs right out of you. Other soups, as well as stir-fries, can be customized with combinations of meat and fish or served vegetarian style. Order a side of their ethereal spring rolls and you have a fine meal. Bring cash—nothing else is accepted—and call ahead because Saigon 39 is open on a limited and ever-changing schedule. But their curry dishes alone are definitely worth a phone call.

THAI PLACE $–$$
9359 W. 87th St.
Overland Park, KS
(913) 649-5420

11838 Quivira
Overland Park, KS
(913) 451-THAI (8424)

4130 Pennsylvania (Westport)
(816) 753-THAI (8424)
www.kcthaiplace.com

There may be no other cuisine as marvelously diverse and intricate as Thai, and Ann Liberda does it to a T. She and her son, Ted, have introduced Kansas Citians to unusual sauces that include everything from slightly sweet coconut milk and refreshing basil and lemongrass to a head-exploding concoction flecked with slivers of bright red peppers we've nicknamed "hurt me." Although it's fun to experiment with new dishes (huge servings make it easy to share), you can't go wrong with the popular seafood pad Thai, a delightful marriage of sweet, salty, and spicy flavors made with shrimp, mussels, squid, and crabmeat in a fermented fish sauce called nam pla. We've decided that most of the menu sounds like a teenager who just came home with a pierced tongue. Just point and smile, and let your friendly server do the rest.

BAKERIES, DELIS, AND DESSERTS

ANDRE'S RIVAZ TEA HOUSE
4929 W. 119th St.
Overland Park
(913) 498-3440)

This combination Swiss-style tea shop, bakery, and candy store (the Overland Park address was added a few years ago) is wildly popular with the hat and gloves crowd, midtown office workers, and even men who do eat quiche. There's usually a crowd; people will gladly wait in line for the day's special such as goulash or smoked pork loin. Of course you'll want dessert. They're all incredible, especially the Linzer torte. Before you leave the shop—and you can bet someone in line hopes you will—stop by the cases of exquisite handmade chocolates and desserts. The artistry of the truffles and chocolate boxes filled with confections is superb. Out of town fans can order from the Web site.

Andre's is open for lunch Tues through Sat. This Kansas City gem is truly a family affair. Marcel Bollier took over for his father, Andre, and now his own son, Rene, is continuing the tradition at the Overland Park store.

D'BRONX DELI & PIZZARIA $
3904 Bell
(816) 531-0550

2450 Grand Ave. (Crown Center)
(816) 842-2211

7070 W. 105th St.
Overland Park
(913) 649-9000
www.dbronx.com

This cheerful, bustling New York–style deli serves massive sandwiches, but is perhaps most beloved for its thin-crust pizza piled nearly 2 inches high with toppings. Its 30-inch version is a party in a box whether you're taking it home for a night in front of the tube, to share with your co-workers, or sneaking it past the hotel's front desk. There are 50 sandwiches on the menu at the original location on Bell, making first-timers a bit crazed. Here's a hint: The Italian meatball is hard to beat. Or try a house specialty, such as the Wild Bill, which is salami, provolone, coleslaw, and spicy mustard and horseradish on rye. The other locations tend to feature just the best-sellers, but the food is still superb. And just in case you doubt the name's authenticity, d'Bronx owners Janet and Robert Bloom are originally from that famous neighborhood. More important, they beat out plenty of famous New York addresses to be named one of the six top delis in the country. The deli is open seven days a week.

FOO'S FABULOUS FROZEN CUSTARD $
6235 Brookside Plaza (Brookside)
(816) 523-2520

3832 W. 95th St.
Leawood, KS
(913) 383-3667
www.foosfabulousfrozencustard.com
What could be better on a sultry night than sharing a Sticky Hickey? Especially when the treat is actually a concrete—a richer, denser version of ice cream mixed with marshmallow, caramel, and chocolate chips. You can choose from dozens of ingredients to mix with your frozen custard, including fruits, nuts, chunks of Snickers and Heath Bar, and flavorings such as maple, rum, and coffee. Make your own recipe or go for a Foo's favorite, such as Mint Oreo Twist or a Blue Devil, which incorporates raspberries, crème de menthe, and chocolate chips. Divine. And JoCo rejoiced when Foo's came south with a second location.

MURRAY'S ICE CREAMS & COOKIES $
4120 Pennsylvania Ave. (Westport)
(816) 931-5646
www.westportkc.com/murrays
Murray's may be the reason we don't mind the heat and humidity in mid-July. This tiny spot at the end of a horseshoe-shaped loop in Westport lists 16 or so flavors on the wall with around 200 other recipes waiting their turn. The Chocolate Flake Fromage, a cream cheese–flavored ice cream with semisweet chocolate flakes, has its own fan club.

Other specialties are smooshies, which merge ice cream with such toppings as chunks of candy bars, and lumpies, which are malts made chunkier than normal. Try to control yourself.

Murray's has a few tables indoors and out, but most people prefer to walk around Westport to window-shop and people-watch. During December and January, when Murray's is closed, you'll just have to dream about Fudge Raspberry Rhapsody or One Drunk Monk. But they do a very nice send-off: On the last Sun in Nov all ice-cream tubs are half price. If you plan to visit, here's the scoop: Murray's opens at noon Tues through Sun and closes between 9 and 10:30 p.m. depending on the day. Closed Mon.

NATASHA'S MULBERRY & MOTT $–$$
10573 Mission Rd.
(913) 341-0300
www.natashasmulberryandmott.com
The shop's name is a mouthful, but so is the *pain au chocolate* when you try to consume an entire warm, flaky roll of heaven all at once. We have a general rule about never partaking of pastries baked by anyone this tiny, but rules are meant to be broken. The darling Natasha received her diploma from the French Culinary Institute in New York before returning to Kansas City to open a wedding cake business with her mother, Vicki. A year later, the duo created a cute bakery shop on 39th Street's Restaurant Row before packing it up for a grander (and much more girly) setting in the posh Mission Farms center. Now there's even more room for the tender croissants, delightful cupcakes and macaroons, the impossibly good *pain au chocolate*, and a dizzying assortment of cookies, all from scratch. Natasha recently added ice creams in luscious flavors like red currant pear sorbet, and an espresso bar that opens at 7 a.m. It's a lovely way to spend the morning with a cup of espresso or hot chocolate and a flaky pastry, either in the sunny lounge or flower-filled sidewalk patio. Tasha's weddings cakes, however, are what put her on the map; she crafts exquisite flowers out of sugar and fondant that threaten to take the spotlight away from the bride's gown. Visit www.natashagoellner.com for information on her cakes.

BARBECUE

ARTHUR BRYANT'S BARBEQUE $
1727 Brooklyn (East Side)
(816) 231-1123
www.arthurbryantsbbq.com

Celebrities and presidents have made the pilgrimage to this landmark since 1930, and today, despite the spot's location in a neglected neighborhood, the lunch line still forms by 11:30. Even then you'll wait as much as half an hour to yell "Beef and fries" to the man standing in front of that smoking pit, but it's worth it to get your hands around 4 inches of brisket slapped on two pieces of Wonder bread. The sauce is an alarmingly orange mixture that's a bit more vinegary—and a lot grainier—than anything else in town. It's one reason New Yorker columnist Calvin Trillin named Bryant's "the single best restaurant in the world." You can eat in the joint or have your meal to go, whereupon it will be wrapped in two layers of butcher paper that will only partially protect your car's upholstery.

i Burnt ends might sound like a restaurant reject, but around here it's a delicacy. The dish is cut from the ends of a barbecued brisket and served alone with sauce or as a sandwich. The high-flavor, slightly chewy treat is on the menu at just about every barbecue joint in town.

BB'S LAWNSIDE BAR-B-Q $
South Kansas City
1205 E. 85th St.
(816) 822-7427
www.bbslawnsidebbq.com

For a full shot of what Kansas City does best—blues and barbecue—you can't beat Lindsay Shannon's roadhouse. The Louisiana-style gumbo is mighty good, but BB's excels at hickory-smoked ribs. Grab your barbecue and a locally brewed Boulevard Beer and pull up a chair at one of the long tables filled with temporary strangers. Once the ragtime, boogie-woogie, or blues starts up you'll be sitting next to your new best friends. A seat at the bar will give you a vantage point for plenty of people-watching. BB's is open for lunch and dinner Wed through Sun, and there's live music every night. If you're in town on a Tuesday Bluesday, be sure to check out the resident band, Trampled Under Foot, a trio made up of two brothers and a sister. That is, if you can get in; the International Blues Band of the Year always fills the house. Check out the listing in Nightlife for more information about this popular joint.

DANNY EDWARDS FAMOUS KANSAS CITY BARBECUE $
2900 Southwest Blvd.
(816) 283-0880

Owner Danny Edwards learned well from his pop, legendary smokemaster Jake Edwards. He dry-rubs his ribs in a secret spice mixture before smoking them out back for about eight hours. The result is a deep-down flavored slab that's tender but with just enough chewy texture to make you work at falling in love. The brisket sandwich—arguably the most tender in town—is the top seller, with ribs and burnt ends running close behind. Danny also does a mean barbecued chicken. Now that Danny has moved from his tiny 18-seat spot downtown to these more spacious 60-seat digs, he may have to come up with a new motto to replace the "Eat it and beat it" painted on the 45-pound, concrete pink pig.

FIORELLA'S JACK STACK BARBECUE $–$$
13441 Holmes (Martin City)
(816) 942-9141

9520 Metcalf
Overland Park, KS
(913) 385-7427

4747 Wyandotte St. (Country Club Plaza)
(816) 531-7427

22nd and Wyandotte (Freight House District)
(816) 472-7427
www.jackstackkc.com

Zagat reviewers say this is the best barbecue in the nation and there are plenty of local fans who agree. Forget the mental picture of the typical barbecue joint. The location in the bustling Freight House area is a fancy-pants version

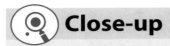 # Close-up

Kansas City Barbecue

Welcome to the barbecue capital of the world. Oh, we know: The Carolinas claim to be the cradle of American barbecue, and Texas has the brisket circuit sewn up. But here in the Midwest we've perfected the technique so well it's often referred to by the generic term "Kansas City barbecue," as if the city and the food are forever intertwined.

To really appreciate barbecue you've got to talk the talk. First off, true aficionados consider "barbecue" a noun, not a verb, although the rest of us tend to use it both ways. It refers to beef or pork that's been slow-cooked over wood—often hickory, cherry, or apple to add a subtle flavor—for hours. And we do mean hours. It's a commitment of time and constant attention, turning it into a recreational sport that calls for cold beer and good friends. A brisket or slab of ribs can take eight hours or more of monitoring the fire to make sure the temperature doesn't vary more than a dozen degrees. This patient technique makes barbecue distinctly different from Kansas City's preferred method of cooking steak, grilling quickly over a flame stoked as high as 1,400 degrees F.

The result is a succulent morsel of meat. But saying ribs are so tender they fall off the bone is not necessarily a compliment; it may mean they've been parboiled—a real no-no that local experts call faux 'cue. Say it fast and you'll get the message.

And don't expect your barbecue to show up slathered with sauce. Although meat is often dry-rubbed with a spice mixture before going into the smoker, the sauce—if applied at all—is mopped on right before serving or during the final minutes of cooking so the sugars in the sauce don't burn. That's another thing: Although there are exceptions such as the vinegary version at Arthur Bryant's, for the most part Kansas City sauce is on the sweet side thanks to its molasses-spiked tomato base. If you want more sauce with your brisket sandwich, you'll usually find a bottle or two of the thick, mahogany-colored liquid on the table, often sporting the restaurant's label. Don't even think about asking for the recipe. Around here ingredients are guarded as carefully as Sharon Stone's birthdate.

If you're getting the idea that barbecue isn't merely a food group but our city's true identity, you're halfway there. Or as members of the **Kansas City Barbecue Society** like to say, "Barbecue. It's not just for breakfast anymore." Membership in the KCBS—the world's largest barbecue organization, with more than 10,000 members worldwide—is $35 a year. Contact them at 11514 Hickman Mills Dr., Kansas City, MO 64121. Or call (816) 765-5891 or (800) 963-KCBS, or visit www.kcbs.us. You can even take classes to become a judge at one of the 300 or so barbecue contests they sanction every year.

KCBS members—and the rest of us—are eternally grateful to Henry Perry. He introduced the food group to Kansas City in the late 1920s when he started selling ribs out of a trolley barn at 19th and Highland. A slab back then—wrapped in pages of newsprint—cost 25 cents. Henry's barn became 'Cue University for such local legends as George Gates and Charlie Bryant. Charlie

with a gorgeous bar, soaring ceilings, and cushy booths. One diner walked in, whistled, and said, "This is where gluttony gets an etiquette lesson." The original restaurant in Martin City looks like a house that's been expanded a few times to make room for relatives. The second location, on Met-

calf, is an attractive space with a huge parking lot that is still overflowing on weekends.

The menu at all four locations is filled with a mind-boggling selection of barbecued meats, hickory-grilled poultry and fish, and certified Angus steaks. Trust us: order the thick-cut onion rings, which come to the table stacked like a kid's

eventually bought the place and expanded it with help from his brother Arthur. After Charlie died Arthur tinkered with the sauce—the original was so hot it nearly caused blisters—and moved the business to 1727 Brooklyn. The lunch lines have never stopped.

As for its preparation, though the main ingredients and basic techniques passed down from Henry are universal, the sauce recipe and even the hardwoods used for smoking often are closely guarded secrets. In Kansas City, saying one barbecue restaurant is the best in town can start a heated debate. Heck, we can't even agree on one single spelling of the name: barbecue, barbeque, BBQ, or bar-b-que. When it comes time for locals to pick their favorites, the criteria are usually split into categories like best fries, best ribs, best brisket, or best sauce.

We'll let you decide. But pace yourself; there are 80 or so barbecue outlets in town. We've listed some of the top achievers in this chapter. But before you go, here's a quick primer, courtesy of the Kansas City Barbecue Society, to help you place your order.

- **Baby back ribs:** Also known as loin back ribs, these are cut from the pork loin and usually weigh about two pounds per slab.

- **Barbecue:** Meats slow-cooked over hardwood (some folks use charcoal or a mix of the two) at a temperature of 200 to 375 degrees F.

- **Burnt ends:** Blackened, somewhat charred pieces of brisket that are too charred to slice. These are served with plenty of sauce and highly prized at restaurants. Sometimes they're called "brownies."

- **Glaze:** A finishing sauce applied to meat—what's called mopping—during the final minutes of barbecuing.

- **Long end spare ribs:** The first six ribs from the breastbone on back.

- **Pit:** The cooking unit used to barbecue. You'll see everything around here, from black barrels on legs to cement or brick open structures. A good smokemaster can produce great barbecue from a hole in the ground.

- **Rib tips:** The breastbone at the top of a slab of spare ribs.

- **Rub:** A dry marinade—usually a closely guarded mixture of dry spices and herbs—that's liberally massaged into meats to impart flavor.

- **Short end spare ribs:** The last seven or eight ribs in a slab of spare ribs. We're calling dibs right now.

- **Wood chips:** Small chips of wood used to impart smoky flavor to barbecued meats. Hickory is perhaps the most popular, but plenty of experts use fruitwood like apple or cherry because it's slightly sweeter. Some people cut the bitterness of hickory by mixing in fruitwood.

toy on a copper skewer. Other side dishes include a rich cheesy corn casserole and hickory pit beans thickened with chunks of burnt ends, ham, and meat drippings.

Jack Stack serves five types of ribs, including pork and beef spare ribs, baby back, and lamb ribs that got rave reviews in the *London Times*.

Along with steaks, sausage, pork chops, and crown prime rib, there are fire-grilled chicken, fish, and shrimp.

All four locations are open for lunch and dinner seven days a week. Jack Stack's also ships their award-winning ribs and other smoked meats anywhere.

GATES BAR-B-Q $

1325 E. Emanuel Cleaver II Blvd.
(816) 531-7522

2001 W. 103rd St.
Leawood, KS
(913) 383-1752

3205 Main St. (Downtown)
(816) 753-0828

1221 Brooklyn (East Side)
(816) 483-3880

10440 E. 40 Highway
Independence, MO
(816) 353-5880

1026 State Ave.
Kansas City, KS
(913) 621-1134
www.gatesbbq.com
It's always fun to watch a tenderfoot walk through the door and take a step backward when assailed by a loud "May I help you?" from behind the counter. The menu is printed on the wall above the open kitchen, but if you get flustered just remember you can't go wrong with the ribs and fries. Or go for the mixed plate to try the ribs, beef brisket, and beef sausage. Gates offers four flavors of sauce, and the mild version makes a fine ketchup substitute for dipping fries. And don't be surprised if you find yourself heading back to the line after your meal, this time yelling back at the order taker, "Yeah, you can help me. Give me a slab to go."

L.C.'S BAR-B-Q $

5800 Blue Pkwy. (East Side)
(816) 923-4484
Although not as famous as Arthur Bryant's, L.C.'s is usually on the top-five list of people who really know their smoked meat. The sauce is sweet and tangy. The sweet potato fries are deep-fried strips of heaven. You'll want to eat until you hurt. Table space is generally gone by a quarter to noon, and when there's a Saturday game at Kauffman Stadium, cars line up early. Be forewarned, though: This is far from a fancy location. Perhaps there's a good reason for the bars on the windows, and even the smoker in the parking lot is chained to a utility pole. Lunch and dinner are served Mon through Sat.

OKLAHOMA JOE'S BBQ $

47th and Mission Rd.
Kansas City, KS
(913) 722-3366

11950 S. Strang Line Rd.
Olathe, KS
(913) 782-6858
www.oklahomajoesbbq.com
No doubt Jeff and Joy Stehney heard every imaginable joke using "gas" and "restaurant" in the same sentence when they started serving barbecue in a space shared by a filling station and convenience store. Now they're laughing all the way to the bank as people line up noon and night for award-winning fare. While competitors often excel at one or two items, at Oklahoma Joe's everything is superb. Favorites include lip-smacking ribs, burnt ends, and Carolina-style sandwiches, that Southern treat of pulled pork topped with spicy slaw. They'll slap smoked meats on anything here, including salads. Just don't skip the fries. In supersize-me portions, they're some of the best in the city. The line starts to form again for the dinner specials where the mix is half dine-in, half rib slabs to go. Can it get any better than this? Well, yes. They could be open on Sunday. And if they would just do something about that name. Though we still favor the original location, we're happy to have an Oklahoma Joe's in Olathe now. But it's still not open on Sunday!

ROSEDALE BARBECUE $

600 Southwest Blvd.
Kansas City, KS
(913) 262-0343
Naturally this joint knows how to smoke meaty ribs and flavorful brisket. They've been doing it since 1934, longer than anyone else in Kansas City. Lines extend out both side doors by noon. It can be a madhouse, but you can always show up when the crowds are gone; it's open until 10 p.m. Mon through Sat and until 8 p.m. on Sun.

Fans go for the hearty beef, pork, and ham sandwiches, or "half bird and fries," tasty barbecued chicken and crispy zigzag-cut fries served hot in a waxed paper bag. The baby back ribs are tender and lean but are available only on Sun.

CAJUN/CREOLE

JAZZ—A LOUISIANA KITCHEN $-$$
1823 W. 39th St.
(816) 531-5556

1859 Village West Pkwy.
Kansas City, KS
(913) 328–0003
www.jazzkitchens.com

Every night is Mardi Gras at these rowdy spots that serve up traditional Cajun dishes such as blackened seafood, gumbo, oysters on the half shell, and po'boy sandwiches. Or just order the all-you-can-eat hushpuppies for $139; the order includes a free bottle of Dom Perignon. At night this becomes party central as live jazz, Dixieland, and blues play five nights a week. During the day the original location on West 39th is often a hangout for interns from the KU Medical Center up the street looking for a little relaxation and roux between rounds. Jazz is open from 11 a.m. to midnight daily. Catch some terrific local blues talent at the Village West location, several nights a week.

CASUAL DINING

BLANC BURGERS + BOTTLES $-$$
4710 Jefferson (Country Club Plaza)
(816) 931-6200

10583 Mission Rd. (Leawood)
(913) 381-4500
www.blancburgers.com

Blanc likes to say they've done for the gourmet burger what Alexander McQueen did for couture fashion. Staying with the metaphor, let's examine their version of the LBD—a classic burger. The typical lettuce and tomato topping is taken up a notch with aged white NY cheddar, housemade pickles, and made-from-scratch ketchup on a brioche bun. A bison burger achieves star power with pepperjack cheese, peppadew pepper jam, and mayo, while the Inside Out is stuffed with blue cheese. Keep that napkin handy.

Not big on beef? Go for grilled mahimahi, a spice lentil burger, or a salad. Just save room for the sides that arrive in miniature shopping carts: sweet potato fries, truffle fries, and thick onion rings. The crunchy batter is made from Kansas City's own Boulevard Pale Ale. Local vendors are also tagged for the milkshakes (with or without booze), including Foo's Fabulous Custard and Shatto Milk. In fact the dairy farm had to buy more cows to keep up with Blanc's needs. Burgers are around $9; worth it for a custom blend of tenderloin, ribeye, and strip steak. The Quick-Fix lunch menu lets you choose a burger and a side for eight bucks. There's a full bar and a mind-boggling selection of flavored sodas that provide a pretty pastel display in the spare, white decor. So *that's* where they get the name!

HARRY'S COUNTRY CLUB $-$$
112 Missouri Ave.
(816) 421-3505
www.harryscountryclub.com

Harry Murphy's relaxed neighborhood honky tonk may fool you. Sure there are ice-cold yard beers. Two-fisted turkey sandwiches. Pan-fried catfish. A fried bologna sandwich and bottle of Pabst Blue Ribbon will set you back just $3.75. But you might be surprised to see some upscale items on the menu, including a seductive penne with spicy vodka, tomato, and cream sauce. Those who are too refined for brewskis can indulge in flights of premium tequila, which simply means three one-ounce pours of different brands for $12, or choose to fly first class with samples of the premium aged fire water for $17. Whiskey flights also are departing from Harry's Country Club, with three different one-ounce pours for just $10—including top-notch bourbons and single malts. And what's good grub and booze without live music? Wed through Sat during good weather, the friendly deck's the place to be. There's often a cover charge, but the view of a glittering downtown skyline is free.

THE MIXX $

4855 Main St.
(816) 756-2300

1347 Main St.
(816) 283-0300
www.mixxingitup.com

The pretty proprietor of the Mixx comes by her culinary instincts naturally. Jo Marie Scaglia's dad, Mario, is part of the family that brought Kansas City the grinder—an Italian roll stuffed with meatballs, sauce, and cheese. Jo Marie's legacy is introducing the most inventive way to order a salad or sandwich since . . . well, since sliced bread. The fun starts at the counter, when diners order a basic salad, then customize it from 50 ingredients ranging from orange wedges to fried capers. Add roasted chicken or other goodies, choose a house-made salad dressing, and then watch the chef assemble your fresh masterpiece. If you're not feeling creative, stick with a specialty salad like the Knife & Fork with grilled steak, roasted potatoes, and caramelized onions. At less than 10 bucks it's slightly more moolah than a fast-food joint, and the portions at the Mixx are big enough to share.

Sandwiches are also DIY affairs, or choose a proven winner like the Thanksgiving Favorite with roasted turkey, cranberry chutney, and lettuce on a ciabatinni roll. The Mixx also shines with savory stews and chowders and a daily pasta special. Kids get grilled cheese sandwiches or Mom's Buttered Noodles, and everybody needs to grab a cupcake or cookie. Wine and beer are available as well. Jo Marie is now sharing the love at a second location in the Power & Light District. Expect lines at both places at the noon hour; both are open for lunch and dinner seven

i Dining out with little ones? Lots of our restaurants cater to kids, with special menus, coloring books, or toys to keep them happy and occupied. Some of the best are Yahooz! in Leawood, the Crayola Cafe in Crown Center, and Winstead's, where children can share a Skyscraper ice-cream soda and listen to the jukebox.

days a week. And check out Jo Marie's sister Kathy Scaglia Green's hip bistro in the Freight House District, Twenty 20.

STROUD'S $

5410 Northeast Oak Ridge Dr. (North of the River)
(816) 454-9600

4200 Shawnee Mission Pkwy. (Fairway)
(913) 262-8500
www.stroudsrestaurant.com

This is the home of legendary pan-fried chicken, where folks are willing to wait for hours for a table. The rickety 1920 roadhouse under a bridge was part of the charm, as was singing along to the piano player. That's why our hearts were broken when we learned Stroud's South would be torn down as part of a construction project. The new location is smack dab in yuppie country, but we don't care. The food is the same, thanks to Mike Donegan, the last of the three guys who started Stroud's decades ago. If you want history with your fried chicken, there's always the original Stroud's Oak Ridge Manor, a homestead that dates back to a log cabin built in 1829.

Whichever you choose, you won't mind the wait: The crowd is festive, there's a full bar, and the aroma of fried chicken serves as a constant reminder of the final reward. Once seated, remember that everything is served family style, so whatever chicken dinner you order will arrive at the table on large platters and in bowls to pass around. Don't worry, we've never seen a table run out of fluffy mashed potatoes, slow-cooked green beans, peppery cream gravy, cottage fries, or french fries. To start you'll have your choice of chicken noodle soup or salad, and every dinner ends with a basket of warm cinnamon rolls. Like magic your server will show up with doggie bags and packets of hand wipes.

But back to that chicken. Stroud's serves it steaming hot from the 14-inch cast-iron skillets. The crispy golden brown crust falls away to reveal tender, juicy chicken that was deemed "the best chicken on the planet" by the *New York Times*. Other fare includes pork chops, chicken-fried steaks, pan-fried catfish, and deep-fried shrimp. You can start your diet tomorrow. The waitresses are friendly, efficient, and polite enough to laugh at whatever chicken joke you care to share. And if you're looking for a reminder of your visit beyond that doggie bag, buy a "We Choke Our Own Chickens" T-shirt.

The Fairway location is open for lunch and dinner seven days a week; the Oak Ridge Manor serves lunch on weekends and dinner nightly.

TWENTY 20 $
2020 Baltimore
(816) 471-2020

This sliver of a bistro on one of the busiest corners in the Freighthouse District gets positively jammed on the first Friday of every month, thanks to its proximity to the Crossroads Arts District. Well, that and the fact that owner Kathy Scaglia Green hires a DJ to pump out the tunes for patrons sitting outside with cocktails and wine. What's on the menu board is pretty heart-thumping, too, such as Kathy's salmon salad and big, fat sandwiches. Her pastas, such as a rigatoni with sausage and spicy red sauce, and pizzas are favored neighborhood noshes. There's a brisk lunch business, with people dining in the upstairs loft, dotting the outdoor cafe tables, or grabbing a to-go box. And when you see that Twenty 20 is the caterer for an event, you know it's going to be good.

ℹ️ An On the Town Passport Unlimited card (888-273-6392; www.passport unlimited.com) gets you a free entree when you pay for one of equal or higher value. The roster includes around 40 places ranging from brewpubs to fine dining, and you could easily recoup the annual membership fee over a long weekend in town.

WESTPORT FLEA MARKET $
817 Westport Rd.
(816) 931-1986
www.westportfleamarket.com

Joe Zwillenberg got more than a deed when he bought this hamburger joint in the center of a ragtag collection of flea market booths; he got hero status. He saved it from becoming a hot pants–wearing chain known as Hooter's and has turned what has always been a popular spot into a local phenom. Joe Joe kept the grunge factor: patrons still have to navigate a chockablock entrance, find a table amid all the pinball machines, order at the counter, then wait for the cheeky announcer to call their name. He'll sing, yodel, and make wacky rhymes with your moniker.

While you're waiting, notice the wall of awards announcing Best Burger in KC. It is that, indeed. Joe buys his beef from McGonigle's, one of the true great butcher shops left in Kansas City. The Mini-Market Burger, at 5½ ounces, is plenty of protein, especially when you doll it up at the condiment table filled with lettuce, sliced tomatoes and onions, real mayo, and pickles. The Flea Market Burger is a 10-ounce bad boy. The curly fries are good and greasy. The menu also lists daily specials including catfish and steak, but who cares? It's all about the burger.

So now you know what to order; all you need to know is when. Wednesday night is a trivia party when the joint is packed with teams who know all the battles of the Crimean War and every TV theme song ever written. It's great fun just to watch. Fri and Sat are karaoke nights and you can just picture how crazy that gets. Sun there's free live music and half-price burgers and booze.

WINSTEAD'S $
Country Club Plaza (see Web site for additional locations)
101 Brush Creek Blvd.
(816) 753-2244
www.winsteadskc.com

Since 1940 this has been the place to come for burgers and shakes, and other than a few menu updates not much has changed since then. The waitresses still wear jaunty uniforms, the jukebox still plays great tunes—no quarters required, just punch in your favorite tunes—and most important, they continue to live up to their 60-year motto, "We grind U.S. choice steak daily for the sandwich."

For newcomers, it's only fair to tell you that the famous Winstead's steakburgers are flat, thin circles of beef. In fact the onion slice is thicker than the burger, so you won't be remiss if you order a double. But it's the combination of flavors—the grilled beef with slightly crispy edges, fat slice of sweet onion, tangy mustard-and-ketchup sauce, pickle sliced the long way, and unadorned bun—that beats all other burgers hands down. It's even wrapped in paper and presented on your plate like a gift. To complete your experience get the Special Chocolate Frosty, "the exclusive Winstead drink you eat with a spoon." They mean it; try to suck this creamy concoction through a straw and we know for a fact your head will cave in. During hot summer days the limeade is a refreshing substitute, made with plenty of shaved ice and a perky hat of lime sherbet. For families or a table of teens it's great fun to order a Skyscraper Soda; this monster of an ice-cream treat is served in a glass about a foot tall and is meant to be shared by two to four people.

CHINESE

BLUE KOI　　　　　　　　　　$-$$
1803 W. 39th St. (Midtown)
(816) 561-5003

107th and Mission Rd. (Mission Farms)
Leawood, KS
(913) 383-3330
www.bluekoikc.net

The sponged aqua walls at Blue Koi aren't the only cool thing about this dumpling and noodle shop. Here's where we learned to drink bubble tea, an iced milk and tea drink with tapioca balls that float to the bottom of the glass, waiting for you to slurp them up through a straw. Purists will find an extensive list of aromatic brews, including a slightly floral-scented jasmine, to go with your meal. But it's the Chang family's comfort food that has people filling the long, narrow space for lunch and dinner. The Chinese pot roast, a slab of slow-roasted, fork-tender beef ladled over wide strips of noodles, is addictive. Or try Ants on a Tree, a Taiwanese dish of sautéed minced pork and shredded cabbage served with amber-colored cellophane noodles. Or play mix and match with the extensive menu. Seven types of dumplings are available to order either boiled or pan-fried as a meal or an appetizer to share. Vegans will be happy to find several tempting dishes, including a vegetarian dumpling, lettuce wrap, and braised tofu with shiitake mushroom entree. The savory fare is now also available in fancier digs, at Leawood's swanky Mission Farms, where JoCo's kids can discover bubble tea.

BO LINGS　　　　　　　　　　　　　$
9055 Metcalf Ave.
Overland Park, KS
(913) 341-1718

4800 Main St. (Country Club Plaza)
(816) 753-1718

9574 Quivira Rd.
Lenexa, KS
(913) 888-6618

7105 W. 135th St.
Overland Park, KS
(913) 239-8188

8870 Northwest Prairie View Rd. (Zona Rosa)
(816) 587-7880

20 E. 5th St. (River Market)
(816) 841-5465
www.bolings.com

When Kansas Citians are hungry for Chinese food, those in the know head for one of Richard and Theresa Ng's restaurants. Their original place, a beautiful showroom in pale teal and dark wood in the Plaza's Board of Trade Building, gained them a loyal following. For the business lunch crowd, it was a welcome rest from steakhouses and sandwiches. Johnson County fans were thrilled when they opened new locations closer to home.

Richard's food is fresh, flavorful, and authentic; in fact he often visits Hong Kong's best restaurants for ideas to bring back home. The extensive menu includes Cantonese lettuce wraps, General Tso's chicken, shrimp and scallops in garlic sauce, sizzling black pepper beef, and fried noodles. Even the rice is special: a blend of aromatic jasmine and fluffy American long grain. A house specialty is succulent Beijing roasted duck. These plump, rice-fed ducks are cooked in custom-designed hanging ovens that let the fat drip away as the skin becomes crisp and russet colored. The duck is then carved and tucked into soft steamed buns along with slivers of cucumber, green onion, and sweet plum sauce. It may become your new favorite dish.

On Sat and Sun dim sum is served at the Plaza, River Market, and Metcalf locations. This wildly popular event offers over 50 appetizers, including steamed barbecue pork buns, shrimp dumplings, and stuffed eggplant. The younger set has discovered this fun and relaxing way to while away a weekend afternoon, so reservations aren't a bad idea. All six locations are open seven days a week.

GENGHIS KHAN MONGOLIAN GRILL $

3901 Bell (Midtown)
(816) 753-3600

8634 N. Boardwalk (Northland)
(816) 587-8883
www.genghiskhankc.com

This large corner restaurant with exposed brick walls and wooden floors is always packed thanks to the variety of food, a fun atmosphere, and incredible value. Although the menu offers tempting dishes such as braised meats in clay pots, regulars ignore the printed list and head for the all-you-can-eat buffet.

For lunch grab a plate and start piling on your choice of 25 fresh vegetables and sliced beef, chicken, pork, crab, catfish, and squid. At night the selections expand to include shrimp, scallops, lamb, Chinese sausage, and mahimahi. Then add a splash of sauce from more than a dozen ingredients; recipes are provided or create your own. Finally, hand your overflowing plate to the cook, who will grill it before your eyes.

Expect a crowd by noon, when this becomes a hangout for interns and staffers from nearby University of Kansas Hospital, vegetarians, and anyone else looking for fresh flavorful food at a

bargain price. Lunch starts at just $9.50, and dinner is around $13 depending on whether your creation includes meat. Unique cocktails, like the refreshing mango sangria, add to the fun. The original location is open Mon through Sat; the Northland experience is closed Mon.

FRENCH

Even though our first official settler was French, it would be some 150 years before we acquired more than one restaurant serving Gallic food. Today we have some of the finest French bistros this side of the Atlantic, attended to by chefs who, more often than not, came here for love and ended up falling in love with the city as well.

AIXOIS $$

251 E. 55th (Midtown)
(816) 333-3305
www.aixois.com

Pronounced *ex-WAH*, this bistro is named for Emmanuel Langlade, the owner and chef who, along with lovely wife Megan, have fashioned a place made for a romantic rendezvous. The ambience starts with the Crestwood Shops where it resides, a mix of homegrown home decor boutiques and antique shops, exquisite little clothiers, and a stationery. Inside the bistro, mustard-yellow walls and exposed bricks and ceiling beams set the mood. And though the menu is small, there are enough daily specials to warrant a weekly reservation. Many devotees would be quite happy to order Emmanuel's truite saumon meunière every single day; this ruby trout sautéed in lemon butter and topped with slivered almonds is so popular it's served for both lunch and dinner.

We hate to use the term French fries when describing the pommes frites here, because no fast-food joint ever offered such crisp-tender slivers of spuds. They're served with a number of items, including the peppered flank steak, Kansas City strip, and Prince Edward Island mussels in a luscious cream sauce. Starters are also delicious, especially a classic salade niçoise, a lovely composed salad of tuna, tomatoes, tiny black olives, and hard-boiled egg on a bed of greens with a tangy vinaigrette, and the peppery arugula and strawberries with warm goat cheese. The luxurious pâtés are all made in-house.

If you can't decide which dessert to have, enjoy them all with the assiettes Aixoise, a decadent display that includes crème brûlée, chocolate mousse, fresh fruit with puree, and profiteroles with chocolate. Aixois serves lunch and dinner Mon through Sat. The coffee bar is open seven days a week.

CAFE DES AMIS $$
112½ Main St.
Parkville, MO
(816) 587-6767
www.cafedesamiskc.com

It's easy to pretend you're in a village in France while sitting on this sun-dappled deck with the fragrance of roast duck swirling around you. The clincher is handsome owner Didier Combe's accent as he asks if the escargot is to your liking. Didier's recipes, from his mother's kitchen in Aix-en-Provence, are brought brilliantly to life by his chef. The menu includes classics such as coquilles Saint Jacques and newer masterpieces such as a casserole of organic vegetables, aromatic herbs, and tangy goat cheese. For lunch there are lovely crepes, and at night the filet in a sauce of cognac, peppercorns, and Roquefort will have you swooning. Desserts include crepes filled with a dark chocolate sauce and a shimmering tart served with caramel sauce. Although the deck seating is divine, the bistro also has small—and we do mean small—rooms inside. But no one's complaining; the close quarters give you one more reason to sit knee-to-knee with your sweetheart.

i If preparing barbecue sounds like a huge commitment in time and trouble, we have a solution: Skip the wood, get on the road, and let a master smoker prepare it for you. You'll find some of the city's most popular barbecue restaurants elsewhere in this chapter. Happy eating.

CAFE PROVENCE $$
3936 W. 69th Terrace
Prairie Village, KS
(913) 384-5998
www.cafeprovence.net

So what if the windows here look out over a parking lot rather than the Seine? It's the food that counts, and Chef Daniel Quillac does not disappoint. As for atmosphere, the television at the bar is always tuned to a French station, where even a traffic report sounds romantic. The sunny, saffrony bouillabaisse will make you think you've traveled to Provence. But if you really want to savor your seafood, opt for the mussels in a white wine, garlic, and shallot sauce so decadent you'll beg for more bread. Other classic French dishes include steak tartare and pan-seared frog legs served with a rosy tomato coulis. And, ah, for dessert, there's crème caramel, lemon tart, and profiteroles, which are pastry puffs topped with ribbons of chocolate ganache and served with homemade ice cream. Lunch and dinner are served Mon through Sat.

LE FOU FROG $$–$$$
400 E. Fifth St. (River Market)
(816) 474-6060
www.lefoufrog.com

It only makes sense that this cozy French bistro would land in the historic River Market district not far from where our famous first Frenchman made his home. The rest of us are just glad Chef Mano Rafael left Marseille to follow his heart—and his bride, Barbara, a Kansas City native—to our river town as well. Since opening the restaurant in 1997, Mano has thrilled guests with classic French dishes such as escargot with garlic butter and seared rack of lamb coated with Dijon mustard and herbs. And after more than a decade, there's still a steady buzz about Mano's moules marinieres, which are Prince Edward Island mussels steamed in a broth of white wine, shallots, mustard, and heavy cream. But don't overlook the osso buco Corsican, slow-braised veal shanks in a red wine–veal broth topped with thin slices of prosciutto and shaved mozzarella. Le Fou Frog, which means "the crazy Frenchman," is open for dinner Tues through Sun. It also hosts such events as a Bastille Day celebration, wine tastings, and a Valentine's Day feast that features food declared to be aphrodisiacs. To turn even a winter's evening into a party, a heated tent is available year-round. One bit of warning: This place is very noisy and boisterous, and that's just how the owner and most of the patrons like it. But if you're looking for a quiet, intimate evening, this may not be your best choice.

TATSU'S   **$$**
4603 W. 90th St.
Prairie Village, KS
(913) 383-9801
www.tatsus.com

Don't let the location in an unassuming strip mall dissuade you from coming here. Just pop in a French CD and pretend you're driving your Renault past the Eiffel Tower rather than a fire-house in Johnson County. Japanese-born owner and chef Tatsu Arai has been adding a delicate touch to classic French cuisine, to the delight of his longtime fans, since 1980. Specialties include braised oxtails cooked in a red wine sauce and Jacques a la Moutarde. And after you've fallen in love with the house-made salad dressing, you'll be glad to know it's available by the bottle. By now we hope you've ordered the Grand Marnier soufflé. It's a lovely sight on a pool of crème anglaise and stripes of dark chocolate sauce. And notice, please, the two dollar signs in Tatsu's heading. It is truly amazing to find food and ser-vice this splendid for so few francs.

INTERNATIONAL

LA BODEGA   **$$**
703 Southwest Blvd. (Midtown)
(816) 472-8272
www.labodegakc.com

This boisterous cafe is where you'll find out which of your friends learned to share in kindergarten. For at La Bodega, most of the menu is composed of hot and cold tapas—little savory appetizers—that are meant to be passed around the table. We've come to love the Basque way of socializing

so much we often graze this way for hours, with a different dish arriving every few minutes to a round of applause. Complete the Spanish tradi-tion with a glass of sherry or indulge in big rosy pitchers of La Bodega's now famous sangria. Just don't let the fruity goodness fool you; it's potent.

Top-selling cold tapas include marinated olives, roasted red peppers stuffed with tuna and rice, and asparagus spears wrapped in smoked salmon. Hot versions to try are skewered chicken and chorizo with garlic-cumin mayo, squid sau-téed in olive oil and garlic, and Pimento Del Piquillo Relleno, meatballs in a spicy garlic cream sauce. If you still have room for entrees, two of the most popular are grilled steak with blue cheese and the Spanish paellas. Skip the dessert and spend your last pesos on the special coffee made with several types of liqueurs. As you're sip-ping you'll have time to study the colorful decor, especially the mosaic bar and fabulous mural by local artist Peregrine Honig.

PIROPOS   **$$–$$$**
4140 N. Mulberry Dr. (Briarcliff Village)
(816) 741-3600

1 W. First St. (private dining)
Parkville, MO
(816) 741-3600
www.piroposkc.com

In Buenos Aires the women are so beautiful that admirers have created an art form—loosely translated into *piropos*—for paying them compli-ments. The lovely Cristina Worden received a par-ticularly fine *piropo* from husband Gary; he built a restaurant to showcase her country's cuisine.

The view of a glittering downtown skyline in the distance will have you whistling in admira-tion. In winter, the fireplace is another enchant-ing view.

At Piropos the food is the star, especially since it's based on ingredients we appreciate in the Midwest: excellent steaks and fresh salads. Be sure to try the trio of sauces served in tiny pots with the empanadas: creamy garlic aioli; criolla made with peppers, tomato, celery, and vinegar; and chimichurri, that Argentinean staple made with parsley, garlic, vinegar, and olive oil. The fact that nearly half the population of Argentina is made up of Italians is evident in pasta dishes, such as ricotta and spinach–stuffed ravioli with a walnut-studded butter sauce. But it's the grilled meats that stand out at Piropos, including succulent steaks, lamb, and pork chops. You'll find yourself asking for more sauces for dipping. For dessert, whisper yes to anything made with *dulce de leche*—a caramel known in South America as milk candy—which is drizzled over creamy flan, chocolate cake, and apple-filled crepes. Piropos serves lunch Mon through Fri and dinner daily. The original Parkville location is open for special (and we mean special) events only.

RE:VERSE $$
618 Ward Pkwy. (Country Club Plaza)
(816) 931-7811
www.reversekc.com
La Bodega owner James Taylor had an instant hit when he opened this hip place on one of the Plaza's most visible corners. The Beat Generation theme doesn't matter to the mostly twentysomethings at the bar, but the retro cocktails certainly do. The list includes grasshoppers, stingers, and martinis and a refreshing mojito made by adding white rum to a muddled mix of mint, sugar, and lime. The cocktails keep coming until 1:30 a.m., and insiders often head to the sexy Red Room lounge downstairs, where a DJ or live music is on tap several nights a week.

The decor is just as stylish as the crowd, with lipstick-red walls and ceiling, stainless steel panels, and viewing screens that let you peek into the kitchen. The menu stars tapas, like its sister restaurant on the Boulevard: spicy tidbits to share with dining partners. The trio of ahi tuna slices is a nice choice; they're seared, tied with scallions like little packages, and served with a peanut-chili sauce. The sautéed calamari and spicy chorizo is a sensual delight on a stark white plate.

Re:Verse is open for lunch Mon through Sat and dinner seven nights a week. The Sunday brunch on the sidewalk often becomes a party as friends text friends, encouraging them to join them for a Bloody Mary and eggs with chorizo.

For early birds, re:Verse serves espresso starting at 6:45 a.m. and breakfast from 7 to 10:30 a.m. Mon through Fri.

ITALIAN

GAROZZO'S RISTORANTE $–$$
526 Harrison (East Side)
(816) 221-2455

1547 Northeast Rice Rd.
Lee's Summit, MO
(816) 554-2800

13505 S. Mur-Len
Olathe, KS
(913) 764-6969

CAFE GAROZZO
9950 College Blvd.
Overland Park, KS
(913) 491-8300
www.garozzos.com
Some people have a standing reservation at the original Garozzo's on Harrison every Fri night. Is it the 5-inch-high lasagna, Frank Sinatra tunes in the background, or owner Mike Garozzo singing along in his gravelly voice? Sorry, Mike. It's the food.

Here's where many of us tasted our first chicken spiedini, that flavorful rolled breast of chicken smothered in a piquant garlic-lemon sauce. It's a recipe Mike brought from the Italian section of St. Louis known as the Hill in 1989.

Spiedini fans may find it hard to branch out, but the menu offers other wonderful items, particularly specialties named for Garozzo family and friends, such as the Gambretti Angelina, charbroiled jumbo shrimp in a white wine butter sauce with mushrooms and fresh broccoli. The Bistecca Salvatore Alla Siciliano is a 16-ounce porterhouse that's breaded, charbroiled, and basted in amogio sauce, that garlicky lemon concoction that defines so many dishes here.

All entrees are served with a house salad, pasta on the side, and bread to dip in a plate of olive oil, freshly ground black pepper, grated Parmesan cheese, and a sprinkling of red pepper flakes. If you're lucky somebody will order the

Three Way Pasta, a platter overflowing with ravioli, spaghetti, and mostaccioli and topped with a softball-sized meatball. We've been waiting to see it polished off in one sitting.

i We love to eat. On average, every man, woman, and child in Kansas City spends $938 dining out each year, according to the National Restaurant Association. That puts us third in U.S. metropolitan areas; just $30 less than first-ranking New York City and $17 less than Washington, D.C. We spent $29 more per person than San Francisco!

JASPER'S $$–$$$
1201 W. 103rd St. (South Kansas City)
(816) 941-6600
www.jasperskc.com
For nearly five decades the Mirabile (pronounced Mir-AH-bill-ee) family, led by Jasper Sr., collected culinary rating stars, diamonds, and a multistate fan club for serving classic Italian food. The patriarch passed away, but the quality has never waned. His son, Jasper Mirabile Jr.—friends call him JJ—has added his own energy and passion to the place, making this party central on a Sat night as regulars slide into a cushy booth and new fans are soon treated like family.

Jasper's respect for traditional cuisine earned him a guest-chef spot at at the James Beard House—the first Italian chef so honored, and the first chef from Kansas City—a trip he revisited to glowing reviews in 2010. And he's always improvising: A tour of Venice inspired entrees such as grilled sea bass with truffle sauce and fire-roasted duck with blood orange and dried cherry balsamic demi-glace.

JJ also finds time to share his passion with others. He teaches cooking classes at the Culinary Center of Kansas City (see www.kcculinary.com for schedules), the Brookside farmers' market, and even Hen House grocery stores where his primo pasta sauce is available. And when not dining with JJ, you can listen to his radio show—on which he interviews top national chefs—every Saturday morning.

But we suggest you show up in person. Reservations for parties of six or more are accepted, but if you have to wait, enjoy a flight of wine at the first Italian enoteca in Kansas City in the entrance. After dinner, be sure to buy one of Jasper's cookbooks; chances are Jasper is in the house, happy to autograph your copy. Pick up the next day's lunch or dinner at Marco Polo's Italian Market on the premises.

LIDIA'S $$
101 E. 22nd St. (Freighthouse District)
(816) 221-3722
www.lidiasitaly.com
It was quite a coup when famed restaurateur and public TV cooking show host Lidia Bastianich chose Kansas City for her first restaurant outside New York. Locals who'd been dazzled by her northern Italian cuisine at Becco and Felidia helped create a buzz that hasn't abated a decade later. Buzz is right; the three-story, open room is often jammed with patrons ordering from the the expansive, evocative menu. Can't decide? Do what so many of us do: order the pasta trio, which takes "all you can eat" to an entirely new level as servers circle the rooms to refill plates with pastas fresh from the kitchen. The selection changes daily but usually includes a ravioli, sauced ribbon shape, and aromatic risotto. For around $13 it is without a doubt the most delicious bargain in town. The regular menu includes roasted veal shank with saffron-scented barley risotto and grilled salmon over braised lentils with a zesty chive-mustard sauce. Lidia has left her namesake restaurant in the capable hands of chefs Dan Sweeny and Cody Hogan, and a young pastry chef who is making the entire town swoon with her luscious desserts and gelato flavors. No room for dessert after your fifth helping of pasta? Then end the evening as the Italians do, with a *caffe corretto*, "corrected coffee," that's braced with shots of grappa and liqueur.

MEXICAN/SOUTHWESTERN

LA FONDA EL TAQUITO $
800 Southwest Blvd. (Midtown)
(816) 471-1675

Drive up and down Southwest Boulevard and you'll find the real deal: Mexican restaurants where the owner's grandmother stirs the pork chili while a younger sister presses tortillas one at a time. El Taquito is just such a place. Like true family-style Mexican food, the flavors are not hot, but you can crank up the heat by adding freshly made salsas in temperatures ranging from mild to wild. Flavorful pork is used for the taquito carnitas, soft-shell tacos that satisfy right down to your soul. The taquitos can also be ordered with chicken or chorizo. Burritos are popular as well, but leave room for the sopapillas, fried bread dusted with cinnamon sugar, or the smooth flan.

On Fri and Sat nights live Latino music turns the front area into a salsa and merengue dance floor. Things cool down a bit a few hours later, just in time for a Sunday brunch when huevos rancheros and other classic dishes liven up the menu. La Fonda is open seven days a week.

TARAHUMARA MEXICAN RESTAURANT $
10001 W. 87th St.
Overland Park, KS
(913) 403-9211
www.tarahumaramexicanfood.com
Your mouth may stumble over the name of this rustic restaurant, but local foodies are raving about this place—despite the fact that it's in the suburbs instead of midtown's Southwest Boulevard. Although you'll find all the usual suspects, from enchiladas to tamales and burritos, Tara is known for its specialties. Chuletas Adobadas are pork steaks in adobo sauce; Puerco en Salsa Verde, chunks of pork that have been cooking for hours served in a tomatillo sauce; and Bistek con Papas, grilled steak served with potatoes, jalapeños, and onions. Regulars simply go for the addictive soft tacos filled with barbacoa and cilantro for $1.50 each. Just add a bowl of chunky guacamole and an icy margarita, and who needs a strolling mariachi band? Along with classic margaritas, Tarahumara serves Mexican and domestic beers. And mole? Olé!

SEAFOOD

Fresh seafood lovers, your ship has come in. Thanks to overnight shipping, several restaurants receive fresh fish and shellfish shipments six days a week. Then they fry, grill, roast, blacken, or pan sauté them with finesse. Following are some of the seafood restaurants that really float our boat.

BRISTOL BAR AND GRILL $$–$$$
5400 W. 119th St.
Overland Park, KS
(913) 663-5777

51 E. 14th St. (Power & Light District)
(816) 448-6007
www.bristolseafoodgrill.com
Fans of this Kansas City classic gladly followed it from its perch on the Country Club Plaza to the suburbs where it still packs them in. Now, with a location in the Power & Light District, even more of us can enjoy the slightly sweet drop biscuits that servers bring around throughout your meal, as well as the beloved Sunday brunch. This button-popping display features dozens of dishes including seafood pasta, cheese grits, crab soufflé, peel-and-eat spiced shrimp, carved prime rib, scrambled eggs and egg casseroles, fresh fruit, a Belgian waffle bar, and decadent desserts such as Key lime tarts, bread pudding, and chocolate-dipped strawberries. At lunch and dinner, however, it's the seafood that rules. Several types of fish are available seared, grilled, baked, or blackened, including yellowfin tuna, salmon, and mahimahi. The Bristol is open seven days a week. The Power & Light location has become a popular happy hour hangout, especially on Fri when live music and hand-crafted cocktails go nicely with appetizers. Be sure to sign up for special offers—like a $25 gift cerficate on your birthday. Go fish!

MCCORMICK & SCHMICK'S $$–$$$
448 W. 47th St. (Country Club Plaza)
(816) 531-6800
www.mccormickandschmicks.com
Here's where the beautiful people show up to see and be seen and partake of happy hour appetiz-

ers. The rest of us get happy by heading to a dinner table. And if you want to get positively silly, reserve one of the booths (called a "snug") with curtains that can be drawn discreetly shut. Good luck choosing from this eye-popping menu of no less than 30 fresh seafood entrees. And they do mean fresh: Fish is shipped in six days a week. You might start with oysters on the half shell from Washington, Long Island, Prince Edward Island, and British Columbia; a sampler plate will get you a few from each location. During cold weather the traditional oyster stew is the perfect comfort food.

The menu changes daily based on the latest coastal catch but usually includes specialties such as salmon roasted on a cedar plank and served with a pinot noir sauce or stuffed with crab, shrimp, and Brie; and cashew-crusted tilapia with a Jamaican rum butter sauce. Carnivores will still find plenty to love with grilled steaks and chops. For dessert, don't miss the now-famous Chocolate Bag; a dark chocolate sack filled with white chocolate mousse. Now don't you wish you'd requested one of those secluded snugs?

SOUL FOOD

PEACHTREE $-$$
31 E. 14th St. (Power & Light District)
(816) 886-9800

1672 Northwest Chipman Rd. (Lee's Summit)
(816) 554-8733

THE PEACHTREE BUFFET
6800 Eastwood Trafficway
(816) 923-0099
www.peachtreerestaurant.com
Real lard. Real butter. Real home cooking made with soul. That's Peachtree's way at both the original all-you-can-eat buffet on Eastwood and the pretty new place in the Power & Light District. The buffet tables practically groan under the weight of all the fried chicken and catfish, smothered pork chops, macaroni and cheese, candied yams, and salad fixings—more than 20 selections prepared fresh daily. Save room for the

famous peach cobbler and bread pudding, but you might want to order a dozen sweet potato corn bread muffins to go. The decor in the Power & Light District and the Lee's Summit locations are more upscale, with a full bar, but the fixin's are just as soulful. Order favorites from the menu, such as Ole-time Salmon Croquettes or a juicy steak, before heading to live music or a movie nearby.

STEAKHOUSES

As the city that gave the world the Kansas City strip—please don't ask for a New York strip around here—we're known for our steaks. This particular cut came to be in 1946 when Eddie Williams bid $35.05 per pound—10 times the going rate—for a champion Hereford at the American Royal livestock auction. It made T. O. Pride's 16-year-old owner $44,375 richer and created national attention for Kansas City steaks. Following is a cowtown primer on cuts of beef, along with a few suggestions about where they do them up royally.

Filet: Selected from the finest beef tenderloin, this cut is the tenderest, most melt-in-your-mouth of all red meats. Usually available in 6-, 8-, and 10-ounce cuts.

Kansas City strip: A beautifully marbled, boneless cut loaded with flavor. Typically available in 10- and 12-ounce sizes.

T-bone: A very thick, very juicy cut that's fit for a king or queen. Better save room for this one; it's often served in 22-ounce cuts.

Rib eye: Very juicy and flavorful, this steak is hand-cut from the naturally aged prime rib.

BENTON'S STEAK AND CHOP HOUSE $$$
Westin Crown Center Hotel
1 Pershing Rd.
(816) 391-4460
www.bentonskc.com
Ah, decisions, decisions. Shall we have the Western Auto sign, the Marriott Hotel light display, or the Liberty Memorial flame? Those aren't menu items, they're just three of the spectacular views from Benton's floor-to-ceiling windows 20 floors

above the Westin Hotel. The interior is nearly as spectacular, especially the 16 original works by namesake and beloved Kansas City artist Thomas Hart Benton. Chef Martin Hueser deftly supervises a panorama of dishes, from double-cut pork chops to tasty holdovers, such as steamed dumplings, from the days of the popular Asian eatery downstairs, Trader Vic's. And if you think a steak is a steak is a steak, you'll be pleasantly surprised. Benton's starts with twenty-one-day-aged certified Angus beef flavored with a signature seasoning that adds a unique, tangy hickory flavor. Benton's is also the place to find bison prepared several ways—leaner and, some say, more flavorful than regular beef. Benton's also prides itself on serving wild Canadian sockeye salmon, a fine finny choice, along with lobster and crab cakes.

The Sunday brunch is a celebration of eye-popping choices—over 100 items in all, including healthy fresh fruit, an omelet station, and carving stations with prime rib.

Another "prime" time to come is Thurs through Sat evenings, when the pretty lounge offers live jazz to go with the view. Check the Web site for wine flights and appetizer specials. In fact, that's where we snagged a coupon for a free flambéed dessert prepared tableside one evening. Or you could simply watch the flame over the Liberty Memorial to your left.

THE CAPITAL GRILLE $$$
4740 Jefferson St. (Country Club Plaza)
(816) 531-8345
www.thecapitalgrille.com
When readers of *KC Magazine* named this the best steakhouse in town, they raised a few eyebrows. Frankly, it's rare that a transplant—and a national chain at that—can win the hearts of such a loyal crowd. But this ultraplush restaurant earns its accolades. There's even a signature martini, the Stoli Doli, made with slices of pineapple marinating in glass crocks of Stolichnaya vodka on the bar. Trust us; they're as potent as they are delicious.

As you're escorted to your table, you'll pass the glass case where beef is dry aging for fourteen to twenty-one days. When they're at the peak of flavor, steaks are hand-cut, well seasoned, and seared at 1,100 degrees Fahrenheit to seal in the juices and provide that distinctive caramelized crust. Dinners can start with cold baby lobster with confetti mayonnaise, a sinfully rich lobster bisque, or the "Wedge," an enormous portion of iceberg lettuce with blue cheese and crumbled bacon. As for lunch, the steak salad is large enough for two, or one diner with dreams of a second meal.

Service is refined yet friendly, with servers who say "My pleasure" to any request—and mean it. Don't be surprised if you receive a handwritten note a day or two after your visit. An impressive wine list includes more than 300 bottles ranging from $27 to well over $500. And true wine connoisseurs will appreciate the fine crystal glassware without a rolled rim. At about $12 a stem, it's an investment in quality that sets the right tone. Wine lockers are available to store your personal collection; the brass plaques lining the wall read like a "Who's Who" of Kansas City elite.

If you need one more reason to make a reservation, consider the deep-dish Key lime pie with toasted pistachio crust. The restaurant is open for lunch on weekdays and dinner seven days a week, including a 9 p.m. last call on Sun.

HEREFORD HOUSE $$–$$$
5001 Town Center Dr.
Leawood, KS
(913) 327-0800

19721 E. Jackson St.
Independence, MO
(816) 795-9200

8661 N. Stoddard Ave. (Zona Rosa)
(816) 584-9000

PRIME RIB GRILL BY HEREFORD HOUSE
100 E. 20th St.
(816) 842-1080
www.herefordhouse.com
Since 1957 the Hereford House has been sating the carnivorous tastes in Kansas City. The thrill begins with a charred carpaccio sliced paper

thin and served chilled with a peppy chipotle mayonnaise. The steaks, of course, are delicious, either simply grilled or topped with a cracked pepper and blue cheese sauce or Dijon mustard and brown sugar glaze. Fish is done right here as well, particularly the cedar-plank salmon that's oven roasted and served with a garlic herb butter. Side dishes include the signature cowboy baked beans and twice-baked potato. As for the creamy Italian and cheddar cheese salad dressings, regulars refer to them as "pink" and "yellow" and usually order a little of both.

Frequent visitors to Kansas City may blink twice when looking for the original Hereford House at 20th and Main. Alas, it was torn down in 2010 due to a fire. Beef eaters, take heart: Hereford House owner Rod Anderson opened the Prime Rib Grill across the street. The lunch crowd has mooo-ved over to the new digs for all their favorites, like the French dip sandwich. Truth be told, we opt for the tasty salmon burger instead. And every Tues and Thurs night, your friendly server will bring you succulent slabs of prime rib until you say "uncle." Leave room somehow for the heavenly deep-dish pecan pie or Grandma Ginger's date-nut cookies.

All four restaurants are open seven days a week. The Leawood location offers kosher dinners with advance notice.

J. GILBERT'S $$–$$$
8901 Metcalf
Overland Park, KS
(913) 632-8070
www.jgilberts.com
Hello, handsome! We're not flirting with the waiter, we'll talking about the masculine yet elegant interior of this eatery set on a busy Johnson County street. Just let your hostess know if you prefer a cushy booth away from the crowd, or near the cozy fireplace.

Although J. Gilbert's fashions itself a steakhouse, it offers some excellent seafood, chicken, and pasta dishes, such as a five-spice chicken penne with a smoked Gouda sauce. But this place definitely knows how to put the sizzle into a steak. They select only corn-fed Black Angus

beef, then sear the steaks on a wood-fire grill hot enough to seal in the flavorful juices within seconds. Purists will go for the tender filet mignon, and those who hanker for something fancy might like the bourbon-based sauce. The side dishes really shine here as well, especially the poblano potatoes au gratin.

J. Gilbert's provides the right atmosphere for a romantic anniversary dinner, yet is casual enough for families. It's open for dinner only. Show up for your reservations early enough for an order of the house-made potato chips topped with blue-cheese sauce.

JESS & JIM'S STEAK HOUSE $$
517 E. 135th St. (South Kansas City)
(816) 941-9499
www.jessandjims.com
This down-home place landed forever on the culinary map in 1972 when Calvin Trillin announced in *Playboy* that it served the best steak in the universe. Bingo: the 25-ounce Playboy Strip was born.

The restaurant's namesakes are gone, but the tradition lives on with Jim's kin, the VanNoy family. There are 10 cuts of steaks available, including filets ranging in size from 5 to 14 ounces, and an eye-popping, button-flying 30-ounce porterhouse. Steaks are served sizzling on big hot silver platters. You can order them any way you like, but please note that steaks cooked beyond medium well are not guaranteed.

Other entrees include lobster—available either steamed or battered and fried—frog legs, chicken gizzards, and shrimp. And most come with your choice of a football-sized baked potato, fabulous cottage fries, soup or salad, and homemade garlic toast. There's even a surprisingly varied wine list that includes several decent cabernets.

The restaurant is open for lunch and dinner Mon through Sat.

THE MAJESTIC RESTAURANT $$$
931 Broadway (Downtown)
(816) 471-8484
www.majestickc.com

This slim three-story building once housed Fitzpatrick's saloon and a bordello, making it a popular place for gangsters and political bigshots during the 1930s. Pressed tin ceilings, tile floors, and stained-glass lights reveal its turn-of-the-20th-century age and helped put it on the National Register of Historic Places.

Since 1993 the landmark has gone from making history to serving historically good steaks. The Majestic is justly proud of its dry-aged prime beef. True carnivores will simply point to the 12-ounce Kansas City strip. And here's good news: unlike some steakhouses that serve a cut of beef looking forlorn and lonely on a plate, here diners get salads and side dishes. And new owners, Frank and Jolyn Sebree, have added a few French dishes from their time in Europe. One delectable example is the free-range chicken roasted with herbes de Provence. We're not sure where the idea for fried green beans came from, but we're not complaining. They appear on the lunch and dinner menu. At night, add a lobster tail to any item for around $26. The music hits all the right notes as well; there's someone playing the circa 1910 piano in the front of the bar every night during happy hour. That's a perfect excuse for an evening of lower-priced cocktails and a trio of sliders—miniature burgers in your choice of lamb, salmon, BLT, or filet mignon. Downstairs, live jazz is on tap Fri and Sat. More good news: parking is free in the lot at 919 Broadway.

PLAZA III THE STEAKHOUSE $$$
4749 Pennsylvania (Country Club Plaza)
(816) 753-0000
www.plazaiiisteakhouse.com
Not much has changed since this granddaddy of local steakhouses opened in 1963. But that's just fine with its loyal fanbase. Standout appetizers include the famous Plaza III Steak Soup, a thick broth of ground beef and vegetables, and a spinach salad with spiced roasted walnuts and hot bacon dressing. But let's get down to why Plaza III is consistently rated one of the country's top steakhouses. It's the beef. They hand-select only corn-fed, center-cut USDA-graded prime beef and then age it from three to four weeks in

their own beef locker. Optional diable, béarnaise, and pan-gravy sauces are available but totally unnecessary with steaks of this caliber. If you're not in the mood for steak, lobster and salmon are also on the menu. The extensive wine list has won acclaim from *Wine Spectator*.

i Beyond barbecue and steaks, we have a few other hometown recipes to sample. The Plaza III steak soup is a perennial favorite, as is the baked potato soup at the Grand Cafe. You'll also want to try a brew from Boulevard Brewing Company and finish your meal with java from the Roasterie Coffee. Several top restaurants also serve their own blends.

SULLIVAN'S STEAKHOUSE $$–$$$
4501 W. 119th St.
(913) 826-6551
www.sullivanssteakhouse.com
Since opening in 2008, Sully's has become the hot spot for Johnson County's elite who like their steaks juicy, their martinis bold, and their jazz smoking. Speaking of smoking, cigars are allowed on the patio. We'll skip the stogies, thank you, and opt for the house-made potato chips dripping with bleu cheese, or what the restaurant calls the "Best Burger in Town." They're just two of the temping appetizers on the $5 Swinging at Sully's menu on Thurs and Sun nights. But the menu is pretty compelling any day of the week. The Business Lunch is a bargain for $18 with a choice of salad or soup, entrée (including a 6 oz. filet mignon), and the renowned horseradish mashed potatoes.

Naturally, dinners focus on a selection of steaks and chops along with seafood, including live Maine lobsters. The bar serves an impressive list of high-end cognacs, single malt scotches, and three-ounce pours of ports. Then there's the Knockout, Sullivan's lethal martini made with orange vodka. It's a pretty sweet way to end a weekend while listening to jazz from some of Kansas City's top performers like Mark Lowrey. Thank goodness the nice folks at Sully's keep the doors open late on Sun.

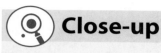

Close-up

Brunch

Some folks save all their calories for Sunday, when several restaurants offer items a la carte or a brunch buffet. Show up and you'll be rewarded with made-to-order omelets, boiled spiced shrimp, carved prime rib of beef, fresh pastries, and everything in between. And on special occasions such as Easter, Mother's Day, and Thanksgiving, lots of other places fire up the chafing dishes, so call ahead and ask. If a restaurant listed below does not appear elsewhere in this chapter, we include the address in its description.

Ophelia's on Independence Square serves brunch items from its inventive menu and is a great place to begin a trip to the nearby Truman Library and Museum. The big-daddy brunch is part of **Benton's** charm, along with the stunning view of midtown.

At **YiaYia's Eurobistro**, where the service is like a big comfortable hug, a diverse brunch menu greets you every Sunday. Two standouts are Corey's crab omelet and the Big Guy, an eye-popper that includes eggs Benedict, lox and bagel, a blueberry pancake, strawberry French toast, oven-roasted potatoes, and bacon or sausage. **Succotash** (2601 Holmes in the River Market, 816-421-2807, www.succotashkc.com) doesn't just serve its Burrito of Love on Sundays; this hip little bruncheonette is open for three meals every day but Tuesday when dinner is not available. Owner Beth Barden's sense of humor is evident in her menu names, such as the Count of Monte Delicious, made with ham and a sage-cheddar on slightly sweet French toast, and the ginormous red-orange chandelier in the entrance. She also has plans to become a 24/7 destination. Burrito or not, we'd love that. Brunch may be the best—certainly the quietest—time to try **Tomfooleries Restaurant & Bar** (612 W. 47th St., 816-753-0555) because all the twentysomethings are still in bed. You'll be treated to an amazing number of pastries, hot dishes, cold shrimp, made-to-order omelets with 50 choices of ingredients, and unusual buffet items such as cold pizza and hot corned-beef hash.

VEGETARIAN

Vegans and the diet conscious can usually find at least one or two meatless meals on the menus of most of the restaurants listed above. But the following places cater to those who love veggies and grains.

BLUE BIRD BISTRO　　　　　　$–$$
1700 Summit (West Side)
(816) 221-7559
www.bluebirdbistro.com

At this storefront cafe located above the downtown bluffs, you'll see a diverse crowd enjoying inventive dishes and a cozy atmosphere. Although dishes with free-range chicken and chemical-free beef and pork have been added, many still consider this their favorite vegetarian menu. The emphasis on locally produced ingredients is evident with a menu peppered with names of farms and growers. Never is that more delightful than the monthly Farmers Table, where friends and local food tenders come together over five courses of superbly prepared and beautifully presented dishes. The Wednesday Night Tables are communal affairs where conversation is shared along with the risotto, roasted wild salmon, or flavorful bison. Naturally there are vegan choices—a roasted acorn squash stuffed with savory organic quinoa is one example—and you can get tofu with your eggs just as easily as bacon from a rancher a few miles away.

There's also a full bar, where you can try a chilled Japanese sake. Come for breakfast Mon through Sat starting at 7 a.m. Lunch and dinner are served those days as well, with brunch on Sun.

EDEN ALLEY CAFE $
707 W. 47th St. (Country Club Plaza)
(816) 561-5415
www.edenalley.com

Hidden in the basement of the Unity Temple on the Plaza, this fun and funky place evokes the feeling of a hippie hangout from the 1960s. The patrons, however, are a mixed bag. At any given table you can see suits from surrounding offices, book club participants, and, yes, vegetarians looking for delicious dishes starring whole grains, beans, and greens. Even little vegans in training have their own menu and play area.

The day's menu appears on a blackboard above the tiny kitchen, and always includes tasty salads and a veggie burger that could change your mind about meatless fare. Other frequent offerings include pizza and cheesy quesadillas. With what you've saved in animal fat, you can splurge on a yummy dessert. We lost count at some 80 flavors of cake, from the sinfully rich Mighty Mocha to a lavender lemon berry.

Bring your sense of humor; folks here realize good, healthy food should be fun. Witness the title of the Eden Alley cookbook: *Stir-Well to Heaven*. And be sure to bring cash, too, because Eden Alley doesn't take credit cards or checks. It's open for lunch only on Mon and Tues, and lunch and dinner Wed through Sat. Hope for good weather—the outdoor patio provides premium people-watching. Better hold onto that wedge of cake.

NIGHTLIFE

To taste the true essence of our town, you simply must spend an evening listening to jazz. It was that syncopated, soulful, savory stew of many different musical styles, after all, that put Kansas City on the musical map.

That, and the atmosphere that surrounded it. During the Jazz Age, Kansas City earned the name "Paris of the Plains," not so much for our wide boulevards but for the variety of vice available 24 hours a day. At one time this wide-open town was home to hundreds of nightclubs, speakeasies, cabarets, dance halls, and honky-tonks, chiefly clustered around 12th Street and Vine on the east side of town.

Along with jazz, Kansas City had another thriving entertainment option in the 1920s and 1930s: female impersonators. The city's most popular drag club was Dante's Inferno on Independence Avenue. The club is long gone, but its sign lives on in the front window of Retro Inferno, an ultracool vintage furniture store downtown (see more details in Shopping).

Those honky-tonk days are long gone, but on any given night and even some afternoons you can still hear jazz pouring out of clubs and restaurants, on street corners on the Country Club Plaza, and at annual festivals such as the Juneteenth Celebration and Parkville's River Jam. (see Annual Events and Festivals for information). But today "Satin Doll" shares air space with other musical styles, including rock, R&B, zydeco, Irish folk songs, country, and reggae.

When you get enough people together to listen to music, it's a sure bet many of them will want to get up and dance. Whether you want to scoot your boots, learn the tango, or practice your West Coast swing, you'll find an open dance floor somewhere in town.

Night owls can also find plenty of other entertainment around here. We have our share of comedy clubs and bars and taverns, including some that serve up their own microbrewed beer. Before you head out, however, a bit of housekeeping: In both Kansas and Missouri, the legal drinking age is 21. Most of our nightlife is clustered in the downtown, Westport/midtown, and Plaza districts, and a few spots are within walking distance of one another; club-hoppers will most likely need a designatied driver.

Enough of the rules, already—let's go! To make it easier to locate your personal predilection, we've divided this chapter into entertainment categories.

COCKTAIL LOUNGES, WINE BARS, SPEAKEASIES, AND TAVERNS

These days, the person serving you a cocktail isn't a bartender, he (or she) is a mixologist. Sure, you can still get a pour of scotch or a pull of our hometown brew from Boulevard Brewing Company, but we've embraced the martini madness in earnest. Here are some of our favorite places to belly up to the bar.

BLONDE
100 Ward Pkwy.
(816) 931-2525
www.blondekc.com
The bar area is crowded with pretty people, the dining area subs as a tiny dance floor with DJs spinning hip-hop to techno sounds, and the mezzanine area offers plush chairs and even a bed for lounging.

Blonde introduced Kansas City to bottle service, a swanky way to entertain your group of up to 10 with premium liquor and mixers. And this blonde isn't all about eye candy: The food is quite good. We enjoy the flats (grilled steak or chicken with tomatoes, rosemary, and cheese), the satays, and Devil Chips, which are potato chips drizzled with blue cheese. Blonde is open until 1 a.m. Mon and Tues and until 2:30 a.m. other nights including Sun.

i If you've had too much nightlife around the holidays, get a ride or call a cab when it's time to hit the road. Each year Holiday Cab offers free rides home (the first $25 worth of fare, or about 20 miles) between Christmas and New Year's from 7 p.m. to 3 a.m. Call (816) 276-7899, or ask the bartender for the free cab.

BOOZEFISH WINE BAR
1511 Westport Rd.
(816) 561-5995
www.boozefish.com

Maija Diethelm created a European-style bistro on a busy midtown street, where girlfriends show up every first Wednesday of the month for Cosmos and Manicures Night, neighbors roll in for Saturday brunch, and theater-goers drop in on the way home. It's a lively place to test this year's beaujolais nouveau, or relax on a date night with a carefully culled list of wine over dinner or simply the fromage et saucisson. And isn't it romantic to feed each other bites of smoked salmon while listening to jazz? Here's something else we appreciate: a back parking lot.

THE CASHEW
2000 Grand
(816) 221-5858
www.thecashew.com

What do you call a more upscale version of a string of bars called the Peanut? The Cashew, of course. And while the Peanut (5000 Main St., 816-753-9499, plus five other locations) is known for hot wings, the world's best BLTs, and peanut shells on the wooden floor, this more refined legume serves cashews in a bowl.

On balmy nights you'll see urban professionals and a few artists from nearby studios hanging out over beers and martinis when the garage doors are up and the view of downtown is spectacular. So's the red sangria and the Cashew "3" Martini, made with soy vodka. It's a cool place to start the gallery stroll through the Crossroads Arts District on First Fridays. Or come for the live music Mon through Wed. The Cashew also rents out its second floor for private parties. Or have a really small private party in the photo booth tucked in a corner.

CIGAR BAR
1519 Grand Blvd.
(816) 421-7222

Slightly on the seedy side, this long, slender room has everything you want in a bar—a cheesy lounge singer, Al Latta, who performs at 8:30 p.m. Tues through Sat; pretty cocktail waitresses with plenty of cleavage; and a print of a naked woman smoking a cigar behind the bar. She's the only one partaking; Missouri's bars and restaurants are now smoke free. While old timers (and bar owners) are unhappy, even they would admit the food tastes better without the blue haze. The lasagna is fabulous, as are the rest of the mostly Italian dishes served here. That's one of the reasons the person sitting next to you at lunch could be a titan of industry or a stripper from the club down the street. The Cigar Bar is open from 11 a.m. to 3 a.m. Mon through Sat and 6 p.m. to 3 a.m. Sun.

JP WINE BAR
1526 Walnut St.
(816) 842-2660

4311 W. 119th St.
(913) 345-9444
www.jpwinebar.com

In trendy shades of chocolate and chartreuse, this wine bar and coffeehouse came on the scene in an ideal location halfway between the hip Crossroads Arts District and the hot-as-a-pistol downtown loop. Here's where the urban sophisticate drops by after work or couples end the night over a pinot and a cheese platter that's as pretty as the room. When the second location opened in the One Nineteen shopping center, suburbanites joined the fan club.

JP's features wine flights, refreshing mojitos, and concoctions that marry wine with alcohol. But don't worry about wine snobs; here they call sweet red wine Stickies, and smooth whites are Like Butta. On the Missouri side you can join the wine club, which allows you to store your wine (or liquor bottles, for that matter) and get invited to exclusive events. JP's opens at 6 a.m. with coffee drinks, then lunch is served from 11 a.m. to 4 p.m. with salads, sandwiches, and soups, like a luscious acorn butternut squash number. Small plates and cheese platters (along with terrific desserts) are available from 4 to 11 p.m. Hang up your cup or glass at 1:30 a.m. Not open on Sun.

KELLY'S WESTPORT INN
500 Westport Rd.
(816) 561-0635
www.kellyswestportinn.com
History buffs might like to know that Kelly's is the oldest building in Kansas City. Well, at least they have a bronze plaque saying it is. Even the owners aren't sure. What they do know is that this corner establishment was once a grocery store run by Daniel Boone's grandson and became a saloon by 1933. Since then it's been where a cross section of the city—lawyers, salespeople, real estate agents, and artists—meets for lunch on Friday and never seems to make it back to the office. By evening the crowd is younger and rowdier and, in summer, barely dressed. Kelly's is such a tradition on St. Paddy's Day that in 1989 they closed the doors for fear that the floors would cave in. On weekends those wooden floors are wall-to-wall with returning college kids and boomers who make regular pilgrimages to their favorite hangout.

MANIFESTO
1924 Main
(816) 536-1325

A fedora or flapper dress wouldn't be out of line for this basement speakeasy that's so secretive, it doesn't have a Web site or sign on the door. But we've got the goods for you, toots. Call or text the number above, or use the discreet call button in the alley behind 1924 Main Restaurant. Only if there's room in the 30-seat lounge, you'll be buzzed in to walk along dark hallways and down narrow stairs.

The exclusivity—and the candlelight—only adds to its charm. So does the skill level of the bartenders, including owner Ryan Maybee, who craft each cocktail with love. Skip the cosmo or margarita; the inventive libations incorporate ingredients as far-flung as applewood-smoked Jim Beam and maple syrup in the Smokin' Choke, and roasted butternut squash puree for the Winter in Buenos Aires. Can't decide? Ryan or Beau will gently quiz you on your tastes and mood, then shake a potion you'll deem just right. Just be patient. Magic takes time. Bar food from 1924 Main upstairs is available, including fried green beans with an aioli dipping sauce. Manifesto is a grand way to start or end an evening.

i Around here, Sunday is made for S.I.N. That's nothing naughty; it's the acronym for Service Industry Night, when restaurants and bars offer steals and deals on food and liquor to other chefs, waitstaff, and managers. No secret handshake necessary; they'll recognize you from your comfortable shoes and it's-been-a-long-week attitude.

MARTINI CORNER
31st and Main
www.martinicorner.com
When hipsters in Kansas City mention "the corner," this is what they mean: an entire neighborhood of bars a few blocks from Crown Center (the KCTV5 Tower is an excellent landmark). It all started with the Velvet Dog (400 East 31st St., 816-753-9999), Kansas City's original martini lounge. The retro decor, terrific jukebox, and bocce ball court out back make it one of those great neighborhood bars your dad may have vis-

ited long ago. Play pool indoors or out while you chow down on such typical bar fare as chicken fingers and deviled eggs. Across the street, the Mint (334 East 31st St., 816-561-2640) is where a young, often gay, crowd dances to a DJ. Private events like fashion shows pack the place to the rafters. On breezy summer nights, the young business crowd spills out of the patios and tiki bar at Sol Cantina (408 East 31st St., 816-931-8080), where happy hour starts just after siesta time—3 to 7 p.m., with reverse happy hour from 10 p.m. to midnight. Keep the margaritas coming, por favor. For sustenance, there are the famous fish tacos, bruschetta, paninis, and other tasty grub.

A pool table, a dozen TVs, pizza, stromboli, and friendly owners. What more could you want? That's the setup at Tower Tavern (401 East 31st St.), which stays open until 1:30 every night. Here's where you'll see locals chatting at the bar after work or on weekends when flip-flops are the footwear of choice.

The Drop (409 East 31st St., 816-756-DROP, www.thedropbar.com) has morphed from a bar with great bruschettas to a great restaurant that also serves well-made drinks. The key is Eddie Crane's vision of what a cool neighborhood bistro should be: friendly and welcoming with comfort food. The addition of chef Kelli Daniels put it on the foodie's list for lunch and dinner with duck confit over cranberry risotto and diver scallops with mustard bread pudding. Meanwhile, Eddie developed adult versions of Jell-o shots in flavors like lemon drop and mojito. At $12 for three, they are as potent as they are fun. And where else can you get warm cookies with an ice cold glass of milk?

THE WINE BAR
13657 Washington St.
(in Lukas Liquor Super Store)
(816) 942-8707
www.kcwinebar.com
Hidden inside this enormous liquor supermarket really is something super: a wine bar that invites you to experience more than 90 wines plus premium ports and single-malt scotches. The technology alone is enough to make you woozy: the Enomatic, an Italian-designed wine-serving

system, ensures that the vino is always fresh. And there's always delicious fare, including small plates and lovely cheese platters, to go with your wine. Special event dinners are just that—very special.

WINE FLIGHTS BAR AND BISTRO
5408 W. 152st (Leawood)
(913) 402-9800
www.awineflightsbar.com
RJ and Sherri Hamiel have created a haven for wine lovers in the middle of suburbia, complete with a gorgeous decor, palm trees, and fountain out front. And a flight of wine—a trio of small pours of one variation or from a particular grape—is a fine way to educate your palate. No pop quizzes here or pressure, for that matter. RJ's motto is "it's just juice." When you discover a wine you love, you can order a six-ounce pour or share the bottle with friends. Wine Flights has a 1,200-bottle wine cellar, so chances are there's a label with your name on it.

Sherri's food will entice you to linger over lunch or dinner, with a menu that ranges from artisanal cheese plates to seafood ravioli. The Chilean sea bass with sweet corn relish is a bargain at around $17. A vintage port will complement chocolate dessert quite nicely.

COMEDY CLUBS

Since the days of burlesque, Kansas City has always been a circuit for top-name comedians, a tradition that continues today thanks to more than our share of comedy clubs. Over the past decades we've welcomed such up-and-comers as Rosie O'Donnell, Ellen Degeneres, and a guy named Jerry Seinfeld. At one time, our first official comedy club, Stanford & Sons, was ranked first in the Midwest and third in the nation by *Rolling Stone* and *Variety*.

COMEDYCITY
817 Westport Rd. (in Westport Flea Market)
(816) 842-2744
www.instantcomedy.com
Home of Kansas City's original Comedy Sports, where tag teams improvise to suggestions from

the audience. During the early evening performances, held Fri, Sat, and Sun, you won't hear the "blue" language used in other clubs; this is good, clean family fun that's appropriate for groups of all types and sizes. But the 10 p.m. Sat night show is strictly for adults when things get a little wilder. And when the audience participates and the players are on, this can be a hilarious night out. With its new digs in the back room at Westport Flea Market, you have even more reason to get tickled. The Flea is famous for its burgers and brewskis.

> **i** If you're taking a cab, be aware that—unlike in some other major cities—taxis here don't cruise, so allow time for the doorman to call one, and make sure you keep the cab phone number handy.

STANFORD & SONS
1867 Village West Pkwy.
(In the Legends at Village West)
Kansas City, KS
(913) 480-7500
When Craig and Jeff Glazer—along with comic David Naster—opened a comedy shop above dad Stanford Glazer's restaurant in 1979, it catapulted the Westport neighborhood into the city's nightspot scene. When Craig convinced Robin Williams to try out new material here in 1981, *Variety* picked up the story and the rest is history. After a brief stint in Overland Park, Craig built a 6,000-square-foot, half-million-dollar club in Wyandotte County's mega-successful Village West near the Kansas Speedway. With 300 fixed seats and three levels of plush seating, the club has attracted celebrity and up-and-coming comics. You'll recognize names from TV shows such as *Last Comic Standing* and movie roles. If you think you have a shot at stardom, bring three minutes of material to open-mic night every Tuesday.

GAY AND LESBIAN CLUBS

BALANCA'S
1809 Grand
(816) 474-MEOW (6369)
www.balancaskc.com

Gay, straight, singles, couples, biker chick, or accountant—well, maybe not an accountant—but everyone else will feel welcome here. In fact, owner Lori Burroughs won't tolerate closed-minded jerks. It can get pretty rowdy here, and that's just the way Lori likes it. The upstairs lounge is a teensy bit more chill, and here's where you come for a game of darts or pool before heading back down to the Pyro Room, where DJs and sometimes live music get the floor crowded. The 3 a.m. closing time makes it the place plenty of folks head for a nightcap or late night snack; the kitchen stays open 'til 2. The action starts at 9 p.m. Tues through Thurs, 6 p.m. Fri and Sat. And if you were here Sat night you'd understand why it's closed Sun and Mon. That's when all the kitties sleep.

BISTRO 303
303 Westport Rd.
(816) 753-2303
www.bistro303kc.com
Talk about night and day! At noon a mix of gal pals and execs from nearby offices come here for the lobster roll or Cobb salad. The space is bright with windows and floor-to-ceiling mirrors; the fact that one of the owners is also a respected antiques dealer shows in the lavish decor.

Come evening, twinkling votive candles and the city's most sophisticated gay men are reflected in the mirrors. It can get pretty crowded, making it a challenge for the attractive servers to deliver your pommes frites with roasted garlic aioli. Breath mint, anyone? Sunday brunch is another opportunity to see and be seen while dining very well. Smokers are welcome on the back deck.

> **i** Kansas City is home to a vibrant, growing gay and lesbian population that includes high-society sophisticates and the bohemian set made up of actors and artists. We list several nightspots that cater to them, but the truth is that straights are just as welcome. It's all about tolerance, except when it comes to dressing with style. No slobs allowed.

MISSIE B'S
805 W. 39th St.
(816) 561-0625
www.missiebskc.com

This good-time place opened its doors in April 1994 as a piano lounge, and when Belle Starr began doing Monday-night drag shows, that became its claim to fame. The region's best female impersonators perform here five nights a week; add twice-weekly karaoke and you've got plenty of reasons to buy those new silver heels you've been eyeing. The outrageous Dirty Dorothy takes the stage, complete with a naughty Wizard of Oz getup, every Sat from 10 p.m. until 3 a.m. Closing on weeknights is 2 a.m.

OUTABOUNDS SPORTS BAR
3601 Broadway
(816) 756-2577

People thought Doug Knetzer and Alan Rogers were crazy to open a gay sports bar, but look who's crazy now—as in happy crazy. It's wall-to-wall on Chiefs Sundays and just about any other time a game is on one of the multiple plasma-screen TVs. The bar food and decor are pretty standard, except the poster of local legend George Brett has longer hair. And just like any sports bar, when the favored players come on the screen, the entire place cheers—but here it might be more for how cute he looks in his uniform. But it's all in good fun. Although it's mainly a gay hangout, the friendly staff welcome straight folks as well.

SIDEKICKS SALOON
3707 Main
(816) 931-1430
www.sidekicks-saloon.com

Who says gay men can't wear cowboy hats and line dance? At this saloon and dance hall, everyone's welcome, but it mainly caters to the gay crowd of cowboys and leathermen. Fri night features drag shows, and Sat night brings on dancing to country and pop music. Tuesday is a retro-music affair, and on Wednesday get ready to vote for your favorite contestants in their boxers. Drag queens and singers are on the stage most Thursdays. Hours are 2 p.m. to 3 a.m.

LIVE MUSIC

Some of the venues below offer a true nightclub atmosphere with cocktail tables surrounding a stage and an appreciative audience that's actually there to listen rather than gab with tablemates. Answer a cell phone here and you might find yourself stared down or even out on the street.

There are also dozens of places—restaurants and hotel lobbies all over town—where trios or piano players provide background music to clinking glasses and conversation. But whether you take your jazz with a side of sirloin or like it a la carte, you'll discover talent that can soar above the din.

Some locations charge covers ranging from $3 to $5 depending on the night and the talent; many invite you to sit and enjoy the music gratis as long as you order an occasional cocktail or two.

Blues and Rock 'n' Roll

Rhythm and blues was the father of jazz, and Papa never really left the Kansas City music scene. These days there are as many blues venues in town—and at least as many fans—as there are jazz emporiums. You can catch a case of the blues nearly anywhere, any night in Kansas City. For times and locations, check out the schedule on the Kansas City Blues Society's site at www.kcbluessociety.com.

BB'S LAWNSIDE BAR-B-Q
1205 E. 85th Terrace
(816) 822-7427
www.bbslawnsidebbq.com

Owner Lindsay Shannon combines his passions for blues, beer, and barbecue in this homey roadhouse, which plays live music Thurs through Sun. The food's pretty hot, too; try the spicy jambalaya, Smoky Jo's Gumbo, or ribs and burnt ends. And to wash it all down, order a "Bucket of Blues," which will get you five Pabst Blue Ribbons in a galvanized tin. Get here early for Tuesday Bluesday, when Trampled Under Foot (just TUF to their fans) crank up the sound. These siblings from Kansas City have garnered international acclaim.

THE BEAUMONT CLUB
4050 Pennsylvania (Westport)
(816) 561-2560
www.beaumontkc.com
If an old-timer walked into this cavernous space wearing a "Let's Rodeo" belt buckle, he'd wonder where his favorite cowboy bar went. It moooo-ved on, mister. Now the Beaumont hosts bands with a more kinetic beat, including punk rock and indie electro, as well as classic rock tribute bands. In fact, it's nothing if not diverse. A recent evening brought in a burlesque review, and there are free salsa dance lessons every Sat from 10:30 p.m. until last call at 3 a.m. The Beaumont added an outdoor bar and live music venue recently, where young music lovers can party in the heart of Westport.

i Like it or not, folks, Kansas and Missouri bars and restaurants are now smoke free. Some establishments have patios and decks that allow smoking; a few even still have humidors on the premises.

CROSSROADS KC
18th and Oak
(816) 221-LIVE (5483)
www.crossroadskc.com
Leave it to local artist Stretch for adding a fan-friendly concert venue to his East Crossroads neighborhood. Here's where music lovers come to hear big-name national groups, grab a slice of pizza and beer from Stretch's Grinders Pizza, and enjoy low prices and a killer view of the Kansas City skyline. It's rustic, and there are no refunds if it rains, but hey, it's rock 'n' roll, folks. Tickets are available online, including reserved seating and even VIP treatment. Free parking surrounds the area.

KNUCKLEHEAD'S SALOON
2715 Rochester
(816) 483-1456
www.knuckleheadskc.com
Blues, rockabilly, classic rock, underground folk. It's all at this wildly popular bar that hasn't a whiff

of pretense to it. Readers of *The Pitch* have named it Best Blues Bar for five years running because the cover charges are fair, the atmosphere is fun, and the place scores top talent from national and local scenes. That means in one week alone you might hear Terry Clark, CMA's Female Vocalist of the Year, as well as Miss Major and Her Minor Mood Swings. Want to take it down a notch? Spend the evening swaying to gospel music in the lounge. Feel like a VIP? Reserve a reclining seat in the Caboose. Tickets to the hottest bands go fast, making reservations a must. And if you enjoy hearing up-and-comers—or want to chime in—show up at the open jams every Sat and Sun starting at 1 p.m.

THE UPTOWN
3700 Broadway
(816) 753-8665
www.uptowntheater.com
God bless Larry Sells, the man behind the restoration of this magnificent movie palace. When it opened in 1928, the Uptown thrilled patrons with its elaborate Mediterranean courtyard design complete with balconies, twinkling stars, and mechanical flying birds. Ten years later the theater copyrighted the "Fragratone" system, which piped fragrances through the ventilation ducts.

Through the years all the greats played here, from Bob Hope to Bob Dylan, and it continued to serve as a live concert venue until it closed in 1989. After a $15 million restoration, it has reopened in all its glory. Shows range from Kansas City's own Pat Metheny to tribute bands covering Queen. The new Conspiracy Lounge offers salsa dancing and special events. Tickets may be purchased at the Uptown or through Ticketmaster.

Casino Entertainment
Although Kansas City's four casinos provide plenty of gaming action, you can exchange the blackjack tables for a cocktail table to hear live music in a variety of pavilions and piano bars. In Attractions we provide additional details about each casino.

AMERISTAR CASINO
8201 Northeast Birmingham
(816) 414-7000, (800) 499-4961
www.ameristarcasinos.com/kc
Consistently voted "Best Casino" by readers of *KC Magazine*, Ameristar could also win prizes for the entertainment lineup in its Star Pavilion. Since 1997 it has brought in such acts as Keith Urban, Tony Bennett, and even the Smothers Brothers to its elegantly appointed stage. Tickets range from $12 to $65. Or head to the more intimate Casino Cabaret.

ARGOSY CASINO
777 Northwest Argosy Pkwy.
Riverside, MO
(800) 270-7711
www.stayargosy.com
With a $105 million makeover, this stunning casino has plenty of action outside the blackjack tables. The local jazz and rock stars in the Casino Stage Bar and Crazy Olives Bar and Restaurant are as cool as the margaritas and martinis. One of our favorites, Lonnie McFadden, brings soulful R&B, a right-on impression of Louis Armstrong, and even some old soft-shoe to the stage. And if a steak is calling your name, the Journey is the place for wood-fired beef. As for us, we think we'll journey upstairs to one of the stunning new suites. See more details in Accommodations.

HARRAH'S
One Riverboat Dr.
(816) 472-7777
www.harrahsnkc.com
Although Harrah's bills itself as the place for serious slots, when it comes to music the emphasis is on fun. Your first hint is the sound of jazz horns or head-thumping rock coming from the VooDoo Lounge, one of the city's best nightclubs. The lineup continues to thrill, with such headliners as Robert Cray and jazz stylist Dave Koz. Even when there's no live music, it's still the place to hang with old friends or flirt with new ones as attractive bartenders mesmerize you by tossing the shakers overhead. Got enough liquid courage yet?

Then head to the dance floor with great lights and a fantastic sound system as the DJ plays the hits. VooDoo is definitely the place to wear your trendiest club gear. And the mezzanine-level VIP section gives you the best shot of the entire venue—your own private sanctum to do that voodoo thing you do.

For a more laid-back (way, way back) vibe, there's Toby Keith's I Love This Bar and Grill. The Whiskey Girls will pour you a cold one as you listen to live country music.

ISLE OF CAPRI CASINO
1800 E. Front St.
(816) 855-7777, (800) THE ISLE
www.kansas-city.isleofcapricasinos.com
You can't miss this casino, with lights outlining the paddleboat so bright it rivals the nearby downtown skyline. Inside, the music is lively as well, with local groups making Sat evenings special with everything from jazz to rock to funk.

Country

Although we sometimes try to ignore our cowtown heritage like it's a pesky younger brother who follows us around, there's no disputing our Western roots. Throughout much of 1980, in fact, the most popular radio station and most of the jukeboxes in town played nothing but country hits. Most of us have hung up our spurs these days, but you can still join in a line dance at these two nightspots when the mood strikes.

DENIM AND DIAMONDS
1725 Swift
North Kansas City, MO
(816) 221-7300
www.denimdiamondskc.com
Loosen up those new Levi's with free dance lessons Wed, Fri, and Sat from 7:30 to 8:30 p.m., then be ready to two-step all night. The crowd often breaks into a line dance, and even if you don't know the steps you'll have fun. Double D is known for some of the prettiest cowgirls in the Midwest, especially on Wed, which is Ladies' Night.

PBR BIG SKY
111 E. 13th (Power & Light District)
(816) 442-8145
www.pbrbigskykc.com
Here's where cowboy cool meets urban chic. Truth be told, you won't see as many Stetsons here as other country bars, but the vibe is still "let's party." There's often a line waiting to get in on a Saturday night, but that's a fine way to meet your next dance partner—or someone to spot you on the bull-riding machine. Live music ranges from country to southern rock.

IRISH PUBS

The success of our stockyard industry in the West Bottoms was built, for the most part, on the broad backs of Irish workers who moved here in the late 1800s. They brought their music, dance, and a passion for a pint to their new home, and the rest of us become at least a little Irish when we partake of it. No wonder ours is the third largest St. Patrick's Day parade in the country. But you won't have to wait until March: There's an Irish festival or sing-along nearly every weekend somewhere in Kansas City.

O'DOWD'S LITTLE DUBLIN
4742 Pennsylvania St.
(816) 561-2700

8600 Northwest Prairie View Rd. (Zona Rosa)
(816) 268-6330
www.odowdslittledublin.com
On summer nights the upstairs deck of this Plaza establishment is packed with young, attractive people whose motto seems to be "the more the merrier." Many a date has been made on the slender staircase that joins the two floors. You can enjoy live Irish music seven nights a week (Eddie Delahunt is a popular draw) with your ale and traditional Irish fare. With its busy Plaza corner location, it's a fine place to meet up with friends or make new ones. And it's not always Irish eyes that are smiling. O'Dowd's hosts several of Kansas City's best bands, including Drew Six, a high-energy group with a sexy lead singer. And because Northlanders deserve some fun as well,

there's a second location in the Zona Rosa entertainment district. Bob Reeder is the guy leading the sing-along Thursday nights with live music throughout the weekend.

O'MALLEY'S PUB
500 Welt St.
Weston, MO
(816) 640-5235
www.westonirish.com
When a German immigrant named John Georgeans started a brewery (the oldest brewery west of the Hudson River) in the early 1840s, he dug three rooms 55 feet underground and lined them with limestone blocks to create an even temperature for the fermenting process. At one time the brewery produced up to 20,000 barrels of beer a year before it was closed during Prohibition. Today the tri-level space is home to Sean O'Malley's Pub, which is the perfect escape on a hot summer evening. When entertainers take the stage, the atmosphere is unlike anything else in town. Every October, Sean hosts an Irish Festival with three additional stages outside (see more in Annual Events and Festivals). There's authentic Irish food, imported libations, and great entertainment, including bawdy limericks.

Jazz
THE BLUE ROOM
1600 E. 18th St.
(816) 474-2929
www.americanjazzmuseum.com
Back in the 1930s and 1940s, the Blue Room, located in the swank Street Hotel, was one of the hottest nightspots in the country. Six decades later it serves as a museum by day, with a wall of images of local musicians who made Kansas City swing. The glass-topped cocktail tables are display cases filled with such rare artifacts as Count Basie's 1936 Musician's Union card, while the jukebox serves up tunes and videos from performers such as Louis Armstrong, Charlie Parker, Billie Holiday, Fats Waller, and John Coltrane. Don't miss seeing Charlie Parker's saxophone or Ella Fitzgerald's rhinestone eyeglasses among the displays.

At night the Blue Room comes to life as a jazz club where four nights a week it welcomes local and national jazz greats. Indigo Hour gets the weekend started right with an appetizer buffet from 5 until 7:30 p.m. (the only time food is served), then a headliner show at 8:30. The crowd tends to be older and well dressed. The Blue Room is part of the American Jazz Museum but has its own entrance. There is a small cover charge.

THE GEM THEATER
1615 E. 18th St.
(816) 474-6262
www.americanjazzmuseum.com
Opened as a movie theater in 1912, the Gem has a facade that's still beautiful, with its stained-glass and distinctive neon marquee. But inside it's been updated to a 500-seat theater with the latest in lighting, sound, and acoustical design. The theater has hosted concerts, workshops and symposiums, and an annual Jammin' at the Gem Concert Series featuring outstanding national performers such as Lionel Hampton and James Moody. Call for event information, or check the Web site.

JARDINE'S RESTAURANT & JAZZ CLUB
4536 Main St.
(816) 561-6480
www.jardines4jazz.com
This cozy club has become one of Kansas City's hottest night spots to hear some of the city's top performers seven nights a week, including Angela Hagenbach, Lonnie McFadden, Mark Lowrey, and the Barclay Martin Ensemble. The late-night jam session is also popular every Saturday after midnight when musicians show up after ending gigs elsewhere; anyone with a voice or a horn is encouraged to get up on stage.

And here's good news for night owls: Jardine's is one of the rare places that serves dinner until midnight on weekends. There is usually a cover charge.

THE MUTUAL MUSICIANS FOUNDATION
1823 Highland Ave.
(816) 471-5212
www.thefoundationjamson.org
This living shrine to jazz is where Charlie Parker, Jay McShann, Bennie Moten, Lester Young, Mary Lou Williams, and other greats got their start and where today, on Fri and Sat, musicians jam from around midnight until dawn—or as long as the audience is there. There's no cover charge for musicians and music students; everyone else gladly pays $8. There's a full bar and food is served all night.

Located in the 18th and Vine District, the building was designated a National Historic Landmark in 1982 after undergoing major reconstruction.

PHOENIX JAZZ CLUB
302 W. Eighth St.
(816) 472-0001
www.phoenixjazzkc.com
You can't miss this cozy neighborhood club; just drive around downtown until you hear music or spot the giant smiling face mural painted on its brick wall. Folks inside are grinning as well, thanks to the friendly atmosphere. Expect visits from top performers such as internationally respected jazz stylist Karrin Allyson (who lived in town for a while), as well as local favorites. The menu features steaks, pasta, and fresh seafood for lunch and dinner, but the main pull is the live music and casual vibe. Originally the Phoenix Hotel built in the 1880s, today it's where to get your weekend started right. A jazz brunch is served the second Saturday of the month, when part of the $20 cover charge goes to a local charity.

i Although you'll see plenty of jeans and even shorts during summer, lots of jazz club patrons tend to dress up a bit on Saturday night. So pull out that cocktail dress and black suit when you paint the town red. Didn't pack the fancy duds? Don't worry: You'll be welcome no matter what you're wearing.

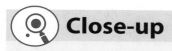 **Close-up**

Kansas City—and All That Jazz

During the 1920s and 1930s, Kansas City was at the heart of the music scene. Because the city was a railroad hub, some of America's best musicians would stop here on their way to or from New Orleans, Chicago, or New York, and many, such as Bill "Count" Basie, liked what they saw and heard and soon made the city their home.

Kansas City was a prosperous place during these decades and patrons had their pick of grand palaces, such as the Pla-Mor, which opened Thanksgiving Day 1927 at the northwest corner of Linwood and Main. The "million-dollar ballroom" featured an enormous dance hall along with a bowling alley, swimming pool, and ice-skating rink that doubled as the home ice for the town's minor league hockey team. Local stars shared marquee space with top-name touring acts such as Louis Armstrong. And Hoagy Carmichael premiered a new tune called "Stardust" on the Pla-Mor's stage.

The city's seedier side was represented by such joints as the Chesterfield Club, where waitresses were clad in nothing more than cellophane.

But no matter whether the nightclub was ritzy or raunchy, it was packed with talent. Local musicians such as Count Basie, Charlie Parker, and Joe Turner eventually influenced jazz across the nation. Basie practically invented the infectious, syncopated style called swing at his piano at the Reno Club, bringing in soaring solos to drive the crowds wild.

Parker is generally considered most responsible for the creation of bebop, taking the music known as jazz into its modern incarnation. Certainly, others like Dizzy Gillespie and Thelonious Monk contributed mightily. But even among his peers, Parker was recognized as a leader, one of the rare musicians who actually earned the tag "genius." Had he not died in his thirties he might have gained even more of a mainstream following.

The legendary "cutting session" between tenor sax greats Lester "Pres" Young and Coleman "Bean" Hawkins depicted in Robert Altman's film *Kansas City* really happened. It went down on December 18, 1933, and continued until the wee hours at a joint called the Cherry Blossom. Pianist and bandleader Count Basie kept time.

Some say famed saxophonist Charlie Parker came by his nickname "Yardbird," later shortened to just "Bird," because of his fondness for fried chicken. But others say his handle came from his "free as a bird" lifestyle that would cause his untimely death.

As musicians such as Basie and Parker became better known, they often left for the East Coast and bigger gigs. But it was the fall of political boss Tom Pendergast (read more about his reign in the History chapter) that marked the end of the Jazz Age in Kansas City. Once reformers closed the nightspots, the remaining bands took the A Train to places like New York and Chicago.

So the term "Kansas City jazz" is a handy handle for a musical mix that owes its life to gospel, ragtime, blues, swing, and bebop. No wonder it's so hard to define. Our advice? Don't overanalyze it. Just listen.

You'll have plenty of chances. Kansas City has given birth to some remarkable jazz talents over the decades, and it continues today. A few, such as singer Kevin Mahogany and Grammy-winning guitarist Pat Metheny, have moved away. But others are happy to call the heartland home between tours to Chicago, New York, and Europe. While they're touring there are others to keep your fingers snapping: A two-page list of local musicians printed in *JAM,* the Kansas City Jazz Ambassadors' bimonthly magazine, includes 85 bands, 55 vocalists, and one tuba player. You'll find them performing almost every night at some nightclub or restaurant or headlining at music festivals all over town. Look for listings in the *Kansas City Star's* **Friday Preview** or *The Pitch,* or check the calendar at **www.kcjazzambassadors.com.** By the way, when Charlie Parker's plastic horn came up for auction at Christie's in New York, forward-thinking Kansas Citians, led by then-mayor Emanuel Cleaver II, outbid a Japanese investor to bring it back home for $145,000. The instrument is now displayed at the American Jazz Museum at 18th and Vine.

SPORTS BARS

Kansas City is officially a sports town, so nearly every bar in town—even the more sophisticated versions with highly polished wood and real ferns—has a big screen or two tuned to a game, tournament, or race. And when a professional sports team or college game is on the tube, one of these bars is the place to go to commiserate or celebrate with friends.

810 ZONE
4686 Broadway (Country Club Plaza)
(816) 268-9663)

4800 W. 119th St. (Town Center Plaza)
(913) 469-9663
www.the810zone.com
The name of this bar and grill isn't the code name for a football play (810 . . . hike!); it refers to the hyper-popular Sports Radio 810 station. That means it's the ultimate spot for sports fans where live broadcasts, buckets of Corona, and dozens of TVs (including four HD big-screens) are always on tap. Naturally the walls are lined with sports memorabilia, and the crowd gets noisy when the game is on. Even tough guys might need help hoisting the menu describing burgers, pizzas, sandwiches and salads, even a deep-fried Twinkie. And at the more swanky Plaza location, you can even play Pebble Beach, or at least pretend, on the amazing golf simulator. Another plus here: two for one burgers every Tuesday.

THE GRANFALLOON BAR & GRILL
608 Ward Pkwy.
(816) 753-7850
www.thegranfalloon.com
First off, you're wondering what the name means. Kurt Vonnegut, Jr. coined the word for a "proud and meaningless association of human beings." What's not meaningless is the fun quotient at one of the Plaza's most popular places to watch some college football, challenge someone to game of pool, rock out to live music, or chow down on Taco Thursdays. What's not to love? The food is better than a lot of sports bars, rooms are available for private parties, there are three Golden Tee golf simulators, and some of the most attractive people in town like to hang here.

SHOPPING

In the mid-1800s, as the last civilized stop on the way out West, Kansas City welcomed wagon trains and riverboats with provisions, pickaxes, and camaraderie. Shoppers still come here in droves, although today they show up for style rather than mere sustenance.

In fact, several times a year entire busloads of ladies disembark at the shopper's paradise known as Kansas City. Shoppers from hundreds of miles away make annual, sometimes quarterly, pilgrimages to our city-sized antiques centers, enormous outlet malls, and one-of-a-kind emporiums such as Nell Hill's in nearby Atchison, Kansas.

Of course, the high-winter holidays wouldn't be the same without a visit to the Country Club Plaza, our 14-block extravaganza of retail stores and entertainment with 250,000 glowing Christmas lights outlining every building, spire, and arch.

And for those who enjoy one-of-a-kind shops rather than big-name stores that could be in any city in North America, there's the Crossroads Arts District, a vibrant neighborhood with more than 80 art galleries, boutiques, and showrooms, all within a mile walking radius. We'll give you the full tour in this chapter's Shopping Districts section, but we've also singled out a few shops in cross-referenced categories, such as antiques.

Our shopping opportunities are so stupendous that when people call us a sports town, they're often referring to the action in the aisles, not the stadiums. Our renowned buying power and sophisticated lifestyle have naturally attracted giant retailers, often for their first forays into the Midwest. Examples include Nordstrom, Ralph Lauren, and Crate and Barrel. And where these giants go, smaller exclusive boutiques and stores such as Armani, St. John Knits, Dean & Deluca, MAC Cosmetics, and Apple follow, giving us enough cachet to be considered the heartland's Rodeo Drive.

And don't overlook the dozens of one-of-a-kind shops you'll find only in Kansas City. Asiatica creates exquisite garments from antique kimonos, and Retro Inferno sells designer furniture from the 1930s to 1970s in prime condition, just right for that so-in loft look. Both shops were "discovered" by collectors in New York and Los Angeles before their own hometown. Ditto for local artists Markus Pierson, whose famous Coyote series is owned by the rich and famous, and his wife, Sherl Pierson, whose collages grace the homes of Whoopi Goldberg and Sir Elton John. The Piersons' work can be acquired through Blue Gallery (see separate listing under Art). Metal sculptor Tom Corbin (see separate listing) counts Jack Nicholson, Tom Hanks, and Alec Baldwin as fans, and Joscelyn Himes (www.jhtextiles.com), whose studio and shop is in the Crossroads Arts District, creates ethereal fabrics for the design collections of Bill Blass, Donna Karan, and Vera Wang.

The shops in this chapter are grouped by category of goods and then listed alphabetically. All the shops are in Kansas City, Missouri, unless otherwise noted.

Many of these special places are unadvertised, and several are off the beaten path. When the shopkeepers ask how in the world you discovered them, just say an Insider gave you the scoop. So put on those comfortable shoes, grab that credit card, and let's go shopping!

ANTIQUES AND COLLECTIBLES

It's true: We're one of the country's best-kept secrets when it comes to the quality and value of the antiques available here. And often, just to make the hunting even more delightful, we've grouped dozens of shops together in a huge antiques mall or neighborhood. You can literally shop all day at one location, returning to your vehicle just long enough to store another treasure in the trunk. When it's time for a break, a cafe or coffee shop is usually just a shopping bag's throw away.

ANTIQUITIES & ODDITIES ARCHITECTURAL SALVAGE
2045 Broadway
(816) 283-3740
www.aoarchitecturalsalvage.com
If the name doesn't get you, just driving by the beautiful two-story Broadway Bank–turned–antiques shop with intriguing treasures peeking through the windows will. For decades, Architectural Salvage has been collecting interesting and priceless pieces from razed buildings, churches, and movie palaces and selling them to interior decorators, set designers, and savvy shoppers.

Here's where to find massive carved wooden doors, rusted gates, salvaged church pews, stained-glass windows, Tara-sized porch columns, discarded fireplace mantels, and red velvet fold-down seats. You can spend hours just digging through boxes of doorknobs and cases of rescued hardware. Pace yourself, and leave the nice clothes at home; it can get pretty grungy here. But to find that perfect gargoyle for your garden, what's a little 80-year-old dust? The store is open 10 a.m. to 5 p.m. Thurs through Sat or by appointment. Owner Rick Bettinger may have just the baluster or newel post you need.

THE CURIOUS SOFA
3925 W. 69th Terrace
Prairie Village, KS
(913) 432-8969
www.curioussofa.com

Stopping by Debbie Dusenberry's antiques and home furnishings shop is like a minivacation as your senses are assailed by scented candles, offbeat treasures longing to be touched, and a danceable French tune on the stereo. On any given day you might find a peeling-paint medicine cabinet, funky mirror covered in shells, or beaded Barbie-size chandelier. Her selection of new and antique jewelry is divine.

Here, vintage is cleverly mixed with made-to-look-old new items, such as the sofas tufted to within an inch of their lives. The store itself is a charmer; Deb transformed a standard space into a vintage wonderland with tin ceilings, cubbyholes, and her legendary more-is-more sensibilities. We dare you to visit Curious Sofa and not fall hopelessly in love. For just a taste, visit her flirty, evocative, totally sexy Web site, or, as we like to call it, foreplay.

45TH & STATE LINE ANTIQUE, ART & DESIGN CENTER
45th and State Line Rd.
(816) 531-4414
If you have a penchant for the old, the unique, or the collectible, then snoop to your heart's content in this quaint historic district that features over 20 antiques shops and galleries, all within charming row houses. Despite the number of shops in one place, they rarely repeat each other, so it's a sure bet you'll be here for hours. The prices bring back buyers again and again.

One not to miss is Christopher Filley (816-561-1124), where unique antiques and decorative arts are stacked to the rafters. Although it specializes in garden art including architectural remnants, statues, bird fountains, and pitted stone balls, you'll also spy hand-carved *santos*, a nice selection of mercury glass, mirrors set inside enormous industrial gears, and other delightfully quirky finds. Prices are not marked, but don't be afraid to ask Christopher or his associate, Rich Hoffman. You'll get a price and perhaps a fascinating story about the item's history. The Knotty Rug company (913-677-1877), where owner Darrel Wingo's motto is "the knottier the better," is where to find that perfect Oriental or French needlepoint, all displayed in lovely settings. European Express (816-753-0443) may sound like a fast-food cafe, but it's actually three floors filled with antiques, including enormous armoires and marble washstands. And make sure to stop by Rick Bumgardner's Morning Glory Antiques (816-531-5554), and . . . oh, what the heck. Visit them all; each is totally different, all are wonderful. And the proprietors are truly happy to greet you and answer questions.

LOCUST GROVE ANTIQUES & INTERIORS
25180 Missouri Highway JJ
Weston, MO
(816) 640-3203
www.locustgroveweston.com

Locust Grove isn't an antiques mall, but with its barnlike size it may as well be. It's amazing that two partners own the entire inventory, which is part antique, part new, all sensational. Kate Parsons, a talented interior designer, teamed up with daughter Christy Shafer to create small vignettes of themed treasures to make browsing fun and collecting a breeze.

A recent walk-through spied a pair of carved hatchets, a tapestry throw, 200-year old olive jars from Turkey, an antique bedroom set, vintage linens, and needlepoint pillows. They also have some of the most incredible faux florals and botanicals available, including dried wreaths. Locust Grove is definitely worth the 40-mile drive out of town, especially if you're heading to Weston (see Day Trips and Weekend Getaways) for the afternoon or weekend. The shop is open every day but Mon.

MISSION ROAD ANTIQUES
4101 W. 83rd St.
Prairie Village, KS
(913) 341-7577
www.missionroadantiquemall.com

Better get plenty of rest the night before you plan to attack this 50,000-square-foot mall, considered to be one of the finest in the Midwest. The building is as historical as some of its contents; 60 years ago it was a stable for Thoroughbred horses, including the 1938 Kentucky Derby

winner, Lawrin. Today 350 dealers display their wares, which include European antiques, primitives, stained glass, vintage housewares, Oriental porcelain, estate jewelry, military collectibles, and more. The mall is open daily, 10 a.m. to 6 p.m. Some vendors specialize in one category, such as original oil paintings or Christmas decorations, but most offer an engaging array of goods. And just as you've reached sensory overload, there's a cozy cafe in the mall to offer a place to sit down to some tasty food. The Bloomsbury Bistro's menu changes weekly, but expect to find items such as veggie lasagna and chicken salad along with soups and wraps. Homemade desserts include pies and German chocolate cake. The bistro is open 11 a.m. to 3 p.m. Mon through Sat and is closed Sun.

RIVER MARKET ANTIQUE MALL
115 W. Fifth St.
(816) 221-0220
www.kansascityrivermarket.com

No wonder this mall has been voted "Best Antique Shop in Kansas City" by readers of *The Pitch*. First, there's the size. With more than 30,000 square feet of booths and showcases spread out over four floors, it's enough to make you just plain giddy with anticipation of what you'll find. Here's just a teaser: American, European, and primitive furniture including mission and Wakefield; pottery and glassware featuring plenty of Roseville; vintage clothing and jewelry; quilts and lamps; antique toys; and old advertising art. The vendors are friendly enough to answer questions and point you to another booth if you're seeking something specific. Did we say friendly? What other antique mall provides layaway, local delivery (for a fee) and will even hold your item for up to 30 days? Open 10 a.m. to 6 p.m. seven days a week.

WEBSTER HOUSE ANTIQUES
AND RESTAURANT
1644 Wyandotte
(816) 221-4713
www.websterhousekc.com

Even this beautiful building is an antique, considered to be Kansas City's oldest surviving school.

While renovating the Romanesque Revival building, built in the late 19th century, workers removed plasterboard to find blackboards with homework assignments written in chalk.

Thanks to owner Shirley Bush Helzberg's vision, you'll want to spend the day here. Along with shopping for marvelous antiques, there are gifts for the home, baby, bath, and kitchen, and even a glorious selection of jewelry, some by local artisan Jane Signorelli. As for the aroma wafting around the Chinoiserie and Chippendales, it's probably executive chef Charles d'Ablaing's latest creation. We tempt you further in our Restaurants chapter.

BED AND BATH GIFTS AND SKIN CARE

DERMADOCTOR
1901 McGee
(816) 472-2627
www.dermadoctor.com
What better gift to take back from your visit to Kansas City than that of gorgeous skin? If you're lucky enough to live in Kansas City, you've seen the arresting, purple sign announcing you've found one of the country's most celebrated dermatologists. Dr. Audrey Kunin's Web site is quoted in all the best women's magazines, she's appeared on TV to lend beauty secrets, and now she has a home for all her potions. The doc's new headquarters—incorporating a laboratory and sleek sales area—is where to find her entire skin-care line, as well as well-chosen products from other collections. Plus, you can get a tour (via a high-tech camera) of your own face. It will have you heading to the display of skin creams pronto.

INDIGO WILD
3125 Wyandotte
(816) 221-3480, (800) 361-5686
www.indigowild.com
This tiny company produces delightfully scented bath and beauty products made of good-for-you ingredients. The Zum bars, for example, include goat's milk, pure essential oils, and herbal extracts and come in lots of yummy scents, such as lavender-mint and sandalwood-citrus. The

bars, which look like tie-died artwork, with swirls and chunks of colors, come in fun, corrugated shapes. The company also makes soy candles, baby care products, body lotions, and all-natural lip balms in flavors such as tangerine. That's Zum kiss! They've recently added all-natural household cleaning products such as sweet orange laundry soap (doesn't that sound delightful?) and a sink scrub with ingredients you can actually pronounce. Now you can toss those rubber gloves. Products are available by phone, online, or through a clever catalog. Or stop in to visit; they're open seven days a week. Just don't be surprised if your greeter has a cold nose. Employee pets, usually rescued animals, are welcome.

PERFECT SCENTS
5010 Main St.
(816) 753-8117
www.perfectscentskc.com
"Come inside and play," Nancy McAnany beckons to those who enter her shop of earthly and ethereal delights. Since 1989 she's been turning customers into alchemists as they create unique body lotions, massage oils, and home products using dozens of aromatic essential oils. Nancy figures there are at least 3,424 different custom-scented products you can conjure up. Or choose one of her designer oils that smell like expensive versions without the hefty price tags.

The shelves and counters reveal other treats, such as orange-flavored lip balm, gentle baby care products, lamp rings that send a subtle fragrance throughout the room, and car diffusers that do the same for that long drive home. And who could resist the red mineral facial treatment she calls the "Hoover vacuum cleaner" of masks?

BOOKSTORES

Naturally we have the national book dealers, but we also have an amazing number of independent booksellers who succeed because of their special services. Rainy Day Books, for instance, consistently brings well-known writers to town for speaking engagements. At Reading Reptile customers wouldn't think of being disloyal. So here, dear readers, are some of our best and brightest booksellers.

I LOVE A MYSTERY
6114 Johnson Dr.
Mission, KS
(913) 432-2583
www.iloveamystery.com

It's no mystery why this place is so popular with book lovers: It's stocked with more than 24,000 new and used mystery books, including a large selection of signed first editions and all things Sherlockian. But it's the decor that sets it apart. Visitors are greeted at the door by a gargoyle, while a life-sized skeleton guards the coffee bar. Daggers, skulls, and poison bottles are tucked into nooks and crannies, but never fear. You're welcome to sit down in an overstuffed chair and settle in for a read or a nap. And signing up for a book club wouldn't kill you, would it?

PROSPERO'S BOOKS
1800 W. 39th St.
(816) 531-WORD (9673)
www.prosperosbookstore.com

Since November 19, 1997, owners Will Leathem and Tom Wayne have created more than a bookstore; they've built a place to celebrate the written and spoken word. In 2002 they moved book, stock, and barrel to a historic hardware building, restoring pressed tin ceilings and rolling library ladders. A dramatic staircase links the main floor and basement, marrying the late 1800s with today's urban chic. The casual reader or antiquarian collector can find a gem here, while listening to the city's longest-running and largest open-mic poetry readings. Songwriters perform here as well. And the fact that it's surrounded by dozens of indy and ethnic restaurants means you can spend time here before or after brunch, lunch, or dinner. Chances are Prospero's will be open.

RAINY DAY BOOKS
2706 W. 53rd St.
Fairway, KS
(913) 384-3126
www.rainydaybooks.com

Vivien Jennings and Roger Doeren somehow manage to convince top authors that they can't sell a single book unless they appear in Kansas City. Since 1975 Rainy Day has hosted thousands of book signings—several a month—for authors including Ray Bradbury, Anne Rice, John Grisham, Martha Stewart, Garrison Keillor, and Nigella Lawson.

This corner store in Fairway near the Country Club Plaza is all that a bookseller can hope to be: a friendly place where there's someone on the staff who can recommend a book whether the subject is murder, cooking, home repair, romance, or coping with a baby sister. Rainy Day also sponsors writers' seminars throughout the year to encourage local authors to keep those bookshelves filled. And Vivien writes a regular column, "Book Ends," in a weekly society magazine, the *Independent*. Heavens, if she can find time to read, anyone can.

READING REPTILE
328 W. 63rd St.
(816) 753-0441
www.readingreptile.com

Is this someone's living room or a bookstore? Actually, it's both. Since 1988 owners Pete and Debbie have made this cheery shop their home-away-from-home, where they've brought up their four adorable kids, made lasting friendships, and introduced hundreds of children to the joys of the written and spoken word. They hold free story hours for preschoolers and school-aged children every week and host book clubs for young readers.

Once a year Reading Reptile sponsors a two-day event (a literary love-in, they call it) so that children, adults, teachers, and librarians can meet some of the top authors and illustrators. The store is fun, the Web site is a hoot, and the T-shirts, in which a fellow implores his dog to "Read, dammit!" would make a fine gift for the serious booklover.

STEALS AND DEALS

ACT II
1417 W. 47th St.
(816) 531-7572
www.actiiinc.com

Yes, it's true that Act II is a consignment shop, but owner Gloria Everhart is so picky about quality that the goods might as well be right off the retail rack. Savvy women and men shop here first for eveningwear with labels from Bill Blass, Calvin Klein, St. John, and other designers. The after-five and ball gown selection is amazing thanks to the number of black tie affairs held each year in Kansas City; some social denizens attend four or more a season and wouldn't dare wear the same sequined number twice.

Gloria also sells tailored suits, casual clothes, outerwear—yes, even furs—and like-new handbags and shoes. The store is just up the hill from the Plaza.

BOB JONES SHOES
1914 Grand
(816) 474-4212
www.bobjonesshoes.com
You're bound to find your sole-mate at Bob Jones. At any given time more than 100,000 pairs of designer shoes line the racks at up to 70 percent off retail. Sure, a few in the back room are a little dated, unless you want bright blue pumps with 6-inch heels, but 98 percent of the inventory consists of top names found at the finest department stores. For women that includes Enrico Gori, Via Spiga, Stuart Weitzman, Joan & David, and Calvin Klein. Men can choose from Johnston Murphy, Kenneth Cole, Bostonian, Rockport, and more. Bob Jones also carries a limited number of athletic shoes and unique women's handbags. Just look for the wooden Indian in front.

BUSHNELL FACTORY OUTLET
8500 Marshall Dr.
Lenexa, KS
(913) 752-6166

445 Northwest Murray Rd.
Lee's Summit, MO
(816) 525-2220
www.bushnell.com
Take a look at the pair of binoculars in your hall closet or backpack; if they're good, chances are "Bushnell" is printed on the case. This Kansas City–based company has been manufacturing high-performance optics for more than 50 years, but until these outlets opened, you'd have to pay retail prices at sporting goods stores. You'll still pay retail for some merchandise, including first-run binoculars, telescopes, night-vision scopes, and laser rangefinders. But you'll find significant discounts, from 25 percent to 50 percent off retail, on discontinued items, and up to 75 percent off retail on factory demonstration goods that are still in great shape.

The outlets hold plenty of attraction for any birder, astronomer, or sports enthusiast, even if that means someone who pulls a beer tab at a football game instead of a trigger in the woods. Plus Bushnell carries Bolle and Serengeti, some of the most stylish sunglasses in the world.

CARGO LARGO
13900 E. 35th St. South
Independence, MO
(816) 350-6101
www.cargolargo.com
This may be the only place on Earth to find a limited-edition Italian fountain pen worth $3,000, an antique Japanese tansu chest, a 10-pound bag of kitty litter, and a Big Bird costume all in the same place. But don't bother rushing over for the yellow feathered suit: it's long gone by now. In its place is something else just as bizarre. Cargo Largo handles about 15,000 shipments of lost, unwanted, or otherwise undeliverable cargo every week, all discounted up to 80 percent off the retail price.

In fact, its parent company, Kansas City–based Recovery Management Corp., is the biggest single buyer of all misdirected freight in the country. And although it does a big Internet business, most of the goods end up on shelves in this airplane hangar–size warehouse. Here's a recent haul for one shopper: a Winston fly-fishing rod at half its $700 price, an Oriental rug for $60, a fax machine, a floor lamp, Doc Marten boots, and massive quantities of caulking supplies. He passed on Budweiser neon sign in the shape of a football helmet. Hours are 9 a.m. to 8 p.m. Mon through Sat; 11 a.m. to 6 p.m. Sun.

Cargo Largo also holds a Thursday-afternoon bid sale, which is more fun than a barrel of monkeys; a container of live simians is perhaps the only thing you won't see. Items include retail, commercial, industrial, and hard-to-classify categories. The sale is held in Unit 800 of Carefree Industrial Park (call Cargo Largo for directions) every Thursday.

FARMERS' MARKETS

We're blessed to be surrounded by dozens of small farms and orchards, many of them certified organic. Farmers drive to town in the wee hours every Sat and Sun to bring us fresh sweet corn, snap beans, juicy peaches, and tomatoes so good you can eat 'em like apples.

BROOKSIDE MARKET
63rd St. and Wornall Rd.
(Border Star Montessori School parking lot)
www.farmerscommunitymarket.com
This lively mix of local and certified organic famers provide freshly picked vegetables and fruits, fragrant herbs, edible cut flowers, and free-range egg and honey products. Green Dirt Farm, in Weston, brings lamb products and artisanal cheeses. Opening day at Brookside is mid-Apr and it goes until mid-Oct. You'll want to schedule the entire day here; after you pick up a dozen ears of sweet-as-sugar corn and get a bag of brownies to go, visit the Brookside shops just across the street.

i **The holiday shopping season officially begins Thanksgiving night when the Plaza lights are turned on. Stores on the Country Club Plaza stay open until 9 p.m on Thursday nights year-round to give you an opportunity to hit your favorites while in town. And beginning Thanksgiving night, the stores stay open every night except Sunday during the holidays to help make the season bright.**

CITY MARKET
Fifth and Walnut
(816) 842-1271
www.kc-citymarket.com
This is the big kahuna, the biggest open-air market in six states, where nearly 200 vendors hawk

fresh produce on Wed, Sat, and Sun year-round. For the pick of the crop, it's best to get here early, around 7 a.m. on Sat, 9 a.m. otherwise. That's when all the chefs arrive to sniff cantaloupe, inspect zucchini, and plan for that evening's special. That pale yellow ear of corn might end up in a chipotle-laced chowder tonight.

Restaurants aren't the only ones buying in bulk; you'll see couples lugging flats of strawberries to cars parked down the street. And beyond ripe produce, expect to see a hodgepodge of arts and crafts such as twig furniture, jewelry, and paintings from local artists. It's always a party atmosphere, especially on weekends, when crowds can swell to 30,000 or more a day.

KC ORGANICS
Minor Park (Just east of Holmes on Red Bridge Rd.) and 117th and Nall (Leawood)
(816) 444-FOOD (3663)
www.kcorganics.com
This market doesn't draw nearly the crowds of others in town. But that's just fine with the picky consumers who show up every Sat from May through mid-Oct. Shorter lines mean you can actually talk to the farmers about their green beans, fingerling potatoes, apples, peaches, and exotic-looking Japanese eggplant. But don't expect picture-perfect specimens. A few bug-ravaged tomatoes prove that everything is certified pesticide- and chemical-free.

Many of the growers also bring prepared foods such as jellies, jams, salsas, and even hand-milled soap. You may also be treated to live music and cooking demonstrations. The second location, in Leawood's beautiful Park Place open-air shopping area, is open Wed, 10 a.m. to 2 p.m., Aug through Sept.

MARCHE DU JOUR
3920 W. 69th Terrace (Prairie Village Shops)
(573) 584-3385
www.widgeonwood.com
Every Sat from May through Oct, Mother Nature shows up in the guise of Sally at Widgeonwood Farms (even the name sounds like something organic) with just-picked heirloom tomatoes, wild

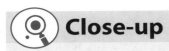

Close-up

The Country Club Plaza

What do you get when you combine an art and sculpture gallery, shopping center, flower garden, and jazz club? You get the Country Club Plaza, and admission to this outdoor extravaganza is free of charge.

Nestled against the banks of Brush Creek, this architecturally stunning, 14-block plaza offers everything you could want—shopping, dining, hotels, services, and entertainment—all within walking distance. Or if you're so inclined, you may view the elegant surroundings from a horse-drawn carriage.

The Plaza was the brainchild of Jesse Clyde (J. C.) Nichols, a real estate developer who changed a swampy tract of land into the country's first shopping center in 1922. He envisioned a shopping area that was automobile-friendly at a time when many thought the auto was a passing fad. And he wanted his little village filled with the romantic courtyards, ornate towers, red-tiled roofs, elaborate ironwork, art, and sparkling fountains he had admired in Spain. Today the artwork alone is worth far more than the $1 million he originally paid for the 55-acre site.

In the early 1920s new shops opened and thrived on the Plaza, and soon long-standing downtown stores opened second locations here. It became the center of style and fashion. The permanent wave was introduced in a Plaza beauty salon, and top Hollywood movies debuted at the ornate Plaza Theater. J. C. continually looked for ways to attract shoppers.

In 1925 a single strand of lights heralded the start of the holiday shopping season. It's a celebration that has grown into a world-famous event as 250,000 jewel-colored bulbs outline every spire, swag, and tower beginning Thanksgiving evening. The lights continue to shine until mid-January.

During the Depression the Plaza Art Fair began in 1932 as a promotional tool to encourage visitors. More than 70 years later, the event is the Midwest's premiere art fair, drawing an annual crowd of more than 275,000 during the three-day event. Before J. C. Nichols died in 1950 he had seen his idea influence other developers around the country. Miller Nichols built on his father's dream, adding hotels and apartments to the Plaza's landscape and buying outstanding artwork and fountains from around the world to adorn his museum without walls. Some of the most spectacular pieces include the J. C. Nichols Memorial Fountain by Henri Gerbert, the Pool of the Four Fauns, the 130-foot-tall reproduction of the famous Giralda Tower of Seville, and the endearing Sleeping Child sculpture that slumbers in the median of a busy street. Find photos and maps at **www.countryclubplaza.com.**

For some, shopping is an art form, and the Plaza provides plenty of opportunity to practice it. Among more than 150 unique stores you'll recognize such retailers as Brooks Brothers, Coach, Eddie Bauer, Betsey Johnson, Gap and Gap Kids, J. Jill, St. John, Tiffany and Co., AIX Armani Exchange, Banana Republic, MAC Cosmetics, Anthropologie, and Barnes & Noble Booksellers. But we're perhaps even more proud of the hometown retailers presented here. They include Halls (see

plums, slender asparagus stalks, and other organic delights. But some regulars come to Marche du Jour to stock pantries rather than vegetable bins. Each week brings new jars of treats, such as dilled green beans, Italian parsley pesto, port wine cranberry relish, tomato-basil-Vidalia dressing, and wild plum butter. There is rarely enough to go around; get there by 9 a.m. or you may be disappointed. Sally also makes decadent sweets, including

biscotti dipped in white chocolate, chocolate English toffee, and chocolate raspberry truffle sauce.

OVERLAND PARK FARMERS' MARKET
Marty St. between 79th and 80th Sts.
(913) 642-2222
www.downtownop.org

It can get pretty crowded on a summer Wed or Sat morning as people stand in line for just-

separate listing under Fashion and Accessories), an elegant emporium with fashions for men and women, fine jewelry, giftware, and accessories for the home; jewelry stores including Tivol, Swirk, Vinca, and Helzberg Diamonds; Diebels Sportsman Gallery; Three Dog Bakery with treats for pets; Superlatives, a world-class antiques and home decorating shop; and Scandia Home by Ursula Terrasi, where the service matches the exquisite display of European linens and gifts.

The culinary arts are well represented as well. Nearly 40 restaurants, bistros, and pubs will tempt you. Frequent travelers will be happy to know their favorites are here, including Ruth's Chris Steakhouse, McCormick & Schmick's Seafood Restaurant, the Capital Grille, Houston's Restaurant, P. F. Chang's China Bistro, and the Cheesecake Factory. But don't miss some of our hometown dining experiences; one taste of Bo Lings Chinese Restaurant, Baja 600, re:Verse, Starker's el Restaurant, or Plaza III the Steakhouse and you may find a new favorite. The Plaza is also home to 14 or so specialty food options, including the Better Cheddar, a purveyor of gourmet food and wine; Panache Chocolatier, where you'll find decadent fudge, truffles, and addictive chocolate-dipped popcorn; and Topsy's Popcorn Shop, the place to get freshly popped treats and perhaps the world's best limeade. And because you shouldn't have to go too far without an espresso, LatteLand has two separate locations on opposite ends of the Plaza.

Just as J. C. Nichols intended, the Plaza is a self-contained city with personal services galore. Get your shoes shined or repaired, suits tailored, and boxes shipped, handy for all those purchases you plan to take home. Kansas City's musical heritage is well represented on the Plaza. Beginning each May, free "Plaza Live" concerts bring some of the area's best jazz, blues, and folk musicians to the outdoor courtyards. The entertainment goes from 5 to 8 p.m. every Thurs, then again each Sat and Sun from noon to 5 p.m. It's the perfect way to enjoy a latte or lap some ice cream, sit on the side of a fountain or find a bench, and listen to stylists such as Ida McBeth confessing the blues. Music lovers can also hear tunes at several venues throughout the Plaza, including the InterContinental and Raphael hotels.

It's true, there is a lot to see and do on the Plaza. May we give you a lift? One of the most exciting ways to experience the magic is in a carriage. Two companies, Pride of Kansas City and Surreys Ltd., will escort you around the open-air marketplace in a festive old-fashioned carriage pulled by horses. For a truly enchanting evening choose Cinderella's Coach, a pumpkin-shaped carriage outlined in sparkling white lights.

If all this shopping, dining, and sailing has you exhausted, sweet dreams are just a stroll away at four hotels—the InterContinental (formerly the Fairmont), Raphael, Four Points by Sheraton, and Hampton Inn & Suites—and the Southmoreland Inn, an award-winning bed-and-breakfast. In the Accommodations chapter, you'll get officially tucked in.

The Country Club Plaza was a gift to Kansas City from J. C. and Miller Nichols. And this visually stunning, wildly exciting fantasyland of shopping, dining, music, and entertainment is our gift to the rest of the world.

picked watermelons, fat blueberries, Big Boy tomatoes, and peaches-and-cream corn, a variety so sweet and tender you can practically eat it raw. There's always a display or two of cutting flowers in bouquets, locally produced honey, and more. To keep things lively, several times a month a live band will entertain the crowds at the Clock Tower, an old-fashioned public square a few stairs up from the market area. Get there early for a seat outside, or duck into Farm to Market Cafe or Homer's Coffeehouse for a cappuccino and a muffin and grab a chair on the patio.

FASHION AND ACCESSORIES

ASIATICA LTD.
4824 Rainbow Blvd.
Westwood, KS
(913) 831-0831
www.asiaticakc.com

Fans of this shop report Asiatica sightings all over the world—in a posh hotel lobby in New York City, in the shadow of the Sistine Chapel—because its fashions, made from old Japanese kimonos, are so distinctive. Each year Elizabeth Wilson travels to the Far East to hand select vintage fabrics or exquisite new textiles, then brings them back home to get glorious new lives as vests, flowing jackets, blouses, and wraps.

CHURCHILL
5240 Belinder
Fairway, KS
(913) 262-5240
www.shopatchurchill.com

Chances are, the booty in the coveted Oscar swag bag is on Churchill's shelves before the telecast is over. Just how does a tiny shop in the heart of Kansas City get such a scoop? Leave it to Churchill's vivacious owner, Sally Hilkene.

Sally's unerring eye for taste serves her well, as she fills her shop with an eclectic collection of treasures for the home and personal adornments. Fancy the handbag the young Hollywood star was sporting in a celebrity magazine? Check with Sally first. Though Sally follows the trends, her inventory consists of pieces that will stand the test of time. And speaking of that, did you see her selection of divine watches?

FENG
5029 W. 119th St. (Hawthorne Plaza)
Leawood, KS
(913) 498-0530
www.fenglookeast.com

Just look at the handcrafted door handles and you know you're entering the shop of a woman who digs the details. In feng (as in feng shui, the Asian art of design and placement that brings harmony) Beth Zollars has created an oasis of style and refinement in the middle of suburbia. Just for an hour you'll be transported to a chic neighborhood in SoHo or L.A. or Hong Kong, filled with precious antiques, designer fashions, and one-of-a-kind accessories that you simply must have.

HALLS
211 Nichols Rd. (Country Club Plaza)
(816) 274-3222

200 E. 25th St. (Crown Center Shops)
(816) 274-8111
www.halls.com

Kansas City's only true, homegrown department store was created in 1913 by Hallmark Cards founder Joyce C. Hall. It continues to be the town's crown jewel. Here's where Kansas City's women and men of style find clothes—from ball gowns and tuxedos to tees and jeans—acquire fine stationery and home decor, register for weddings, and purchase corporate gifts. The shoe department is divine and Jennifer in couture can zip you into an Oscar de la Renta or Badgley Mischka (and never, ever let you attend the Symphony Ball wearing someone else's dress). Naturally, Halls has an extensive Hallmark card department. The Plaza location also houses the Midwest's only Steuben Gallery, and the beyond-fabulous Jewel Room shows off several exclusive lines including Van Cleef & Arpels.

Halls is also the anchor of the Crown Center shopping complex, offering business and dressy attire to the urban set. An extensive housewares department, gourmet food section, and paper-goods selection make up the three-story mix.

MITZY LONDON'S
4541 W. 119th St. (Leawood)
(913) 661-1775
www.mitzylondons.com

Frankly, we'd follow adorable Kelly Cook anywhere, especially when it's to her fabulous shop that invites your girly-girl self to come out and play. Against a color scheme of deep pink and black, you may see moms shopping with pre-teen daughters, girlfriends meeting before a lunch date at one of the nearby restaurants, or an entire bridal party sitting down to high tea in the room in back. The fashion will catch your eye; Kelly hand picks each frothy cocktail dress or bright trench, every exquisite shoe, all the must-have accessories. And her hand is also in the home decor including fabrics, pillows, and giftware. Can't choose between the LBD and the red number? Here, have another cup of oolong and a cupcake.

NOLTE'S BRIDAL
5057 W. 119th St.
Overland Park, KS
(913) 345-1122

4149 N. Mulberry Dr.
(816) 587-5575
www.noltesbridal.com

Weddings are all about the dress; once that's conquered, everything else falls into place. If only it were that simple. That's what a seasoned wedding planner is for. Michael Nolte has been fitting Kansas City's most knowing brides for more than 30 years. Naturally, Nolte's carries the best designers, including Vera Wang, Badgley Mischka, Monique Lhuillier, and Priscilla of Boston. And now, based on decades of tweaking styles, the wedding planner has his own line of exquisite wedding gowns. At the Briarcliff Village location (possibly the most glamorous wedding salon in the land), the ever-charming owner introduced an exciting collection of cocktail dresses and formal gowns for weddings and beyond.

MIRIAM GARVEY
2710 W. 53rd St.
Fairway, Kansas
(913) 722-2101

On any given Saturday, you may run into three friends (two with dogs, one with a teenage daughter) seeing what's new at this hipper-than-hip store in the Fairway Shops. What's the draw? Clearly it's the runway-hot collection of clothes Miriam Garvey displays throughout the tiny shop. You'll pick her out right away—she's a ravishing redhead. Oh, wait, that's her equally beautiful daughter, Leslie. All the names you read about in *W* and *Bazaar* are found here: Nanette Lepore, Tracy Reese, Bob Hale, Seven for all Mankind. With Miriam's just-us-girlfriends guidance, you can put together an outfit for daytime or cocktail that looks smashing on you, but never contrived. Add a bracelet or earrings from their fun displays and poof! You will turn heads at the soiree. When Miriam says she dresses the most beautiful women in Kansas City, she means beautiful both inside and out. Just like her.

SOHO 119
4419 W. 119th St. (Leawood)
(913) 338-5800
www.soho-119.com

The phrase "one stop shopping" may have been coined at this store in the upscale One Nineteen shopping mecca. The fashion will lift your spirits with the season's most exciting garments. The spa can lift other parts of you with a cabernet massage and cosmetic treatments including Botox. And before you glide out the door looking even more ravishing, text your girlfriends to invite them for wine and an antipasti platter in the tiny restaurant or at a café table on the sidewalk.

And speaking of ravishing, that describes the woman behind all this glamour, Carmela Spinelli, who brought her New York fashion sense to the Midwest. Be sure to sign up for Soho 119's regular fashion and skin-care events.

STANDARD STYLE BOUTIQUE
5076 W. 119th St. (Town Center Plaza)
Leawood, KS

447 W. 47th St. (Country Club Plaza)
(913) 685-4464 (for both stores)
www.standardstyle.com

It was a good day when Matt and Emily Baldwin followed their hearts (and Matt's family) and moved back to the Midwest from California. They brought with them a passion for fashion, and opened a boutique that showcases the most sought-after designers in the world. With nearly 150 lines in all, women will lust after casual to glam clothes from Jean Paul Gaultier, Marc Jacobs, Trina Turk, and DVF. Guys will locate just the right screen printed T-shirt, jacket, and jeans for the nightclub that night. And Matt recently launched his own line of denim in flattering shapes for both sexes. We happen to love the fact that this movie-star gorgeous couple is one of us: friendly, helpful, and fun.

WILL WYATT'S COWBOY COUTURE
15245 Metcalf Avenue
Overland Park, KS
(913) 681-9455
www.willwyatts.com

Cowboy and *couture?* If you're thinking that's an oxymoron, partner, then you haven't been to Will Wyatt's. This barn-sized, western ware emporium features gorgeous fringed blazers, tooled leather vests, dusters, halters with plenty of bling and enough boots to outfit Wyoming (in prices ranging from under $150 to scootin' past $1,200). True rodeo aficionados will recognize designer names like Tasha Polizzi, Lucchese, Tres Outlaws, Montana Dreamwear, Cripple Creek and Old Gringo. There are also home furnishings fit for a cattle baron, and gifts for buckaroos of all ages.

Owners Bryden and Jennifer Becker also have one of the largest displays of western jewelry in the Midwest: stunning necklaces by Coreen Cordova, Rocki Gorman, and local artist Jessie Rose, and silver belt buckles by Clint Orms. Of course, there are hats by Stetson as well as custom numbers by Trent Johnson of Greeley Hat Works.

FINE ART

We have more than our share of talented artists in Kansas City, thanks in part to the influence of the Kansas City Art Institute and Hallmark Cards. We cover the galleries that show their work in the Arts chapter. But in the meantime, here's your chance to visit the studios, showrooms, and even classrooms where they create their craft.

BLUE GALLERY
118 Southwest Blvd.
(816) 527-0823
www.bluegalleryonline.com
Owners David and Kelly Kuhn have a knack for attracting artists with a salable look. Nothing here is so out-there that you instantly feel like the only person in the world without a tattoo or pierced appendage. Not that that's a bad thing, mind you.

Like many gallery owners, David and Kelly will bend over backward to help you own the art you fall in love with. They'll let you take it home to live with for a few days or even come out to take a picture of your intended wall, then digitally drop in the artwork to see how it would look. Out-of-town buyers can peruse art on the Web site and have it shipped. But trust us; you'll want to visit this space yourself, if for no other reason than to meet Stella, the lovable gallery mascot. With any luck, you'll be here for First Friday when Blue is the epicenter for the gallery walk. Sign up for such upcoming events as artist receptions and parties.

Other must-see galleries in the Crossroads Arts District include Sherry Leedy Gallery (2004 Baltimore, 816-842-2626, www.sherryleedy .com) in a two-level converted warehouse that's art in and of itself. Sherry displays outstanding pieces from international as well as emerging regional artists. Leedy-Voulkos Art Center (2012 Baltimore, 816-474-1919, www.leedy-voulkos .com) is owned by Jim Leedy, whom many consider the father of the Crossroads district. Along with regional and national artists, Jim's diverse talents are showcased here. Known for his expressionist ceramics, he has had a major exhibition nearly every year somewhere in America since 1962.

CORBIN BRONZE LTD.
1166 Southwest Blvd.
(816) 766-4012
www.corbinbronze.com
You can see Kansas City sculptor Tom Corbin's work at the Firefighter's Memorial Fountain at Penn Valley Park, the Kauffman Memorial Garden near the Plaza, and in galleries and designers' showrooms across the country. Or simply rent the movies *Ransom* and *A Perfect Murder*, where his stunning furniture and statuettes set the tone for the characters' privileged lifestyles.

His collectors' list includes Ellen DeGeneres, Tom Hanks, and Jack Nicholson. In fact, this artist is so hot, he just moved into a new studio and showroom space in a renovated firehouse. His trademark is slim, ethereal female figures that seem light enough to float despite their bronze heft. Prices range from $200 to more than $100,000 each.

THE KANSAS CITY ART INSTITUTE ANNUAL CERAMICS SALE
4415 Warwick
(816) 474-5224, (800) 522-5224
www.kcai.edu

Discover emerging artists and incredible bargains during this student sale at one of the country's most respected art institutes. The event is always held a few weeks before the Christmas buying season, usually the first weekend in December. Doors open promptly at 10 a.m. on Sat and noon on Sun, but shoppers start showing up hours before to secure a place in line. Insider hot tip: Show up for the Friday-night preview to stake your claim. Once the doors open it's every art lover for himself or herself. Here's the drill to keep from being trampled by the crowds behind you: As soon as the doors open, grab one of the empty cardboard boxes off to the left and start moving around the stations. When you see something you like, grab it or it will be gone.

The proceeds help keep the artists in clay and supplies, so that's a good thing.

RHETT AND KELLY JOHNSON
Dearborn, MO
(816) 450-3616
www.rhettjohnson.com

Rhett is a monumentally talented sculptor who works with such found objects as old cobalt-blue bottles, engine parts, and iron he shapes and leaves outside to rust. His garden art features graceful birds landing on arches and stakes. Kelly creates exquisite beaded art and witty painted papier-mâché masks, which she also sells at Missouri Bluffs, a women's clothing store in Weston, Missouri (see Day Trips and Weekend Getaways). Their studios in Dearborn, Missouri, just north of Kansas City, are open by appointment only and definitely worth the 35-mile trip.

FLORISTS

We wouldn't think of letting you choose a florist out of the Yellow Pages or online list; sending flowers to a friend or choosing a vendor for an event like a daughter's wedding or your own birthday party is just too important. Here are a few of our favorite florists in town. As a bonus, each shop also has an exquisite selection of items for your home and gift giving, including candles and serving pieces.

BECO FLOWERS
1922 Baltimore
(816) 472-4242
www.becoflowers.com

A serene collection of baby artichokes in a wooden bowl. A fat pineapple in a base of bright gerbera daisies. Collette Keenan and Rebecca Ederer like to play with their food. These talented florists also do amazing things with flowers, from show-off displays for an entryway to sweet floral bouquets. There is no minimum price for orders. The florist is also an art gallery, called the CUBE, which showcases a different artist's work every month.

MATNEY FLORAL DESIGN
2708 W. 53rd St.
Fairway, KS
(913) 362-5419

If the flowers at a black-tie gala get more attention than the ball gowns, Chuck Matney is probably to blame. From a single exquisite orchid to stunning arrangements that use Granny Smith apples in tall vases, his designs are fresh, inventive, and in perfect taste.

STUDIO DAN MEINERS
2500 Pennway
(816) 842-7244
www.danmeiners.com

When Dan Meiners moved to a beautifully renovated building near Union Station, he definitely had room to grow. His new digs incorporate his floral design business, a gorgeous event space, and even room for other small companies such as interior designers. But chances are, as handsome as the new headquarters are, you won't notice anything but the blooms.

If you want to get a "Wow!" from someone, send one of Dan's arrangements. His work can be contemporary or very traditional depending on your needs, and he's known for incorporating unusual vessels and groupings. Dan and his talented staff are also high society's first call for weddings and special events.

i When Barnett Helzberg brought the Hope diamond to town to promote his new store on the Country Club Plaza, security was tight as the public took turns viewing the priceless gem. But when it came time to transport the legendary rock to the store's Topeka location, Barnett simply dropped it in his coat pocket and drove away.

FOOD AND GIFTS

ANDRE'S CONFISERIE SUISSE
5018 Main St.
(816) 561-3440

4929 W. 119th St.
Overland Park, KS
(913) 498-3440
www.andreschocolates.com
When Master Confiseur Andre Bollier and his wife, Elsbeth, came here from Switzerland in 1955 to set up a candy shop, few residents had ever tasted premium chocolates; it would be decades before "Godiva" meant anything but a lady with a horse. So the Bolliers served lunches at their tea room while they began educating the Midwest palate. Son Marcel and his wife, Connie, joined the company in 1974, and in 2001 their son René and his wife, Nancy, came on board.

All the chocolates, from truffles to cream- and caramel-filled assortments, are handmade and meltingly delicious. The shop's specialties are treats tied to the seasons, such as hand-painted, edible chocolate Easter eggs; Valentine hearts filled with truffles; and chocolate wine bottles packed with chocolate-covered almonds that are perfect for any celebration. Replace the Andre's label with your own and the glossy brown bottles make extraordinary wedding and anniversary gifts. Chocoholic Johnson Countians were thrilled when the Bollier family opened a second location in Hawthorne Plaza.

THE BETTER CHEDDAR
604 W. 48th St.
(816) 561-8204

71st and Mission
Prairie Village, KS
(913) 362-7575
www.thebettercheddar.com
What sets a specialty gourmet shop apart from a grocery store are unique products and personal service. That's certainly the case at The Better Cheddar, where owner Ron Shalinsky and his gracious staff welcome you like family and encourage you to sample the wares. In fact there are so many chunks of cheeses, crackers with savory toppings, and decadent chocolate truffles to try, it's easy to have dinner while you shop.

Among the hundreds of gourmet selections are jars of The Better Cheddar's own proprietary brand. There's food for thought as well: Hand-printed cards describe each cheese and offer suggestions for use. The Dutch aged cheddar with black pepper, you discover, is terrific with strawberries and makes a very grownup macaroni and cheese dish.

The Better Cheddar's Plaza store also sells a nice variety of wines (with a free tasting each Sat from 2 to 4 p.m.), a perfect accompaniment to the gourmet picnic the staff can prepare with a little prior notice. And their gift baskets are so legendary that regular customers order them delivered sight unseen.

BROWNE'S MARKET
3300 Pennsylvania
(816) 561-0030
www.brownesmarket.com
When Ed and Mary Flavin opened this grocery store in 1887, it was to offer a taste of County Kerry to the thousands of Irish immigrants finding new homes here. The tradition continued when daughter Margaret married Jim Browne, and today the shelves are still stocked with treats from the homeland: sweets such as Hob Nobs and Cadbury Flakes, tweed caps, Aran knit sweaters, teas, and Claddagh windchimes. The deli case features bangers and mash, soda bread, and Irish

stew. And everyone, no matter their heritage, enjoys the chocolate chip, chocolate oatmeal, and white chunk macadamia cookies. Show up on Cookie Tuesday and they're on sale. You might even see an impromptu Irish dance by the family's fifth generation. Browne's is the unofficial starting point for the city's huge St. Patrick's Day parade; the party starts as early as 7 a.m. with an authentic Irish breakfast.

CHRISTOPHER ELBOW ARTISANAL CHOCOLATES
1819 McGee
(816) 842-1300
www.elbowchocolates.com
It's quickly become one of our favorite gifts for an open house or a birthday: a box of Christopher Elbow's chocolates. Each morsel is a work of art: glossy orbs that look like glass marbles, rainbow-colored pyramids, fat squares screenprinted with swaths of color or dusted with cocoa. He infuses the truffles with unusual flavors such as Brazilian coffee, French lavender, Chinese five-spice, caramel banana, and delicate Earl Grey tea.

His gorgeous new digs in the Crossroads includes a "chocolate bar" where you can experience the world's most decadent hot chocolate. What's next, you ask? Decadent ice creams and glaces at a nearby shop ready to open any day now.

FERVERE BREAD
1702 Summit
(816) 582-7323
Fred Spompinato makes breads with a tender texture and chewy crust that can be achieved only by hand kneading, lots of patience, and a special Old World oven. He named his tiny take-out bakery for the Latin word (pronounced fur-VAIR-ay) meaning passion. That may explain why Fred sold his first successful bread company years ago when it became more of a business and less of a craft.

Now he's up to his elbows in dough again and loving every sticky minute. Using organic flours

and natural ingredients, he turns out dense, crusty loaves in six or so varieties, including an aromatic olive rosemary, a country French, and an oval wonder filled with walnuts, apples, and plump apricots. During winter his holiday gift to us is a cranberry pecan loaf enlivened with orange rind. No need to wrap it, Fred, we'll eat it here.

Fervere, which is in the bohemian neighborhood along with Blue Bird Bistro (see Restaurants) and a few artist studios, is open 11 a.m. to 7 p.m. Thurs through Sat. There are always generous chunks of each bread, along with dishes of good olive oil for dunking, ready to sample before you buy.

ORIGINAL JUAN SPECIALTY FOODS INC.
111 Southwest Blvd.
Kansas City, KS
(913) 432-5228, (800) 568-8468
www.originaljuan.com
Forget complaining about the heat and humidity of a summer day in Kansas—it's always hot at Original Juan's, where they cook up 80-gallon vats of incendiary salsas and sauces, even fruit jellies, using chili peppers and little else. Even Wilber Scoville, the guy who devised the rating system for chilis, would whimper with one drop of Da' Bomb's The Final Answer. This deep-red sauce tops out at 1.5 million Scoville units and is available in a box that includes a lock and key. They're not kidding; you must be 21 or over to buy the stuff.

PLANTERS SEED & SPICE COMPANY
513 Walnut
(816) 842-3651
www.plantersseed.com
At Planters the atmosphere is always festive, even without 35,000 people milling around the farmers' market down the street, as regulars show up for a monthly fix of coffee, bird seed, and dog food. Not much has changed since it opened in 1924; the wooden floors may creak a little more now, but you can still get more than 200 varieties of herbs and spices in giant bins. The sales staff can

help you create gifts using complementary items, such packets of chili seasoning and dried beans in a ceramic casserole dish or bags of flavored coffee beans and a grinder in a laminated box.

THE ROASTERIE
1204 W. 27th St.
(816) 931-4000, (800) 376-0245
www.theroasterie.com

As a foreign exchange student in Costa Rica, Danny O'Neill fell in love with the rich, robust coffee served there. Fifteen years later his passion for the brew had him roasting beans in the basement of his Brookside home, and when he mastered the art of air roasting he knew he'd found his calling. He and buddy Norman Killman would roast in the basement, pack in the living room, and deliver the fragrant bags of beans to customers in Norm's '81 El Camino.

That was 1993. And although Norm swears he still has the car, he can certainly afford to drive something a little more exotic; the brand is sold in grocery stores and gourmet shops and served in Kansas City's top restaurants. In fact, several local chefs have commissioned their own special blends, so if you dig the java at the American Restaurant or the Classic Cup, you have Danny to thank. The company makes about 40 blends and flavors in all, including a Kansas City Blend, a combination of Indonesian and Central and South American beans that's hearty yet smooth. But to be sleepless in Kansas City go for the Nitro Express, a darker roast with a pungent, smoky aroma and flavor. You can find the flavor-sealed bags at most area grocery stores. Tour the Roasterie's new facility Sat starting at 11 a.m. We bet there will be coffee.

THREE DOG BAKERY
612 W. 48th St.
(816) 753-3647, (800) 4TREATS
www.threedog.com

Yes, we know the food here is for pooches, but it's so artfully done we couldn't resist. Besides, what better gift to take home to your best buddy than a Scotty Biscotti or Puppy Petit Four? Locals Dan Dye and Mark Beckloff started the company when they couldn't find healthy snacks for their three dogs, Dottie, Gracie, and Sarah Jean. Using dough made from whole wheat flour, unsweetened carob, and low-fat yogurt powder and a $2 bone-shaped cookie cutter, the duo concocted treats their girls loved.

Since Dan and Mark sold the company, they're rolling in dough. The products are available at Three Dog Bakery stores across the country (with one in Japan) and through selected Target stores. If you stop by the Plaza store you'll see several four-footed fans sampling the wares. You can also order through the dog-alog (a catalog simply wouldn't do) or the company's fun Web site.

HOME FURNISHINGS AND ACCESSORIES

BLACK BAMBOO
1815 Wyandotte
(816) 283-3000
www.black-bamboo.com

As an interior designer for an international architectural firm, Tim Butt envisioned beautiful and functional spaces for clients. Through his business travels, he was drawn to the simple, elegant lines of Asian and modern furnishings, so when he opened his shop he filled it with a mix of each. He personally selected pieces from Burma, China, Thailand, Bali, Vietnam, and elsewhere.

In his handsome space, which formerly housed a vintage Corvette restoration shop, Tim gives each piece of furniture its due with room to breathe and great lighting. The inventory includes an ever-changing collection of antiques, such as a lovely blue-painted secretary from the mid-1800s, and sterling-and-jade jewelry and artwork.

The look of the place says expensive, but you might call it Asia minor: Prices range from $3.50 for a silk-screened greeting card that could easily be framed to a large cabinet handcrafted of Asian Yuma for around $3,000. In between is a wonderful array of sofas, chairs, side tables, and accessories—all reflecting Tim's keen sense of style. Lucky you; he also provides interior-design services.

NELL HILL'S
501 Commercial
Atchison, KS
(913) 367-1086

4101 N. Mulberry Dr. (Briarcliff Village)
(816) 746-4320
www.nellhills.com

You might think, *What's the big deal?* at first sight of Mary Carol Garrity's modest two-story building on the corner, but, oh, what wonders await inside. Room after room is filled with European antiques next to all-American red-plaid sofas mingled with Indonesian tables topped with baskets, vases, and dishware. Everything is so artfully arranged you'll want to say, "I'll take the whole room, please." No problem; delivery is free. But the affable Ms. G would rather help you develop your own look, a service she does every day for customers who bring in photos of rooms and a plaintive "Help me, please."

Personal service and inventory aside, some people come to Nell Hill's just for the price tags. Gifts such as silverplate bowls, sets of crisp white linen cocktail napkins, and wire baskets are so well priced it pays to just grab several and figure out who will get them later.

For more treasures, walk just a few paces to her antiques emporium, **Garrity's Encore,** at 121 North Fifth St. (913-367-1523) where tabletop and bedding are on display. Be sure to pick up a copy of one of Mary Carol Garrity's decorating books, including *Nell Hill's Style at Home* and *Nell Hill's Christmas at Home.* Her new store in Briarcliff Village brings her magic closer to home. Here, 16,000 square feet provide enough space for nearly 20 ahh-worthy room environments, each painted one of Mary Carol's favorite colors.

PORTFOLIO KITCHEN & HOME
8027 State Line Rd.
(816) 363-5300
www.portfolio-home.com

You won't leave this stunning showroom with a shopping bag, but you might come away with an entire new kitchen, bath, or dressing room worthy of any diva. Since opening a few years ago,

owner Geri Higgins has become the go-to girl for Kansas City's most persnickety gourmets and style mavens. The showroom displays five complete kitchen environments, including a Zenlike haven, a loft-ready contemporary concept, and an Old World classic style. Though you might be tempted simply to point and say, "I'll take that one," you'll want to have the on-staff designers create your own dream kitchen. Geri takes full advantage of the showroom's refrigerators and multiple burners to turn Portfolio into party central several times a month when she hosts a fund-raiser or other fabulous event. This is one A-list you'll want to join.

i Here's one more reason to shop on the Country Club Plaza during your stay here: The parking is plentiful and free. Covered lots and on-street parking spaces are easy to find throughout the 4-block district.

PRYDE'S OLD WESTPORT
115 Westport Rd.
(816) 531-5588
www.prydesoldwestport.com

It's a three-decade Kansas City tradition: When a young woman gets engaged, she heads to Pryde's to register *before* picking out her dress. Owner Louise Meyers has helped newlyweds, as well as college-bound seniors, singles, and empty nesters, outfit kitchens for more than 20 years. The array of cutlery, cookware, dinnerware, linens, and serving pieces is so staggering you can get lost within the multifloored, many-roomed space. Turn a corner and there's a wall of kitchen utensils you didn't know existed, barbecue tools of every design, candles, glassware, and more. Pryde's has a splendid collection of dinnerware to set an elegant or casual table, including England's finest stoneware, Portmeirion, and Emile Henry from France. But one of the store's best commodities is advice. Louise and her staff are more than happy to help you choose the proper tool for the task, demonstrate a pasta machine, or put together a gift basket for a bridal shower. Gift-wrapping is always free, and Pryde's can ship anywhere.

RETRO INFERNO
1500 Grand Blvd.
(816) 842-4004
www.retroinferno.com
Truth be told, collectors and interior designers on both coasts are more familiar with Rod Parks's collection of mid-20th-century furniture than many Kansas Citians are. With wall-to-wall primo modern designs in his groovy location, it's a sure thing you'll find the Herman Miller, Knoll, Dunbar, McCob, Russell Wright, or Heywood Wakefield piece you seek. Retro Inferno also sells accessories such as vintage cocktail shakers, Murano glassware, pink ice crushers, and even some vintage cocktail dresses that may have spent the evening at the Inferno Lounge, the disco that gave the shop its name. The nightclub is long gone, but the neon light lives on in Rod's front window. And you might even leave with a pocketful of cash; he buys quality vintage furniture and accessories, so that Electrolux gathering dust in the closet could pay for your trip. Here's an Insiders' tip: Park in back rather than the street; you may avoid a parking ticket. Hours are 11 a.m. to 6 p.m. Mon through Sat.

SCANDIA HOME BY URSULA TERRASI
501 Nichols Rd. (Country Club Plaza)
(816) 753-4144
www.scandiadownkc.com
Welcome to Ursula Terrasi's little corner of the world. Literally. This merchant—with the grace of Italian royalty and the warmth of a Midwesterner—searches the globe for luxurious bedding (can you count to 800 threads per inch?), hand-finished furniture, heavenly scented bath potions, and beautiful tableware for her shop on the Country Club Plaza. But it's the meringue-high, down-filled comforters that have shoppers wanting to jump in bed. Each cozy store vignette has been dressed to the nines in sumptuous fabrics and masses of pillows. Now she even has her own line of mattresses.

No wonder Scandia Down is favored for its bridal registry service: Climb into one of these sumptuous confections every night and the honeymoon may never end. And following Mother Nature's course, the shop has a sweet collection of baby giftware. No one leaves empty-handed, now that Ursula has added lovely jewelry and personal accessories.

JEWELRY

HELZBERG DIAMONDS
Various locations at shopping malls and the Country Club Plaza
www.helzberg.com
From one tiny storefront in Kansas City, Kansas, this enterprise has become the personal jeweler to customers at more than 75 stores across the country. Morris Helzberg began the dream in 1915, but it was his son, Barnett, then Barnett Jr., who grew it into one of the most successful retailers in the country. These marketing geniuses added an element of fun to the sometimes all-too-serious task of buying jewelry. In the 1930s the company offered free "aeroplane" rides with the purchase of a $49 Benrus Pilot watch, and to launch the new Country Club Plaza store Barnett Jr. brought in the Hope diamond, which the public could view for free if they made a contribution to the United Way.

This benevolent tradition continues today: Although retired from the gem business, Barnett Jr. and Shirley Helzberg are two of the most generous Kansas City citizens of all time. But it was their engagement in 1967 that sparked one of the store's most successful promotions, the "I Am Loved" pin. Barnett originally thought of the idea as a pre-engagement stall tactic. Since then the red-and-white pins have been used in schools to teach children self-esteem, sent to American troops in Vietnam, translated into eight languages, and featured in the "Charlie Brown" comic strip. To date the store has handed out more than 35 million of the red-and-white tokens of love.

MAZZARESE JEWELRY
4850 W. 135th St.
Leawood, KS
(913) 491-4111
www.mazzarese.com

Like those of so many of Kansas City's finest jewelry stores, Mazzarese's traditions have been passed down through the generations. The youngest members are Tony and Tosca's son and daughter, Mark and Veronica, who have kept the family legacy of quality and brought in exciting new lines and ideas. With a gorgeous new store the company has even more room to show off its diamond creations from cherished lines as well as exclusive designs. Mazzarese is also known for its masterful array of timepieces, from diamond-encrusted look-at-me styles to classic tank watches. Along with stunning diamond and gemstone pieces, the store carries top-name sterling jewelry from John Hardy and a stellar collection of gifts for men.

i Some of the city's best gift shops are found in art museums. The Nelson-Atkins Museum of Art and the Kemper Museum of Contemporary Art both feature shops that offer books, posters, note cards, wearable art (such as jewelry and painted silk scarves), and handcrafted pieces such as vases and teapots.

SWIRK JEWELRY
310 W. 47th St.
(816) 753-1949, (800) MR SWIRK
www.swirkjewelry.com
Seems like 1910 was a good year to open a jewelry store in the Midwest. Swirk's has built a loyal following buoyed by personal service, a small but lovely selection of diamond and gemstone jewelry, many estate pieces, and the fix-anything skill of its repair team. Here's where Kansas City brings its tired timepieces and broken bracelets. Visit the small shop above Buca di Beppo restaurant on the Country Club Plaza. You'll get a handshake whether you buy something or not, most likely from somebody named Swirk.

TIFFANY & CO.
310 Nichols Rd.
(816) 531-7676
www.tiffanys.com
All the classics are to be found in this glittering store: engagement rings from demure to eye-popping, stunning pearl creations, and the finest tableware items and timepieces. Heirlooms all. Manager Melinda Petet is usually around, happy to show you a bold Peretti cuff or Picasso drop—just two of the exclusive designer lines carried here—proving once again that although the Tiffany name has been around since 1837, the styles are endlessly fresh. And in case you're wondering, never fear; come in wearing jeans or furs. You'll always get friendly, courteous service.

TIVOL
220 Nichols Rd.
(816) 531-5800

4721 W. 119th St.
Overland Park, KS
(913) 345-0200

4131 N. Mulberry Dr.
(816) 891-2600
www.tivol.com
In 1910 when jeweler Charles Tivol opened a store in downtown Kansas City his ledger registered $105,000 the first year. Today the store often does that in one sale. It's come a long way from $95 diamond rings, but it's never wavered from a commitment to customer service. It doesn't hurt that Charles's son, Harold, has a knack for marketing; in fact the dapper gentleman still shows up in the company's clever ads. The store moved to its current location on the Country Club Plaza in 1951, where it remains the area's crown jewel with breathtaking window displays and even more stunning creations inside. Top designer names are represented here, and in Kansas City the only proper engagement ring comes in a Tivol's black-and-gold box.

Harold swore he'd never move from the Plaza, and he hasn't, but when daughter Cathy accepted the reins she opened a second location in Hawthorne Plaza to cater to their customers out south. But don't let the luxurious surroundings keep you from entering. The friendly salespeople are happy to let you try on a dozen diamond line bracelets, whether your wrist is clad in denim or mink. The latest in the Tivol string of pearls is the Briarcliff Village location, serving clients up north.

SHOPPING DISTRICTS

BROOKSIDE
Surrounding 63rd St. and Brookside Blvd.
(816) 523-5553
www.brooksidekc.com

This beloved Main Street-ish string of stores has retained its charm while continuing to grow thanks to the vibrant neighborhood surrounding it. More than 70 locally owned businesses are here, many for decades, from the ethnic treasures at World's Window to a fantasy world for little girls and their mommies at Lauren Alexandra (www.kcbebe .com), where a pink tutu has your name on it. Need clean undies? That's just one of the unique fragrances you'll find at 5B&Co. Candles.

Your little wizard will go ga-ga over Brookside Toy & Science, and Brookside Barkery & Bath will keep Fido in fine form. STUFF is a crazy quilt of marvelous gifts, decor, and art from more than 60 local and national artists. The Dime Store is an old-time throwback, complete with creaky wooden floors and penny candy. Fine art is available at Leopold Gallery, and artful food can be had at Avenues Bistro, Julian, or Blue Grotto.

CRESTWOOD
55th St. between Brookside Blvd. and Oak St.

One of the city's first suburban shopping districts, Crestwood is in an area marked by its lovely homes and gardens. Naturally the block is filled with some of Kansas City's most stylish shops, including the Pear Tree, filled with must-have treasures for home and garden; and George Turbovich Designs (816-523-3974), an endlessly fascinating grouping of leather goods, accessories, and antiques hand-selected by its renowned interior-designer owner. Plan to spend a day as you peruse each antiques shop and boutique. To tide you over, there are cafes, including Aixois and Café Europa, where you can relax over lunch or dinner.

CROSSROADS ARTS DISTRICT
1-mile-wide area between Downtown Kansas City and Crown Center
www.kccrossroads.org

Every big city has one—a neighborhood where unique boutiques, antiques stores, showrooms, art galleries, and restaurants have popped up to become the trendiest place in town to shop. In Kansas City that destination is the Crossroads Arts District.

Part of its charm is that the studios and storefronts have emerged out of brick warehouses, abandoned office buildings, and lofts, many still sporting handsome concrete moldings and wooden beams. This is shopping the way it used to be, where the person behind the counter is the owner, friends gather over wine in the evening, and there's not a Starbucks in sight.

When a handful of the art gallery owners banded together to stay open late on Friday, First Friday was born. It's become Kansas City's official street party, with crowds walking to the 60 or so galleries and artist studios and shopping in unique boutiques. Restaurants offer anything from a quick bowl of spicy noodles to a white-tablecloth, four-course meal.

THE LEGENDS AT VILLAGE WEST
1843 Village West Pkwy.
At the intersection of I-70 and I-435
(913) 788-3700
www.legendsshopping.com

Call it the shopping mecca a racetrack built. When the Kansas Speedway turned this vast acreage in Kansas City, Kansas, into the hottest thing going, shops soon followed. Cabela's appeals to every sports enthusiast, and you can decorate your entire home in the overwhelming inventory at Nebraska Furniture Mart. The Legends is the nifty open-air shopping and entertainment district to complete the mix with more than 80 tenants, including the city's first Adidas store and Cavender's western wear. The kid magnet, 20,000-square-foot T-Rex Cafe also has landed here first before it becomes a national phenom.

All in all, the Legends is a destination with 1.1 million square feet of retail space plus a luxury movie theater with a VIP section and Pin-Up Bowl (where you can pick up a spare along with a cocktail!). You'll find more than 100 shops to keep you busy, including several factory outlets from exciting fashion brands Ann Taylor, Banana Republic, Gap, and Brooks Brothers. Take a walking tour to learn more about famous Kansans who have been immortalized in bronze sculptures and medallions throughout the beautifully landscaped area. You have your choice of more than 30 restaurants at the Legends, including Kansas City's own Jazz—A Louisiana Kitchen. The Legends also hosts, well, legendary live music events including free summer concerts and family entertainment around the holidays.

PRAIRIE VILLAGE SHOPS
71st and Mission Rd.
(913) 652-3306
www.prairievillageshops.com
Oh, to live in a cute ranch house in Prairie Village where you can walk to everything your heart desires. In this open air collection of shops, services, and boutiques you'll find one-of-a-kind treasures such as Curious Sofa, a gift and home decor emporium as clever as its name. Stop by The Better Cheddar to taste your way through an incredible selection of imported and domestic gourmet goods and then choose a table at Cafe Provence, tout de suite.

ZONA ROSA
I-29 and Barry Rd.
(816) 587-8180
www.zonarosa.com
This exciting mixed-use district in the booming area north of the river hearkens back to the time of town squares where neighbors would gather to catch up with their weeks or listen to the local band. That's the theme behind this collection of more than 80 unique shops, including national chains and a few local boutiques, along with restaurants and services galore. It's all set in a pretty mix of architectural styles with plenty of green spaces, wide sidewalks, old-fashioned phone booths, and fountains (kids are welcome to splash around), encouraging you to park your car and actually stroll as you shop for the latest fashion at Ann Taylor or outfit your entire home at Ethan Allen.

SOUVENIRS AND GIFTS

THE BEST OF KANSAS CITY
Crown Center Shops
1532 Grand Blvd.
(816) 303-7330, (800) 366-8780
www.thebestofkc.com
One taste of our food and you'll want to take it all back with you. Now you can, with a gift basket from the Best of Kansas City. For years they've been putting together big, gorgeous gift baskets bursting with hometown products like Laura Little's Fudge, Andre's Chocolates, Strawberry Hill nut loaves, Fritz's smoked meats, Hereford House Steak Sauce, and Wolferman's muffins. Nonfood items include CDs and books from local talent, coffee mugs, and caps.

KANSAS SAMPLER
9548 Antioch Rd.
Overland Park, KS
(913) 383-2920

4849 W. 117th St.
Town Center Plaza
(913) 491-3004

6858 Johnson Dr.
(913) 432-3355
www.kansassampler.com
When you realize, Dorothy, that you're not in Kansas anymore, you'll wish you had some fun souvenir to remember your trip. Here's just the place to find it. Peg and Tim Liebert have put together a wonderful collection of Sunflower State–themed goodies such as T-shirts, sampler boxes filled with locally made gourmet food and goodies, books about the region, CDs from local artists, and Kansas magnets to add to your refrigerator collection. Favorites are the Pet Tornado and delicious sunflower-seed cookies.

ATTRACTIONS

Looking for a fabulous family vacation? Romantic weekend for two? A new place to call home? Congratulations! You've come to the right place. With so much to see and do, Kansas City is the perfect choice no matter how you define fun.

In fact, here's where our unique mix of citified culture (la-de-da) and Wild West rowdiness (yee-haw!) really pays off. You can spend your day contemplating a Rembrandt or attending a rodeo and then dine by candlelight or campfire . . . all within our city's boundaries.

History buffs will be taken aback; although another city is rightly called the gateway to the West, we were the gate that outfitted more than half a million travelers on the Oregon, California, and Santa Fe Trails during the mid-1800s. You can relive their stories at dozens of museums, historic sites, and restored antebellum homes. And if your taste runs to more modern architecture, things are looking up . . . way up. Our downtown skyline has nearly 60 art deco buildings from the 1920s and 1930s.

Naturally in this chapter you'll also see attractions that have wowed tourists for decades, such as our renowned Nelson-Atkins Museum of Art and the shopping mecca known as the Country Club Plaza. But for those frequent KC visitors who are thinking, *Been there, done that*, get ready for a few surprises. A citywide cultural renaissance is taking place just in time for your visit. We're busy updating and renovating some of our most treasured landmarks and historical districts while adding new destinations on both sides of the state line. That means there's bound to be a snappy little bonus for the art lover, sporting nut, and shopaholic in your entourage. We're proud to show it all to you.

The attractions are grouped by category and listed alphabetically. Because hours frequently change, it's best to call for updated information. You may wish to start at the Observation Points where you can see our city from on high.

ART MUSEUMS

KEMPER MUSEUM OF CONTEMPORARY ART
4420 Warwick Blvd.
(816) 753-5784
www.kemperart.org
When locals describe Kansas City's "other" art museum, they simply say, "It's the one with the spider." This one could be the model for a sci-fi thriller. The sculpture by Louise Bourgeois weighs 1,600 pounds and is roughly the size of a New York apartment. A much smaller crawler can be seen on the building's exterior wall.

Opened in 1994, the museum is a gift from R. Crosby Kemper, recently retired as head of UMB Financial Corporation. At its core is the stunning collection of Kemper and his wife, Bebe, that includes works by Jasper Johns, David Hockney, Robert Motherwell, Georgia O'Keeffe, Willem de Kooning, and Frank Stella. A Dale Chihuly blown-glass chandelier is one of the most stunning displays.

If Wayne Thiebaud's *Cakes and Pies* painting makes you hungry, you'll find relief in Cafe Sebastienne. Consider this delightful restaurant part of the art tour because the walls are filled floor to ceiling with 110 canvases by Frederick James Brown. The works, commissioned by the Kempers, tell "The History of Art," and it's fun to pick out references to masters such as Picasso, Matisse, and Van Gogh. Along with permanent displays, the museum hosts exhibits throughout the year, usually by cutting-edge artists. Want one more reason to thank the Kempers? Admission is free. The museum is open every day except Mon, and the cafe serves lunch Tues through Sat, Sunday brunch, and dinner Fri and Sat. When you visit, take time to walk around the grounds of the Kansas City Art Institute next door; several of the students' sculptures are good enough to be in the museum.

NELSON-ATKINS MUSEUM OF ART
4525 Oak St.
(816) 561-4000
www.nelson-atkins.org
See Close-up on pages 106-107.

NERMAN MUSEUM OF
CONTEMPORARY ART
Johnson County Community College
12345 College Blvd.
Overland Park, KS
(913) 469-8500
www.nermanmuseum.org
Imagine the silence on the end of the line when museum director Bruce Hartman called big-time art dealers in New York to schedule a buying trip for a gallery at the Johnson County Community College in Overland Park. Now imagine their surprise when they see the art displayed in this glorious new space designed by architect Kyu Sung Woo. It has placed Kansas firmly on the international art scene.

Named for local philanthropists (and revered collectors of postwar art) Jerry and Margaret Nerman and their son Lewis, the 38,000-square-foot space is the largest contemporary art museum in the four-state region and the only contemporary art museum in Kansas. The spare, minimalist structure, composed of two glass and pale limestone boxes that jut out of the college's austere brick facade, is the architect's latest masterpiece. Kyu Sung Woo is also known for the Olympic Village in Seoul and the Arts of Korea Gallery at the Metropolitan Museum of Art. Actually, JCCC has been famous for its outdoor Oppenheimer Sculpture Garden for years, gifts of Tony and Marti Oppenheimer that include the striking 6-foot *Walking Man (on the Edge)* by Jonathan Borofsky. The couple donated to the new museum's acquisitions as well.

The building's interior is a planned process of continual discoveries where elements are gradually revealed—giving visitors a sense of surprise at every turn. But it's the art that will have you swooning. Within the 4,000 square feet of permanent collection space you'll find the works of 21 big names, including Frank Stella, Leon Golub, Uta Barth, Brian Finke, Amy Sillman, and Aaron Young, as well as artists with Kansas City connections—James Brinsfield, Warren Rosser, and Eric Sall. Highlights are Kehinde Wiley's *Alexander the Great, Variation*, an immense painting of an African-American man, and Do-Ho Suh's *Some/One*, a shimmering, almost fluid suit of armor constructed of thousands of dog tags.

There is also a changing art gallery, the Oppenheimer New Media Gallery, as well as education and community spaces, and Cafe Tempo (which seats around 100).

CASINOS

In Kansas City you'll have a chance to go rollin' on the river. Sort of. Our riverboat casinos are, shall we say, permanently docked. But that doesn't mean you won't have a boatload of a good time as long as you're 21 or older. And here's an easy way to cruise over to the boats: Catch a ride on the Casino Cruiser, the No. 173 Metro Bus, which makes the loop from Crown Center and downtown hotels to the casinos. For information call the Metro at (816) 221-0660, jump on board www.kcata.org, or ask your hotel's front desk for more information.

AMERISTAR CASINO HOTEL
3200 Ameristar Dr.
(816) 414-7000, (800) 499-4961
www.ameristarcasinos.com
You'll find two casinos for the price of one here, with more than 3,200 slot and video poker machines (the most in the city) plus more than 140 table games, including craps, roulette, and mini-baccarat. In fact, Ameristar boasts the largest poker room in the Midwest. Go fish.

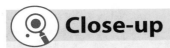 **Close-up**

The Nelson-Atkins Museum of Art and Bloch Building Expansion

At the heart of Kansas City's vibrant art scene is the Nelson-Atkins Museum of Art, ranked among the top 15 art museums in the United States. The city owes this Beaux Arts treasure to two primary people: the larger-than-life founder of the *Kansas City Star*, William Rockhill Nelson (see his profile on page 249), and a reclusive schoolteacher, Mary Atkins, who married late but well. Nelson bequeathed $11 million to the city for art acquisitions, and his daughter and son-in-law donated the family's 20-acre estate, Oak Hall, for the site. At Mary's death, her late husband's estate was worth $1 million, enough to help fund the $3 million museum, completed in 1933. An imposing rectangle six stories high and larger than a city block, its classic design boasts 32 gigantic columns on both sides. Set far back on its sweeping, terraced lawn, it gives an air of a royal palace.

From literally nothing—not one single piece of art to its name—the Nelson has amassed nearly 35,000 pieces in its collection, from precious ceramic objects found in ancient Chinese tombs to an exceptionally beautiful Pawnee headdress dating to 1840. The Claude Monet *Boulevard des Capucines* is enchanting, while *Persephone* by local artist Thomas Hart Benton isn't nearly as shocking as when first, um, revealed.

But perhaps the most exciting acquisition isn't something that can hang on a wall—it literally is a wall, or actually several of them. The Bloch Building, which opened in June 2007, was deemed "the most anticipated building of 2007" by *Time* magazine. This is, according to the *New Yorker*, not just architect Steven Holl's "finest building so far but also one of the best museums of the last generation." Just don't be alarmed when you first spy this series of five irregularly shaped structures rising out from the east lawn. The size is deceiving; picture a 67-story skyscraper resting on its side partially submerged in the earth. The architect calls them lenses, and they are indeed constructed of milky glass. By day they look somehow unfinished, but at night they dazzle with a pale-blue glow. The interior walls beg to be touched— luminous polished white plaster and sections of the glass walls lead you through narrow corridors to the galleries belowground. The Bloch Building was made possible primarily by the co-founder of H&R Block, Henry Bloch, and his wife, Marion. The new building expanded the museum by 71 percent to some 400,000 square feet. And what's a building without art? In early 2010, the Blochs donated 29 works of art from their breathtaking French impressionist collection to the museum. It is the largest gift the museum has ever received. The new building also provides space for the immense contemporary and African collections and the celebrated Hallmark Photographic Gallery. The latter is a gift from the Hall family—a collection of more

This pleasure palace also holds the cards to lots of other entertainment, including live music venues and several dining options. There's also an attached 184–guest room luxury hotel.

ARGOSY CASINO
777 Argosy Dr.
Riverside, MO
(816) 746-3100, (800) 900-3423
www.argosycasinos.com

Casino decor can range from over-the-top to elegant, and Argosy is definitely the latter. A gorgeous new hotel pampers guests in 250 rooms, 8 exquisite suites, and a full-service day spa. The public areas and restaurants follow a romantic theme with midnight-blue skies and twinkling stars. It's particularly appealing in Journey Wood Fired Steaks, where chefs grill steaks to perfection over mesquite—a nice dining choice even if you don't plan to play. At Crazy Olives, order your

than 6,500 works by 600 artists. The galleries include canvases by Willem de Kooning, Jackson Pollock, and Franz Kline. And we've fooled plenty of new visitors by pointing them to Duane Hanson's lifelike *Museum Guard*, and saying, "Go ask that guard where the bathroom is." It will only work once.

With the expansion comes breathing room for the Nelson's massive collections of European, Asian, and American Indian art, much of which has never been seen for lack of space. In addition, there's a more thoughtful approach to the displays; decorative arts, paintings, and sculpture from similar periods are grouped together to provide a fascinating look at life during that time. Highlights include rooms decorated with European and American furniture and art from 1200 to 1960, including furniture by Frank Lloyd Wright, Gustav Stickley, and Ludwig Mies van der Rohe. Educational areas have also been expanded, including the Ford Learning Center. Nelson-Atkins Friends of Art members receive significant discounts for classes, along with other valuable privileges. Check membership levels, for as little as $50 a year, on the Web site.

Seven large sculptures by Isamu Noguchi sit in a contemplative space that serves as a visual bridge to the sculpture garden outside. Once again, the pieces are gifts from the Hall Family Foundation. The Kansas City Sculpture Garden is delightful any time of day or night. This 22-acre urban oasis is dotted with 30 stellar pieces of art by such masters as Renoir and Alexander Calder, and the Oldenburg–van Bruggen whimsical and often-photographed 18-foot-tall *Shuttlecocks*, from the Sosland family, which turn the green space into a giant's badminton court. And if you find your jaw dropping as you count the number of large Henry Moore pieces, yes, you're quite right: We have 13 of these masterpieces. Once again, a tip of the hat to the generosity of the Hall family. Audio guides are available at the information desk. As you stroll the 0.7 miles, take care to notice that much of the time you're literally walking over the Bloch Building.

A visit to the museum should include a meal at what *Travel Holiday* magazine called "the prettiest cafe in the Midwest," the open-air Rozzelle Court restaurant, with stone columns, massive trees, and a cascading fountain. The cafeteria-style line might pull you back from your mental vacation, but the menu of artistically arranged salads, delicious soups, and desserts won't disappoint. Rozzelle is open for lunch Tues through Sun, 11 a.m. to 3 p.m. and dinner from 5 to 8 p.m. Thurs through Sat. Seasonal terrace seating looks onto the museum's spectacular new entry plaza with Walter De Maria's *One Sun/34 Moons* as its centerpiece. This sculpture is situated over the parking garage—surely the most beautiful place for cars in the country—where it casts a heavenly glow. The watery view will cost you; parking is $5, but free for members. Admission to the museum, however, is free. To plan your visit, check out **www.nelson-atkins.org** or call (816) 561-4000.

favorite martinis, appetizers, and sandwiches to go with a side: live entertainment. Terrace Buffet's cozy environment will tempt you with breakfast, lunch, and dinner selections seven days a week.

For real action go from the dining table to a gaming table. There are 42 in all, plus what *Casino Player* magazine calls "Missouri's loosest slots." You can try your luck at 1,800 of them for a nickel to $10 a pull. The Casino Stage Bar is where to find live entertainment Thurs through Sat.

HARRAH'S NORTH KANSAS CITY CASINO & HOTEL
One Riverboat Dr., North Kansas City
(816) 472-7777, (800) HARRAHS
www.harrahs.com

Harrah's offers the whole package: an exciting casino, a luxury hotel, five restaurants, and fabulous live music in the rockin' VooDoo Lounge. You may never want to leave, especially when you see the gorgeous two-story casino. Take your winnings, or at least your hunger, to a buffet bonanza, Italian restaurant, or sizzling filet dinner at the Range Steakhouse. Or count your coins back in your suite and order room service, available 24 hours a day.

i When planning a day at an area attraction, don't forget that Kansas City's weather can change at the drop of a rain hat. Check the weather to see if you need to bring a warm wrap, umbrella, or sunscreen—or all three. Updated weather can be found online at www.kansascity.com.

ISLE OF CAPRI CASINO
1800 E. Front St.
(816) 855-7777, (800) THE ISLE (843-4753)
www.isleofcapricasino.com
Welcome to the islands, mon, and have a nice day. The Isle of Capri is like visiting a tropical resort with bright colors, a two-story waterfall, lush landscaping, and the sound of island drums. If your button-down shirt gets in the way, simply replace it with a festive print at the Banana Cabana kiosk. The casino floor offers more than 1,000 slots and 30 table games and a chance to win big at Missouri's only Free Pull Machine. If you've worked up an appetite, you'll find several eateries, ranging from steakhouses to ice cream parlors.

ENTERTAINMENT DISTRICTS

Oh sure, you'll want to spend at least one day on our famous Country Club Plaza. But don't miss our other areas that offer festivals and fairs along with enough nightclubs, unique shops, and restaurants to keep you entertained for an afternoon or a weekend.

THE COUNTRY CLUB PLAZA
(816) 753-0100
www.countryclubplaza.com
No matter what you've read or heard about the Plaza, you're bound to be amazed by its beauty. Picture 14 blocks of Spanish-style buildings filled with retailers and restaurants, nightclubs and coffeehouses, antiques shops, and tiny boutiques. And in every corner and alleyway, courtyard, and median you'll discover a sculpture in bronze or marble, a lacy wrought-iron gate, a painted tile mural, a fountain, or flower bed. Entire books have been devoted to the Plaza, and you'll need three brochures just to try to see it all: a walking tour of artwork and fountains, a dining and entertaining guide, and a retail map. You'll find all of these and more on the Web site above.

Show up in spring and you'll share sidewalks with the 6-foot-tall Easter bunnies that have delighted generations of children and adults; this is also the season when flowering bulbs fill the gardens and people fill the sidewalk cafes. During summer you'll enjoy the free weekend music series, as well as the ice cream, iced cappuccinos, and icy martinis waiting at dozens of cafes and shops. In September the Plaza Art Fair turns the place into a giant neighborhood block party with 250 artists, live music, and food vendors. And starting on Thanksgiving night, miles of colored lights outline every spire and arch and swag— the Plaza's holiday gift to the world.

Plan to leave plenty of room in your suitcase; the Plaza puts Rodeo Drive to shame with more than 180 stores and boutiques. You'll find fashion's aristocracy, such as Armani, Brooks Brothers, BCBG, Ann Taylor, Betsey Johnson, and St. John and three glittering floors of fashion, housewares, and giftwares at our hometown department store, Halls. Make yourself over at MAC Cosmetics or Bare Escentuals, or make over your home with something from Pottery Barn, Restoration Hardware, or Scandia Home by Ursula Terrasi. Younger kids will go for places like Zoom, a fabulous toy store. Whew! Ready for a break? Then you'll love the fact that the Plaza is home to 40 restaurants, bistros, and pubs, from one-of-a-kind eateries like re:Verse, Starker's Restaurant, and Bo Lings Chinese Restaurant, to national favorites like McCormick & Schmick's, the Capital Grille, and Cheesecake Factory.

If you're ready to have someone else do the walking for a change, take a carriage ride with Pride of Kansas City Carriage (816-531-1999) or

Surrey's Carriage (816-531-2673). These tours-on-the-hoof are fun during the day but really turn on the romance at night with white lights and glowing lanterns. Parking is plentiful and free.

CROWN CENTER
2450 Grand Blvd.
(816) 274-8444
www.crowncenter.com
In 1968 Joyce C. Hall, founder of Hallmark Cards, and his son, Don J. Hall, turned an eyesore called Signboard Hill into one of the city's most vibrant entertainment centers. Crown Center became one of the nation's earliest mixed-use developments and a model for how to do urban redevelopment right. At the information booth near the main entrance, pick up a map of the outdoor sculptures, including an Alexander Calder, plus fountains and landmarks throughout the 85-acre complex and surrounding neighborhood.

But what makes this complex the Rockefeller Plaza of the Midwest is Crown Center Square, with fountains and terraced lawns where events take place all year. The Entertainment Pavilion with its free-form tent is home to free family activities, including concerts and outdoor movies, throughout summer, and from Nov to Mar it's transformed into the city's only outdoor ice-skating rink. Each winter the 100-foot mayor's Christmas tree becomes the square's glowing focal point.

Within Crown Center are more than 50 unique shops—standouts include home-grown Halls and Function Junction—and restaurants, a movie complex, and two live stage venues: the American Heartland Theatre and the Coterie Family Theatre. The Hallmark Visitor Center provides a look at the greeting card company's history (you'll learn why the wackiest line is called Shoebox), and at Kaleidoscope kids can exercise their creative muscles.

POWER & LIGHT DISTRICT
1100 Walnut Downtown
www.powerandlightdistrict.com
This $850 million retail, entertainment, and housing district has brought Kansas City's long-slumbering downtown back among the living. And how! The district connects the areas between Bartle Hall Convention Center, the new Sprint Center, and downtown's hotels. At its heart is the 17-story H&R Block world headquarters, that glowing green oval that also includes an art gallery and theater. And proving that they don't build 'em like they used to, two magnificent theaters were renovated as part of the mix—the Midland and the long-vacant Empire Theatre, which was renamed as AMC's flagship Main Street Theatre. Dining options are plentiful, with Kansas City favorites the Bristol Seafood Grill joining popular national names such as Gordon Biersch Brewery, Lucky Strike Lanes, and 801 Chophouse. Howl at the Moon offers a sing-along venue, while Mosaic Lounge's DJs spins your favorites all night long. One entire block is reserved for Kansas City Live!, a multilevel design with tented space for live music performances. Visitors and residents alike will be encouraged to stay and play with sidewalk bistros, pretty landscaping, and green spaces.

RIVER MARKET
North of 5th St. from Broadway Bridge to Heart of America Bridge
(816) 842-1271
www.kansascityrivermarket.com
When it comes to attractions, this one really produces, literally. Since 1857 it's been home to the biggest farmers' market in the Midwest. But there's plenty happening here besides ripe tomatoes. The River Market is a laid-back neighborhood that's fun to explore on foot. You might even find a treasure to ship back home at the Kansas City Artists Coalition (816-421-5222) at 201 Wyandotte, where a variety of artists show work from cutting-edge to classic.

Then follow your nose to Planters Seed and Spice Company at 513 Walnut, where you'll find bins overflowing with every fragrant herb, seed, and coffee bean imaginable. Antiques hunters will go nuts in the 30,000-square-foot River Market Antique (816-221-0220) at 115 West 5th St. Other antiques are on view—this time reclaimed treasures from a boat that sank in 1856—at Ara-

bia Steamboat Museum, 400 Grand St. (see listing in Museums).

Newer shops are taking residence as well, including Urban Dwellings Design (412 Delaware, 816-569-4314), a shop and design studio filled with furnishings that would feel at home in a sleek condo or a traditional abode. You wouldn't be the first to show up and tell designer/owner Jaclyn Banash, "I'll take everything." The trio of friendly birds, however, isn't for sale. New restaurants have joined the neighborhood as well, prompting a monthly wine walk. You'll want to start or end at the Farmhouse (3rd and Delaware, 816-569-6032), known for its focus on local produce. How handy to have a farmers' market close enough to smell the tomatoes!

VILLAGE WEST
Intersection of I-70 and I-435
Kansas City, KS
(913) 788-3700
www.legendsshopping.com
This shopping, dining, and entertainment district surrounding the Kansas Speedway quickly became the state's biggest draw. Sports enthusiasts can find all camo, all the time at Cabela's (where little ones can stare for hours at the big fish in the huge aquarium), moms can outfit an entire home at Nebraska Furniture Mart, and we can all get a little retail therapy at dozens of specialty and fashion stores, many of which are the first ones to open in the Midwest.

Find a hot bargain at an outlet stores, then chill out over a cool drink at one of the many restaurants and bars. We guarantee kids will think the country's first T-Rex Cafe is dino-mite. Just save room for Sheridan's frozen custard after dinner.

If all that's not enough, Village West tempts you to stay longer with live entertainment, a 60-foot fountain display, and a walking tour that celebrates 80 famous Kansans (we're waiting for our plaque to go up any day now).

WESTPORT
Westport Rd. between Main St. and
Southwest Trafficway
www.westportkcmo.com

Westport got its start in 1833 when John Calvin McCoy built a trading post on the northeast corner of Westport Road and Pennsylvania. By 1836 the area's colorful population of 50 or so included scouts Kit Carson and Jim Bridger as well as John Sutter, a guy who skipped town to escape creditors and look for gold. The area also played a bloody role in the Civil War when the Battle of Westport became known as the Gettysburg of the West. Learn more at www.westporthistorical.org.

Today Westport is still a stopping point for thirsty and hungry travelers. Lucky for you, prairie dog is no longer on the menu; instead you'll find dining choices including award-winning bluestem, chic (and gay-friendly) Bistro 303, and Westport Flea Market, home of the town's best burger—make that the world's best burger—plus bars and live music venues. And instead of spurs and cattle prods, shops offer candles, handcrafted jewelry, and garden art.

Most of us agree that a trip to Kansas City isn't complete without visiting Kelly's Westport Inn (500 Westport Rd., 816-561-5800, www.kellyswestportinn.com), the city's oldest standing building. Built in 1837, it was once a grocery store operated by Albert Boone, grandson of Daniel.

HISTORICAL CHURCHES

CATHEDRAL OF THE IMMACULATE CONCEPTION
416 W. 12th St.
(816) 842-0416
www.kcgolddome.org
In 1882 the dome of this neoclassic-style church was the highest point in the city. Today it's dwarfed by its steel-and-glass neighbors, but the gleam from the 23-karat gold leaf dome outshines everything in sight. Masses are held at 12:15 p.m. Mon through Fri; at 2:30 and 4:30 p.m. on Sat; and at 9 and 11 a.m., and 6 and 8 p.m. Sun.

COMMUNITY CHRISTIAN CHURCH
47th and Main
(816) 561-6531
www.community-christian.org

When Frank Lloyd Wright designed this church in the 1930s, technology couldn't produce the shaft of light he envisioned coming from the top of the dome. The beam would have to wait another 60 years for artist Dale Eldred to make it work, but even he wouldn't be around to see it. A year after his death, in December 1994, the Steeple of Light, which includes four xenon lights at 300 million candlepower each, was switched on. The lights shine heavenward every weekend and nightly through the holiday season.

COMMUNITY OF CHRIST TEMPLE AND AUDITORIUM
1001 W. Walnut
Independence, MO
(816) 521-3045
www.cofchrist.org
With its silver spiral reaching skyward, the Community of Christ Temple is one of the country's most visually stunning structures. From the inside, looking up toward the ceiling as it rises 195 feet, the design becomes organic—a giant seashell glowing bright white.

In 1831 Joseph Smith designated Independence as the new site for the city of Zion, and today this international Mormon headquarters serves a denomination of 250,000 members. Visitors are welcome to experience the Worshiper's Path, a reflective walkway filled with symbolic artwork leading to the 1,600-seat sanctuary. The room is large, but when the 102-rank pipe organ is played, the very walls seem to vibrate with the powerful sound. Time your visit for one of the free recitals, which are held daily. The auditorium was designed in the 1920s and features a 5,800-seat chamber with seating in the round beneath a domed ceiling. Within the space is the Children's Peace Pavilion, an interactive museum dedicated to promoting peace through example.

THE CHURCH OF JESUS CHRIST OF LATTER-DAY SAINTS
937 W. Walnut
Independence, MO
(816) 836-3466
www.lds.org

Learn about the key role the Church of Jesus Christ of Latter-day Saints (the Mormons) played in the early and often tempestuous history of Independence. The visitor center houses rare artifacts and artwork documenting the history and beliefs of the Mormons. Exhibits include a re-creation of a log cabin; the two-story mural titled *The Second Coming of Jesus Christ* is splendid. The center is 1 mile south of the Truman Library on the corner of River Road and West Walnut and is open from 9 a.m. to 9 p.m. daily for free guided tours.

UNITY WORLD HEADQUARTERS
1901 Northwest Blue Pkwy.
(816) 524-3550
www.unityworldhq.org
Unity Village's beautiful, 165-foot-tall bell tower can be seen for miles throughout the southwest part of the city; its teachings touch lives around the world. Unity has been offering nondenominational ministry, prayer, and education since 1889, and its monthly spiritual publication, *Daily Word* (www.dailyword.com), is translated into nine languages with an annual circulation of 1.3 million. Its Silent Prayer ministry receives more than two million requests for prayer assistance annually.

Unity Village's Mediterranean-style buildings, two of which are on the National Register of Historic Places, are situated among 1,400 acres of beautifully landscaped grounds, with meditation chapels, fountains, and reflecting pools. The showplace rose garden, with more than 800 rose bushes and 50 varieties, is at its prettiest June through Oct. Free tours start at the visitor center and are available 9 a.m. to 4 p.m. Mon through Thurs, 10 a.m. to 1 p.m. Fri through Sun. The guided walking tour, which includes a 12-minute video presentation about Unity's history, takes about an hour and is equal to 2 city blocks; there are two flights of stairs. The tour can be modified to be wheelchair-accessible with advance notice. Guided tours must be booked in advance; call (816) 251-3578.

HISTORICAL HOMES

If you like looking at homes—really old homes—we've got 'em. Several of these mid-1800s era houses are on the National Register of Historic Places. Although you'll see a wide variety of styles, from simple cabin to opulent Victorian, there is a recurring theme. Most of these homes were directly on or near the famous trails heading west; in one case the backyard was turned into corduroy by thousands of wagon wheels.

BINGHAM-WAGGONER ESTATE
313 W. Pacific
Independence, MO
(816) 461-3491
www.bwestate.org
If there ever was a superhighway in the mid-1800s, it was the Santa Fe Trail, and this estate had a front row seat. In fact, in 1999 wagon "swales" were discovered on the southern 19 acres, which suggests this was a shortcut to the trail. You can see these paths by going behind the house, crossing the footbridge, and looking along a line of trees.

History was made inside the 1827 house as well. Of its many colorful residents, the most famous was George Caleb Bingham, an artist and early-day political activist who used brushstrokes to demonstrate his feelings about the Civil War. When a Union general issued the infamous command that left countless residents of Jackson County homeless, Bingham painted *Order No. 11* here. Other works are in the American Paintings section of the Nelson-Atkins Museum of Art. In 1870 he sold the home and moved to Kansas City.

The Waggoner family purchased the house in 1879 and produced its Queen of the Pantry Flour in the mill across the street. Three generations of this family occupied the home over the next hundred years. Today the house and its acreage are recognized as one of the more significant historical sites in western Missouri. Inside are many furnishings of the time, including a massive dining room table and a walk-in icebox. The home is open for tours from Apr to Oct and during the Christmas season. Admission is $4 for adults, $2.50 for seniors, and $1 for ages 6 to 16.

1859 JAIL, MARSHAL'S HOME, AND MUSEUM
217 Main
(816) 252-1892
www.jchs.org
Just think: In the mid-1800s prisoners didn't have TVs or phones. Okay, no one did. But you'll still be amazed at these dungeonlike cells that held Frank James, William Clark Quantrill of Quantrill's Raiders, and others crossways with the law. Actually, the cell that held Frank James was opulently outfitted by his many adoring fans, and he took his meals with the jailer's family. But in other "guest" quarters, barred windows, double iron doors, and leg chains provide a chilling look at frontier justice. The jail and the marshal's home have been restored to period and contain an outstanding historical collection. Tours are given seven days a week Mar through Dec. Closed Thanksgiving, Christmas, Jan, and Feb. Admission is $3.50 for adults, $2 for ages 6 to 16, and free for under 6.

HARRY S. TRUMAN HOME
219 N. Delaware St.
Independence, MO
(816) 254-9929
The simple charm of the Summer White House speaks volumes about the man who chose to be buried in his hometown rather than beside a towering monument in Washington, D.C.

Bess Truman's grandparents built the Victorian home in 1885; she grew up here, and she and Harry lived here when they weren't in Washington, D.C. The furnishings are just as they were when she died in 1982, right down to the dishcloth by the sink and Harry's hat by the door. The house is open year-round and tours are conducted every 15 minutes. We suggest you arrive early because tickets are issued starting at 8:30 a.m. on a first-come, first-served basis. Tickets are available at the Truman Home Ticket and Information Center at Truman Road and Main Street, where you can watch a short slide show about the Trumans. Admission is $4, free for those under 17. Guided walking tours of the neighborhood leave from the center daily from 9 a.m. to 4:45 p.m. Memorial Day through Labor Day.

HARRY S. TRUMAN OFFICE AND COURTROOM
112 W. Lexington
(816) 795-8200
The office where the 33rd U.S. president began his political career as a county judge is chiefly unchanged since the day he left for a higher calling. An audiovisual show traces Truman's life before his presidency. Tours are available Tues through Thurs and Sat; the courthouse is closed on federal holidays.

INDEPENDENCE SQUARE
(816) 252-0608
www.theindependencesquare.com
Independence has it all: infamous outlaws and a hometown hero, bloody border battles of the Civil War, and opulent homes. At its heart is Independence Square, which marked the beginnings of Harry S. Truman's political career and the journey for thousands heading west. Within the old-fashioned town square you'll find the 1859 Jail and Truman Office and Courtroom (described above) as well as antiques shops, unique stores, and restaurants. And there's a phosphate or banana split waiting for you at Clinton's Soda Fountain (100 West Maple), where a young Harry once scooped ice cream and mopped the floor. He'd later say his weekly salary of three silver dollars looked like three million.

JESSE JAMES BANK MUSEUM
Court House Square
Liberty, MO
(816) 781-4458
www.jessejames.org
Did the James Gang really steal $60,000 from this bank in February 1866? We'll never know for sure, but it makes a great story. Regardless of who done it, this is the site of the first daylight peacetime bank robbery in the United States. You can tour the bank with its stone vault, iron safe, and

Civil War–era teller's window. The bank museum is open year-round. Admission is $4 for adults, $3.50 for seniors, $1.50 for ages 8 to 15, and free for those under 8.

JESSE JAMES FARM AND MUSEUM
21216 Jesse James Farm Rd.
Kearney, MO
(816) 628-6065, (800) FUN-CLAY
www.jessejames.org
Where else but in the Wild West would people idolize a man who robbed trains and banks? But Jesse James wasn't just a typical hoodlum. His boldness and flamboyance—helped along by sensationalized newspaper articles and dime novels—turned him into a modern-day Robin Hood. Jesse was born in this house in 1847, the son of a Baptist minister. The young man's religious upbringing apparently didn't take; after a stint in the Civil War he joined with other former Confederate guerrillas to lead the James Gang.

A tour of the home begins with a short film recapping the exploits of James and his older brother, Frank. Artifacts include Jesse's boots and spurs and Frank's letter of surrender. You can also stroll along the stream where the boys played as youngsters and pass Jesse's original burial site, where his mother once sold souvenir stones from his grave. The woman figured since visitors were taking them anyway, she might as well make a profit. The home is open year-round and often hosts dramatic reenactments. Admission is $7.50 for adults, $6.50 for seniors, $4 for children 8 to 15, and free for those under 8.

JOHN WORNALL HOUSE MUSEUM
146 W. 61st Terrace
(816) 444-1858
www.wornallhouse.org
Today this stately 1858 Greek Revival structure sits peacefully amid other lovely homes near Loose Park. But during three days in October 1864, the antebellum home's wide front porch was stained with blood when it served as an army hospital. The home's 500-acre farm was at the vortex of the Civil War's largest battle west of the Mississippi.

As a museum, the Wornall House provides an intriguing look at the lives of early settlers. Well-informed docents and staff take visitors through rooms filled with period furnishings, including a foursquare grand piano in the parlor and Lincoln rocker in the master bedroom. From Oct through May actors re-create a typical day in the mid-1800s. Several programs are mounted throughout the year, such as holiday candlelight tours and Civil War reenactments on the grounds. The museum is part of a 25-stop driving tour of the Battle of Westport; other sites include Loose Park and a rise near the Big Blue River that was known as Bloody Hill. Brochures are available from the Parks and Recreation Department (816-513-7500, 4600 East 63rd St.). The museum is open Tues through Sun; closed in Jan. Admission is $6 for adults, $5 for seniors and students, and free for ages four and under.

RICE-TREMONTI HOME
66th and Blue Ridge Blvd.
(816) 358-7423
www.rice-tremonti.com
In 1844, Archibald Rice's 160 acres were a popular place to camp while waiting for spring before heading west on the trails. The homestead wasn't as fancy as some others still with us today, but that's the key to its fascination; its furnishings provide a glimpse into the way families lived in what was once wilderness. The home is now on the National Register of Historic Places.

One of the most interesting attractions is a replica of Aunt Sophia's cabin, where the family's slave lived. Sophia would cook the meals here and then carry them to the main house. Tours are available Sat and Sun from May through Sept.

THOMAS HART BENTON HOME AND STUDIO
3616 Belleview
(816) 931-5722
www.mostateparks.com/benton
If you're a fan of this famous Kansas City artist, this tour is a must. If you're not familiar with his work, there's ample opportunity to discover it in the Benton section of the Nelson-Atkins Museum

of Art and a mural that fills a wall at the Truman Library.

His painting style was bigger than life, a colorful montage of voluptuous women, powerful men, and landscapes that seemed to rise and swirl as if in a tornado. The Benton home remains exactly as it was when the artist went outside to sign a painting and dropped dead in 1975. His brushes and paints, pipe, and harmonica are casually placed as if waiting for his big rough hands to take them up. His wife, Rita, died a few months later, but her famous spaghetti sauce lives on. Make sure to pick up a copy of her recipe in the kitchen. The tour is open seven days a week; admission is $4 for adults, $2.50 ages 6 to 12. If you have time, stroll around the lovely Belleview homes district; minimansions line the streets, and the landscaping is exquisite, particularly in spring when the pink and white azaleas are in bloom.

UNION STATION
30 W. Pershing Rd.
(816) 460-2222
www.unionstation.org
After a second flood devastated the Union Depot in the West Bottoms, the city knew it needed to build a rail station on higher ground. Several years and $5.8 million later, the result was the City Beautiful movement's most spectacular testament to date. When Union Station opened on October 30, 1914, it was the third largest train facility in the world after New York's Grand Central and Pennsylvania Stations. More than 100,000 people jammed the 400- by 800-foot Grand Hall for the grand opening ceremony, with thousands more pushing into the football field–size North Waiting Room.

This magnificent Beaux Art structure was more than a train terminal; it was the city's town hall, where people came to dine at Fred Harvey's restaurant and dance on New Year's Eve. "Meet me under the clock" was a common phrase as friends looked for familiar faces under the 6 ½-foot-wide dial. Army boots echoed through the marble halls as more than half of all World War II soldiers boarded trains here.

i When you go to Union Station, remember that there really was a Union Station Massacre. It happened on June 17, 1933, when four people were killed during an attempt to free a notorious federal prisoner. You can still see the stray machine-gun bullet lodged in a wall near Union Station's east entrance.

But by the 1950s travel by rail was a thing of the past, and the station's depot was relegated to a walk-up window on one side. The last Amtrak train pulled out in 1985. Finally, city leaders had two choices: Restore it or tear it down.

They decided to bring it back to life, financed with a bi-state cultural tax in 1996, the first such two-state, five-county program in the country. After more than $250 million and years of work, Union Station and its new Science City museum opened in November 1999. As you walk through the Grand Hall and North Waiting Room, be sure to look at the ornate ceilings 95 feet above you. These plaster swirls and ribbons, oak leaves, and rosette medallions—sky-blue, gold, and terra-cotta—were meticulously restored by artisans, including a team from Liverpool, England, that helped restore the fire-ravaged Windsor Castle. Crystal chandeliers, all 3,000 pounds of them, sparkle like new.

Union Station is once again a place to celebrate and meet friends under the clock before enjoying an elegant meal at Pierpont's, where the gorgeous bar alone is enough to make a conductor whistle.

VAILE VICTORIAN MANSION
1500 N. Liberty
Independence, MO
(816) 325-7430
www.vailemansion.org

As pretty as a wedding cake, this 31-room mansion features gables and towers, lacy trim, and Gothic windows. Its highest peak is adorned with grillwork that looks like a crown, a fitting reference for a town called "Queen City of the Trails."

The house was built in 1881 for Harvey Merrick Vaile, a prosperous lawyer, rancher, and, as

you'll see, rather wicked fellow. The home was filled with unheard-of conveniences like flushing toilets and a 48,000-bottle wine cellar. In the master bedroom a reclining woman (minus more than just her high-button shoes) was painted on the ceiling. Other interesting but less scandalous artwork appears elsewhere: As was the norm, the builder used inexpensive pine in the upper floors and then had it painted to look like more costly mahogany or cherry wood. If you look closely at the faux graining in the second-floor smoking room, you'll notice faces and animals incorporated into the swirls and dips.

After the owner's death in 1894, the home became a sanatorium and then a nursing home. It was nearly demolished before the DeWitt family bought it in the 1960s. The family, along with members of the Vaile Victorian Society, restored this home to a fare-thee-well and are pleased to invite you in. The home is open seven days a week from Apr through Oct and certain days in Dec, when it is beautifully decorated for holiday tours. Admission is $5 for adults, $3.50 for seniors, and $2 for ages 6 through 16.

i One of the most freewheeling ways to see our sites is on a Segway. Zip by Union Station, get a taste of the Crossroads Arts District, tour the Country Club Plaza, or take a Segway Safari at the Kansas City Zoo. Tours last from 45 minutes to just over two hours (about the time it would take us to learn to operate the motorized wheels) and cost $40 to $80. Contact Segway Experience at (816) 531-0600 or www.segway experience.com.

HISTORICAL MUSEUMS AND SITES

AMERICAN JAZZ MUSEUM
18th and Vine
(816) 474-8463
www.americanjazzmuseum.com

Jazz. It was America's music, and in the 1920s and 1930s no place played it with more passion than Kansas City. Some of the greats, like Count Basie,

Bennie Moten, and Charlie "Yardbird" Parker, got their starts, made their names, or honed their craft here. Many stayed; some headed to the even brighter lights of New York. The American Jazz Museum is the first in the country devoted exclusively to this art form.

Dozens of interactive displays provide a glimpse of this historical, hysterical time when music poured out of dozens of nightclubs 24 hours a day. You can become part of it, if only for an hour or so, by listening to hundreds of the greatest jazz recordings ever made, including Ella Fitzgerald scatting through "A Tisket, A Tasket" and Big Joe Turner singing—what else?—"Goin' to Kansas City." Little hipsters aren't left out. In the Wee-Bop Room, children can play audio engineer at the mixing station; experiment with harmony, melody, and rhythm; and learn the range and sounds of different instruments. The museum is open Tues through Sat 9 a.m. to 6 p.m., Sun noon to 6 p.m. Admission is $6 for adults, $2.50 for children. A combination ticket to the American Jazz Museum and the Negro Leagues Baseball Museum costs $8 and $4, respectively.

ARABIA STEAMBOAT MUSEUM
400 Grand Ave.
(816) 471-4030 (information)
(816) 471-1856 (group reservations)
www.1856.com
Who hasn't dreamed of finding buried treasure? Bob Hawley and sons David and the late Greg Hawley, along with Jerry Mackey and their families, put their dreams to work by uncovering the steamboat *Arabia* 132 years after it sank on its way from Westport to Parkville, Missouri. When the 171-foot boat went down, a quick-thinking crew got all 130 passengers off safely, with the exception of one lone mule. But 222 tons of goods drifted to a watery grave, including frontier-bound tools and dishware, shoes, and buttons . . . and 400 barrels of Kentucky bourbon. A few ladies were devastated to learn they wouldn't get the perfume they'd ordered from France.

Using an old river map, the Hawley and Mackey team located the boat in a cornfield ½ mile from the river's edge and began excavation

in 1988. It would be three torturous weeks before they uncovered the splintered remains of the left paddle wheel. Soon the men were bringing up box after box of treasure. The museum is a fascinating look at these remarkably preserved supplies, which *National Geographic Traveler* calls "A King Tut's tomb . . . a time capsule of another age!" It's believed to be the largest single collection of pre–Civil War frontier artifacts in the country. Once inside, visitors will see a replica of the *Arabia*'s side-wheel paddle slicing through the water; there's even part of the walnut tree that was its downfall. After a short movie about the steamboat's history and its excavation you can ask questions, and often the person with the colorful answers is named Hawley.

You can then walk through the display areas by yourself or attend one of the tours—worth waiting for—that begin every half hour. Children eight years old and up will enjoy the museum, and it is wheelchair-accessible. A gift shop sells books about the *Arabia* written by Greg and David Hawley, including a cute children's book, and an 1856 perfume based on bottles found within the dig. Allow at least 90 minutes to see it all. Admission is $12.50 for adults, $11.50 for seniors, and $4.75 for ages 4 to 12.

The museum is open seven days a week, closed on major holidays. The first tour begins at 10 a.m.; the last starts at 4 p.m.

> **i** Call ahead to find out if attractions offer tours, as these can greatly enhance your visit. One example is the *Arabia* Steamboat Museum in the River Market area, where the tour guide is occasionally one of the people who discovered the buried treasure. Often you can reserve space in the tour to guarantee your seat—not a bad idea during the busy summer or on weekends.

ELMWOOD CEMETERY
4900 Truman Rd.
(816) 231-0373, (877) 231-0373
www.historickcelmwood.org
Many of Kansas City's most important civic leaders were laid to rest in this European-style cemetery,

their wealth and social status evident in enormous monuments and mausoleums. Even the grounds are historic, created by the city's most respected landscape architect, George Kessler. The 43 acres served as an early drawing board for the parks and green spaces he would design during his career. Stop by the cemetery's office or go online for biographies of famous people buried here; guided tours are available for groups of 10 or more with advance reservation. There may be a fee; certainly donations are always welcome at this not-for-profit historic treasure.

In a sea of massive monuments, the most impressive by far is the Armour Chapel, a stone Gothic sanctuary dedicated to the memory of meatpacking magnate Kirkland Armour (1854–1901). Other elaborate resting places belong to Jacob Loose, founder of Sunshine Biscuits, whose estate donated the land for Loose Park, and Kersey Coates, an influential leader who helped develop downtown's Quality Hill. His Coates House Hotel was one of the finest in the Midwest.

A much smaller tombstone was laid for a very large woman, 6' 10" Leannah Loveall Kearnes, also known as Annie Chambers. Kansas City's most notorious madam, Annie changed her ways late in life and left her City Market property to the City Union Mission. Along with famous people, more than 700 Civil War veterans are buried here, as well as many who died in border wars. There are also a large number of Jewish burials from Congregation B'nai Jehudah Temple in two southwest acres, all facing east.

Self-guided tours of Elmwood are welcome until dusk Mon through Fri. Please check with the office before attempting to take any monument rubbings. At this time there is no fee.

HARRY S. TRUMAN LIBRARY AND MUSEUM
500 W. U.S. Highway 24
Independence, MO
(816) 833-1400
www.trumanlibrary.org
Independence is still wild about its native son, the 33rd president, who grew up in this town. When the library opened in 1957 it became only the second such archive in the country.

After a $22.5 million renovation completed in 2001, the museum and library does more than just tell Truman's story. As he wished, it challenges visitors to explore the decision-making process of that era and how it affects our lives today. Two new permanent exhibits include "The White House Decision Center," a behind-the-scenes look that lets visitors take on the roles of the president and his aides in a re-creation of the West Wing. A multimedia exhibit contains dozens of original artifacts and documents from before, during, and after Truman's presidency. Other features include the gravesites of Harry and his wife, Bess, the documentary film *Harry S. Truman: 1884–1972*, and a replica of Truman's Oval Office where you can listen to a tape of his voice and see the original THE BUCK STOPS HERE desk plaque.

This is a fascinating look at a leader who may be better regarded today than when he was in office, as we find a new appreciation for his honesty and frank-talking ways. And visitors are often surprised to discover the many ways Truman changed history: He proposed the first national health care plan, announced the end of the war in Europe, and signed peace treaties with other countries. He was also the president who dropped the first atomic bomb. The gift shop offers such keepsakes as replicas of Truman's famous THE BUCK STOPS HERE desk sign (for just 55 bucks) and pieces of the original red tape, which was strips of scarlet-colored twill used to bind U.S. documents during the Civil War. Now you know!

Museum admission is $7 for adults, $5 for those over 61, and $3 for ages 6 to 18. It's open seven days a week. Plan on spending at least one hour viewing the permanent displays and any special touring exhibit. Or consider making a day of it touring the other "Man from Missouri" attractions in Independence, including Independence Square and the Truman Home, both detailed in this chapter.

i Looking for a gift for your boss back home? Pick up a replica of Harry S. Truman's famous THE BUCK STOPS HERE desk signs, available in the gift shop of his museum. Just present it after you get that raise.

JOHNSON COUNTY MUSEUM OF HISTORY
6305 Lackman Rd.
Shawnee, KS
(913) 631-6709
www.jocomuseum.org

Although baby boomers might take issue with things from their childhoods ending up in a museum, the truth is that everyone will enjoy the 1950s All-Electric House. The ranch-style house, built in 1954 to showcase all the modern electric conveniences, was actually a model home in Prairie Village, a tidy Johnson County suburb. Now this was the life: a painting that slides back to reveal a black-and-white television, a remote control near Dad's recliner that closes the drapes and turns on the stereo, and a bedside dial that controls the lights throughout the house. Guess they hadn't discovered "clap on, clap off" technology yet. Other displays include actual home movies, toys from the '50s, and a snazzy 1955 two-tone Chevy Bel Air.

The main museum chronicles the county's growth from its beginnings as Indian Territory in 1820, its change to farmland, then suburbs, and now its role as one of the fastest-growing areas in the two-state region. Exhibits show—through more than 500 artifacts, documents, photos, and maps—various and often competing versions of "the good life." The first inhabitants, the Shawnee, are represented by items such as ceremonial clothing and an 1859 edition of *Hymns in the Shawnee Language*. There are also interactive displays and profiles of 33 individuals who helped shape the area over the past 175 years. The museum is open from 10 a.m. to 4:30 p.m. Tues through Sat and 1 to 4 p.m. Sun. The All-Electric House is open Tues through Sat from 1 to 4 p.m. Admittance to the museum is free; the house tour costs $2 for adults and $1 for children 12 and under (with tours every half hour). Poodle skirts not required.

KANSAS CITY MUSEUM OF HISTORY AND SCIENCE
3218 Gladstone Blvd.
(816) 483-8300
www.kcmuseum.com

When lumber baron Robert A. Long built his villa called Corinthian Hall in 1911, it cost a whopping $750,000, unheard of in those days. He was content with everything except the view. To improve it he moved three 4,000-square-foot mansions down the street. Perhaps that's where the phrase "not in my backyard" originated. The palatial space is now the Kansas City Museum, which houses interactive displays about the pioneering spirit of our early settlers.

Kids in particular will enjoy exploring the culture of the Osage Indians, visiting Chouteau's trading post, and climbing aboard a covered wagon heading west. Everybody will go for the 1910 soda fountain, where they still scoop a pretty good ice-cream cone. A tour of the mansion gives you a taste of how fortune's favored lived . . . but who needs a bowling alley anyway? The planetarium hosts seasonal star shows and educational programs throughout the year.

Take a self-directed tour Tues through Sun; student and group tours are also available with reservations. Call Union Station (816-460-2020). Admission is free, but suggested donation is $2.50 for adults and $2 for seniors and those 17 and under. Please note that the museum is closed for renovations at this writing; call to check its current status before visiting.

LIBERTY MEMORIAL AND WORLD WAR I MUSEUM
100 W. 26th St.
(816) 221-1918
www.theworldwar.org

At this monument's groundbreaking ceremony in 1921, the crowd watched as General John J. Pershing and the four other principal Allied commanders took the stage. It was the first and only time these men appeared in one place. Five years later, before a crowd of 100,000, President Calvin Coolidge dedicated the country's only memorial honoring the men and women who died during World War I. The city had a reason to be proud; it had taken only 10 days to raise the $2.5 million needed to build the monument. In today's dollars the contributions would be more than $20 million.

New York architect H. Van Buren Magonigle envisioned his 217-foot column as "an altar high raised in the sky with its flame of inspiration ever burning." That flame went out when the monument, crumbling and deemed unsafe, was closed in 1994. After a $30 million restoration project, the Liberty Memorial reopened with great fanfare on Memorial Day weekend 2002.

The project was financed by benefactors, private citizens, and the sale of granite bricks inscribed with names of brave loved ones long gone, including this author's father, John H. Van Luchene.

In 2007 extensive work was completed on the National World War I Museum, and it's as moving as the sight of the monument above. To enter the underground museum you'll cross a glass bridge and have one last view of the tower through the skylights before passing over a field of 9,000 red poppies, each one representing a man or woman who died fighting in the Great War. With over 50,000 artifacts, many never seen before, and interactive displays, it's a fascinating look at the physical, emotional, cultural, and political experiences during this time in history. Immersion galleries bring the combat to life through the eyes and ears of those who served. The museum store offers books, movies, music, and other materials related to WWI. The new Over There Café serves sandwiches, soups, snacks, and desserts, all named for people of the Great War. A kid's menu is available as well.

The museum is open Tues through Sun, 10 a.m. to 5 p.m., with the last ticket sold to tour the tower at 4:15 p.m. Ticket prices range from $6 for children to $12 for adults (those in active service are admitted free with our thanks). Be sure to ride the elevator (included in admittance) to the apex of the tower for a breathtaking 360-degree view of the skyline. Please do note, however, that visitors will need to climb the last 45 stairs.

NEGRO LEAGUES BASEBALL MUSEUM
1616 E. 18th St.
(816) 221-1920, (888) 221-6526
www.nlbm.com
Before the multimillion-dollar contracts, before the megabuck endorsement deals, there were men who played baseball just because they loved the game. And they continued to suit up and take the field even when major league teams shut them out because of their color. This museum, the only one of its kind in the country, follows the history of the Negro National League, beginning with its formation at the nearby Paseo YMCA in 1920. Out of that came the Monarchs, one of the league's most exciting teams thanks to players like Satchel Paige, Cool Papa Bell, Connie Johnson, and John Jordan "Buck" O'Neil. Oh, man, could these guys play ball.

Two short videos tell the stories of games played here and on the road, and an impressive display of memorabilia brings them to life. You'll see documents and photos that demonstrate the highs from wins and fans' adulation as well as the lows caused by segregation and racism. In this regard the exhibits transcend sports and hit at the very heart of our country at the time. Eventually the Negro Leagues ended for the same reason they started: sheer talent. The Brooklyn Dodgers recruited Monarchs player Jackie Robinson in 1945, and others soon followed. The leagues played their last game in 1960.

One of the museum's most striking displays is the Field of Legends, where life-size bronze players are positioned on a ball diamond. The 10 statues represent the first Negro League players inducted into the Hall of Fame in Cooperstown, New York. Trivia games test your knowledge about these heroes.

The museum is open Tues through Sun; admission is $8 for adults, $3 for kids 12 and under.

UNION CEMETERY WALKING TOUR
28th and Walnut
(816) 472-4990
www.uchskc.org
When 49-acre Union Cemetery was deeded in 1857, its planners thought it would provide enough burial space for the towns of Kansas and Westport for all time. Shortsighted? Not for two communities (we didn't become Kansas City until 1889) that had only 3,000 residents between them. It's estimated that 55,000 are buried here,

including veterans from every American war and cholera victims by the score. Some of our city's most famous citizens lie here as well, individuals whose granite-etched names are repeated on city street signs, schools, and historic home sites. Alexander Majors, whose company founded the Pony Express, is here, as is artist George Caleb Bingham. Lesser known (except to those he assisted) is Tillman Crabtree, Kansas City's first policeman. One of his duties was to carry women across the city's muddy streets.

The cemetery is open for self-guided tours seven days a week from 8:30 a.m. to 3:30 p.m. Maps with biographies of the most famous are available in a small box near the entrance gate or at the sexton's cottage, or visit the Web site for an interactive tour and map. Be sure to bring large sheets of paper and charcoal pencils to create rubbings of interesting stones.

i Kansas City's beautiful Power and Light Building, built in 1931, was once Photoshopped into the background of Gotham City in a Batman movie. The art deco structure is now the home of AMC Entertainment.

LANDMARKS

THE KANSAS CITY POWER & LIGHT BUILDING
14th and Baltimore
www.skyscrapers.com (click on "Kansas City")
The same year that New Yorkers were admiring their tallest skyscraper so far, the Empire State Building, we were agog at ours. In 1931 the Power & Light Building became the tallest building in Missouri. Architectural team Hoit, Price & Barnes knew this 31-story art deco beauty would eventually lose its tallest-structure status, so they added a bonus: a 97-foot pillar of lights at top that cycle among white, amber, red, and green. The building's setbacks, which give it a telescoping look, are also dramatized at night with hidden floodlights. The art deco theme is repeated inside with a sunburst motif in the brass elevator doors, radiator grills, and even the water fountain. You

may notice that one side of the building has no windows; its twin tower, planned for the west side, was never built.

CHARLIE PARKER MEMORIAL
1616 E. 18th St.
The name of sculptor Robert Graham's 17-foot bronze head of Charlie "Bird" Parker is *Bird Lives.* He certainly does, through his music. The Kansas City, Kansas, native, who changed the sound of jazz, is memorialized on a plaza behind the American Jazz Museum in the 18th and Vine District. This was a gift to Kansas City from philanthropists Tony and Marti Oppenheimer.

PIONEER MOTHER
Penn Valley Park (south of the entrance to the Liberty Memorial)
The inscription on this large bronze tells the story of thousands of women who gave up homes and families back east to start new lives. The passage from the Book of Ruth reads, "Whither thou goest, I will go and wither thou lodgest, I will lodge. Thy people will be my people, and thy God, my God."

ROSEDALE MEMORIAL ARCH
35th St. and Booth
Kansas City, KS
Based on the Arc de Triomphe in Paris, this monument pays tribute to soldiers who fought in World War I. It was designed by Rosedale resident John LeRoy Marshall and dedicated in 1923. The "War to End All Wars" wasn't, and 70 years later a monument was added to honor the soldiers of World War II, Korea, and the Vietnam conflict. High on a hill, the arch can be seen from miles away.

THE SCOUT
Penn Valley Park between Southwest Trafficway and Broadway (just off 31st St.)
This impressive statue of an Indian on horseback wasn't even meant to be ours; it rested here temporarily en route to its intended home at San Francisco's 1915 Panama-Pacific Expo. But Kansas Citians loved the sculpture so much they raised $15,000 to buy it. Now *The Scout* forever watches over our skyline from a hill in Penn Valley Park.

SKY STATIONS/PYLON CAPS
Atop H. Roe Bartle Hall
13th and Central
When these metal sculptures were mounted on tall, slender pylons 200 feet above Bartle Hall in 1994, they became one of our most dramatic landmarks—and one of the most hotly debated. Some pundits refer to them as "three whirligigs and a curling iron." George Jetson may disagree, but R. M. Fisher's designs were influenced not by the space age but by the art deco designs found throughout our downtown skyline.

NEIGHBORHOOD DRIVES

Take a rubbernecking drive through some of our most beloved neighborhoods filled with charming Tudors or jaw-dropping mansions. Most of the stunners were built between 1900 and 1940, but there are some up-and-comers, particularly on the Kansas side. And take note of the number of trikes and basketballs in the driveways of homes costing $2 million or more. Where do these whippersnappers get all that cash? We know for sure it's not from writing travel guides. Following are some of our favorite drives.

HALLBROOK
West of State Line, north of College Blvd. in Leawood, KS
What Hallbrook lacks in maturity—the area was developed just over two decades ago—it more than makes up for in sheer glamour. Its villas and minimansions lean toward Spanish and country French in design. Look for one jaw-dropper that's based on Tara from Gone with the Wind.

MISSION HILLS
Southwest of State Line Rd. and 53rd St., west of the Carriage Club
This lovely drive is another blessing from landscape architects and builders who let the lay of the land determine where streets and houses should be placed. Roads dip here and there, jogging gracefully around streams and skirting ancient trees. And the homes caught up in all this natural glory are simply magnificent. As you

drive southwest you'll pass Mission Hills Country Club and Kansas City Country Club golf courses on the west.

WARD PARKWAY
Beginning at W. 53rd St., southwest of the Country Club Plaza
No one will ask for your ticket to this attraction: It's a 4-mile drive on one of the country's most beautiful boulevards. We adore it, HGTV devoted an entire hour to it, and if you're visiting friends in Kansas City you're bound to get the grand tour at least once.

Ward Parkway has some of the priciest real estate in town. But even some locals don't know that it didn't cost a dime when J. C. Nichols began developing homes on these 500 acres near the turn of the 20th century. Businessman Hugh Ward donated the land to the city but died before the papers were signed. His wife, Vassie James Ward, followed through on the plan and requested that it be named for her late husband.

The new boulevard became a magnet for money, and during the early 1900s some of the most prominent families chose to build their homes, villas, and mansions here. The Tom Pendergast house at 5650 Ward Parkway is one of the most famous, while certainly the most striking is the Corrigan-Sutherland House on the corner of 55th and Ward Parkway. In 1912 Barney Corrigan commissioned flamboyant Kansas City architect Louis Curtiss to design the splendid 25-room home (a room for each of his 18 children, with space for more, it would seem). The modern Art Nouveau style was constructed of concrete with a Carthage cut-stone facing and magnificent tree-motif stained glass. The estate cost around $200,000, but, alas, the 66-year-old Corrigan didn't live to see it finished. He died on January 6, 1914, on his way to inspect the home's progress. The property was then purchased by the Sutherland lumber family, who remained here for several decades.

Though the homes' opulence turned this into a street of dreams, the green spaces made it a paradise. Today people jog, walk dogs, and bike along its tree-shaded sidewalks, and kids play tag football on wide medians that form miniparks. The boulevard was designed by renowned landscape architect George Kessler along with father-and-son team Hare & Hare. As for the remarkable fountains, sculptures, and urns that grace Ward Parkway, those were gifts from J. C. Nichols.

WESTWOOD HILLS
West of State Line Rd. on 50th St.
Although this is one of the smaller cities in both size (less than 1 square mile) and number of residents (around 390), it's earned the right to its nickname, "the Prettiest Little City in Kansas." Darling cottages and elegant estates are sprinkled along roads that dip and twist, and massive trees cross the streets to create overhead umbrellas. Be sure to stop in for a mango-flavored Jet Tea at the Hi Hat Coffee Shop (5012 State Line, 913-831-0341); there's enough ginseng in this golden-yellow smoothie to power your trip back home.

OBSERVATION POINTS

CITY HALL OBSERVATION DECK
414 E. 12th St.
(816) 274-1444
www.kcmo.org
The only place to get a better look at the city is from an airplane. Our stunning art deco–style City Hall provides a breathtaking view from its 30th floor open-air deck 425 feet above downtown. And while you're waiting for the elevator, check out the friezes and celestial-themed lighting fixtures in the lobby. The art continues outside with 16 panels just above the sixth floor that depict major events in our city's history. This steel and limestone stunner, designed by architect firm Wight & Wight, was completed in 1937 at a cost of $5 million. The deck is open Mon through Fri from 8 a.m. to 4:15 p.m. To reach it take the lobby elevator to the 28th floor, and then take the stairs. There's no charge.

CLIFF DRIVE
Gladstone Blvd. and Elmwood
www.cliffdrive.org

You're just in time to enjoy this 6-mile roadway that was recently restored to its turn-of-the-20th-century splendor. Although today the view from Cliff Drive isn't so hot—a jumble of train tracks and industrial buildings—it's a pleasant diversion with places to pull over and consider what it must have been like to negotiate the curves in a horse and carriage.

You can thank landscape architect George Kessler for retaining its natural beauty back in 1893 along with the surrounding 282-acre North Terrace Park. In fact you might see rappellers risking knees and elbows on the rugged limestone cliff that gives the road its name. For a more civilized look, stay in the car; that way you can also tool around the historic Northeast area, including the Scarritt Renaissance neighborhood bound by Independence Boulevard and the park. More than 120 homes and churches are listed as local historic landmarks. A good place to start is the Kansas City Museum on Gladstone Boulevard (see details in Museums), a mansion-turned-museum that hints at the area's opulence at one time.

LEWIS AND CLARK POINT
Eighth St. and Jefferson
www.lewisandclarktrail.com
Stand at the bluffs overlooking where the Kansas and Missouri Rivers meet and try to imagine what Meriwether Lewis and William Clark were thinking on September 15, 1806. The expedition team was returning from an arduous trip to Oregon. They were exhausted and no doubt thirsty, but they wouldn't find refreshment here. Clark had deemed the Kaw "disagreeably tasted" on their first stopover two years earlier. No doubt.

The three-day encampment is now memorialized by Eugene Daub's sculpture *Corps of Discovery* at Jefferson and Eighth Streets on the bluffs of what is now Quality Hill. Dedicated in 2001, the 18-foot-high bronze depicts Lewis, Clark, their Shoshone Indian interpreter, Sacagawea, Clark's black slave, York, and Lewis's dog, Seaman. It's the nation's largest monument to honor the expedition. Check the back of Seaman's tail for a surprise: the artist's face!

i Looking for a bird's-eye view of our beautiful city? Take the elevator to the top of the Liberty Memorial's 217-foot column in the sky. You'll overlook our skyline and, just below the monument, our grand Union Station.

OUT AND ABOUT

DEANNA ROSE CHILDREN'S FARMSTEAD
138th St. and Switzer Rd.
Overland Park, KS
(913) 897-2360
www.opkansas.org

Let's see: Old McDonald had a pig, and a cow, and a goat . . . and a bison? You'll find them all, along with chickens, sheep, and owls, at this fun-for-all 12-acre farm in south Johnson County. It opened in 1976 and in 1985 was named to honor Deanna Rose, an Overland Park police officer killed in the line of duty.

It's always a fun excursion but especially so in spring, when newborn animals are popping up like daffodils. Although it's fun to watch them be bottle-fed, it's a positive giggle fest to feed the goats from your hands. New to the area are a dairy barn, log fort, a country schoolhouse circa 1900, and a Kanza Indian encampment, complete with earthern lodge and tepees. For details skip over to Kidstuff.

THE KANSAS CITY ZOO
6800 Zoo Dr.
(816) 513-5800
www.kansascityzoo.org

Take a wild animal safari without leaving the country at this natural-habitat zoo set on 200 rolling acres. The areas are divided into different "countries," which you can visit by walking, riding the train, or taking a safari boat ride. In Africa you'll see elephants giving each other mud baths to cool off on a summer afternoon, herds of sable antelope and impala running free, and giraffes necking. The Australian exhibit includes an aviary with 20 species of birds and mammals, and acres where kangaroo, emus, and dingoes roam. Here's where you can catch a ride on a camel or pony.

Some of the older exhibits remain favorites, especially with kids who love to watch the sea lions splash in the pool. Polar bears will make their debut in summer of 2010, and a penguin exhibit isn't far behind.

Nocturnal Safaris give children a chance to play zookeeper for one night at a campout under the stars. This exciting, educational program is ideal for families, scouts, and church groups for ages six and up. Reservations are on a first-come, first-served basis starting Mar 1.

You can also catch a flick (a really big one) at the Sprint IMAX Theatre, which boasts a 6 ½-story-tall screen and 12,000 watts of digital sound. Call (816) 871-IMAX for day and evening show times and ticket information. You can attend IMAX without visiting the zoo (tickets range from $4 to $10), but the best value is a combination ticket. Read more in Kidstuff.

KANSAS SPEEDWAY
1333 Meadowlark Lane
Kansas City, KS
(913) 328-RACE (7223)
www.kansasspeedway.com

"It's purrrty," drawled NASCAR legend Richard Petty when he first saw this $260 million ICS-owned facility that opened in June 2001. It's also *biiiig*. In fact you could fit both Kauffman and Arrowhead Stadiums and their parking lots in the racetrack's infield. And while size does matter, this 1 1/2-mile tri-oval track was designed for the comfort and convenience of the fans and racing. One example is the infield Fan Walk that gives racing fans an up-close look at the garages, inspection stations, and Victory Lane. You can lap up more information in the Sports chapter.

POWELL GARDENS
1609 Northwest U.S. Hwy. 50
Kingville, MO
(816) 697-2600
www.powellgardens.org

This road trip for the soul begins with a 30-mile drive out of town, just enough time to listen to Vivaldi's "Four Seasons" while you anticipate what's coming up . . . literally. With 915 acres of perennial gardens, a shady rock and waterfall trail, wildflower meadow, and a lovely island garden set in the 12-acre lake, the garden seems to offer some new display or event to treasure every spring. One of our favorites is the "Social Irrigation" cocktail party during every full moon in the summer. Daiquiris and daylilies—we'll drink to that. Tickets are $15 for nonmembers, $10 for members, and reservations are required. And a 3.25-mile nature trail, a haven for butterfly- and birdwatchers, winds through lush forests and past orchids with perhaps a deer or two to spy. A new 12-acre exhibit, the Heartland Harvest Garden, offers the nation's largest "edible landscape." You can read more about this magical place in Parks, Lakes, and Recreation.

TOURS

BOULEVARD BREWING COMPANY
2501 Southwest Blvd.
(816) 474-7095
www.blvdbeer.com

Since 1989 John McDonald has been single-handedly (well, actually he has helpers now) resurrecting Kansas City's 150-year-old tradition as a brewery town. That's when he rolled out his first barrel of Pale Ale, and he has since added brews like Unfiltered Wheat, Dry Stout, and Bully! Port, which won a gold medal at Chicago's Real Ale Festival. You can get a mini-lesson on brewing on the Web site. Better yet, hop to it and attend a tour, Wed through Sun by reservation only. You can also purchase some great merchandise with the company's cool logo at the brewery, online, and by phone.

FEDERAL RESERVE BANK OF KANSAS CITY
One Memorial Dr.
(816) 881-2038
www.kansascityfed.org/moneymuseum

If you promise not to walk in and chirp, "Show me the money," we'll let you in on this interesting tour. The guided walk through this new building includes an overview of the Fed's responsibilities in monetary policy and regulation and a look at the bank's operating areas. The real fun comes,

though, when you see the high-speed sorter that can count, sort, and destroy cash faster than a 16-year-old daughter: up to 100,000 bills an hour. The Money Museum tells the story of U.S. currency from its start during George Washington's administration to the current electronic processes. Coin collectors in particular will find the museum interesting. The museum offers both walk in and guided tour experiences. Upon arrival, guests will undergo a security screening and those over 18 are required to show a valid photo I.D. Hours are from 8:30 a.m. to 4:30 p.m. Mon through Fri, excluding bank holidays. And leave your money at home; the tour is free.

HARLEY-DAVIDSON FINAL ASSEMBLY PLANT
11401 N. Congress
(816) 270-8488, (877) 883-1450
www.harley-davidson.com

Get your motor running at this facility, where you can watch the assembly-line action and drool over some shiny new rides. Tours are free, but there are a few rules. Children must be at least 12 years old and accompanied by an adult. No open-toed shoes are allowed. Anyone over 18 will need a photo ID. Cameras are prohibited in the factory area, and all visitors will pass through a metal detector. But don't worry. Lockers are available to store your camera and the four pounds of keys that held up the security line.

Tours last approximately one hour. We suggest you call ahead, because tours are not available on holidays, during summer and Christmas shutdown, and when the plant is off-limits during special production work. The museum and tour center are open from 9 a.m. to 1:30 p.m., and logo merchandise is available in the gift shop. Some enthusiasts barely make it past the parking lot, which looks like one gigantic Harley dealership.

HISTORIC KANSAS CITY FOUNDATION
201 Westport Rd.
(816) 931-8448
www.historickansascity.org

The foundation began in 1974 when concerned citizens, led by the irrepressible Jane Fifield Flynn, began trying to save historic structures from demolition. Since then they've rescued beauties like the Coates House, the President Hotel, and a group of apartment buildings on the Plaza known as Poets' Row. The group gives several public walking tours a year to showcase a different neighborhood or area such as Hyde Park, Union Station, and the Garment District. During these time-machine travels, volunteers describe architecture and tell interesting tidbits about famous residents. Most tours simply require showing up at an appointed time and paying $3 or so; others require preregistration and $10 to $15 each.

The foundation also hosts private walking tours for groups of 10 or more with a two- to three-week advance notice. The donation is $5 per person. Tours last from one to two hours and some are adaptable for vans or buses. Potential areas include downtown's art deco buildings, River Market, 18th and Vine, and Northeast neighborhoods. Volunteers are also available for speaking engagements. Jane is gone, but she left a legacy of these irreplaceable gems.

KANSAS CITY STAR PRESS PAVILION TOUR
www.kcstartours.com

You read it here first, folks. *The Star* boasts one of the most modern newspaper plants in the world—certainly the prettiest one. That's it, the glowing green-glass rectangle just south of downtown. Two city blocks long with more than 420,000 square feet within four levels houses four 68-foot-tall Commander presses. These highly automated presses are fun to watch. For safety reasons, tourgoers must be at least eight years of age. There are other restrictions posted on the registration form available on the Web site. Note that there is considerable walking on the tour, but hey! To see how they print enough papers for one million readers a week, it's worth it. *The Star* also has an impressive number of items available for sale, including books.

THE ROASTERIE
1204 W. 27th St.
(816) 931-4000
www.theroasterie.com

Coffee is routine to most people; hit the button, wait for the hot brown liquid to appear. Slurp. Repeat. Well, we're not most people and we appreciate the talent in buying the best beans, lovingly roasting them, and giving them fun names like Full Vengeance and Nitro. The Roasterie produces award-winning coffee that is available at most local supermarkets, many of our fine restaurants, and online. And now you can learn how to savor the aromas and nuances that put coffee in the same category as wine and chocolate during an interesting, educational tour. Tours are offered every Sat at 9 a.m. and reservations are a must. We're betting they have coffee waiting.

THE ARTS

Kansas City: the art capital of the world. Well, darn close anyway. When you factor in our museums, art spaces and galleries, orchestras, musical groups and soloists, and millions of dollars of public artwork like fountains, sculptures, and murals—well, it's enough to make any city seem downright highbrow. And the phrase "All the world's a stage" may well have been coined for Kansas City; we have more professional theaters than any other city our size in the United States. With more than 320 cultural organizations, our town is an exciting destination and, more important, a great place to live, work, and raise a family.

You can attribute our amazing cache of culture to early philanthropists like William Rockhill Nelson, who decided his adopted hometown deserved boulevards and a world-class art museum, and J. C. Nichols, who gave us enough fountains to make even Rome seem second-rate. That city may boast more fountains, but we have more that actually work.

Current-day angels with names like Hall, Helzberg, Bloch, Kemper, and Kauffman keep the "home is where the art is" tradition going. And now they, along with thousands of musicians and singers, artists, writers, poets, and dancers who call Kansas City home, would like to share the wealth with you.

The listings in this chapter are presented in alphabetical order by category. All organizations are located in Kansas City, Missouri, unless otherwise noted.

ART MUSEUMS

THE KEMPER MUSEUM OF CONTEMPORARY ART
4420 Warwick Blvd.
(816) 561-3737
www.kemperart.org
This dynamic art space features a dazzling core collection that includes work by Georgia O'Keeffe, Jasper Johns, Robert Motherwell, and Frank Stella. The museum also presents exhibits taken from its permanent collection as well as several shows a year starring internationally known artists such as Dale Chihuly and Herb Ritts. It's easy to find the

i Find out about 150 other arts organizations, from individual graphic artists to puppeteers to orchestras, at the Arts Council of Metropolitan Kansas City Web site, www.artslinks.org. You'll also see a listing of events happening in and around Kansas City.

place; just look for a gigantic spider sculpture on the front lawn. Yikes! The museum is open Tues through Sun. Call for the times. Admission is free. The Kemper is described in detail in Attractions.

THE NELSON-ATKINS MUSEUM OF ART
4525 Oak St.
(816) 561-4000
www.nelson-atkins.org
This magnificent neoclassic building put Kansas City on the art map, not just in the country but also in the world. Along with pieces by Rembrandt, Renoir, and Caravaggio, the Nelson boasts one of the world's finest Oriental collections and more Henry Moore sculptures than anywhere outside the artist's hometown. Thanks to the extraordinary Bloch Building expansion, there's 70 percent more to love. We've included a Close-up on the Nelson in the Attractions chapter. The museum is open Tues through Sun.

NERMAN MUSEUM OF CONTEMPORARY ART
Johnson County Community College
12345 College Blvd.
Overland Park, KS
(913) 469-8500
www.nermanmuseum.org

Designed by esteemed architect Kyu Sung Woo, this $15 million museum—the largest contemporary art museum in the four-state region—has placed Kansas firmly on the international art scene.

The stunning minimalist gallery makes art the star with lots of white, light, and open spaces. And if you're wondering what a world-class museum is doing on the campus of a community college, you do not go to the head of the class. The new space is simply a way to display more of the already stellar collection that has been inside and out of the school for years. Central to this has been the Oppenheimer Sculpture Garden, gifts of Tony and Marti Oppenheimer. The couple donated to the new museum's acquisitions as well; the museum takes its name from major donors Jerry and Margaret Nerman and their son Lewis.

Read more about this glorious new space in Attractions. And during your tour, if you see a guy with a permanent grin on his face, that's Bruce Hartman, the museum's director. He's asking himself the same question: "How did I get so lucky?"

DANCE

KANSAS CITY BALLET
1601 Broadway Blvd.
(816) 931-2232
www.kcballet.org

This 50-year-old company of two dozen dancers is thriving under artistic director William Whitener, who has also contributed some of the troupe's newest ballets. Classical, modern, dramatic, and even comedic work makes up the rich and varied dance tapestry, and each year Whitener expands the repertoire. He enjoys shaking up the audience, and challenging the dancers, by bringing in new choreography and giving vibrant

new life to pieces that haven't been performed in decades. One look at *Deuce Coupe*, set to Beach Boys tunes, and you'll realize this ain't your grandmother's ballet.

The tutus come back on, however, for other productions. Four are presented each season, including an annual *Nutcracker*, which is performed at the Midland Theatre during the holidays. Until the company makes its permanent home in the Kauffman Performing Arts Center, the other programs are at the Lyric Theatre. Along with ballet, programs in jazz, tap, yoga, and even tai chi are available. And you might want to keep those dancing shoes handy: Join the Ballet Barre, and you can party with other young professionals ages 21 to 40 during happy hours before performances, salsa lessons, and other events. Membership dues are just $65; check the Web site. And good news for the dancers; in 2010 the ballet company broke ground on a new studio space near Union Station. No more dancing into walls.

KANSAS CITY FRIENDS OF ALVIN AILEY
218 Delaware, Suite 101
(816) 471-6003
www.kcfaa.org

We defy you to keep your feet from tapping along when the dancers match their steps to syncopated rhythms, bending bodies into human pretzels, leotards flying across the stage.

As the only official second home of Alvin Ailey American Dance Theatre, this organization not only hosts performances during the year, but it also instills a love of dance to youngsters through its innovative and powerful Ailey-Camp program. Designed to reach "at-risk" middle-school students in the Kansas City, Missouri, school district, this six-week summer camp uses dance to develop self-esteem and self-discipline and to foster creativity. It's heartwarming and inspirational to sit in the audience on the night the entire class performs in front of parents and siblings. You'll find yourself calling out right along with the proud parents sitting around you. In addition, KCFAA reaches over 35,000 young people each year through year-round programs

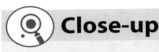

Close-up

Welcome to the 'artland

You won't need a ticket to see some of Kansas City's most exciting odes to culture. Art is all around us, gracing parks and shopping areas, defining neighborhoods, fronting office buildings and libraries, providing beauty on brick walls. It's our public art, and many newcomers to our town are simply blown away at the amazing array.

In Attractions we listed two areas, Crown Center and the Country Club Plaza, that are really outdoor art galleries filled with sculpture, mosaics, and fountains. Our city's most beautiful landmarks were originally established to fill the needs of people and provide water for horses. There were plenty of takers; in 1910 the equestrian population of Kansas City was 70,000. Later fountains fed our desire for beauty and celebration. The **City of Fountains Foundation** (816-842-2299, www.kcfountains.com), established in 1973, partners with the Parks and Recreation Department of Kansas City to maintain existing fountains and help establish new ones.

The InterContinental Hotel

Corner of Wornall Road and Ward Parkway

The hotel's front is defined by one of the tallest man-made fountains, a concave curtain of water 56 feet wide and 17 feet high. The waterfall provides a backdrop for a sculpture of the goddess of the hunt and her entourage of cherubs. Diana has an arm raised as if taking in the magnificent scene before her. But we think she's actually saying, "Hand me one of those fluffy robes, will ya?"

J. C. Nichols Memorial Fountain

47th St. and Nichols Pkwy.

Kansas City's signature fountain was dedicated in 1960 to the memory of J. C. Nichols, the developer of the Country Club Plaza, and Mr. Fountain as far as we're concerned. He was instrumental in turning our town into a water wonderland by acquiring fantastic fountains from Europe and shipping them home. This particular beauty depicts four equestrian figures that each represent a famous river of the world. The multiple water jets spray 30 feet from the center. Even in winter, when part of the fountain has become a blue ice sculpture, it is magnificent. In October, red dye is added to the water to turn it pink for national Breast Cancer Awareness Month.

Fountain Displays

Forget statues on horseback; these three newer fountains offer gushing geysers. The Henry Wollman Bloch Fountain, in front of Union Station, sends dancing water 120 feet high, then

that shatter racial, ethnic, and social barriers to promote awareness and respect.

FINE ART SPACES

Kansas City's vibrant art scene isn't just showcased in museums and galleries. You'll find original works of art displayed in coffee shops, libraries, restaurants, and bank lobbies. Here are a few of our favorite artful haunts.

BELGER ARTS CENTER
2100 Walnut St.
(816) 474-3250
www.belgerartscenter.org

One of the world's most impressive collections of works by Jasper Johns . . . in a warehouse? That's Kansas City, where art enthusiasts are everywhere. You can make special arrangements to view the John and Maxine Belger Family Foundation's collection of some of America's finest contemporary artists by calling the number

lingers in mid-air before crashing to the ground. It propels two tons of water in a single gush from 232 nozzles. The Crown Center Fountain offers a dancing water show every hour on the hour from noon until 10 p.m., synchronized to music recorded by the Kansas City Symphony. Kids of all ages chase the 49 water jets and 48 water shooters that spout up to 60 feet in the air. And at the Legends in Village West, wet is the word at the Civic Courtyard Fountain, which offers a two-tiered display that's mesmerizing to watch.

Boy and Frog Fountain

Nichols Rd. and Central

One of the Plaza's most endearing and amusing fountains, this charmer was purchased in 1929 in Florence, Italy. It shows a toddler who's surprised by a shower from a friendly bronze frog.

The Children's Fountain

North Oak Trafficway and Missouri Highway 9

Local sculptor Tom Corbin truly has captured the fountain of youth in this delightful display of six children frolicking in jets of water. The entire fountain itself is massive; the basin measures 60 feet by 100 feet.

Heritage Fountain

23rd and Topping

This spectacular tower of water in Blue Valley Park can be seen for miles around. Dedicated in 1977, this fountain stands on a site some 400 feet above the base of the park and consists of an 85-foot steel pylon with 16 water jets at its summit.

The Town of Kansas 1850 Mural

204 W. 3rd St.

Although this isn't a fountain, it does have a watery theme. Close to where our city began is a wonderful monument to the thousands of people who came here by way of the Missouri River. A mural on the side of a brick River Market building depicts a steamboat chugging along next to a raft in the muddy Missouri. Cows and a settlement are seen on the bluffs above, all under a cloudy Midwestern sky. The artwork, based on a well-known 1853 lithograph, was painted by Jesus Ortiz, Alisha Gambino, and Joseph Faus. River Market loft developer Mel Mallin came up with the idea, raised the money, got the building owner's blessing, and hired the artists. A few years later, this spunky octogenarian commissioned the same team to paint a mural depicting the Lewis and Clark Expedition's stop at our river area. It's located in the River Market area. Bravo, Mel!

above. Better yet, attend any of the regular art showings in the center's immense spaces in the Belger Cartage Services century-year-old building in the Crossroads Arts District. Since the first exhibition in 2000, the Belger has staged more than 20 major art shows, including an exciting variety of 2-D, 3-D, and 4-D artworks.

The galleries are free and open to the public Wed through Fri from 10 a.m. to 4 p.m., Sat from noon to 4 p.m., and open until 9 p.m. on the first Friday of each month.

H&R BLOCK ARTSPACE
16 E. 43rd St.
(816) 561-5563
www.kcai.edu/campus/artspace

When the Kansas City Art Institute got a grant from a Missouri cultural trust program, it was able to renovate a small warehouse near its campus into a gallery and arts education space. That cash infusion begot more, this time from benefactor Henry Bloch, and voilà: a home-away-from-school for art students. The gallery hosts several exhibits a year that bring this concrete shell to life with ideas and vitality. Granted, a few exhibits have guests whispering, "Am I missing something, Edna?" but most are insightful works by very talented and as yet undiscovered artists.

KANSAS CITY ARTISTS COALITION
201 Wyandotte
(816) 421-5222
www.kansascityartistscoalition.org
Since 1975 the Kansas City Artists Coalition has provided support, exhibition space, and a voice for established and emerging artists both local and regional. More than 400 artists use its white walls as an ever-changing art gallery, and dozens of artists have nervously watched the public pick apart or praise their first exhibitions here. Art lovers show up in droves (and SUVs) every February for the KCAC Benefit Art Auction, when some of the region's best artists donate work to be auctioned to the highest bidder. This is a chance for the artists to give back to an organization that played an important part in their early careers.

The coalition also produces the wildly popular Open Studios Tour every other year. These open houses all over the city give art lovers a chance to meet the artists and their environments.

LITERARY ARTS

PROSPERO'S BOOKS
1717 W. 39th St.
(816) 960-7202
www.prosperosbookstore.com
Described as an artistic community masquerading as a used book store, this is the home of The Pit, Kansas City's largest open-mic poetry reading. And if you're picturing a handful of hopefuls waiting their turn, you'll be surprised to see the crowd. Each month between 40 and 100 writers show up to read original works to a sensitive and encouraging audience; after all, most of them have faced that microphone.

Readings begin at 5:30 p.m. on the fourth Sunday of each month. The bookshop also publishes some of the best work in *Prospero's Pocket*

Poets. And if music is more to your liking, Prospero's turns into an intimate space for original music by some of the area's best songwriters on most Fridays and Saturdays. You'll hear a broad range of folk, Celtic, punk, jazz, and country.

THE WRITER'S PLACE
3607 Pennsylvania
(816) 753-1090
www.writersplace.org
Entire books could be written about, not just in, this literary community center. The large stone structure with a turret was built as a private residence in 1909, then spent time as an apartment house, brothel, and church until becoming a homey place for writers to take classes, get advice, and share their work in 1992. You might call it a ghostwriter's place, because several workers and guests have seen, felt, or heard a presence they call Clara. Apparitions aside, the center houses a gracious lounge on the first floor, which is used for public events or smaller meetings, plus a gallery displaying art and texts. Classrooms, an extensive library, and offices take up the second and third floors.

The Writer's Place is a wonderful resource for local authors to share ideas, get tips from published writers, or commiserate over rejection letters. Several programs are held throughout the year, including book and poetry readings, a monthly book club, student writing competitions, and art exhibits. The public is invited to attend or participate for a small fee, and membership to the organization costs around $45 a year. And you may get to meet Clara.

MUSIC

Ah, the city where the blues and jazz officially met. Naturally we offer plenty of opportunity to explore the music scene of harmonicas, electric guitars, and drums. If you need a nudge, check out the dozens of nightclubs and restaurants offering live music seven days a week in the Nightlife chapter. But you'll also find classical music throughout our fair city. Hear that? Someone is tuning up right now. Please take your seat.

THE FRIENDS OF CHAMBER MUSIC
4635 Wyandotte, Suite 201
(816) 561-9999
www.chambermusic.org
In the late 1970s, Cynthia Siebert took a chance that Kansas Citians would sit through an evening of chamber music, let alone pay for the privilege. She was delighted by the enthusiastic response, and today as executive director she continues to bring in the world's finest chamber music, pianists, and early-music ensembles. To her credit, and to the audience's delight, she seeks out performers who bring passion and a freshness to their craft, not just a famous name. The series of 14 concerts takes place at four remarkable venues: the Folly Theatre, Grace and Holy Trinity Cathedral, Carlsen Center, and Redemptorist Church in midtown. Single tickets are not available but may be purchased for a minimum of three concerts. After that, they figure they have you hooked and you'll gladly pony up for an entire season subscription.

KANSAS CITY SYMPHONY
1020 Central, Suite 300
(816) 471-1100 (office)
(816) 471-0400 (tickets)
www.kcsymphony.org
With the hiring of Michael Stern as musical director in 2005, the symphony got the likable rock star it needed to bring the crowds back. He's handsome, charming, funny, and has a full head of beautiful hair—in short, everything you want in a conductor. A night at the symphony is whatever you make it: black tie or jeans, romance or revelry. Fond memories of the last time you heard "Symphonie Fantastique" or an exciting new venture into the music of Phillip Glass. You'll hear it here first, thanks to a full season that includes a dozen or so classical concerts at the Lyric Theatre, the Music Hall, and other venues such as Yardley Hall at Johnson County Community College.

The symphony also presents a Pops series of crowd pleasers like the Count Basie Orchestra or Neil Sedaka. Its Family Series introduces youngsters to the joy of classical music, pain free. Just try to keep a four-year-old from dancing in the aisle to "Snoopy Does the Samba." The symphony's musicians also take it on the road often for wonderful (and often free) concerts, like Celebration at the Station on Memorial Day, when cannons punctuate "1812 Overture" and fireworks dazzle thousands of patrons sitting in the green space between the Liberty Memorial and Union Station. Tickets vary by performance, with prices ranging from $15 to $40. Check online; the symphony sometimes has nonadvertised deals such as $13 tickets that are upgraded to the best available seats in the house—free. Now that's what we call a musical score!

LYRIC OPERA OF KANSAS CITY
712 E. 18th St.
(816) 471-7344
ww.kcopera.org
Not crazy about opera? The Lyric may change your mind. Since 1958 it has been presenting glowing productions that have turned blasé audiences into opera lovers. What's the secret? For one thing, although the performances are in the original languages, supertitles shown above the stage let you know what that large man is bellowing about. Four productions are offered each season, including a blockbuster like *Aida* or *Madame Butterfly* and an American opera (for which supertitles may still be necessary). Long-term subscribers may have noticed an upgrade in singers and production values since 1998, when artistic director Ward Holmquist took the helm.

QUALITY HILL PLAYHOUSE
303 W. 10th St.
(816) 421-1700
www.qualityhillplayhouse.com
When you're hungry for a sophisticated evening filled with the singable tunes of Cole Porter, George Gershwin, and Henry Mancini, this intimate theater has your seat ready. J. Kent Barnhart serves as emcee and musical director—and brilliant pianist—for cabaret reviews that have covered themes such as great duets, musical divas, and Sinatra songs. Kent's other talent (along with a quick wit and perfect timing) is choosing the right singers for the selections. In Kansas City he's

blessed with some standout performers who can give us goosebumps with showstoppers like "My Man" from *Funny Girl* and "Try to Remember" from *The Fantasticks*.

The two-hour shows are slick and professional, and the small, seven-row arrangement ensures a great seat. The audience laps it up seven nights a week. To be sure, more than a few get in with a senior discount, but you'll also see plenty of young music lovers in the audience, especially those who appreciate haunting lyrics and music to hum all the way home. Quality Hill Playhouse produces four shows a year, with performances every night and matinees on Sun and some weekdays. Single tickets are $23, with discounts for groups and seniors. Covered parking is adjacent to the playhouse.

THEATER COMPANIES

ACTORS THEATRE OF KANSAS CITY
30 W. Pershing Rd., Suite 850
(913) 677-5374
www.kcactors.com

This is a relatively new troupe of some of the city's most talented thespians who banded together to present plays that don't get as much, well, play as they should. *Who's Afraid of Virginia Woolf?* made audience members appreciate their own spouses during a recent series, for instance. The productions aren't elaborate, but we'd put the quality of the acting against any in the country. ATKC schedules three plays each season during the summer, all performed at the H&R Block City Stage Theatre, relocated in Union Station. Tickets are available through the Central Ticket Office, 4949 Cherry St. in the University of Missouri–Kansas City Performing Arts Center, (816) 235-6222, or on the company's Web site.

AMERICAN HEARTLAND THEATRE
Crown Center, Third Level Shops
(816) 842-9999
www.ahtkc.com

The actors must have been chanting "Break a leg!" nonstop when this theater opened on April 1 more than 20 years ago. Luck was obviously on its side, however, because the American Heartland continues to thrive. What keeps it so fresh is the variety of productions that include musical comedies, mysteries, and drama. The 420 seats rise sharply from the stage, ensuring that everyone has an unobstructed view. Unique features include a full-service bar (patrons can take beverages to their seats), a private suite for 36 guests, and free covered parking. Single ticket prices range from $19 to $27.50, with the holiday shows costing a few dollars more.

BARN PLAYERS
6219 Martway
(913) 432-9100
www.thebarnplayers.org

"Hey kids! I've got a barn, and my sister can sing and dance. Let's do a musical!" That's probably close to what happened in 1955 when this group held its first production, making it the longest continuously operating community theater in Kansas City. The group presents three productions a year, ranging from *California Suite* to *Little Shop of Horrors*. The group also has a scholarship fund for college-bound high school students interested in the performing arts.

THE COTERIE THEATRE
Crown Center
(816) 474-6552
www.thecoterie.com

This professional theater for young adults has been a Kansas City favorite for more than 20 years, thanks to artistic director Jeff Church's mission to create an experience that all age groups can enjoy—with or without the kids in tow. The Coterie focuses on imaginative adaptations of beloved stories and fairy tales but isn't afraid to tackle deep subjects, like the Holocaust. The artistic integrity is so high that *Travel + Leisure* rated it one of the country's top-ten children's theaters. A new grant is allowing the Coterie to expand its classroom space and construct a lobby. See Kidstuff for information about auditions and tickets.

HEART OF AMERICA SHAKESPEARE FESTIVAL
Southmoreland Park
47th St. and Oak
(816) 531-7728
www.kcshakes.org

One of our most beloved summertime traditions started when a feisty redhead, Marilyn Strauss, brought her Tony award home and decided what this town needed was more Shakespeare. That was more than 20 years ago, and since then, for four glorious weeks starting in late June, we watch sword fights and ladies swooning from balconies as some of the city's finest actors bring the Bard's words to life. It all takes place under the stars in the tiny, urban Southmoreland Park near the Nelson-Atkins Museum of Art. Come early for the pre-show and either bring a picnic basket or purchase anything from hot dogs to salads, kettle corn to snow cones, and even wine and beer at the concession stand. You can rent lawn chairs for $5 rather than lug yours around, or better yet, get a reserved seat up front for $15. Call the office number listed above at least 48 hours before the performance date. There's no admission fee, but of course you'll want to donate to keep this wonderful theater experience alive.

KANSAS CITY REPERTORY THEATRE
UMKC Campus, 50th and Oak
(816) 235-2700
www.kcrep.org

From its humble beginnings in a wooden playhouse on the University of Missouri–Kansas City campus in 1964, this company has grown into a nationally respected theater that attracts actors and directors of national and international acclaim. Now, with new artistic director Eric Rosen, its um, well, rep has skyrocketed, thanks to this young man's bold choices in offerings. The *Wall Street Journal* called the production of *The Glass Menagerie* "one of the top two shows in the country" in 2009. He's also mounted first-time plays in Kansas City, including the wildly successful *A Christmas Story: the Musical*, which he plans to take to Broadway within the next few years. The Kansas City Rep produces six main productions during its Sept through June season, each running a minimum of 24 times.

THE NEW THEATRE RESTAURANT
9229 Foster
Overland Park, KS
(913) 649-7469
www.newtheatre.com

This dinner theater puts the emphasis on dinner, with a tempting buffet of entrees and side dishes that might have you wondering why they bother with a show. More lobster risotto, please! But you'll be glad you waited for the production; chances are the person on stage is a beloved TV star like Jamie Farr, Marion Ross, or Loretta Swit. With all that, plus nearly 700 seats in a beautiful stepped arrangement that gives everyone a great view, it's no wonder the *Wall Street Journal* calls this "the best dinner theater in the country."

Founders and co–artistic directors Dennis Hennessey and Richard Carrothers put on five shows per season, four of which star characters like Ritchie's Mom or Hot Lips. But audiences also enjoy seeing local actors on stage, like Lori Blalock, Jim Korinke, and Debra Bluford. Apparently it's a recipe that works. The New Theatre enjoys an average 94 percent attendance 52 weeks a year. And 40,000 to 50,000 of those people are out-of-towners, including several hundred who fly in from California and catch a show before heading to Branson or back home. Yes, indeed, it does cater to the mature audience. But you'll also see plenty of young adults laughing at the jokes. Ticket prices range from $28 to $48 including the buffet, but better hurry. The majority of seats belong to season ticket holders.

STARLIGHT THEATRE
4600 Starlight Rd. in Swope Park
(816) 363-7827
www.kcstarlight.com

Starlight opened its theater under the stars on June 25, 1951, with *Desert Song*. At the time about 40 professional, self-produced outdoor theaters existed in the country; today only two remain, both in Missouri. During its early days, seasons consisted of 10 shows that included operettas and new Broadway musical comedies. One of its unique features came from a disgruntled star. In 1958 Jerry Lewis was unhappy with the distance between the stage and the audience. An extension, paid for by the comedian, was built to cover the orchestra pit and remained in place until a new stage was built in 2000.

By the 1970s, facing the exorbitant costs of mounting lavish Broadway musicals, Starlight turned to variety shows, and attendance dropped every year. Now the big shows are back, with five Broadway-style shows each May through Sept, including classics like *Sweet Charity* and *Hairspray*.

A $10 million, 12,000-square-foot, fully enclosed stage allows for huge, complex sets, such as a helicopter landing in *Miss Saigon*. The design incorporates two new towers to complement the existing ones that are the theater's trademark.

Tickets cost from $9 to $70—quite a range, but with 8,000 seats the cheap ones seem an acre away from the stage.

BROADWAY ACROSS AMERICA
Music Hall
301 W. 13th St.
(800) 366-0583
www.broadwayacrossamerica.com

Here's where Kansas City gets to see those thrilling Broadway productions like *Wicked* and *Young Frankenstein*, not long after they win Tony statuettes in New York. Sets are breathtaking displays, such as a miniature lake lit with thousands of candles for *Phantom of the Opera*.

The venue is pretty spectacular, too: the gorgeous 1930s art deco music hall at 13th and Wyandotte, with romantic private balconies overlooking the stage and sumptuous decor. Broadway Across America mounts six major shows a year as well as special engagements such as concerts. And although individual tickets are available, it's the season ticket holders who get the best deals. With prices ranging from $140 to $200 per season, the package includes first dibs on special engagements.

THEATRE IN THE PARK
Shawnee Mission Park
79th and Renner Rd.
Shawnee, KS
(816) 464-9420 (info line), (913) 631-7050
www.theatreinthepark.org

A summer night, a star-filled sky, and Curly singing something about a beautiful morning. There are few better ways to spend an evening than watching talented local actors and singers bring new life to classic Broadway shows, especially if you've packed a wedge of cold watermelon in your picnic basket.

The season consists of four musicals, and more than 3,000 people show up each night, far more than just parents of lead actors. The crowd attests to the fact that the talent is top-notch. Ticket windows open at 6:30 p.m., and our advice is to get there early because the line can get long. Better yet, order season tickets online or by mail so you can relax and enjoy the show. The programs begin at 8 p.m. A concession stand and public restrooms are available. Admission is $8 for adults, $6 for children ages 4 to 12, and free for those under three.

i Not sure what to wear to the ballet, symphony, or opera? Although opening night is usually business dress or evening wear, other performances are typically "anything goes." To learn more, including program guides, terms, and even when to applaud (when everyone else does!), check out the major performing arts groups' Web sites. They'll also give you age restrictions for children.

UNICORN THEATRE
3828 Main St.
(816) 531-PLAY (7529)
www.unicorntheatre.org

"Edgy," even "risky," are words often used to describe the topics portrayed on Unicorn's stage. In fact, artistic director Cynthia Levin likes to describe it as contemporary, controversial, and consistent. Naturally it appeals to a dedicated audience of free thinkers who want something more to discuss post-performance than what the protagonist was wearing . . . or not.

The professional theater has produced more than 200 plays, with more than 45 world premieres, since it began in 1974 as an acting workshop in what is now the River Market area. In the late 1990s Unicorn moved to its current location in the midtown business district, transforming an old garage into a modern, intimate arrangement utilizing a thrust stage and a seating capacity of 150. Regular performances are shown Tues through Sun, with ticket prices ranging from $20 to $30.

THEATER VENUES

The play's the thing—and so is the musical, comedy act, and concert. Kansas City is home to some stellar theaters, including three historic buildings that are nearly as interesting as what's on stage. And you can share in the buzz about our new Kauffman Performing Arts Center, due in 2011.

CARLSEN CENTER AND YARDLEY HALL
Johnson County Community College
12345 College Blvd.
Overland Park, KS
(913) 469-4445
www.jccc.net
Part of the behemoth community college campus on a windswept hill, the Carlsen Center is a 165,000-square-foot complex that houses four theaters, an art gallery, and an espresso bar along with classrooms and offices. Its size allows for a sweeping lobby with an 85-foot glass ceiling above a granite entry floor.

The exterior is brick, with a graceful arched doorway providing the only adornment, but it's the interior bricks that will catch your eye. Kansas artist Donna Dobberfuhl has created a series of figures that portray the history of theater, dance, and music. The carved-brick sculptures appear on the walls facing the entrance to Yardley Hall, an auditorium known for its superb acoustics and comfortable seating. Since its opening in 1991, the space has hosted such productions as Broadway plays and the Moscow State Sym-

phony Orchestra, as well as current popular singers. More than 200 performances are held here every year, making the extensive free parking a real perk.

FOLLY THEATRE
12th and Central
(816) 474-4444
www.follytheatre.com
The Folly, which opened on September 23, 1900, has gone through many names, including the Standard, the Century, Schubert's Missouri, and (unofficially) the Grand Old Lady of 12th Street. Despite a few face-lifts on the inside, the south facade given her by local architect Louis Curtiss is still intact. It's a stately face with simple lines embellished only with an elegant three-story Palladian window.

The Marx Brothers, Shirley Booth, and Humphrey Bogart performed here as well as an unknown 16-year-old making her debut in 1929. The world soon knew her as Gypsy Rose Lee.

The hall limped through the Depression and finally closed in 1974. Two local philanthropists, Joan Kent Dillon and William Deramus III, saved her from the wrecking ball; she reopened in 1981 and and remains a vital part of our entertainment scene. She hosts the Friends of Chamber Music, the Harriman Arts Program of William Jewell College, and the Civic Opera Theater of Kansas City, as well as an international jazz series. When you visit the Folly, take a moment to realize that her bricks were laid by Civil War veterans.

KAUFFMAN CENTER FOR THE PERFORMING ARTS
16th and Baltimore
(816) 994-7200
www.kauffmancenter.org
A new crown jewel for the city is on the horizon—literally—on a hillside setting overlooking downtown to the north and Crown Center and our visual arts districts to the south. The Kauffman Center will be a world-class attraction consisting of 400,000 square feet of space. More than just audiences and civic leaders are thrilled about the news; the $326 million center will be home to

the Kansas City Ballet, the Kansas City Symphony, and the Lyric Opera, companies in desperate need of growing room. In addition, the 1,600-seat concert hall and 1,800-seat proscenium theater will attract Broadway shows and other large productions.

The architect, Moshe Safdie, who has transformed urban areas from Canada to Jerusalem, is known for dramatic curves, intriguing textures, and a generous use of windows and open space. While Kansas City holds its breath (the center is literally breathtakingly beautiful even during its construction phase), it waits for the official opening in fall 2011.

THE MIDLAND THEATRE
1228 Main St.
(816) 471-8600 (event line)
(816) 471-9703 (administrative offices)
Listed on the National Registry of Historic Places, the Midland is the grandest historic theater within a 250-mile radius of Kansas City. It was built by Marcus Loew in 1927 for an extravagant cost of $4 million. One of only 300 theaters designed by celebrated architect Thomas Lamb, it's often been called Lamb's "favorite theater" and was certainly the most elegant of its day with over 6 million inches of gold leaf. Its five massive Czechoslovakian hand-cut crystal chandeliers, precious antique furniture, and spectacular wood and plasterwork are irreplaceable in today's market. The enormous auditorium seats 2,800 and is five stories high, with balconies and stylish opera boxes. It was the first theater in the country to have air-conditioning and is now among only 25 of its kind still standing.

The Midland presented silent pictures and stage shows during its early years. It was pur-chased by Kansas City's American Multi-Cinema (AMC Theatres) in 1966. The theater showed motion pictures until 1981, when once again it became the venue for Broadway plays, concerts, ballets, and special events. Stars such as Tony Bennett, Dolly Parton, and Harry Connick Jr. have performed on this stage during the past several years.

THE MUNICIPAL AUDITORIUM, MUSIC HALL, AND THE LITTLE THEATER
301 W. 13th St.
(816) 513-5000
www.kcconvention.com
The Municipal Auditorium, an art deco wonder that was built in 1935 for $6.5 million ($2 million over budget), fills a city block with its hulking mass of limestone. Linear geometric designs and bas-relief medallions are its only external adornments, a severity that makes entering the grand foyer even more of a thrill.

The auditorium houses three large spaces—a multipurpose arena, the Music Hall, and an elegant little ballroom known as the Little Theatre—each with its own lobby. The Music Hall, built in 1936 as a home for the Philharmonic Orchestra, is entered through a splendid art deco lobby on 14th Street. It features pale gray Italian marble floors and walls, which create a nice echo until the room fills with theatergoers; chandeliers; and beautiful floor-to-ceiling murals. It seats 2,500 patrons in elegant splendor amid tones of burgundy, deep green, and gold and has an antique pipe organ that once accompanied silent movies. The Little Theatre is accessed through a door on 13th Street and boasts a sweeping doublewide stairway. The space seats 3,000.

KIDSTUFF

As you'll see, Kansas City is a great place to be a kid, raise a kid, or act like a kid again yourself. You can even pet a kid at a children's farmstead in southern Johnson County. From hands-on creative workshops to captivating historic sites, there's something for every tot and teen in your entourage. In fact, we're so kid happy here we don't have just one action-packed theme park, we have two.

And just to prove you can bring a kid to culture and still make him think, Kansas City offers lots of fascinating museums, including the interactive Science City at Union Station. There are plenty of indoor and outdoor activities so that youngsters can burn off all that energy, as well as kid-approved restaurants where they can gain it back.

Although we adore children, we're also partial to parents. That's why we tell you about several attractions that are cheap or absolutely free. You'll find other family activities and events to help fill the photo album in the Festivals and Annual Events chapter and the Attractions chapter. But the following ideas should keep the youngest members of your party busy for days. Soon you'll be hearing, "Mom? Dad? Can we move to Kansas City?"

The attractions in this chapter are listed alphabetically by kid-friendly category. All are located in Kansas City, Missouri, unless otherwise noted.

HAVE A BALL

COOL CREST FAMILY FUN CENTER
10735 E. Missouri Hwy. 40
Independence, MO
(816) 358-0088
www.coolcrest.com

The Patterson family has been entertaining everyone from tiny tots to tottering grandparents since 1950 at this 4 1/2-acre playground. There's something to keep everyone happy, including four 18-hole miniature golf courses, go-karts, batting cages, and a 7,000-square-foot game room with video and pinball machines galore. The nifty '50s-style pizzeria serves up cheesy pies plus hot dogs, ice cream, and slushees. Cool Crest is lovingly maintained and seems to have another new attraction every year. Event planners can help make sure your birthday party or group outing is a success. Cool Crest is open year-round, and golf is available when weather permits. Prices vary based on activities, but the best deal is an unlimited Fun Pass. Open seven days a week, but the hours vary depending on the day; call ahead for details.

FAMILY GOLF PARK
1501 Northeast MO 40
Blue Springs, MO
(816) 228-1550
www.familygolfpark.com

If your kids can't find something exciting to do at this huge play area, it's time to ship them home. This beautifully landscaped park features 36 holes of miniature golf that wind through a lake setting, a par-3 golf course, putting green, game arcade, and bumper boats. Ker-splash! The golf practice facility is open year-round, and golf lessons are available for ages 8 through 12 and 13 through 16. Hours are 10 a.m. until dark Mon through Sat, and noon until dark Sun. Rates vary depending on the activities. Group packages make this an ideal place for kids' birthday parties. The staff can even arrange for pizza delivery and ice cream. And big people, listen up: You can reserve the golf park for corporate outings. Activities may include miniature golf, water balloon toss, bumper boat relay, and even a hula-hoop contest (sorry, sir—you'll have to ditch that tie). Check online for options and prices, or give them a call.

INCRED-A-BOWL
8500 W. 151st St.
Overland Park, KS
(913) 851-1700
www.incredabowl.com

This 65,000-square-foot, state-of-the-art center includes a 40-lane computerized bowling alley, an arcade filled with more than 100 of the latest interactive and virtual reality games, a three-story set of play tubes for the tykes, a new laser tag center, and a miniature golf course. Whew!

The complex's claim to fame, however, is Cosmic Bowling every Fri and Sat night until 1:30 a.m., with groovy black lights, fog, glow-in-the-dark balls and pins, and upbeat music. Incred-A-Bowl also has a pro shop, gift store, and snack bar. And they've hosted more than 6,500 birthday parties here. Activity options are endless, and they even provide a helper for the harried parents. Now if only those shoes weren't so dorky.

KALEIDOSCOPE
25th St. and Grand Blvd.
(816) 274-8301
www.hallmarkkaleidoscope.com

Every child is an artist at this workshop run by Hallmark Cards. In fact, the entire place looks like a giant greeting card, with themed areas where children ages 5 through 12 can spend an hour creating masks and other crafts with leftover materials from the card maker. Your child can come away from this visit with a new sense of expression and self-confidence.

Admission is free, limited to one 45-minute session per child, and open to walk-in visitors on Sat throughout the year and Mon through Sat in summer. Reservations are required on weekdays during the school year and for groups of 20 or more at any time. Tickets are available starting at 10 a.m. for walk-in sessions. Children must be accompanied by an adult. Call to check on what hours it's open.

Kaleidoscope also offers wonderful workshops taught by staff and volunteers where children can build or decorate a take-home project like a birdhouse or tie. There's a small fee

for these programs, and reservations are required. And don't miss the free worksheets that detail additional activities families can do together at home; they're available at the receptionist's desk on the way out and can be downloaded from the Web site; get your five-year-old to show you how!

And here's another bonus: The Hallmark Visitor Center, also in the Crown Center complex, gives children in third grade and above a chance to learn how the Hallmark artists make their magic. Adults will adore the displays as well. This would be an ideal time to visit: 2010 marks the 100th anniversary of the company.

The visitor center is open Mon through Sat. For more information call (816) 274-5672 or point your paintbrush to www.hallmarkvisitorscenter.com.

The center is wheelchair accessible and can accommodate children with special needs.

HOT DOG! TIME TO EAT!

THE CRAYOLA CAFE $
2450 Grand Ave.
(816) 398-4820
www.crayolacafe.com

This colorful restaurant in the Crown Center Shops caters to kids with a tin of crayons and ready-to-color placemats at each seat. And you'd swear a five-year-old—and a picky eater at that—dreamed up the menu. It features s'ghetti and meatballs, grilled-cheese sandwiches, a peanut butter wrap, and mini corn dogs. The grown-up menu includes healthy salads and burgers with all the works.

FRITZ'S RAILROAD CAFE $
250 N. 18th St. (Kansas City, Kansas)
(913) 281-2777

2450 Grand Ave. (Crown Center)
(816) 474-4004

13803 W. 63rd St. (Shawnee)
(913) 375-1000
www.fritzskc.com

Get your vacation on track at this train-inspired restaurant in the Crown Center Shops, the original place in KCK, or the new location in Shawnee.

It's quite a trip to call in your order on the telephone at your booth and then watch it chuga-chug-chug to your table on an overhead electric train. The outrageous fun will delight your kids, and so will the menu of made-to-order burgers, hot dogs, sandwiches, and shakes. Parents will get on board as well, with tasty items like bowls of Fritz's famous chili. The KCK location serves breakfast as well. All three are open seven days a week.

T-REX CAFE   **$–$$**
1847 Village West Pkwy. (The Legends of Village West)
Kansas City, KS
(913) 334-8888
www.trexcafe.com
Turn a corner at the shops in the Legends and—eeek! You've just come face-to-ugly-face with a life-size dinosaur! The first T-Rex Cafe in the country (there's now one at Disney World) serves up fun, food, and even a little education for kids of all ages. Little ones can tear into mac 'n' cheese or Dexter's Dino Dogs (three mini hot dogs), while carnivorous adults will be sated by a rib eye steak or barbecue ribs.

Before or after the meal, eager tykes can unearth the past in the interactive Paleo Zone. Excavate fossils in the Discovery Dig, explore the mine to find hidden treasures, or pan for precious stones in the Discovery Creek.

ICE IS NICE

CROWN CENTER ICE TERRACE
2450 Grand Blvd.
(816) 274-8411
www.crowncenter.com
This is a scene worthy of Currier and Ives: couples, arm-in-arm, gliding across the ice to music, children in snowsuits making frantic arm circles to keep from falling . . . oops, too late. The setting for this living Christmas card is Crown Center, which appropriately enough is the Hallmark Cards headquarters. A free-form tent provides shelter so even during inclement weather the ice is perfect.

The terrace is open seven days a week, 10 a.m. to 9 p.m. from Nov through Mar. Fees are $6 per person and free for adults over 60 and children 4 and under; skate rental is $3.

THE ICE AT PARK PLACE
117th and Nall
(913) 663-2070
www.destinationparkplace.com
At this old fashioned, open-air town square in the heart of Leawood, kids and adults can skate before popping into a neighboring restaurant for hot chocolate (or something a little more bracing for the parents). When the ice melts, the same area is a prime picnic spot. Fees are $6; children four and under are free, and skate rental is $3.

PEPSI ICE MIDWEST SKATING RINK AND FITNESS CENTER
12140 W. 135th St.
Overland Park, KS
(913) 851-1600
www.icemidwest.com
This sparkling, sprawling center features three ice rinks used for hockey and ice-skating competitions and practice. In fact this facility is home to one of the country's oldest ice-skating groups, the Silver Blades, and the only place in Kansas City to play adult hockey.

The ice is available for free skating at various times during the week, usually from 10 a.m. to early afternoon on weekdays, and two sessions on Sat. Check the Web site or call for specific hours. Fees are $7.50 for adults, $5.50 for children under seven years of age, and $3.50 for skate rental. Lessons are also available, and the rink can be rented for birthday parties. The center also has a fitness center, game room, and deli.

SNOW CREEK SKI LODGE
MO 45, 5 miles north of Weston, MO
(816) 640-2200
www.skisnowcreek.com
We'll admit Missouri is a few peaks short of Colorado, but that doesn't mean kids can't have

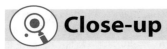

Close-up

The Kansas City Zoo
6800 Zoo Dr.
(816) 513-5700
www.kansascityzoo.org

The Kansas City Zoo had humble beginnings when it opened in December 1909 as a shelter for abandoned circus animals. Since then it's gone through as many skins as a python. Today more than 1,000 animals roam freely within its 200 acres of natural habitats. And while there's no guarantee you'll see a lion—he may be snoozing in the brush out back—you'll appreciate the realistic environment almost as much as these beautiful beasts.

The zoo is continuing to grow and improve, and will soon open a $10 million polar bear exhibit where the magnificent northern species will cavort and swim within a 140,000 gallon pool. A climate controlled viewing area will keep the rest of us toasty, and offer a superb place to host parties. The Rain Forest exhibit is already a hit with little zoologists; here's where calling someone a crested screamer is perfectly acceptable. To really experience the new zoo, pick up a map at the entrance or, better yet, download a copy from the Web site to study before you arrive. Wear comfortable footware; like the animals on view, you'll be hoofing it. Or take the train, which circles the central portion of the zoo with stops at Australia ($2.50 per person round trip); a tram, which runs to the African Market and back (75 cents each way); or a cruise on Lake Nakuru from the African Boathouse. There's plenty to see on foot, and the fun starts right in the front area called the KidZone. That's where you can ride on a cheetah or a rhino. Not real animals, of course; they are part of 36 hand-carved wooden animals that grace the new Endangered Species Carousel. Rides are $2 per person. Nearby is the new Discovery Barn, an enclosed, air-conditioned environment that lets you lock eyes with a lemur, squirrel monkey, or fascinating meerkat. Nearby is one of the most popular sights—the sea lion pool, where several times a day the sleek entertainers dive, splash, and bark in unison for their pay—fish tossed by their trainer. The Tiger Trail celebrates the return of the beautiful big cats. It's mesmerizing to watch the Sumatran tigers, Langka and Manis. Fewer than 250 are thought to exist in the wild. The Australian tour begins at an aviary with over 20 species of birds and mammals from the world's smallest continent. Then watch kangaroos, emus, dingo, wallaby,

fun on skis here. This ski lodge is on a natural hill with a 300-foot vertical drop and enough varied terrain to give beginners and experts a (ski) run for their money. Trails are accessed via two triple chairlifts, one double chairlift, and three rope tows. Thanks to 60 snow-making positions, the snow base ranges from 24 to 60 inches, enough to provide powdery fun for the crowds that pack this place on evenings and weekends. There are plenty of gentle slopes and flat areas for beginners to practice their wedges without getting blasted by the big kids. And the new Tornado Alley snow tubing area is a 700-foot-long slope where kids of all ages can get a heart-pounding ride. Prices range from $26 to $42, with the

slope's own version of happy hour on certain days with a reduced fee of $30 for a four-hour session. Are your fingers numb yet?

A 10,000-square-foot lodge features a cafeteria, bar, and lounge and also houses the ski school and gift shop. The rental shop offers shaped skis with plenty of junior sizes, plus snowboards and ski boards—just the ticket for Jason's Run, an area with enough jumps, bumps, mounds, pipes, and tabletops to keep expert boarders counting the days until Snow Creek opens in mid-Dec. Weather permitting, the lodge stays open seven days a week through mid-Mar.

Prices range from $30 to $69 for a one-day pass; helmets, which are required, are $10 to

and cassowary thriving in their natural habitats. If you want a bird's-eye view, take a camel ride; kids can also saddle up for pony rides.

One of the newest additions is the African exhibit, 95 acres of land that's home to more than 400 animals. Take a tour through Botswana, where the elephants roam, keeping cool by taking mud baths during summer's heat. Sometimes these pachyderms become Picassos as they paint on canvas; you can even purchase one of the masterpieces in the gift shop. Crossing into Kenya, animal lovers can gaze over 17 acres of plains filled with sable antelope, beisa oryx, impala, and greater kudu . . . as in, "Kudu hand me the camera, please? I think I just saw a cheetah!"

Hop on a safari boat ride to tour Lake Nakuru, where you might see a baby hippo or Kifaru Malika, the East African rhino, one of only 660 black rhinos in existence today. Our zoo has been blessed with two giraffe births in recent years, and it's always a delight to watch these graceful animals grow up. And up.

In the Congolese Forest you'll see leopard, bongo, and lowland gorillas, and in Tanzania the chimpanzees will keep you entertained. In the final stop, Uganda, you'll view baboons, lemurs, jackals, and an enormous Aldabra tortoise.

Parents will also be glad to know there are several snack bars throughout the zoo as well as two sit-down restaurants. But, especially during the hot days of summer, it's a good idea to bring plenty of water along with sunscreen and hats.

The zoo also features the Sprint IMAX Theatre, which puts you right in the center of the action with a 6½-story-tall screen and 12,000 watts of digital sound. Call (816) 871-IMAX for day and evening show times and ticket information. But for our money, the biggest thrill for kids is a Nocturnal Safari, where they spend the night at a campsite after a day of playing junior zookeeper. Next morning, is that a tummy growling or a big cat waking up nearby? Never fear, the campers are safe and breakfast is waiting. The zoo is open daily year-round from 9:30 a.m. to 5 p.m. Apr 1 through Oct 14 and 9 a.m. to 4 p.m. the rest of the season, except for Nocturnal Safaris described above. It's closed Christmas Day and Jan 1. Admission ranges from $5 to just under $10. Parking is free and right outside the entrance.

rent. Group rates and season passes are available. Lessons cost around $18 an hour for beginner or refresher; private lessons are also available. See you on the slopes, you snow bunny, you.

LIONS AND TIGERS AND GOATS, OH MY!

DEANNA ROSE CHILDREN'S FARMSTEAD
138th St. and Switzer Rd.
Overland Park, KS
(913) 897-2360
www.opkansas.org

If your children have never been up close and personal with a cow—or even if they have—

they'll love this miniature 12-acre farm. The farmstead opened in 1976 and in 1985 was dedicated in memory of Deanna Rose, an Overland Park police officer killed in the line of duty. Within the barnyard is Bluefeather the bison, plus rabbits, pigs, chickens, sheep, and goats that like to play king of the mountain in their rocky playing field. In spring the place is filled with fuzzy little newborns; it's quite a treat to feed the babies from a bottle. Older animals, particularly the goats, are tame enough to eat from the palm of a two-year-old. Make sure you bring plenty of quarters to buy feed from the vending machines.

There are other activities to keep your child, and you, entertained for hours. Turn off the cell phone and put down the PDA. Rent a fishing pole for catch-and-release action, ride the ponies, or simply walk along the brick pathways past flowers and vegetable gardens maintained by the Johnson County Extension Master Gardeners, and there's usually an expert or two on hand to tell you exactly how they get those begonias so perky. Newer attractions include an Indian encampment, a prairie playground including a log fort, and a country schoolhouse.

Some of the other recent additions are real gems: For around $4 kids can pan for gemstones in the new mine, and a play barn features an open-air bridge leading to two tube slides. The Tiny Tot play area is reserved for children six and under. A combo pack for around $10 is a good value if you plan to stay and play all day.

When those tuckered-out tykes are ready for lunch, the concession stand is ready with hot dogs and PB&Js, snacks, and juice. Admission is free Mon through Thurs, and $2 Fri through Sun. The park is open 9 a.m. to 5 p.m., seven days a week, from early Apr through the end of Oct. Summer hours, 9 a.m. to 8 p.m., are in force Tues and Thurs from Memorial Day to Labor Day.

LOOP-THE-LOOPS AND LOTS OF WATER

WORLDS OF FUN AND OCEANS OF FUN
4545 Worlds of Fun Ave.
(816) 454-4545
www.worldsoffun.com
Kansas City sent the fun-o-meter off the charts when Worlds of Fun opened in 1973 with 175 acres of roller coasters, rides, and musical shows. The park continues to add new attractions and thrills every year. The latest to join the speed demons is the $8 million Prowler set among the wooded African area. Hold onto your hats (and stomachs) as you plummet 85 feet into a ravine. The Patriot, the longest and tallest inverted roller coaster in the region, climbs a 149-foot lift hill before plunging you down a curved drop at nearly 60 mph. The 3,000 feet of track include an 89-foot vertical loop, inclined bank curve, and zero-gravity roll. No wonder flip-flops are not

allowed! Daredevils must be at least 54 inches tall to ride.

And the Boomerang is a 12-story-tall scream machine that rockets forward and backward through corkscrew turns, upside-down loops, and 125-foot lifts at up to 50 mph. You might want to rethink those breakfast plans. A more sedate choice might be the Skyliner Ferris wheel, which provides a panoramic view from 60 feet up.

Worlds of Fun also keeps the smaller kids in mind with their very own Camp Snoopy. This one-acre playland has a three-story interactive funhouse that lets kids slide and jump into 5,000 foam balls. A kiddy train and Red Baron airplane ride round out the activities.

To make your stay more enjoyable, there are food concessions and stroller rentals available. Worlds of Fun is generally open daily from late May to early Sept at 10 a.m.; closing times are as late as 10 p.m. Day passes range from $16 to $41 depending on the age and day. Kids age two and under get in free. Discounts are available on the Web site. Parking is $10 a day. A Ride & Slide pass gets you into both Worlds of Fun and Oceans of Fun for $35 to $56; a gate connects the two. Next door is Oceans of Fun, a 60-acre wet and wild adventure that includes a million-gallon pool with 4-foot-high waves, sandy beach, children's "sprayground," 43-foot water slides, and Castaway Cove, an adults-only pool with swim-up refreshments. Oceans of Fun is generally open daily from late May to early Sept at 10 a.m.; closing time varies. A single day pass ranges from $16 to $48. Prices may change; call for specifics.

Now you can stay where the fun is. The Worlds of Fun Village resort features 20 cottages and 22 log cabins (which sleep up to six guests) and 82 deluxe RV sites so close to the thrills you can practically feel the whoosh of the Patriot roller coaster. A swimming pool, Jacuzzi, video arcade, laundry room, and shower facilities are available in the clubhouse, and there's 24-hour security. Staying here gets you discounted tickets to the parks. RV sites are open early Mar through mid-Nov; cabins and cottages are available early Apr through the end of Oct. Check online for rates.

MUSEUMS FOR YOUNG MINDS

Mention a museum to kids and watch how fast they run from the room. We understand. But if you can get them in the door of one of these exhibitions, you may have a hard time getting them to leave. Pick something your child is passionate about, like dinosaurs, or give him or her something new to learn about, such as astronomy. Suddenly that next science project is in the bag.

When available we've listed the museum's Web site so you can preplan your visit to get the most out of your valuable time. Here's another plus: The wide variety of choices means there's something to interest every age group from toddlers to 'tweens and above. And don't miss our premier children's interactive museum, Science City.

SCIENCE CITY AT UNION STATION
30 W. Pershing Rd.
(816) 460-2000
www.sciencecity.com
For children (or adults, for that matter) who consider science their least-liked subject, the Science City interactive museum will change their minds. Rather than viewing artifacts displayed behind glass, children are encouraged to play, interact, and learn with over 50 hands-on science activities. Land a space shuttle in a NASA-style simulator. Explore new and exciting traveling exhibits each year inside the exhibit gallery. Build a robot using LEGOs.

Science City also showcases Dino Lab, the result of a partnership between Union Station and the University of Kansas. You can watch a scientist prepping real dinosaurs for display in this unique laboratory, the largest of its kind in the United States.

And here, they have camping down to a science with overnight camp-ins for groups of 50 or more; it's a popular getaway for scouts. Science City offers plenty of places for pooped-out scientists and their parents to refuel without leaving Union Station. Science City is generally open from 10 a.m. to 4 p.m., but times and days vary depending on the season. During winter, for instance, it is closed Mon through Wed; check the Web site to plan your visit. General admission is $10 for ages three and older. Parking is free for up to three hours; if you're staying longer, get your parking ticket validated at the event you're attending.

The Theater District, which is separate from Union Station, comes alive in the evening with four exciting stages. The City Extreme Screen's five-story-tall screen and two- and three-dimensional projection bring films to life. City Dome combines video, lasers, special effects, and multichannel sound to create a planetarium show that's out of this world. City Stage is a 200-seat live theater venue offering a variety of shows from musical revues to hilarious science demonstrations. Single theater admissions start at $8 or can be purchased in combination with Science City. The Theatre District is open until 10 p.m. and is located in the lower level on the west side of Union Station.

i Lose your marbles? The Toy and Miniature Museum may have found them. With over a million glass spheres of all colors and sizes, it boasts the largest collection in the United States, perhaps the world.

THE TOY AND MINIATURE MUSEUM OF KANSAS CITY
5235 Oak St.
(816) 333-9328
www.toyandminiaturemuseum.com
Tell your children to "think small," and then take them to this fascinating museum filled with one of the world's most extensive collections of miniatures, antique toys, and folk art. Girls of all ages are drawn to the exquisitely furnished dollhouses as well as a fantastic display of Barbie and her pals (darling, you certainly don't look 50!). Boys will flock to the transportation room with trains chugging overhead and cast-iron scooters, stagecoaches, and cars below. One of the museum's most enduring exhibits is the display of miniatures such as an American Indian bowl with $1/8$-inch-long frog handles

and an 8-inch-high English Georgian secretary desk with working locks and 19 secret compartments. Be sure to request a floor plan so you won't miss anything within the 38-room house. The guide also suggests questions to ask children, providing thought-provoking history lessons along the way. The museum is open 10 a.m. to 4 p.m. Wed through Sat, and 1 to 4 p.m Sun. It is closed Mon and Tues, on major holidays, and during the two weeks following Labor Day. Admission is $6 for adults and $4 for children ages 3 through 12.

WONDERSCOPE CHILDREN'S MUSEUM
5700 King (Shawnee)
(913) 287-8888
www.wonderscope.org
Although it's true that some other museums are fancier than Wonderscope, parents tell us that children beg to return here again and again. Its new home provides even more places for toddlers to 10-year olds to play and learn in a nuturing, fun, and safe environment. Special programs and events range from storytelling to the KABOOM science demonstrations. Budding preschool artists will enjoy the art workshops, while some kids head right for the indoor sandbox. Although food isn't allowed in the exhibit areas, you can enjoy lunch and snacks from home in the indoor picnic area. Wonderscope is also a favorite place for birthday parties; call for information about cost and availability.

The museum is open 10 a.m. to 5 p.m. Mon through Sat and noon to 5 p.m. Sun. It is closed Mon from Sept through Feb and anytime the Shawnee Mission School District has a snow day.

i When visiting Union Station's Science City, don't miss the Henry W. Bloch Fountain out front. This ever-changing liquid ballet pumps 9,225 gallons of water per minute through 232 computer-controlled jets shooting as high as 120 feet.

RIDE 'EM COWBOY (AND COWGIRL)

AMERICAN ROYAL MUSEUM AND VISITOR CENTER
1701 American Royal Court
(816) 221-9800
www.americanroyal.com
Okay, so your young 'uns don't get to ride a horse or rope a steer at this museum. But they can pretend they're riding Blaze as they try out a variety of saddle styles in the Traditions area. Lots of activities and displays keep little cowpokes entertained, and for students and 4-H members interested in agribusiness, this place is a must. The center opened in 1992 as a tribute to the hundred-year-old American Royal, Kansas City's annual horse and livestock shows, rodeo, and parade.

Kids get a kick out of stepping on a livestock scale to compare their weight to that of pigs, chickens, and feeder steer. And little girls can dream while gazing at a dazzling crown from the American Royal Queen contest.

The museum is open year-round, and trained docents are available for tours. Activities are scheduled throughout the year, including spring field trips when kids can take pony rides, make butter, grind wheat, plant a soybean, and learn how to line dance. Call extension 125 for specific dates and costs and to make reservations for specific events.

SEE WHAT'S IN STORE

Following are shops where your kids can spend their allowances, or the entire family can play, poke, and peruse without spending a dime.

BROOKSIDE TOY & SCIENCE
330 W. 63rd St.
(816) 523-4501
www.brooksidetoyandscience.com
You don't need a child to enjoy this store; in fact there are plenty of solo adults walking around with big silly grins in place, reliving a childhood for an hour or so. Every conceivable toy, game,

and model car kit is here, along with a very nice display of telescopes and microscopes. As the ... this is science project headquar... ... ...cational toys to ... ...d Mary Jo Ward, ...floored wonder... ... ...pride in the fact that they ... ...ions of any ki...d.

...independent ...tore (rare these ... ...reserve with the big chains. And he... ... ...reason to shop here first: Kids are enco... ...bring in old toys in good con... ...ss fortunate children.

MOON MARBLE COMPANY
600 E. ...
Bonner Springs, KS
(913) 5...1422
www.m... ...

... himself, so chil-... ...ng with keep-
ing aisles filled with yo-yos, magic tricks, game boards, and old-fashioned tin toys, Bruce Breslow makes marvelous marbles while you watch. And of course there are plenty of the round wonders to buy—whole buckets of them—as well as collectible marbles from all over. This fascinating place—popular with Boy Scouts and their pops—is open Tues through Sat, 10 a.m. to 5 p.m. Demonstrations usually take place Tues, Fri, and Sat from 10:30 a.m. until 3 p.m., as long as there's a willing audience (and a marble artisan). Large groups are welcome, but call to schedule a demonstration.

ZOOM
300 Ward Pkwy. (Country Club Plaza)
(816) 842-8697
We happen to love locally owned toy stores with cool stuff you won't find in big, national chains. That's the beauty of Zoom; every item is personally chosen because it's fun, educational, or a gift a child will treasure forever. And since moving to this new corner spot on the Plaza, John and Jackie Middelkamp have even more room to display their 250 lines of toys. Little girls and 'tweens will go gaga for the expanded section of pretend make-up kits and spa treatments for those so-important sleepovers. Hello Kitty items are well represented as well. Science kits will fascinate both boys and girls, as will arts and crafts packages and other activities for kids from infants to early teens. And if you want to impress that kids who's waiting for a gift from a traveling parent, there are plenty of personalized items including water bottles.

Kites, mobiles, books, puppets, and more are all delightfully displayed, and what's more, there are people eager to help you choose just the right gift for any age. Long-time fans of Zoom will be happy to know that the famous lunch box collection, from vintage to contemporary, made the move. It weaves throughout the store near the ceiling.

TAKE IT OUTSIDE, KIDS

Kansas City is dotted with dozens of parks and lakes where kids can find enough beaches, nature trails, and campsites to fill a summer or a lifetime. You'll find descriptions of some of our favorite parklands in the Parks, Lakes, and Recreation chapter. In the meantime we'll introduce you to the following places created with kids in mind, including a park that's friendly to wheelchairs. Most parks are open from daylight to dusk daily. Call ahead for opening and closing times.

ERNIE MILLER PARK AND NATURE CENTER
909 N. Kansas
Olathe, KS
(913) 764-7759
www.erniemiller.com
Introduce your nature boy or girl to this 113-acre park that's been preserved in all its glorious natural state. Three trails wind through ecological habitats such as grassland, meadow, and forest. It's a terrific place for birding—look for woodpeckers, sparrows, owls, and woodland songbirds—as well as sighting other wildlife, like white-tailed deer. Pick up a pocket-sized guide at the Nature Center (or print one from the Web site), where you can spend time with a terrific wildlife diorama and interpretive displays. Gen-

eral hours are 9 a.m. to 4:30 p.m. Mon through Sat and 1 to 5 p.m. Sun.

PENN VALLEY SKATE PARK
31st and Penn Lane
(816) 513-7500
www.kcmo.org/parks
Kansas City Parks and Recreation made a lot of kids happy when it opened a skate park on the west side of a beautiful urban park. It features a square shallow end with metal coping, clamshell-shaped midsection, and 10-foot-deep huge bowl. The park, open from 7 a.m. to 10 p.m. (unless wet or rainy) is for skateboarding and in-line skating only, and protective equipment must be used at all times. Competitive or demonstration events require special approval; call the number listed above. One blogger writes that "the trans throws you awesome." We're guessing that's a good thing. For links to other facilities in Kansas City (including Blue Springs and Independence), visit www.skateboardpark.com.

OVERLAND PARK SOCCER COMPLEX
13700 Switzer Rd.
(913) 685-1512
www.opkansas.org/soccer-complex
How much do the good folks of Overland Park love their kids? About $36 million worth. That's the price tag for the new 96-acre soccer complex, the first of its kind in the country. Everything is primo here, including the 12 lighted, regulation-size fields with synthetic turf and the clubhouse.

The expense has already paid off for Johnson County, and by more than just having a spectacular space for this soccer-hungry community of kids. The complex has already signed the US Youth Soccer National Championship with more big name national competitions on the way. But back to the local needs: rentals for games and tourneys range from $20 to $50. Prices are less for special-needs children. The complex is open seven days a week, from 7 a.m. until 11 p.m.

THEATERS FOR YOUNG THESPIANS

How many movie stars can pinpoint the moment they decided to become an actor? Plenty, and often that moment came while watching a play or musical as a child. Perhaps your youngster will catch the acting bug as well, or at least be entertained for an hour or so at one of these made-for-kids theaters. Some of them even offer acting classes (read more in the Education and Child Care section of the Relocation chapter), and one provides a forum for young playwrights.

THE COTERIE
2450 Grand Blvd. (lower level of
Crown Center Shops)
(816) 474-6552
www.thecoterie.com
Since 1987 this professional acting company has been introducing young people to the joys of live performances. The subject matter is often thought-provoking, with such titles as *Free to Be . . . You and Me* and a look at the horrors of the Holocaust. But there's lighthearted fare as well, including a musical starring that silly Pooh Bear. It's easy to add to the experience by attending after-performance workshops or by taking acting classes that are available for preschool through 12th grade.

Each May the Coterie mounts a Young Playwright's Festival to showcase local talent. Another reason *Time* magazine named it one of the five best theaters for young adults in the nation? The Lab for New Family Musicals, another idea from the gifted artistic director, Jeff Church. It's already paid off with works from talents such as Harry Connick Jr. Tickets to performances are $10 for students 18 and younger, $15 for adults. A season pass is an exceptional value.

THEATRE FOR YOUNG AMERICA
Union Station
30 W. Pershing Rd.
(816) 460-2083
www.tya.org

For more than 35 years this company's mission has been to foster educational and emotional growth of children through drama. The good news is that children don't even realize they're learning; they're too busy laughing or getting immersed in the actions on stage. TYA, as it's called, mounts five or six shows a year in a range of subject matters from ancient to contemporary. The plays are appropriate for preschool ages and up. The staff and volunteers also offer classes in voice, body movement, and conflict management. Individual classes as well as four-day and one-week residencies are available. Performances are held at the H&R Block City Stage at Union Station, a wonderful facility with comfortable seats and excellent lighting and sound.

TWINKLE, TWINKLE, LITTLE STAR

You promised your child the moon and the stars; well, here's your chance to deliver. Kansas City is blessed with a number of observatories in both urban and suburban settings. Pick a cloudless night to introduce your little star to the wonders of the universe. And for the biggest Big Bang for your buck, head out to the giant telescope at Powell Observatory just north of Louisburg, Kansas.

GOTTLIEB PLANETARIUM SHOWS
Union Station
30 W. Pershing Rd.
(816) 460-2020
www.unionstation.org
One of Kansas City's hidden gems, this planetarium hosts several fascinating kid-friendly programs, including an animated laser light show that includes favorite tunes from classic rock and retro hits. The 360-degree domed screen takes you on an incredible tour of the stars as they appear over Kansas City.

Tickets are $6 or discounted with the purchase of another attraction at Union Station. The planetarium is open Tues through Sun.

POWELL OBSERVATORY
Lewis-Young Park
Louisburg, KS
(913) 438-3825
www.askconline.org
This, to use a purely scientific term, is the big Kahuna. Located far from the lights of the city, Powell Observatory has a reflecting telescope with a 30-inch mirror. It's the largest telescope in a five-state area and among the largest in the country that is available for public viewing.

Members of the Astronomical Society of Kansas City built and maintain the facility and host programs here such as "Starbright Saturday Night." Held every Sat night from May through Oct beginning at dusk, the program includes a discussion about a current astronomical event and a short video. A tour of the observatory concludes with taking turns viewing the stars, galaxies, nebulae, moon, and planets through the 30-inch and 16-inch telescopes. Society members are usually outside with their own telescopes and are happy to let visitors take a peek. The suggested donation is $5 per adult and $3 for children. Bring lawn chairs or blankets, and don't forget the bug spray!

WARKOCZEWSKI OBSERVATORY
800 E. 52nd St.
(816) 235-1606
Locate Orion faster than you can say, "Warkoczewski," through this 16-inch telescope mounted on the roof of Royall Hall on the University of Missouri–Kansas City campus. The observatory is named for the late Stanley Warkoczewski, a retired sound engineer who, along with his wife, Helen, spent 10 years constructing the telescope in his basement before donating it to the school. Stan died in 1997 at the age of 91, but we think he's up there, just to the east of Pegasus.

The observatory is open one hour after sunset on clear Fridays from Apr through Nov. It's best to call the number above to confirm that it will be available.

ANNUAL EVENTS AND FESTIVALS

A while back a gentleman wrote to the editor of the *Kansas City Star* complaining about what he considered a tragic lack of things to do in our town. Where, he implored, could he take his family when they came to visit in early July? For the next week or so, letters to the newspaper answered him with long lists of fascinating attractions . . . and more than a few offers to help him move out of town.

Perhaps he had missed the previous week's edition listing (for one Saturday alone) festivals celebrating Slavic, Greek, Scottish, African-American, and Hispanic cultures; three garden tours; a rock fest; a folk dance; three free jazz concerts; a fishing derby; the Monkees at the Midland; real monkeys at the zoo; a sailboat regatta; and Elvis Presley's cousin singing "Blue Suede Shoes." And that doesn't even include standbys such as Worlds of Fun, Oceans of Fun, the Truman Library, theaters, art exhibits, or lazy afternoons at a park or lake. Mister, if you can't find something to do in that group, you're not trying hard enough.

So here's our calendar for the rest of you. As you'll see, around here we'll throw a party or start a parade based on little more than the fact that that it's Tuesday. Our Wild West roots also show up in rodeos and barbecues, including the granddaddy of 'em all, the American Royal, but those of you with more refined tastes won't be disappointed. Flamenco guitar in a rose garden, check. *Nutcracker Suite* from a balcony, check. A 10-city-block outdoor art show, double check.

One of our finest treasures, our diversity, is evident in the number of ethnic festivals held throughout the year. You'll have a chance to taste spanikopita, kimchee, bangers and mash, or alligator on a stick (tastes just like chicken) while listening to a bagpipe, electric guitar, bouzouki, fiddle, steel drum . . . or accordion if you must.

And few cities celebrate the holidays as passionately as we do, with an old-fashioned Easter parade, and no fewer than 24 separate fireworks displays on the Fourth of July. Even our Halloween is spook-tacular, with a dozen haunted houses and pumpkin patches. Winter brings holiday tours of historic homes and the world's most thrilling display of Christmas lights. So come soon, and come often. No matter when you arrive we'll have something wonderful waiting for you.

JANUARY

COUNTRY CLUB PLAZA HOLIDAY LIGHTS

Just in case you haven't seen the Plaza illuminated with 75 miles of jewel-colored lights, you still have until mid-Jan before they're put away for another year. Our favorite view can be seen coming down from the hill on Wornall that runs between the InterContinental and Raphael Hotels. A celebrity steps on stage to flip the switch on Thanksgiving night, then the magic goes away in mid-Jan.

ICE SKATING AT CROWN CENTER ICE AND PARK PLACE

www.crowncenter.com and www.destinationparkplace.com

Put on your woolies and catch some frozen action at the city's two outdoor skating rinks. You'll be warmed by the entire storybook scene. And when you're ready to duck inside, you'll find dozens of shops and restaurants a snowball's throw away.

KANSAS CITY RESTAURANT WEEK
www.kansascityrestaurantweek.com
When's the last time your favorite restaurant had a sale? That's the idea behind this fantastic program where dining rooms offer multi-course lunch and dinner for around $15 and $30. If your New Year's resolution was to save money, you're golden. If you vowed to lose weight, not so much. Kansas City launched this event in 2010 with more than 100 restaurants signing up; 10 percent of the proceeds went to the Harvester's food bank.

MARTIN LUTHER KING JR. CELEBRATION
William Jewell College
Liberty, MO
(816) 781-7700
www.jewell.edu
Several communities and churches throughout the Kansas City area honor Dr. King's memory with music, dance, and educational programs so that children and teens can learn about his teachings. The City of Liberty has hosted one of the largest, "Building a Community: Shaping a New Generation," since 1985. Past years have showcased local groups including the Wylliams/Henry Danse Theatre and the William Jewell Concert Choir. The event is free to the public.

SNOW CREEK SKI LODGE
Weston, MO
(816) 640-2200
www.skisnowcreek.com
You can hit the ski slopes and still be home in time for dinner at Weston, Missouri, just 40 minutes away. The mini-ski resort offers enough variety to give beginners and expert skiers an afternoon or evening of fun. The 24- to 60-inch base is courtesy of Mother Nature, helped along by 60 snowmaking machines, and trails are accessed via chair lifts and rope tows. Après-ski activities take place in the lodge that sports a cafeteria, bar, and lounge, along with a rental shop where the hottest things going—literally—are the snowboards. Weather permitting, the lodge stays open seven days a week through mid-Mar. Check out more of the cool news in Kidstuff.

FEBRUARY

ART AUCTION
Kansas City Artists Coalition
210 Wyandotte
(816) 421-5222
www.kansascityartistscoalition.org
Hope you have some dough left after the holidays, because you'll want to buy something at this annual event that showcases about 200 artists in categories from ceramics and glass to pastels, found-art sculpture, and oils. The work is displayed in the gallery for a week or two before the gala, which includes a silent auction and live bidding.

GROUNDHOG RUN
Hunt Midwest Underground Facility
Subtropolis
(816) 756-0780
www.childrenstlc.org
There may be 4 inches of snow on the ground, but it's a relatively toasty 58 degrees in this underground cave. More than 3,000 runners vie for prizes in this 5K and 10K race. More than the balmy temperatures, the participants love the flat running surface. Entrants pay around $15, which gets them a T-shirt and the knowledge that they helped raise funds for the Children's Therapeutic Learning Center.

METROPOLITAN LAWN & GARDEN SHOW
Bartle Hall, 13th and Central or American Royal Center
(816) 931-4686, (816) 513-5000
www.patrihaproductions.com
What perfect timing! Just when Midwesterners can't take another day of gray skies and brown lawns, it's time for the Midwest's premier lawn and garden show. Landscape designers try to outdo one another with fabulous displays of flowering bulbs, trees, and the latest in water gardens. And if you're still on the fence about fencing, patio materials, and decking, this is the place to ask questions of the dozens of vendors on hand. The three-day event typically takes place in early Feb. Admission is $8.50 for adults;

children under 12 get in free. See the description below for a two-for-one show price.

REMODELING & DECORATING SHOW
Bartle Hall, 13th and Central or American Royal Center
(816) 931-4686, (816) 513-5000

Homeowners who are tackling a major remodeling job will find great products and ideas here, or at least someone to commiserate with. Even folks living in sparkling new houses will want to watch demonstrations on faux painting, wallpapering, and turning bedsheets into fancy curtain swags. More than 250 companies show the latest home decorating trends as well as products and services for roofing, skylights, kitchens and baths, spas, pools, and windows and doors. Demonstrations continue throughout the weekend. See the lawn and garden show for ticket information.

ANNUAL KANSAS CITY BOAT SHOW
Various locations
(816) 513-5000, (816) 931-4686
www.pathrihaproductions.com

We may be landlocked, but Kansas City has more than its share of recreational lakes dotting the landscape, and the fabulous Lake of the Ozarks is just a few hours away. For nearly 30 years this show, the Midwest's biggest, has put thousands of boating and fishing enthusiasts, as well as party-cove sun worshippers, in the mood. All manner of luxury cruisers, fishing boats, ski boats, personal watercraft, and apparel are see-worthy. Adult tickets are $8.50; tadpoles under 12 get in free.

WORLD OF WHEELS AT BARTLE HALL
13th and Central
(248) 650-5560
www.worldofwheels.com

You'll see plenty of flash, add-ons, and paint here . . . and that's just the bikini contest participants. Every year about this time, Bartle Hall practically vibrates with testosterone as they roll in every kind of hot rod, rebuilt classic car, and fancy detailed motorcycle imaginable. Some of the most popular displays are customized vehicles and bikes that feature incredible paint jobs and pounds of extra chrome. Proud owners vie for top prizes; others just show up to drool. The ticket price of $12.50 will also let you stand in line to ogle celebrities, women wrestlers, and scantily clad beauties . . . just don't ask to look under the hood.

ANNUAL MARDI GRAS FESTIVAL
Power & Light District
www.powerandlightdistrict.com

Bourbon Street comes to Kansas City at this festival of blues and zydeco music, with thousands of your closest friends packed into the KC Live! centerpiece of the P& L District. More than 30,000 beads are tossed to participants, and it's all free. Plenty of food and libations can be had at the clubs and restaurants surrounding the main stage.

POLAR BEAR PLUNGE
Shawnee Mission Park
7900 Renner Rd.
Overland Park, KS
(913) 236-9290
www.ksso.org

Brrrrr! Since 1998 hundreds of folks have braved icy waters and potential head colds to jump into Shawnee Mission Park Lake. There'd better be a good reason, you say? There is: Money raised goes to benefit Special Olympics Kansas. Once participants stop shivering (tents are provided for changing into dry clothes), it's time to head to the post-plunge party at a local brewpub. Say, barkeep, can you warm that beer for me, please? Prizes are awarded for wimpiest plunge and most outrageous plunge wear, among others. Special Olympics is an international program of sports training, education, and athletic competition for individuals with intellectual disabilities.

MARCH

FIRST FRIDAYS IN THE CROSSROADS ARTS DISTRICT
(816) 472-4546
www.kccrossroads.org

Although this street party–cum–gallery opening happens the first Friday of every month, the crowds really start showing up around March when the weather's better. This near-mile-wide downtown neighborhood, bounded by 15th Street and I-35, is home to more than 100 independent studios and galleries. Pick up a map from one of the art spaces, or print one from the Web site. During special events, a colorful trolley will take you around the area for free. Most galleries are open until 9 p.m.

BREAKFAST WITH THE EASTER BUNNY
Powell Gardens
Kingsville, MO
(816) 697-2600
www.powellgardens.org
Could anything be sweeter than a three-year-old girl in an Easter bonnet or a toddler in his first tie? While they're waiting for the Easter bunny they can dig into pancakes with mom and dad. Later, kids up to age 10 scatter throughout the gardens looking for plastic eggs filled with toys and candy. Seeing Powell Garden's display of thousands of spring bulbs is reward enough for most adults. Breakfast is $9.50 for adults, $5 for children 10 and under. Reservations are required.

ANNUAL HOME SHOW
Bartle Hall, 13th and Central
(816) 513-5000
www.kchba.org
Keeping up with the Joneses is a national obsession, and for over 50 years this show has been showing area residents how to do it right. At more than 600 displays in space equivalent to eight football fields you'll see the latest techniques, products, and services available to remodel, decorate, secure, or beautify your home. If you're in the market for a new home, you'll have a chance to meet with area builders and look through sample house plans.

And because this event is combined with the Kansas City Flower, Lawn, and Garden Show, you'll get expert advice on landscaping and get a chance to marvel at the floral displays. Demonstrations showing everything from tree prun-

ing to floral arranging are staged throughout the weekend. The Home Builders Association of Greater Kansas City sponsors the three-day showcase. Admission is $10 for adults, $9 for seniors and students. Children 12 and under are admitted free. Psssst: there's often a $2 discount coupon on the Web site.

SNAKE SATURDAY PARADE AND FESTIVAL
Downtown North Kansas City, MO
(816) 274-6000
www.nkc.org
This pretty little community practically doubles in size—or at least in shades of green—as 100,000 people show up the Saturday before St. Patrick's Day for an all-day party. A parade winds its way downtown with more than 150 cars, bands, and floats, and the post-parade activities offer something for the entire family. Enjoy carnival rides, arts and crafts booths, and enough green beer to forever change the course of the Missouri River. Irish dance troupes and musical groups perform as well. The free fun starts at 11 a.m. at 14th and Swift and snakes its way north.

BROOKSIDE ST. PAT'S WARM-UP PARADE
Meyer Blvd. and Wornall
(816) 523-5553
www.brooksidekc.org
Since 1980, this has been where Kansas City kick-starts the parade season. It's an impressive sight as floats, bands, clowns, community groups, antique cars, and dogs dressed in green wind their way through this pretty neighborhood. The parade starts around 2 p.m., but pace yourself: The big parade is less than 24 hours away.

ST. PATRICK'S DAY PARADE
Downtown
(816) 931-7373
www.kcirishparade.com
Although our official St. Patrick's Day parade got a late start compared with some other cities, we soon showed them how to transform green crepe paper into a world-class float. Outrageous radio host Mike Murphy got the ball rolling on March 17, 1972, while having lunch (and perhaps a beer or

two) with three friends at a downtown restaurant. They decided what Kansas City needed was a St. Pat's parade, by golly, so they whipped up a sign, put a green bow on somebody's dog, and began a tradition that's become the third largest parade in the country. These days about 350,000 people crowd the streets to cheer on more than 200 colorful floats, politicians in convertibles, high school marching bands, pretty girls dancing jigs, pipe and drum corps, an Elvis look-alike or two, and a contingency of kazoo players. Recently, the parade route moved south, starting at 33rd and Broadway around 11 a.m. For those really in the spirit, the day starts at Browne's Market (3300 Pennsylvania Ave.), where an authentic Irish breakfast is served along with music and dancing as early as 6 a.m.

APRIL

CIVIL WAR ON THE BORDER
Mahaffie Stagecoach Stop
1100 Kansas City Rd.
Olathe, KS
(913) 782-6972
www.olatheks.org
As the first overnight stagecoach stop on the Santa Fe Trail outside Westport Landing, this place saw its share of wranglers, riders, and families heading west. It also got caught in the border skirmishes between Missouri and the Free State. In fact, these battles predated the Civil War by four years. Reenactors dressed as infantry, cavalry, and artillery soldiers will relive Civil War days, as Yanks and Rebs mix it up during this two-day event. The cannon booms will be enough to knock you out of your seat! Demonstrations throughout the weekend will shed light on the frontier-town lifestyle, and the vittles and sarsaparilla will tide you over until the next stagecoach pulls up bound for Dodge.

KANSAS CITY FILMFEST
AMC Main Street Theatre (Power & Light District)
www.kcfilmfest.org
This successful festival showcasing the best of film shorts and features has a new name and a new location: The all-digital AMC Main Street Theatre near the Power & Light District. Seminars, workshops, and panels in all areas of filmmaking are on the agenda along with award ceremonies and receptions. That gives participants a chance to mingle with the next Steven Spielberg or Brad Pitt. And, of course, there will be five days of viewing some of the world's best films and videos. Check the Web site for details regarding dates and venues, ticket prices, and workshops.

PEMBROKE HILL SCHOOL CLOTHESLINE SALE
State Line Rd. and Ward Pkwy.
(816) 936-1200
www.pembrokehill.org
This is without a doubt the most incredible garage sale in the Midwest. It takes volunteers weeks just to sort, tag, and display the wares, including everything from baby clothes to furniture, shoes to golf clubs, and antiques to jars of marbles. For those who don't know, Pembroke is a school for mostly privileged students, so their families' cast-offs often sport designer labels. Oh, you'll still find the occasional lamp you wouldn't wish on your brother-in-law, but for the most part it's all primo stuff. Call the school for dates, or watch for the big banners displayed on the school grounds a week or two in advance. It costs $5 to shop from 4 to 8 p.m the day before it opens to the public (worth it!); otherwise it's free.

KANSAS CITY ROYALS OPENING DAY
Kauffman Stadium
(800) 6ROYALS
www.kcroyals.com
The boys are back, the wait is over, and baseball season is officially open at "The K." Opening weekend usually falls within the first week in April, and people dress in blue and challenge their vocal cords. After a major renovation in 2009, the ballpark is bigger and brighter than ever. For fans that means more food courts and bars, a terrific playground for kids, and far more bathrooms. That's a home run in our book. Learn more about this beautiful ballpark and the Royals in Sports.

SPRING HOMES TOUR
(816) 942-8800
www.kchba.org
Find your new home or just see how the other half lives at the second largest scattered home show in the country. For more than 48 years members of the Kansas City Home Builders Association have been giving us their best and most beautiful every spring with abodes ranging from $120,000 to over $4 million. Yowza! The last group usually boasts closets big enough to have their own ZIP codes. Many are fully furnished, giving lookers a chance to check out the latest in decorating trends. The two-week tour spans eight counties and includes close to 500 homes. Visit the Web site for an interactive map of homes; you can search by location, builder name, or price. Free admission, but there is a price: You may not want to go home again.

SYMPHONY DESIGNER'S SHOWHOUSE
Different location each year
(816) 968-9711
www.kcsymphonyalliance.org
For over 40 years, some of the area's most beautiful homes and talented interior designers have come together each spring to create this benefit for the Kansas City Symphony. Each year a different home is selected, but it's always a magnificent specimen, often a mansion along Ward Parkway. The empty house is open for a week or so in Feb for public previews before a single can of paint is opened and then closed while more than 40 interior designers, landscape professionals, builders, architects, and artists work their magic. Preview tickets cost $5, and admission for the completed showhouse, which is usually open for three weeks, costs $15 at the door or $13 when purchased in advance at various outlets. No infants or children under eight years of age are admitted. It's the longest running designer showhouse in the country; to date this annual project has raised over $5 million for the Kansas City Symphony.

MAY

ABDALLAH SHRINE RODEO
Leavenworth County Fairgrounds
Tonganoxie, KS
(913) 362-5300
www.shrinerodeo.com
Yippee ti yi yo! It's the biggest Shrine rodeo in North America, and we've got it. It's quite a thrill to watch 150 professional cowboys and cowgirls compete for big prizes in Brahma bull riding, steer wrestling, and calf roping. The clowns jumping in and out of barrels keep the competition light, and kids can get involved in a shoe race where they have to sprint across the arena, try on shoes from a barrel, and flip-flop back. The pre-show is always a kick, with Shriners dressed in costume riding outrageously decked-out go-karts. Tickets are $10 to $25 for the two-day event.

i For up-to-the-minute listings of events, check the *Star* Friday Preview (www.kansascity.com), *The Pitch* (www.pitch.com), www.gointokansascity.com, and the current issue of *KC Magazine* (www.kcmag.com).

ART IN COLUMBUS PARK
9 blocks east of the River Market
www.columbusparkart.com
This casual gallery walk is a bit like what the wildly popular First Fridays in the Crossroads felt like a decade ago; a handful of galleries and studios opening their doors, serving wine, and introducing artists to art lovers. The longest line isn't to get into an emerging artist's quarters, it's waiting for a table at Garrozzo's Italian restaurant, where the aroma of garlic overpowers any hint of oil paint. The event is held every third Friday of the month, Apr through Dec, 6 to 10 p.m. It's free, but a small donation to keep the doors open and cheese and crackers on the table would be much appreciated. The Web site offers a handy map of participating galleries along with examples of art available.

ANNUAL BACHATHON
Grace and Holy Trinity Cathedral
13th and Broadway
(816) 474-8260
www.kcago.com

Some 24 years ago someone at this downtown cathedral got the bright idea that folks might like to hear six nonstop hours of J. S. Bach's most famous concerti and cantatas. They were right, and today standing-room-only crowds fill the chapel to hear a 28-voice choral ensemble and artists playing the 33,000-pipe house organ. Although most guests choose to listen to a few selections and quietly leave (wait here, I'll be bach), it's not unusual for true music lovers to stay put for the entire program. If that's you, bring a cushion for the pew. Cookies and beverages are available, and the Norman French style cathedral is gorgeous. Good eye; yes, those two stained-glass windows *are* by Tiffany.

ANTIQUES ON THE COMMON
Greenwood, MO (approximately 25 miles southeast of Kansas City)
(816) 537-7822
www.antiquesonthecommonshow.com

If only magazines like *Country Living* would stop showing up, we could keep this one-day antiques extravaganza our little secret. But nooooo, they have to tell the world about the goods brought in from dealers in 15 states, the jaw-dropping prices—and the blueberry cream pie. It takes Claire Fellows about two months to set up all the tents and picnic areas, one day to sell out, and about two weeks to recuperate before she starts it all again for the September sale. Expect to find an enormous variety in every price range. If the $5,000 cabinet is too rich for your blood, check down the way; there's a less-rare version for $180. Other goodies include highly collectible tramp art, baskets, penny rugs, and tons of folk art.

BROOKSIDE ART ANNUAL
63rd St. between Wornall and Main
(816) 523-5553
www.brooksidekc.org

The art fair season officially opens at this outdoor exhibit held in the charming village known as Brookside. It seems more tents are added each year, but still the sidewalks and streets overflow as 70,000 people wiggle their way in for a better look at silver earrings, a photo of the Plaza lights, an azure glass vase, or a pastel landscape.

About 195 artists are represented, grateful for a chance to talk to art lovers and sell work without paying commission. The fair, usually held the first weekend in May, also corresponds nicely with your hankering for a cone from Foo's Fabulous Custard.

CELEBRATION AT THE STATION
Union Station
www.celebrationatthestation.com

What could be more thrilling than our beloved Kansas City Symphony playing the "1812 Over-ture," punctuated by the sound of live firing cannons? It's a fitting finale to an evening of music set against the beautiful Union Station before turning around to see another majestic sight—fireworks against the Liberty Memorial. Grounds open at 3 p.m. with food, drink, and family entertainment before it's time to stake out the prime location for a picnic blanket. Some people simply plop down on the stone walls surrounding the area behind the Henry W. Bloch Fountain, temporarily quiet for the event. The rousing celebration is free.

FIESTA HISPANA
Barney Allis Plaza
12th and Wyandotte
(816) 452-4712
www.fiestakc.org

There's more entertainment than toys in a piñata at this festival honoring our city's vibrant Latino community. For two days puppeteers, Tejano singers, music and dance troupes, and exhibits keep the crowds entertained while an exhibit hall showcases the culture's proud heritage. It's a fitting tribute to national Hispanic Heritage Month. Admission is free.

FIESTA IN THE HEARTLAND
Crown Center
(816) 472-6767
www.hccgkc.com

Just as not everyone wearing a "Kiss me, I'm Irish" button on St. Pat's Day has ties to Ireland, not everyone dancing salsa at this celebration is Latino. About 10,000 festivalgoers crowd City Market each May to hear nationally known Tejano singers and Latino bands, practice salsa and cha-cha slide dances, and sweat off about three pounds in the jalapeño-eating contest. ¡Olé! Admission is $5 per day or $10 for the festival for adults. Seniors and children under 10 are free with one paid admission.

GREAT AMERICAN BARBECUE FESTIVAL
Capital Federal Park at Sandstone
Kansas City, KS
(847) 232-9688
www.thinkbbq.com

Gee, that's all we need, another barbecue festival. Actually, we say bring it on! When a group of 'cue lovers founded this upstart in 2005, 180 competing teams showed up. Now more than 200 slow-cooking masters vie for top prizes, and with the move in 2010 to the beautiful Sandstone Park, it can only get better. A Kidz Zone with a carnival, sports celebs, and other attractions make this Memorial weekend smokin' hot. There are open and invitational contests; check the Web site for official rules and an application. In its first few years, the event raised more than $100,000 for local charities. That's nice, but can you point me to the rib-eating contest?

KIDS FISHING DERBY
Old Lake Jacomo on Beach Rd.
Blue Springs, MO
(816) 229-8980, ext. 16

Hey, kids, grab your fishing poles and head out to this fishing contest made just for little tadpoles. Since 1988 this one-day event, open to kids ages 2 through 15, reels 'em in with fun-filled activities and a casting contest. The first hundred kids to show up get a free cane pole; registration begins at 8 a.m. Children should bring an adult (aw,

shucks), fishing pole, bait, and bucket to hold all that catch.

HERITAGE HIKES
Various locations
(816) 235-1448 (Communiversity)
(816) 931-8448 (Historic Kansas City Foundation)
www.historickansascity.org

Each spring the Historic Kansas City Foundation and Communiversity join up for educational and entertaining strolls through the city's varied and vibrant neighborhoods and historic sites. Past hikes, which usually lasted three hours or so, have included the Northeast, downtown, and Hyde Park districts, giving walkers an up-close look at everything from Victorian homes to turn-of-the-20th-century warehouses-turned-condos. Reservations are necessary, and fees range from $10 for one hike to $25 for three. Other walking tours are hosted throughout the year for around $3 each; contact the foundation for dates and details.

PLAZA LIVE! COURTYARD CONCERTS
Locations around the Country Club Plaza
(816) 753-0100
www.countryclubplaza.com

You may not hear the tune "The Best Things in Life Are Free," but you'll experience it firsthand during this free music concert series that lasts from May through the fall. Some of the area's top musicians plug it in and lay it down at courtyards throughout the Plaza, including the Penguin located by Scandia Down, Mermaid near Eddie Bauer, and Neptune outside Houston's. The music ranges from jazz and pop to blues and Dixieland, with performers like Skip Hawkins Trio, Boulevard Band, Krazy Kats, Max Groove, Ida McBeth, and Angela Hagenbach. Listen up from 5 to 8 p.m. Thurs and Fri and 2 to 5 p.m. Sat and Sun.

TRUMAN DAYS
Independence Square
Independence, MO
(816) 325-7111
www.visitindependence.com

We prove we're still wild about Harry every year as we celebrate his birthday. It's a fine excuse to visit the museum, home, and courthouse that bear the name of the beloved 33rd American president.

JUNE

CORPORATE WOODS JAZZ FESTIVAL
Antioch and College Blvd.
Overland Park, KS
(913) 661-5475
www.jazzinthewoods.com
An opportunity to hear three days of nonstop music from Kansas City headliners—free? Count us in, along with about 40,000 other jazz lovers who've been showing up for the fresh air, great music, and Cajun sausages for nearly 20 years now. Lineups include top-name touring artists as well as hometown favorites like Ida McBeth, Angela Hagenbach, and the New Red Onion Jazz Babies.

The venue couldn't be better. The rolling hills of Corporate Woods, a 294-acre office park blessed with 30 varieties of trees, jogging trails, and a winding woodland stream, provide opportunities to get some private time with your own Sophisticated Lady. As for the Cajun 'dogs, they're just one of dozens of festival foods to tempt you, including barbecue, onion blossoms, frozen margaritas, beer, and frozen treats. Bring lawn chairs, picnic baskets, kids, and dogs. Parking is plentiful around the corporate park.

DOG-N-JOG RUN-FUR-FUN
Mill Creek Park
(913) 596-1000
www.hsgkc.org
For over 20 years, 800 to 1,000 dogs and their owners have come out to enjoy this pretty park on the Country Club Plaza while they help contribute to the Humane Society of Greater Kansas City. Amazingly, the fur rarely flies, as most doggies enjoy the company. Plus they get massages and treats for rewards. Vendors are also on hand with pet-related products, and purebred rescue groups have terrific dogs available for adoption;

in fact purebreds account for 25 percent of shelter animals. Participation in the fun run costs $15. But where do you pin the medal on Bowzer?

DOWNTOWN OVERLAND PARK DAYS
Metcalf Ave. between 78th and 83rd Sts.
Overland Park, KS
(913) 642-2222
www.downtownop.org
Downtown Overland Park celebrates the big five-oh in 2010, and it's throwing a party. Actually, it's an annual event, but this year is even more special. The two-day event includes R&B music, roving entertainers, a beer garden, and an old-fashioned street dance. An Avenue of the Arts features more than 70 local and regional artists and crafters, and the kids' carnival keeps little ones entertained with a petting zoo, clowns, and games. The farmers' market will stay open until all the luscious fresh produce has sold out, and even then you won't go hungry; more than 50 food vendors will tempt you with grilled chicken, barbecue, snacks, and frozen treats. Downtown's unique shops and restaurants will also be open to serve you. Donation is $2 at the gate.

GREAT LENEXA BARBECUE BATTLE
Sar-Ko-Par Trails Park
Lenexa, KS
(913) 541-8592
www.lenexa-kansas.com
Mmmm, smell that hickory smoke? Just follow it to find one of the country's biggest barbecue battles. The word "battle" is right: Each year about 180 teams compete for the chance to take home the coveted trophy. A panel of 250 judges rates seven categories of meat, including brisket, pork, chicken, ribs, and sausage, and although that might sound like a cushy job, it's actually hard work. The fun begins on Friday evening as the smoke masters prepare giant cookers and closely guarded sauce recipes. Entertainment includes live music and kiddie games. The best part comes after the grand champion is crowned and the crowd is invited to taste the best barbecue in the state of Kansas.

HEART OF AMERICA SHAKESPEARE FESTIVAL
Southmoreland Park
47th St. and Oak
(816) 531-7728
www.kcshakes.org
The play's the thing, and since 1992 this lively event has been our opportunity to brush up on the Bard. For four weeks from late June through July, professional actors, many of whom also appear at Kansas City Repertory Theatre, perform one or two of Shakespeare's plays on a rotating basis each Tues through Sun. There is no performance on July 4. The plays are different each season, but you can expect a sword fight or two, love lost then found, and at least one episode of mistaken identity. The play begins at 8 p.m. Admission is free, but donations are welcome. A limited number of reserved seats are available for $20 and may be purchased through the Central Ticket Office (888-286-4849) at least 24 hours in advance. Most folks simply bring a lawn chair, a blanket, and a picnic basket. Concession stands offer hot dogs, kettle corn, snow cones, and wine or beer.

PARKVILLE DAYS RIVERFEST
English Landing Park
Parkville, MO
(816) 880-9026
www.parkvillemo.net
What an enchanting evening this makes, sitting under the stars listening to jazz with the fairy-tale spire of Park University glowing in the distance. There's always an impressive lineup of local musicians. And although it's highly unlikely you'll get bored with the music or tents of arts and crafts, you can always stroll along the groomed trails or visit the nearby nature sanctuary. There's no charge for the jazz fest, and you may bring a cooler for snacks but no alcohol. Food, beer, wine, and other beverages are available at the festival.

JAZZOO
Kansas City Zoo
(816) 513-5800
www.jazzookc.org

Things can get pretty wild at this black-tie gala, and we're not just talking about exotic animals pacing a few hundred feet away. Jazzoo has Kansas City's social elite doing the jungle-boogie all night long, spurred on by music, dancing, and fine wines. And with the aroma of gourmet food prepared by 80 top chefs, it's amazing there aren't a few uninvited guests, like a hungry lion or two. In 2010, guests had another reason to chill out: the opportunity to help fund the new polar bear exhibit. Tickets (at $150 a pop) usually sell out within days.

LAKE FEST
Missouri Town 1855
Fleming Park, Blue Springs, MO
(816) 795-8200
www.jacksongov.org
This is an incredible evening for the entire family, with boat and personal watercraft rides, water games, arts and crafts, and foods of the summer. Live entertainment and a fireworks display continue the fun into the night. The fun begins at 5 p.m. Admission is $7 per vehicle, $3 per walk-in.

LEE'S SUMMIT FESTIVAL OF THE ARTS
Downtown Lee's Summit, MO
(816) 246-6598
www.leessummitdowntowndays.com
Invite some folks over to your block party and watch your population double overnight. That's what happens as soon as music—including rock, country, acoustic, bluegrass, and jazz—starts playing in every corner, alley, and parking lot within the 6-block downtown area. Add more than 400 crafts, food, and commercial booths and, buddy, you've got yourself a festival. Plenty of people agree; the three-day fair, usually held the first week in June, can bring in as many as 80,000 guests. And just to prove they're good neighbors, admission is free.

OLD SHAWNEE DAYS
57th and Cody
Shawnee, KS
(913) 248-2360
www.oldshawneedays.org

On any given day, Old Shawnee Town offers an interesting look at frontier living in the late 1800s. Its 17 original and replicated structures include the 1843 territorial jail, a general store, a bank, and a funeral parlor. But during the annual Old Shawnee Days festival, the place really comes alive (even the funeral parlor) with a parade, carnival, and big musical guests. Other activities have included historical reenactors, a live alligator wrestling show, and a cutest baby contest. No doubt these last two events were held on opposite sides of the fairground. All the usual festival food is available, and admission is free.

RIVERFEST
Berkley Riverfront Park
(816) 550-4722
www.kcriverfest.com
We take it back to where it all began for our town, the Missouri River, to celebrate Independence Day just a little early. Held in Berkley Riverfront Park just east of the City Market, what this annual event lacks in years (it started in 2004), it more than makes up in spirit. The weekend offers plenty of entertainment for all ages and interests including freewheeling motocross, kids' carnival complete with face painting and magic shows, nonstop musical acts, and a spectacular fireworks display that can be seen all over the city. Things can get toasty here around July, but we have a solution: a brewfest with tastes from local breweries. Just the thing to go with grilled hot dogs and other goodies. Tickets are $6 for adults; children five and under are free. Check the Web site for ticket discounts and park-and-ride instructions. It can get crowded.

ROSE DAY IN THE PARK
Loose Park
(816) 784-5300
www.kcmo.org
We can't think of a more lovely way to spend the first Sunday in June than surrounded by thousands of rose bushes in Kansas City's prettiest urban park. It's even more spectacular after a $400,000 restoration in 2009. This event is hosted by the Rose Society of Greater Kansas City, a club

founded in 1931 to prove that roses could indeed grow here despite our Zone 5 rating and rather stubborn clay. And grow they do. The Laura Conyers Smith Municipal Rose Garden started with 120 bushes, and now the 2½-acre park has more than 4,000 plants in 125 varieties. This fragrant sea of pink and salmon, red and flame, lavender and deepest lipstick also includes a fountain and reflecting pool, benches, and pretty limestone and timber pergolas. No wonder more than 250 weddings take place here every year.

SCOTTISH HIGHLANDS GAMES
Riverfront Park
Riverside, MO
www.kcscottishgames.org, www.kcscot.com
The motto of this annual festival is, "Be a Scot, even if you're not." It's easy to sign up with so much Celtic music and mirth. Traditional costumes and dancing are also on tap, including the thrilling Scottish National style made popular by River Dance. Children will enjoy storytelling, face painting, and a chance to pose with Nessie, the Loch Ness Monster. And of course you'll have a chance to cheer on 50 or so big, burly men in kilts as they hurl 16-pound stones and Scottish war hammers for prizes (hopefully not at the audience). Tickets to the two-day event are $15, $10 for kids 12 and under.

ST. DIONYSIOS GREEK ORTHODOX CHURCH FESTIVAL
8100 W. 95th St.
Overland Park, KS
(913) 341-7373
www.stdionysios.org
Why anyone would miss this festival is Greek to us. Every year for nearly 50 years, the church grounds have been transformed into an *agora* (marketplace) with a boutique filled with embroidered blouses, "worry beads," and sailor hats and a taverna set with succulent food. Fill your plate with leg of lamb, chicken baked in lemon sauce, a gyro sandwich, and traditional side dishes and pastries. While dining you'll be entertained by dancers clapping and twirling to the distinctive sounds of bouzouki. Eat fast—they need your table for dancing!

Parish members are proud of their heritage and their church, and tours are given throughout the two-day festival. The icons, bishop's throne, and the Pantokrator painted on the ceiling are beautiful . . . but isn't the music starting up again? *Opa!* Admission and parking are free, and proceeds from sales of food and goods go to benefit church community services.

SUGAR CREEK SLAVIC FESTIVAL
11520 E. Putnam
Sugar Creek, MO
(816) 833-0192
www.slavicfest.com
Here's your chance to overcome your polkaphobia with a healthy dose of Slavic food, dance, and the happy sounds of accordion music. The festival started in 1986 to celebrate customs brought over from Slovenia, Croatia, Hungary, Romania, and Poland in the mid-1800s. The savory food includes sarma (stuffed cabbage rolls), kielbasa (Polish sausage), and povitica (rolled walnut bread). Traditional Slavic music and dancing are the mainstays of the two-day event, and guests have a chance to join in the kolo circle dances.

URBAN TOUR
Various locations in downtown Kansas City
www.downtownkc.org
If you've been dreaming of downtown living with a penthouse view, this two-day tour is right up your alley. There are hundreds of homes to check out, from renovated warehouse lofts to sleek condos and apartments. Many are clustered within walking distance; buses are provided to take you to the next neighborhood. A $5 ticket gets you access to the entire list, or pay around $40 for the VIP tour and cocktail party the evening before.

JULY

MISSOURI RIVER MILES 340 CANOE AND KAYAK RACE
(913) 244-4666
www.rivermiles.com
"This ain't no mamma boy's float trip," the Web site warns, and it's true: just you, your canoe or kayak, and 340 miles of wind, heat, bugs, and rain. And leave it to Scott Mansker, the guy who founded this little cruise in 2006, to put it smack in the hottest time of the year, late July. This race will test your mettle from the first time your paddle hits the water in Kansas City to the last gasp in St. Charles. Did we mention you have just 100 hours to finish? Your reward, other than a trophy, is the chance to witness incredibly beautiful bluffs and forests, hear townspeople cheer you on along the route, and get your mug on the Web site for next year.

SUMMERFEST
St. Mary's Episcopal Church
13th and Holmes
(913) 645-7965
www.summerfestconcertsinkc.com
This four-program series is incredibly popular thanks to the talents of its 10-member chamber ensemble and a repertoire that appeals to a wide audience. Each program also includes a guest artist, such as a soprano soloist, who adds depth to the selections. After you've fed your soul, take care of the rest of you with a postconcert artist schmooze. And as if all that weren't enough, the Sunday concerts are presented in a stunning Gothic church that was built in 1888. Saturdays are performed at White Recital Hall. A subscription to all four concerts costs $80, single tickets are $25.

THEATRE IN THE PARK
Shawnee Mission Park
79th and Renner Rd.
(913) 312-8841 (info line), (913) 631-7050
www.theatreinthepark.org
Thirty years ago this organization opened with a few boards laid on bricks and dressing rooms in nearby bushes. Today it's one of the hottest tickets in town as 3,000 patrons show up to watch Broadway productions like *Annie*, *Evita*, and *The Music Man* performed by nonprofessional actors, many of whom could one day be holding a Tony of their owny. The summertime experience gives hundreds of actors, dancers, and singers of every age group a chance to perform. Four different

musicals are presented each season, and each runs for two weeks on weekends. The ticket gates open at 6:30 p.m., and because there are no prior sales, the line often starts an hour earlier; the programs begin at 8:30 p.m. A concession stand is on-site, as are public restrooms. Admission is $8 for adults, $6 for children ages 4 to 12, and under four free. Bring a picnic basket and lawn chairs and be ready to cheer for somebody's kid.

Fourth of July Fireworks Displays and Festivals

Ever since private fireworks became verboten in KC, we've had to get our thrills at giant community displays. Let's see: a few Black Cats and sparklers or 20 minutes of dazzling jewels and diamonds exploding in the night sky overhead. We'll take the public fireworks, thank you very much. And you won't have to go far to see some spectacular shows; in fact, in some parts of the city you can watch several going off at once. Following are some of our favorites; a two-page spread of more listings can be found in the *Kansas City Star*. We've also included other family-friendly choices around the holiday.

BOOMS AND BLOOMS
Powell Gardens
Kingsville, MO
(816) 697-2600
www.powellgardens.org
The sounds of the local symphony orchestra will thrill you as fireworks light up the sky like giant multicolored chrysanthemums. Light jazz starts at 2 p.m., the conductor takes up the baton around 7, and the pyrotechnics start as soon as it's dark. Besides the booms, there are blooms like the eye-popping display of daylilies and other lush floral gardens. You can even stay cool with a stroll in a shady glen along a waterfall stream. Cafe Thyme offers a selection of crisp salads, tasty sandwiches, and desserts. Admission to the park is $10 for adults, $8 for seniors, and $5 for children.

INDEPENDENCE DAY AT MISSOURI TOWN 1855
Lake Jacomo in Fleming Park
(816) 795-8200, ext. 1-260
www.jacksongov.org/missouritown
You say you want an old-fashioned Fourth of July? How about the way they did it back in 1855? This re-created village from our city's early days really lives it up with patriotic speeches, a town parade, period costumes and music, and children's games that don't require batteries. And it all takes place at one of the prettiest parks in the city. Admission for the 9 a.m. to 4:30 p.m. event goes for $5 for adults, $3 for youth ages 5 to 13, and free for under 5.

STAR-SPANGLED BANNER SPECTACULAR
Corporate Woods Office Park
Overland Park, KS
(913) 829-8483
www.starspangledspectacular.org
You'll be watching the skies throughout this Fourth of July celebration, first when the Kansas National Guard flies overhead and then during a fireworks display that seems to go on forever. Musical entertainment, food and drinks galore, and an activity area for kids complete the deal. Even better, it's free.

PARKVILLE JULY 4TH CELEBRATION
Historic downtown Parkville
www.parkvillemo.com
It's a full day of festivities starting with an old-fashioned parade plus a carnival, the American Legion's famous hamburgers, strawberry-topped funnel cakes, and sweet, sweet music. And there's nothing prettier than fireworks reflected in the Missouri River, so pick out the ideal spot for your picnic blanket early at lovely English Landing Park; this event usually pulls in 20,000 folks.

KC FRINGE FESTIVAL
Various locations around Crossroads Arts District
www.kcfringe.org
Just a few years old, this robust collection of visual and performance art, fashion shows, music,

dance, poetry, and more takes place the last week in July at dozens of venues located within midtown. It's rather like a few days on a cruise ship; there are too many events on the agenda. You'll hear everything from rock bands to Celtic singers, find art to buy, or watch local actors show off their knickers in a burlesque show. A small fee will get you a wristband and more fun than you can imagine. This is where to find emerging artists and wacky performers along with more mainstream talent.

AUGUST

AVIATION EXPO
Wheeler Downtown Airport
(816) 471-4946
www.kcairshow.org
If things are looking up, it must be because the Blue Angels are in town. The U.S. Navy precision flight team is just one exciting element of the Aviation Expo. Other high-flying action includes the midair acrobatics of the U.S. Army Golden Knights Parachute Team, a demonstration team from Air Force A–10s, F–117s breaking the speed limit, and stunt pilots and wing walkers. Live music throughout the two-day show, a hot air balloon show at night, and free airplane rides for kids add to the list of activities, and food vendors serve up nachos, smoked brats, and snow cones.

Staged by the Mid-America Youth Aviation Association, the two-day expo helps educate young people about careers in aviation and related fields. Crowds have grown to more than 150,000 at the downtown airport, so parking elsewhere (such as the Crown Center) and catching a shuttle is a must. You'll find shuttle information on the Web site along with important safety tips like wearing ear protection and plenty of sunscreen. It gets mighty hot on that tarmac, but that doesn't keep runners from participating in an early-morning race. Note: Due to major renovation work taking place at the airport, the air show was cancelled for 2010. It will be flying high once again in 2011.

ETHNIC ENRICHMENT FESTIVAL
Swope Park
Swope Pkwy. and Meyer Blvd.
(816) 333-1124
www.eeckc.org
Twirling costumes, lively music, and an array of international cuisine; here's a chance to celebrate more than 60 cultures that make our city so vibrant and appealing. For two days, usually the third weekend in August, you can enjoy a different performance on stage every half hour, including steel bands from Jamaica, Samoan dance groups, Scottish pipe bands, Mexican folkloric ballet, Japanese martial arts, and a parade of flags. Craft booths, food vendors, and educational activities are also on tap. And what a bargain! Admission is just $3 for adults; 12 and under are free.

FESTIVAL OF BUTTERFLIES
Powell Gardens
Kingsville, MO
(816) 697-2600
www.powellgardens.org
More than 6,000 guests take turns watching the multicolored miracles in the garden's conservatory during the country's largest butterfly exhibit. As cameras click, an orange-and-black Viceroy sips nectar from a purple ironweed flower, a blue Atala becomes a temporary hair bow on a three-year-old, and a rare orange-barred Sulphur flits by in iridescent splendor. More than 23 varieties emerge during this event, plus there are outdoor butterfly and hummingbird gardens, face painting for the children, and a catch-and-release party. General admission prices are in effect for the festival.

KANSAS CITY IRISH FESTIVAL
Crown Center
(816) 997-0837
www.kcirishfest.org
This annual festival should tide you over during those lean months between March 17 and the Labor Day Irish fest in Brookside. It's also simply a fine way to enjoy the warm weather and celebrate the area's Celtic origins. A highlight of the

two-day event is always the traditional and contemporary Irish music. In the past, local beauty and internationally acclaimed singer Connie Dover has thrilled the crowds along with favorites the Elders, Shenanigans, and Eddie Delahunt. The children's area offers games and arts and crafts like Celtic rubbings, along with Irish dancing, pipers, and exhibits for the whole family. Stout and ale flow, and authentic cuisine from across the pond is available. Tickets are $5 for adults; there is no charge for children under 12.

RACE FOR THE CURE
Union Station
(816) 842-4444
www.komenkansascity.org
In August the streets around Union Station become a moving sea of pink as 20,000 T-shirted runners and walkers move toward the finish line and a cure. The Kansas City affiliate of the Susan G. Komen Breast Cancer Foundation has been going strong since 1993, moving its course several times to accommodate the larger crowds. The 5K run/walk and 1-mile fun run appeal to a wide array of athletes, including those who wear photos of loved ones who have died from breast cancer or have survived it and those who are themselves fighting the disease. Water stations and cheering crowds keep the runners motivated, and music, festivities, and lots of food wait at the finish line. Registration fees range from $25 to $35. Call for this year's date.

SUMMER SKIES
Kansas City Museum
3218 Gladstone Blvd.
(816) 483-8300
Learn to locate the constellations and stars just in time for that camping trip. You'll be able to find Scorpio, Sagittarius, Orion the Hunter, and the Summer Triangle from the museum's planetarium. Make a day of it and tour other exhibits, including photos and memorabilia from the Long family, who owned the original Corinthian Hall. Note that, as of this writing, the museum is closed temporarily for renovations. Please check before making plans to visit.

SEPTEMBER

ANTIQUES ON THE COMMON
Greenwood, MO
(816) 537-7822
www.antiquesonthecommmonshow.com
Although antiques buffs try to keep this one-day sale a secret, word has gotten out and the crowds grow bigger every year. By now 1,500 or so fevered shoppers show up to dig through tent after tent of primo antiques and collectibles. Dealers from 15 states bring in the goods, including early Americana, folk art, hooked rugs, redware (highly prized in New England), baskets, quilts, and country furniture with just the right amount of peeling paint. No matter what your budget ($5,000 or $10) you'll walk away with some treasure. And a full tummy: some of us make the food tent our first stop. In fall, pumpkin pie is added to the menu that includes chicken salad and chocolate cake. Live music adds to the fun. The brain behind it all is Claire Fellows of Country Heritage and Friends, a terrific antiques store in Greenwood. Give her a call for directions and a list of motels and RV campsites; she might even send her recipe for Pig Pickin' Cake.

ART WESTPORT
Westport Square
(816) 756-2789
www.artwestport.net
Westport's motto is if you can't beat the Plaza Art Fair in size, at least have yours a few weeks earlier. And it works. But this weekend-long street party succeeds for another reason: All the work is created by local artists, so there's a sense of community and continuity that gives shoppers a chance to buy from favorites year after year. Expect to see a great variety of styles and genres, including ceramics, oils, pastels, watercolors, metal sculpture, garden art, and handcrafted jewelry. Food vendors line the streets, live music adds to the festival atmosphere, and the people-watching (as always) is as good as it gets. Admission is free, so you'll have extra cash for a new treasure.

BELTON, GRANDVIEW & KANSAS CITY RAILROAD COMPANY TRAIN RIDES
502 Walnut
Belton, MO
(816) 331-0630
www.beltonrailroad.org
It's all aboard for fun as this community relives its past as a railroad town in the 1920s. An authentically re-created open window train takes passengers on a 45-minute round-trip on Sat, Sun, and holidays from Labor Day through the end of Oct. Tickets cost $10 for ages three and older, or $25 to ride with the engineer (no extra charge for blowing the whistle. Special seating is limited and on a first-come, first-served basis. Note that only checks and cash are accepted; no credit cards. Other activities are planned throughout the season, including ice-cream socials and educational field trips, and photos and documents from the railway's heyday are displayed in the gift shop.

FALLDO WALDO CRAWLDO
www.waldocrawldo.com
Just try saying the name of this annual event after visiting a handful of the two-dozen bars and restaurants lining Wornall Road. Thank goodness transportation is provided by party buses. Waldo is a magnet for Kansas City's young crowd, who mingle happily with old-timers who have been coming to Kennedy's, Lew's, and the Piano Bar for decades. The fun starts at 85th and Wornall and continues past 75th. Dress casually but look sharp; there's prime hook-up action for singles. Tickets, which get you drink specials at every location, are $5 before the mid-month event or $10 day of. This is the sister festival of Waldo Crawldo that takes place every June. We know people who have lost their car at the spring event, only to rediscover it in September. You'll want a designated driver for this one.

IRISH FESTIVAL
Crown Center
(816) 997-0837
www.kcirishfest.com
'Tis a long way from St. Patty's Day, but apparently the 15,000 folks who turn up for this week-end don't mind—or don't notice after downing a few Irish stouts. They show up in a sea of green to hear traditional music from local talent like the Elders, Eddie Delahunt, and Bob Reeder and to watch the flashing feet of O'Riada Academy of Irish Dance. Kids will keep busy with puppet shows, games, and face painting, and parents may head right for the corned beef, scones, meat pies, and Irish whiskey. Bring lawn chairs or blankets to stake your claim in front of one of the three stages. You might walk away with more than a hangover; raffle tickets are sold for trips to Ireland and other prizes. Or enter your best pie, photos, or knitting project in a contest. Admission is $10; children 12 and under get in free. Money raised goes to a local Irish culture center.

GREEK FESTIVAL
Greek Orthodox Church of the Annunciation
120th and Wornall Rd.
(816) 942-9100, (816) 491-1990
www.annunciationkc.org
It's hard to imagine what our lives would be like without the influence of ancient Greece. Logic, geometry, medicine, and architecture (even words like sophistication and philanthropy) come from their world. Then there's the food. Here's a chance to experience it all (well, maybe just the food) at a celebration this parish has been hosting for nearly 50 years. It's so famous even the Food Network has covered it. You'll find enough gyros to feed an army, enough paper-thin phyllo dough to cover the world, and enough dancing to make Zorba proud. The crowds are so huge they need three food lines to serve hungry festivalgoers. But don't worry. We've saved some baklava for you. Admission and parking are free. The souvlaki plate will set you back about $12.

HIDDEN GLEN ARTS FESTIVAL
Kansas Hwy. 10 and Cedar Creek Pkwy.
Olathe, KS
(913) 961-ARTS (2787)
www.hiddenglen.org
You might say this art fair has a much larger canvas—the gorgeous, upscale homes and emerald-green golf course of Cedar Creek. But it's the

hundred or so booths filled with fine art from around the country that will attract your immediate attention. Past favorites have included garden art crafted of recycled metal, delicate ceramic teapots, and gem-studded silver jewelry. Artists are available to discuss inspirations and techniques. Little squirts have storytellers, puppets, and a color wheel game to keep them busy while you shop. Concession food and drink and live music ranging from acoustic guitar to jazz bands add to the festivities. True art lovers who want the chance to see the show before the public can become Purchase Patrons for $150, which includes a champagne brunch on Sat morning. Admission and parking for this two-day event are free.

LENEXA SPINACH FESTIVAL
Sar-Ko-Par Trails Park
87th St. and Lackman Rd.
Lenexa, KS
(913) 541-0209
www.lenexakansas.net
Kids may shudder at the thought of a day devoted to spinach, but there's more to this festival than simply greens. It starts with a Kiwanis pancake breakfast and includes a polka dance, Popeye and Olive Oyl characters, and a tossing of the world's largest spinach salad, which is sold by the plateful to those who enjoy the leafy vegetable. Festival-goers will also find antiques and crafts for sale; cooks can enter their spinach recipe to win prizes. The two-day event costs $1 for ages 13 and older.

MARCH OF DIMES ANNUAL BIKERS FOR BABIES
The Kansas Speedway
(816) 561-0175
www.marchofdimeskc.org/biker
This annual charity event brings a new meaning to the phrase "biker babe," as hundreds of motorcycle riders raise money to help save infants at risk. Participants are well rewarded with a free lunch, music and entertainment, great prizes including a new Harley, and a chance to ride through some of the Midwest's prettiest countryside. Past years have brought together 6,000 or

so riders with total contributions over the years of more than $4 million, making it the largest and most successful of rides across the country. The pre-registration fee is $35 ($40 the day of), but most participants spend months raising money for the cause. It's hard to say no to a guy in leather chaps.

OLD SETTLERS CELEBRATION
Downtown Olathe, KS
(913) 782-5254
www.johnsoncountyoldsettlers.com
No wonder this annual event is a blast; Olathe's had more than 112 years to get it right. They certainly pack enough excitement into three days, including free concerts on Fri and Sat nights starring big-time names of the '60s and '70s like Mitch Ryder, Gary Lewis and the Playboys, and Mark Lindsay from the Raiders. But the fun starts much earlier with carnival rides on Thurs and the state's biggest parade Sat morning. More than 150 arts and crafts booths show off local talent, and ice cream keeps everybody cool.

One of the liveliest attractions is the gabfest that allows older residents to tell young whipper-snappers about the good old days, like walking to school through 3 feet of snow. Barefoot. This celebration is a chance to discover a vibrant city with a name that means "beautiful" in the Shawnee Indian language.

OVERLAND PARK FALL FESTIVAL
Santa Fe Commons Park
Overland Park, KS
(913) 895-6357
www.opkansas.org
Get your Christmas shopping out of the way early at this outdoor arts and crafts show that's been steadily growing in size since 1980. Pace yourself; there are nearly 200 artists and crafters displaying hand-made treasures like jewelry, candles, ceramic dolls, stained glass, pottery, dried-floral wreaths, oil paintings, and personalized children's puzzles. Or save all your money for the food booths with the usual summertime treats like Cajun sausages, kettle corn, snow cones, and beer. The farmers' market is also open, offering

the freshest produce from nearby farms and orchards. Tables are set under big white tents, so even if it rains you can sit a spell while listening to local bands play crowd-pleasing blue grass, blues, jazz, and classic rock 'n' roll. While the women shop and kids line up for face painting, guys can ogle the motorcycle show featuring new and vintage bikes.

PIG-PICKIN' CHICKEN-LICKIN' FEAST
Bingham-Waggoner Estate
313 W. Pacific
Independence, MO
(816) 461-3491
www.bwestate.org
At the very least this annual festival—29 years old and counting—wins the prize for the best hunger-inducing name. And you can bet you'll be licking your fingers after a dinner of roasted pig, Stroud's famous fried chicken, and lots of savory side dishes. Other down-home fun includes a quilt show, silent auction, banjo music, and clogging (that's folk dancing, folks). You can also tour the home that was a popular stop along the westward trails (read more about this site under Historic Homes in the History chapter). Advance reservations are required; tickets cost $10.

PLAZA ART FAIR
Country Club Plaza
(816) 753-0100
www.countryclubplaza.com
Some people save up all year to buy a fabulous treasure or two at this three-day event. They'll have plenty to choose from; more than 240 of the nation's top artists turn nine Plaza streets into one big outdoor art gallery. The quality of work is incredible. In a highly competitive jury process, more than 1,200 artists from some 35 states vie for the right to have their work seen by more than 275,000 art enthusiasts. Expect to see ceramics, fiber, glass, graphics and printmaking, metal, painting, pastels, photography, wood, and some of the most exquisite jewelry around. It's also the best people (and pet) watching of the season.

While browsing you'll be treated to the aroma of Thai chicken pizza, Italian sausages,

and black bean chili from more than thirty Plaza restaurants. Desserts, icy margaritas, beer, and other beverages are also on the menu. Music fills the air as well, thanks to three stages offering everything from R&B to classical. Children can create their own masterpiece to take home in the Kid's Art Workshop or view other students' work at the Young Artist Exhibition tent. And of course it all takes place at the Country Club Plaza, which is a work of art all by itself. The Plaza Art Fair is a tradition that began in 1932 and just gets better with time.

PLAZA PZAZZ
Country Club Plaza
(816) 421-1753
www.rmhckc.org
As if the Plaza didn't have enough pizzazz, they throw a block party with music, dancing, and delectable food from the trendiest restaurants in town. The location couldn't be more chichi, either; the streets nestled along lovely Brush Creek on the Plaza are lined with booths and tents that are lit up with tiny white lights as the sun sets. The $75 ticket price goes to a very good cause: two local Ronald McDonald Houses that give shelter and support to families with seriously ill children. The charity houses more than 2,000 families a year, as well as sponsoring a family room at nearby Children's Mercy Hospital. Tickets to the festival go as fast as an order of McDonald's fries.

THE KANSAS CITY RENAISSANCE FESTIVAL
Bonner Springs, KS
(816) 561-8005, (800) 373-0357
www.kcrenfest.com
Buxomy wenches and men in tights? These fetching fantasies have been drawing crowds to this 16th-century shire every fall for more than 30 years. Well, that and continuous entertainment, mouthwatering foods, and a wide array of handcrafted wares. Where else can you witness a sword fight, cheer a jouster on horseback, and flirt with a king, all in one afternoon? With 16 acres and 13 stages of music, plays, and zany comedies, there's almost too much to see in

one day, so you'll be thankful the festival runs for seven weekends beginning Labor Day.

Gypsies, bandits, beggars, the royal entourage, and dozens of other costumed characters stroll the village, engaging visitors in skits and revelry. Music is around every bend: Celtic harmonies, bawdy pub songs and sea shanties, lilting tunes on harps and hammered dulcimers. The village's shaded lanes are lined with shops showcasing goods from more than 160 artisans, including puppets, beribboned hair wreaths, tooled-leather purses, and toy swords.

Kids are in their own little realm with elephant and camel rides, a petting zoo, and dozens of games such as Slay the Dragon and Drench a Wench. Some people show up just for the food, particularly roasted turkey legs big enough for two, pork chops on a stick, root beer floats, and 80 other delights. Cider Jack, wine, and ales are also available. The festival is open rain or shine and parking is free. Before you go, practice saying the standard greeting around Canterbury: "Huzzah!" Tickets are $15.50 for adults if purchased online or at various outlets, or $17.95 at the gate. There are similar price discounts for children and seniors.

RIVERSIDE RIVERFEST
Riverfront Park
Riverside, MO
(816) 741-3993
www.riversidemo.com
What this city lacks in history (it's just over 50 years old) it more than makes up for in fun. Witness the number of activities it packs into one September weekend alone: a pancake breakfast, a vintage car show, a grand parade and carnival, a blues and jazz jam, a battle of the bands, a beauty contest, and two fireworks displays. Whew! There's plenty of entertainment for the kiddies, too, including a petting zoo. The older crowd can pitch horseshoes or compete at bingo. The central event is free, and the fireworks display is priceless.

SANTA-CALI-GON DAYS
Independence Square
Independence, MO
(816) 252-4745
www.santacaligon.com
In the mid-1800s three routes—the Santa Fe, California, and Oregon Trails—led pioneers to new adventures out West, and they all began in or near Independence. This festival has grown in popularity in its 30-plus years, topping out at some 250,000 visitors over the four-day span.

There's certainly enough to keep every one of them entertained. The Main Stage is always a big draw, with past performers like the Dixie Chicks, Clint Black, Eddie Rabbitt, and an Asleep at the Wheel tribute band. The Community Stage hosts local talent, including Native American dancing, square dancing, and must-see events like watermelon seed–spitting contests. No contest about who's got the best food roundup for the weekend; here you can choose from barbecue, jambalaya, hamburgers, corn dogs, ice cream, lemonade, and dozens more. In fact, more than 300 commercial food and game booths are here, along with a large carnival midway. And the juried craft show has been ranked among the top in the nation by the crafters themselves.

For those interested in the historical significance of the trails, the Missouri Free Trappers exhibit portrays the life of the pioneers. Four days of fun, free admittance and parking . . . what more could you want? You'll want to take advantage of free shuttles, especially on Sat afternoon.

STRUT WITH YOUR MUTT
Brookside
(816) 761-8151
www.waysidewaifs.org
Put on the dog while you help raise funds for the Wayside Waifs animal shelter. This walkathon is held every fall, and part of the fun is entering different contests like cutest pooch, best costume, or the owner and pet who most resemble each other (scary judging when the entrant is a wrinkled sharpei). Plus there are vendor booths and doggie treats galore. A fee of $30 gets you a T-shirt and possibly a slobbery thank-you from a schnauzer.

OCTOBER

CANSTRUCTION
Union Station
(816) 329-5013
www.canstruction.org

This annual event builds its own excitement as more than a dozen teams of architects, engineers, and contractors compete to design and build giant structures made entirely out of canned goods. Has anyone entered the leaning tower of pizza sauce yet? At the close of the monthlong exhibition, the canned goods are donated to the Harvesters Food Pantry. Admission is free, but you're encouraged to bring at least one can of food or a nonperishable item to view the display.

CHRISTMAS IN OCTOBER
(816) 531-6443
www.christmasinoctober.org

You've gotta love a community that comes together for two weekends each October to clean up, fix up, and rehabilitate homes belonging to low-income homeowners who often are elderly or disabled. This nonprofit group was started in 1984 by Richard W. Miller and John P. McMeel (of Andrews McMeel Publishing) with a couple of hammers and a few willing friends. These days about 6,000 skilled laborers and hardworking volunteers tackle the jobs.

Each year this group improves more than 500 homes, and because the need can't wait for October, the efforts continue year-round. Union craftspeople like electricians, plumbers, carpenters, and roofers handle the major repairs during the first weekend. A week later a horde of energetic workers with paintbrushes, rakes, and wheelbarrows show up to finish the job. There's a mighty big payoff for a few days of sore muscles and Eggshell Gloss in your hair: joyful tears from an 85-year-old lady who will have a warmer house this winter.

FALL PARADE OF HOMES
(816) 942-8800
www.kcparadesofhomes.com

At this annual show you'll find about 500 reasons to buy a new home as more than 200 builders from eight counties tempt you with their finest houses. You can tour as many as you'd like in every lifestyle and price range, from less than $95,000 to more than $1.6 million. Just why does any one family need seven bathrooms, anyway? Many of the most exclusive homes are dressed to the nines by area interior designers, so you'll come away with lots of decorating ideas. To add to your choices, downtown lofts and condos have been added to the tour. Books with floor plans are available at most of the homes, and a tour map is available online.

HISTORIC KANSAS CITY HOMES TOUR
(816) 931-8448
www.historickansascity.org

Ever drive by a beautiful home and wish you could peek inside? Now you can, with the owner's blessings. Each fall the Historic Kansas City Foundation chooses one neighborhood to feature, always an area filled with turn-of-the-20th-century jewels that have been carefully preserved or lovingly restored. Past tours have included the fabulous Scarritt-Renaissance and Hyde Park neighborhoods. Tickets are $10 and can be purchased at the site. Proceeds help continue the foundation's mission of restoring, renewing, and rediscovering historic buildings, homes, and areas of our city. This is the same organization that hosts several walking tours throughout the year—a chance to marvel at our city's art deco buildings or famous Garment District.

HYDE PARK HISTORIC HOMES TOUR AND FESTIVAL
Hyde Park Neighborhood
(816) 561-HPNA (4762)
www.hydeparkkc.com

Get close and personal with some of the loveliest homes in Kansas City at this annual tour. You'll see everything from charming shirtwaist bungalows to stately stone mansions, brought back to glorious turn-of-the-20th-century grandeur by hardworking homeowners. Tour guides (often the residents themselves) discuss the home's history, interesting details about the restoration, and sometimes-spooky tales about ghostly visits. Typically five homes are on the list, all within a pleasant stroll. Hyde Park's parameters are generally 31st to 47th streets and Gillham to Troost.

JUNIOR LEAGUE OF KANSAS CITY
Holiday Mart
Overland Park International Trade Center
115th and Metcalf
(816) 444-2112
www.jlkc.org

Get on your mark, get set, shop! Lots of ladies finish their entire holiday shopping list in one fast-paced afternoon at this annual buyer's paradise that's two decades old and going strong. More than 200 gift boutiques are side by side, offering jewelry (silver, gemstone, and estate pieces), home decor, gourmet foods, pewterware, and collectibles. Clothing booths tend to carry unique fashions elaborately decorated vests and hats, and fun accessories not available anywhere else in town. And of course you'll find Christmas decorations galore, including tree-trimmers, ornaments, dried floral wreaths, and exquisite Santas with price tags of $300 or more. For the most part, though, prices are so reasonable you'll be glad you grabbed a shopping basket at the door. Single-day tickets are $10 in advance and $8 at the door; multiday tickets, good for all four days, are $18. A Ladies Night Out shop-a-rama takes place the night before the event; tickets are $40. And it's not all about shopping; since 1987, the Holiday Mart has raised more than $5 million for local community programs.

LEE NATIONAL DENIM DAY
(800) 944-5633
www.denimday.com

How cool is this? Wear jeans to work and instead of getting reprimanded you're considered a good citizen. Local business Lee Jeans sponsors this now-national event, with money going to the Susan G. Komen Breast Cancer Foundation. Since it started with a handful of Lee Jeans employees in 1986, this national event has raised more than $80 million for breast cancer programs. So take that $5 bill out of your jeans pocket and send it in.

WESTON IRISH FESTIVAL
O'Malley's Pub
Short and Welt Sts.
Weston, MO
(816) 640-5235
www.westonirish.com

In Weston they turn Octoberfest into O'Toberfest with three days of fun. What else can you do when your name is Sean O'Malley and you own an Irish pub? How nice that he invites all his friends and guests to join in as dozens of top-notch Celtic singers, dancers, and musicians entertain. Headliners have included internationally known Connie Dover, who happens to be a Weston resident when not touring, the Elders, and the Shenanigans. Of course there's also plenty of Irish food and drink, authentic jewelry and clothing to buy, and CDs to have the artists autograph. Gate passes range from $8 to $10 a day. Children under 12 are free, but you may want to plug the little ones' ears when Bob Reeder starts in with his naughty limericks.

Halloween Events

We turn into the City Boo-tiful near the end of October, when you can find about 40 Halloween activities all over town (look for current lists in the *Star*), including haunted houses, acres of pumpkins, and nonscary festivals for little trick-or-treaters. As they say at the pumpkin patch, you can take your pick.

BLUE VALLEY RECREATION PUMPKIN PATCH
Blue Valley Recreation Complex
Overland Park, KS
(913) 685-6000
www.bluevalleyrec.org

For children seven and under, this is better than a bag full of Snickers bars. They'll be having so much fun, and get so tuckered out, they may not miss the door-to-door candy collecting. Activities include hayrides, clowns, face painting, and a moonwalk, and everybody gets a pumpkin to take home. A small fee and preregistration are required.

BOO AT THE ZOO

Kansas City Zoo
(816) 513-5800
www.kansascityzoo.org

Looking for a ghoulishly good time for your young trick-or-treaters? This is a not-so-scary place where they can trick-or-treat from 20 candy stops, watch puppet and sea lion shows, and participate in zookeeper chats and animal feedings. And of course they'll get to see the real live versions of their little kitty-cat costumes. This all-day party is usually held the weekend before Halloween, and usual admission prices ($6.50 to $9.50) are in effect.

POWELL PUMPKIN PATCH

25695 Spring Valley Rd.
Louisburg, KS
(913) 837-2212
www.powellpumkinpatch.com

Drive 30 minutes just to get lost? That's part of the fun at this pumpkin patch with a 20-acre corn maze, the largest in the Midwest. Walking through the mile of trails will take at least 30 minutes, and your reward is a chance to pick out the prettiest or at least most carve-worthy pumpkin from 30 acres of the orange globes. Admission is free; pumpkin prices vary by size.

SPOOKTACULAR AT POWELL GARDENS

Powell Gardens
Kingsville, MO
(816) 697-2600
www.powellgardens.org

This two-day fall festival includes storybook characters, games, costume contests, and lots of treats in a friendly setting. And—mum's the word—the gardens are simply beautiful this time of year. Bring your own trick-or-treat bag. Prepaid registration of $5 to $12 is required. To make sure your little scarecrow doesn't miss out, be sure to register early; this is often a sold-out event.

THE BEAST

1401 W. 13th St.
(816) 842-4280
www.kcbeast.com

Can you tell we've gotten to the haunted house section of our list? This one is billed as "America's largest haunted house," and though we can't vouch for that, it is guaranteed to scare your socks off. Instead of having visitors walk in a line, the Beast has an open design so that guests can wander at will through several themed areas. This may not be appropriate for young children or even older kids who are easily traumatized.

It's open weekends in Sept and Oct and then nightly from mid-Oct until early Nov. The haunting starts at 7 p.m. and lasts until the fog lifts. Yikes! Admission is $20. Combo tickets to the Beast and the Edge of Hell are the best deal, at $33; check online for coupons.

THE EDGE OF HELL

1300 W. 12th St.
(816) 842-4279
www.edgeofhell.com

They call this theater the granddaddy of all haunted houses, and you'll wish Gramps were here to hold your hand. It's Kansas City's biggest and oldest fright fest, with a huge advantage over the others: a five-story slide. See the Beast for ticket information.

WATERFIRE KANSAS CITY

Brush Creek on the Country Club Plaza
(816) 421-2341
www.waterfire.org

The aroma of wood and glow of torches on a crisp fall evening? It's just as enchanting as it sounds as thousands of people surround the meandering Brush Creek on the beautiful Country Club Plaza. The relatively new festival is on fire, literally, as 55 boats travel along with waterway, past musical and dance peformances, food vendors, and other entertainment. The event is free.

NOVEMBER

AMERICAN ROYAL LIVESTOCK HORSE SHOW & RODEO

(816) 221-9800
www.americanroyal.com

See the Close-up in this chapter and get ready to rodeo, pardner.

CROWN CENTER ICE TERRACE
2450 Grand
(816) 274-8411
www.crowncenter.com
Something to look forward to all year long: outdoor ice-skating in Crown Center Square. Opening day for the season is usually the first week in Nov, with a free early-morning skate from 6 to 9 a.m. including complimentary hot chocolate. Free morning skates continue while the terrace stays open, through late Mar. Regular admission is $6 per person plus $3 skate rental. The hours are 10 a.m. to 9 p.m. Sun through Thurs and 10 a.m. to 11 p.m. Fri and Sat. It's lovely to skate when you can see stars, as long as that doesn't mean you've just taken a fall. How many cups of cocoa am I holding up?

PARK PLACE ICE RINK
117th and Nall
Leawood, KS
(913) 663-2070
www.destinationparkplace.com
In winter, this bustling town square in the heart of Leawood gets even cooler as families take to the ice for an afternoon of fun. Rental is around $6, with special buy-one-get-one deals throughout the season. There's even a mini-Olympics week. And when you're ready to unlace the skates, the surrounding boutiques and restaurants will entice you with food and shopping.

THE FAIRY PRINCESS
Union Station
(816) 483-8300
www.unionstation.org
Create a delightful memory as children whisper their wishes to the Fairy Princess, and with a wave of her wand, a gift magically appears! Her highness is always a vision in layers of netting and a glittering crown, and children of all ages are instantly enchanted. Wishes come true every Sat from late Nov until just before Christmas. Visits are free with Union Station admission. Photos are $5. It's an experience they'll never forget; this author certainly never has.

HANDEL'S MESSIAH
Community of Christ Auditorium
Walnut and River
Independence, MO
(816) 235-6222
www.cofchrist.org
When King George II heard George Friederic Handel's *Messiah* for the first time, he gave it a standing ovation. You'll do the same after hearing the 350-voice Independence Messiah Choir and the Kansas City Symphony perform the stirring oratorio. The two groups practice for months for this one performance, a nine-decade gift to the community. The staging adds to the evening: a beautiful church, a monstrous 113-rank organ, and a chorus dressed in tuxedoes and evening gowns rising before you on stepped platforms. By the time the "Hallelujah Chorus" begins, you can't help but join in. The performance is held every year on the Sat before Thanksgiving. Tickets range from $12 to $28 and are available starting in early Sept. Don't miss it.

HOME FOR THE HOLIDAYS TOUR
Various locations
(913) 685-2802
www.jcym.net
We'll bet your home would look spectacular if you had a professional interior designer and dozens of elves decorating it for the holidays. That's what happens during this popular tour when the Johnson County Young Matrons choose five gorgeous homes in an upscale area, lavish them with about a ton of ornaments and fresh greenery, and then invite the rest of us in to drool. The tour is typically held on a weekday, so hundreds of workers call in sick and hope their bosses don't show up until after dinner. Advance tickets cost $12 and are available at area grocery stores. The price increases to $15 at the door—worth every penny for the decorating ideas you'll take back to your own home.

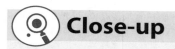

Ropin', Ridin', and Ribs

In Kansas City, when you mention the party, chances are you're talking about the **American Royal.** We've been celebrating this combination grand parade, rodeo, and livestock competition since 1899, so it's definitely here to stay. But for most of us, the American Royal doesn't mean ropin' and ridin', it means ribs. As in barbecue.

Just look for the blue smoke rising from hundreds of cookers taking their own sweet time transforming briskets, ribs, pork butts, and sausages into tender morsels to be offered up to about 600 judges the next day. Have mercy, it smells divine as forests of hickory, oak, apple wood, and cherry give off a sweet and pungent perfume. Adding to the aromatherapy are whiffs of onion, peppers, and molasses as teams mix up carefully guarded sauce recipes or stir big pots of barbecue beans to make the most of meat drippings and chunks of brisket.

Each year teams from around the country show up at the West Bottoms, smokers in tow, to vie for more than $60,000 in prizes and trophies as big as a side of beef. About 65 elite teams, champions all, compete in the International Invitational contest, with about 350 or so more entering the open cook-off.

The annual bash provides plenty of entertainment even for noncookers. It seems more than barbecue is being judged as teams try to outdo one another by personalizing their roped-off areas with outlandish decorations, inflatable palm trees, and live bands. Even the teams' names are a hoot, like Bite My Butt, Pig Newton, Drinkers with a Bar-B-Que Problem, and Any Pork in a Storm. The winners get more than bragging rights and some cash; a title from the American Royal can mean a real boost to business if you own a barbecue restaurant, sell your own sauce brand, or market a smoker.

There is, of course, another side to the American Royal, and without it we probably wouldn't be as well known for our barbecue. The livestock show speaks to Kansas City's century-old importance in the food chain. Here, too, some of the country's best ranchers and 4-H members come to compete for big prizes in categories like Angus bulls, heifers, lamb, and swine.

The American Royal Rodeo is one of the top 10 in the country sanctioned by the Professional Rodeo Cowboys Association and offers such events as barrel racing, saddle bronco riding, calf roping, and the ever-popular mutton bustin'. A Mexican Rodeo Extravaganza salutes the Mexican cowboy heritage with folkloric dancing, mariachi bands, and charro bronco riders. Even folks who don't care about the fine art of lassos show up for the big-name entertainment after the events. Country crooners like Willie Nelson, Faith Hill, Clint Black, and others have appeared. A huge parade down Main Street begins the whole shebang with more than 7,000 participants, including 16 saddle clubs, 25 floats, and 23 bands. A children's rodeo, a horse show, and agricultural exhibitions round out the weeklong extravaganza. So now you know the answer to "Where's the beef?" It's right here in Kansas City, especially in October. And the festivities continue to grow with new events aimed to get more people involved. A new addition is a barbecue competition just for youngsters. An old-fashioned cattle drive makes pedestrians and cars mooove over as four-legged beasts take over the streets. At the other end of our western heritage, "Tablesteaks" brings gentlemen together over good food, whiskey, and cigars. The $175 ticket helps fund the organization's programs.

All the staged events take place at the American Royal Complex, west of downtown in the West Bottoms. For more information, mosey on down to **www.americanroyal.com** or call (816) 221-9800. And if you plan to come, remember: Cowboy boots are more than just a fashion statement.

Holiday Lighting Ceremonies and Displays

Santa doesn't need Rudolph to locate Kansas City. By the first of December we're lit up like a ... well, like a Christmas tree, as every community adds its own special holiday display. Following are some of the best and brightest.

CHRISTMAS IN THE PARK
Longview Lake Campground
Lee's Summit, MO
(816) 795-8200
www.lees-summit.mo.us

Children will have their little faces plastered to the car window when you drive slowly through this display of 175 animated figures illuminated by nearly 300,000 lights. To join them, take I-470 to View High Drive, south to Third Street, and follow the signs, or just listen for the *oohs* and *ahhs* coming from vans full of kids. Free, but donations of $1 per vehicle or $1 per person for buses go to help nearly 40 local charities. The lights turn on in late Nov and continue through Dec 31.

MAYOR'S CHRISTMAS TREE LIGHTING CEREMONY
Crown Center Square
(816) 274-8444
www.crowncenter.com

The holiday season is officially here when the mayor of Kansas City and a celebrity guest flip the switch for more than 7,000 white lights on the tree and an additional 50,000 illuminating Crown Center Square. This glowing, 100-foot-tall tree stands as a symbol of the Mayor's Christmas Tree Fund, which has helped more than 40,000 less fortunate families over the past nine decades. Even after the holidays the tree has a special purpose: Its wood is used to make commemorative ornaments sold the following year to benefit the charity.

OVERLAND PARK MAYOR'S LIGHTING CEREMONY
Between 78th and 83rd Sts. west of Metcalf
Overland Park, KS
(913) 642-2222
www.opkansas.org

Santa arrives a little early at downtown Overland Park, but that's just fine with the kids waiting to take a picture with the jolly old elf. Parents will get in the spirit too, with carolers, holiday crafts for sale, gay music, free cider and cookies, and an electric light parade. The mayor lights the Christmas tree at dusk, and the party continues with free carriage rides for those who bring two canned goods to donate to Harvesters.

CHRISTMAS CARD LANE
Mission Ridge III
Olathe, KS
(913) 764-2913

This neighborhood of more than 200 homes all joins together to create giant holiday card displays, lines of luminaries, and twinkling front-yard trees. The display usually runs from Thanksgiving until Dec 31 and is located north of 151st and west of Ridgeview at Ridgeview and Frontier. No charge, but we'd gladly pay.

COUNTRY CLUB PLAZA

This legendary scene is perhaps our city's most treasured tradition when, starting each Thanksgiving night, more than 75 miles of jewel-toned lights illuminate every spire and swag of the Spanish-style architecture. Even when the temperature is 10 degrees below zero, a crowd shows up to help with the countdown as a celebrity guest pulls the switch. For the past few years the drama has escalated, with a spectacular fireworks display at the InterContinental Hotel.

MISSION HILLS, KS
63rd and Ensley and Eisenhower Lake

We're not sure how this started—as a lark or a mistake—but a few years ago a homeowner tossed a string of white lights into a tree and let it fall naturally. The result was an illuminated modern art sculpture. The look caught on and now dozens of neighbors join in to create a sea of sailboat shapes along the streets of this pretty neighborhood.

WARD PARKWAY AND ROMANY ROAD BETWEEN 69TH AND 71ST STREETS

Make this your second stop after viewing the Plaza lights. It's a fantastic sight, with hundreds of tree trunks wrapped in tiny white lights. The glowing circles are amazing when viewed in perspective from Ward Parkway.

ZONA ROSA
(816) 587-8180
www.zonarosa.com

The arrivals of Santa Claus and the Fairy Princess are just two of the reasons to start the holidays at this open-air collection of shops and restaurants in the Northland. Older Kansas Citians will enjoy seeing sentimental favorites, the giant crown ornaments that used to grace downtown's Petticoat Lane.

DECEMBER

CHRISTMAS IN WESTON
Downtown Weston, MO
(816) 640-2909
www.westonmo.com

For nearly 30 years this charming town has been getting all dolled up for the holidays and inviting us to visit. There's plenty to make the 40-minute drive worth your time: a walking tour of five historic homes, wandering street carolers, carriage rides through town, and visits with Father Christmas. Many of the antiques shops, stores, and boutiques offer hot cider and cookies, too. Tickets are $25. And if you're so enchanted you want to visit Weston again, you'll find information in Day Trips and Weekend Getaways.

JAZZ COMMUNITY CAROL FEST
Community Christian Church
4601 Main St.
(816) 561-6531
www.community-christian.org

Ever hear "Silent Night" performed with a syncopated beat? You will at this happening, happy event that pairs classic holiday tunes with two dozen of Kansas City's finest musicians. Enough gospel and classic renditions are tossed in to keep everyone in the mood; it's simply not Christ-mas until you've heard Ida McBeth sing "O Holy Night." The $20 tickets go fast for this joyful treat that always falls on the first Sun afternoon in Dec.

THE KANSAS CITY BALLET'S *NUTCRACKER*
Midland Theatre
(816) 931-3330
www.kcballet.com

This holiday classic continues to astound audiences, both young and old, with its magnificent sets, costumes, and special effects. (The Mouse King is truly sinister!) The performance features the beloved music of Peter I. Tchaikovsky, choreography by Todd Bolender, three casts of professional artists from Kansas City Ballet, and more than 100 youngsters ages 7 to 17 selected from Kansas City Ballet School. Children love the fantastical characters and perk up when they hear music they recognize. And the setting, the historic Midland Theatre with its gilt trimming and rich velvets, adds to the magic. Tickets range from $15 to $60.

New Year's Eve Celebrations

Prove you can par-tay with the best of them with bubbles, balloons, and boogalooing at your choice of big galas or more intimate affairs. In addition to those listed below, dozens of hotels, nightclubs, casinos, and restaurants offer packages from $40 per person to more than $1,000. In one recent year, the *Kansas City Star* listed more than 50 party events.

POP!
Hyatt Regency Crown Center
2345 McGee St.
(816) 421-1234, (816) 435-4152
www.hyattnye.com

Just you, your sweetheart, and 4,000 of your closest friends. Sound romantic? It certainly is exciting, especially at the stroke of midnight when they release 20,000 balloons. The evening also includes spacious entertainment areas, an indoor laser light show, and a pyrotechnic display. Packages include champagne, buffets, and open bars starting at $180 for singles hoping for a last-minute match and $275 for couples.

UNION STATION'S NEW YEAR'S CELEBRATION
(816) 460-2020
www.unionstation.org

It's been a tradition since 1933 to ring in the New Year at Union Station. At this grand palace there's plenty of room to find a cozy spot for a midnight kiss (dibs on under the clock) or link up with friends to toast the New Year. The evening includes more than just champagne; you can also visit Science City and see live stage shows in the Theater District. Prices start at $60.

VELVET DOG
400 E. 31st St.
(816) 753-9990
www.martinicorner.com

This disco explosion has been the grooviest New Year's bash around since 1996. The crowd becomes one big groove-machine while dancing to a jukebox full of funky '70s disco hits, and next door the Empire Room's DJ takes requests for Bee Gees favorites. Better practice spelling out "YMCA" before you call for reservations. A $30 advance ticket ($40 at the door) will get you into both clubs and includes a limited open bar. This is a definite twenties crowd.

PARKS, LAKES, AND RECREATION

Kansas City and Mother Nature? We're like that. She blessed us with a landscape of shimmering lakes, lush green spaces, golden prairie grass, and acres of woodlands. Everywhere you look we're surrounded by the great outdoors, which might account for the dozens of sports activities and organizations you'll read about in the Sports chapter.

But for now let's see just how easy being green can be. Kansas City, Missouri, alone has 200 parks, including the third largest metropolitan park in the country, and more than 130 miles of boulevards and parkways covering some 10,000 acres. Downtown parks, sometimes shaded more by skyscrapers than sycamores, give city workers a respite from phones, e-mail, and meetings long enough to enjoy lunch alfresco, listen to a jazz concert, or just people watch. In addition, the city is ringed by hundreds of lakes, woods, and parks, places where you can commune with nature, possibly feed apples to bison, and most definitely feed your soul. With an abundance of rolling acres, fragrant floral displays, lakes overflowing with sporting amenities, and cool, sandy beaches, it's easy to say, "You bet!" when someone tells you to take it outside.

And how we do love our gardens. Kansas City gardeners have fought clay, rocks, and a pernicious Zone 5 to create some of the country's most stunning groupings of flowers and plantings. Drive down any street and you'll notice the fruits of their labor as front doors are defined by masses of flowers. Each season brings another reason to celebrate. Spring's irises, tulips, and daffodils give way to mounds of impatiens, splashy azaleas, and daylilies, and then mum's the word each fall. Where the sun won't reach, we plant hundreds of hostas. Backyards are filled with koi ponds, Japanese gardens, shady decks, and New Orleans–style courtyards. And while you may not want to stop the car to peer over a stranger's gate, you can get inspiration and fresh air at one of our public gardens described here. We highly recommend our 915-acre Powell Gardens for starters.

There's far more to describe than one chapter will allow, so in the Close-up we've listed area parks and recreation departments and garden clubs where you can learn about other green spaces, special events, and classes. You may also want to peruse the Annual Events and Festivals chapter for special events regarding flora and fauna throughout the year. Perhaps there's a water garden tour or butterfly festival near you.

Chances are by the time you have that picnic basket ready, you'll have discovered a pastoral spot on which to spread a blanket. To help you find it, we've divided this chapter by activity type. Listings are in Kansas City, Missouri, unless otherwise noted.

LAKES

FLEMING PARK
Missouri Hwy. 40 on Woods Chapel Rd.
Blue Springs, MO
(816) 795-8200
www.jacksongov.org
You bet they're happy campers in Jackson County; they're also happy boaters, fishing enthusiasts, swimmers, and hikers. Fleming Park, a 7,800-acre paradise just 15 minutes east of Kansas City, offers all these activities and more with two lakes, a swimming beach, picnic shelters, archery range, hiking, and camping facilities. We provide camping information in the Accommodations chapter, or call (816) 229-8980 for a free campground guide.

Winding through the grounds are six trails that offer blufftop and lakefront vistas, as well as your choice of a quiet stroll or a challenging hike. The park is also where you'll find Missouri Town 1855, an antebellum farming community of more than 25 buildings dating from 1820 to 1860. This living-history museum uses original furnishings and equipment, interpreters in period attire, and rare livestock breeds to depict the lifestyles of the mid-19th century. Take a self-guided tour or watch for annual events like Children's Day in June, when kids can take out the earbuds and participate in a gunnysack race or pie-eating contest.

Tours are given Saturdays throughout the summer, and tickets ($5 for adults, $3 for seniors and kids from 2 to 13) are available the day of the tour at Missouri Town; preregistration is not available. Call (816) 229-8980 for more information. The Kemper Outdoor Education Center is a haven for nature lovers, nestled on the east side of Lake Jacomo in the Fleming Park Nature Preserve. The center features aquariums, live displays of reptiles (go ahead, *you* touch it), a bird viewing area, and a display of rocks and minerals. The 40-acre site boasts butterfly gardens, ponds, beehives, wildlife-feeding stations, and a 1-mile nature trail through wetlands, tallgrass prairie, and woodlands. Kemper Gardens is a popular spot for summer weddings where the bridge over the garden pool waterfall makes a lovely altar.

i No man is an island . . . but we have one in the area. Twelve-acre Nelson Island is the only publicly accessible island in the Kansas River. It's located at the northern terminus of Mill Creek Streamway Park.

LAKE JACOMO

Set sail on this breathtaking 970-acre lake located in the heart of Fleming Park. Enjoy colorful sailboat regattas, or jump aboard a pontoon boat where the livin' is easy. The marina (816-795-8888) provides everything you'll need for a day at the lake: boat rental, concession stands, state fishing license, and tackle shop. And get that frying pan ready for some crappie, bluegill, largemouth bass, and walleye: Jacomo is an angler's dream come true.

Lake Jacomo is the place to be on any balmy day, but it's particularly appealing during special events like July's Lake Fest, when thousands of folks line the shores and take lake cruises, watch a regatta, and enjoy a spectacular fireworks display. The annual Easter Egg Hunt brings out hundreds of kids to look for goodies.

WYANDOTTE COUNTY LAKE PARK
91st St. and Leavenworth Rd.
Kansas City, KS
(913) 596-7077
www.wycokck.org

You could easily imagine you're in the Lake of the Ozarks while driving through this 1,500-acre parkland with bluffs, heavily timbered woods, and gently rolling hills. Boating and fishing on this 400-acre lake are allowed from the last Sat in Feb through Nov 30. Call about hours and permits. A horse trail and children's playground are other possibilities, and be sure to show up for free model railroad rides each second Satu of the month from Apr through Nov. Just don't expect to feed the geese; it's strictly prohibited.

WyCo Lake, as we call it, has 16 shelter houses, each with water, electricity, restrooms, and playground equipment; there's a reservation fee for each. The handsome James P. Davis Hall provides air-conditioned comfort for up to 150 guests. The lake is also home to the Korea-Vietnam Memorial, the only monument in the United States to honor soldiers from both wars. Dedicated in 1988, the structure includes a wall of marble fronted by two life-size bronze statues representing 111 who died from Wyandotte County.

PARKS AND GARDENS

ANTIOCH PARK
6501 Antioch Rd.
Merriam, KS
(913) 831-3355
www.jcprd.com/parks

Although at 44 acres this isn't the area's largest park, it's packed with lots of activities like tennis and basketball courts, two small catch-and-release fishing lakes, and an accessible playground called Dodge Town where kids can climb in and out of the hotel and general store. Four picnic shelters offer tables, grills, drinking fountains, and restrooms and can be rented for around $30 for a half day from the parks department.

The park is also home to the Helen Cuddy Rose Garden and Memorial Arboretum, a picturesque wedding site found on the northwest corner of the park, as well as the metro's first exclusively Vietnam memorial, which was constructed here to honor those who served.

BONNER SPRINGS PARK
I-70 North
Bonner Springs, KS
(913) 596-7077
www.bonnersprings.org

This 540-acre park is kept busy year-round with more than just picnics and volleyball. Located adjacent to the Agricultural Hall of Fame, the park houses the Capitol Federal Park at Sandstone, where top-selling musical groups perform outdoor concerts. Each fall the area becomes an Old English village during the Renaissance Festival (read about this in Annual Events and Festivals). When the electric guitars and jousting stop, the park offers space for outdoor activities like tennis courts, ball fields, and shady picnic areas.

i Although there's no charge to enjoy most of the green spaces we've described, you will need a little green to rent a shelter or a boat or spend the day at a beach. Call the numbers shown for fee information or to reserve your space. And call early; many of the most popular shelters are reserved far in advance.

DEANNA ROSE CHILDREN'S FARMSTEAD
13800 Switzer Rd.
Overland Park, KS
(913) 897-2360
www.opkansas.org

A favorite destination for families thanks to its petting zoo, wagon train rides, and other activities, the farmstead also contains a delightful garden maintained by the Johnson County Extension Master Gardeners. Surrounded by a white picket fence, the old-fashioned garden contains a butterfly garden; herbs; shade garden planted with hostas, lilies, and columbine; and a vegetable garden, all along a winding brick walkway. Usually a garden expert is there, measuring the marigolds or tending to tulips, so you might get some advice during your visit.

ENGLISH LANDING PARK
Parkville, MO
(816) 505-2227
www.parkvillemo.com

This long and narrow 68-acre greenway stretches along the natural bends and limestone bluffs of the Missouri River, providing wonderful views from its hiking trails, picnic shelters, and playgrounds. Most of the amenities are just across a turn-of-the-20th-century truss bridge. You'll find lots of folks enjoying ripe peaches and other fresh produce from the farmers' market alongside the trail. The park hosts several festivals throughout the year, including the Parkville Jazzfest and Christmas on the River.

For even more adventure, head to the Parkville Nature Sanctuary, which offers 115 acres of woods and wetlands, a waterfall, a beaver colony, and a glimpse of the area's storied past as a river town. You'll find a trailhead just north of the soccer field parking lot. And if you've had enough of the great outdoors, head back to Parkville's Main Street, where shops, galleries, and a wide array of restaurants await.

HERITAGE PARK
159th St. and Pflumm Rd.
Olathe, KS
(913) 831-3355
www.jcprd.com/parks

This 1,238-acre park was dedicated on Independence Day 1981 and includes enough amenities to warrant a parade. Facilities include 10 picnic shelters; a 45-acre lake; a marina with pedal boat

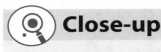

Close-up

The Men Who Turned Kansas City Green

When people visit Kansas City and swoon over our vast parks and boulevards, they're paying tribute to landscape architects George Kessler and the father-and-son team of Sid and Herbert Hare.

When a 21-year-old George Kessler came to town in 1890, he saw little more than scattered homes on little hills, occasionally separated by junglelike foliage. He soon partnered with William Rockhill Nelson, who owned and edited the *Kansas City Star* and who was desperate to turn the little town into a picturesque and pleasant city. Together they, along with other concerned citizens like August Meyer, created the City Beautiful project. By 1895 Kessler was replacing shacks, dumps, and rickety signboards with verdant hillsides, tree-shaded lakes and walks, and smooth, spacious boulevards.

For 30 years he worked with the Kansas City Park Board to create Gladstone Boulevard and Cliff Drive, the Paseo, and Liberty Memorial and to turn a depressing Vinegar Hill into the majestic Penn Valley Park. Kessler did more than just green up Kansas City. During his 40-year career he designed 26 communities, 26 park and boulevard systems, nearly 50 parks, and 46 estates and residences in 23 states, Mexico, and China. You can learn more about his work through the **George Kessler Society** by visiting www.georgekessler.org.

Sid Hare started his career as superintendent at Forest Hill Cemetery, where he became a national authority on expanding the roles of cemeteries as botanical gardens, bird sanctuaries, and arboretums. In 1910 he started a landscaping consulting firm with his son, Herbert, who had studied with the famous Frederick Law Olmsted. During their 28-year partnership, father and son continued Kessler's tradition of wide, beautiful boulevards and parks throughout Kansas City's landscape.

Their trademarks were winding roads contoured to natural topography, preserving trees and valleys, and retaining (or creating) scenic vistas. In 1913 J. C. Nichols hired the Hares to work on the Country Club District area. In addition to laying out approximately 2,500 acres, the firm designed the grounds for many homes, including some of the 50-acre estates that made up the original Mission Hills. Herbert was responsible for designing settings for many of the imported sculptures and fountains that Nichols placed throughout his developments.

Hare & Hare also collaborated with architect Edward Buehler Delk in planning Nichols's Country Club Plaza. Other memorable works include the Rose Garden in Loose Park, which Sid completed in 1937, a year before his death, and the setting for the Nelson-Atkins Museum of Art. Herbert went on to contribute projects throughout the country, including Kansas City's masterful Linda Hall Library arboretum. He passed away in 1960, soon after completing plans for Lake Jacomo.

The legacy of Kessler and Hare & Hare continues today through programs like MetroGreen, a large-scale system of interconnected corridors that will span more than 1,000 miles to link city to countryside, suburb to urban area. More than a system of trails and bike paths, MetroGreen will conserve the unique native landscape—bluffs and woodlands and prairies, parks and boulevards—to ensure that future generations will enjoy them as well.

and sailboard rentals; concession stands; play areas; fields for softball, soccer, and football; and an 18-hole championship golf course and driving range. There's even an off-leash dog area. We're tuckered out just thinking about it.

One of its most unique features is the Black Bob Shelter House, which is on an island and also accessible by foot from the marina area. It can handle up to 300 and is available by reservation only. The shelter includes 30 tables, a large barbecue grill, electricity, and restrooms. Extremely popular, it is often rented months (even years) in advance.

THE EWING AND MURIEL KAUFFMAN MEMORIAL GARDEN
4800 Rockhill Rd.
(816) 932-1200
www.kauffman.org

This exquisite walled sanctuary is one more lasting legacy from the couple who gave so much to Kansas City. And although it's not large, there is much to see as you walk through each display. Brick pathways lead you past elegant ironwork, sculptures, and stained-glass windows providing a delightful mix of vistas and textures. A teak bench provides a place to pause and murmur a quiet thank-you to the Kauffmans, whose gifts are ever blooming. Garden pavilions provide shade, and pergolas brace bright blossoms nodding on vines. A lush mix of flowers and plants is changed three times each year, so the garden looks completely different from month to month.

A reflecting pool runs the length of the Parterre Garden, where slender female sculptures by local artist Tom Corbin are captured in midpirouette. The secluded Secret Garden really does have a secret: three hidden fountains that shoot arcs of water above your head at random moments. This is also the gravesite for the beloved Ewing and Muriel Kauffman. The garden is open every day except some holidays, and there is no admission fee. No pets are allowed except assistance dogs.

LINDA HALL LIBRARY
5109 Cherry St.
(816) 926-8747
www.lindahall.org

Most people come to the Linda Hall Library seeking knowledge and information. With more than one million volumes, it is the largest privately supported library of science, engineering, and technology in the United States. But those seeking tranquility will find it in the 14-acre urban arboretum with 450 or so trees representing 160 varieties. In late April the tree peonies, saucer-size beauties in vibrant colors, begin to bloom; they constitute one of the largest collections in the Midwest. By May the antique shrub roses scent the air as you stroll by. A butterfly garden is planted with happy marigolds, color-box zinnias, Mexican sunflowers, and nectar-rich fennel. A new area contains 50 species of indigenous perennials. Tours of the gardens can be arranged, or you may pick up a printed guide at the library's front desk for $5.

i Although perhaps you'll never have a park named for you like Mr. Swope, Powell, or Loose, you could leave a legacy with a park bench, tree planting, or rose bush. Several of our public parks and gardens can arrange for a lasting memorial in your honor.

LOOSE PARK
51st and Wornall Rd.
(816) 561-9710
www.kcmo.org/parks

Loose Park wasn't always so serene. At one time this was the site of the bloody Civil War Battle of Westport, but today the only reminders are historical markers placed throughout the 75 acres. An 8-foot-high bronze statue of Jacob Loose watches over the garden named in his honor. And early-morning joggers, Plaza workers breaking for lunch, late-afternoon lovers, and children counting ducks (just don't feed them, please) are all drawn to this space up the hill from the Plaza.

Within Loose Park is the Laura Conyers Smith Municipal Rose Garden, with a reflecting pool, a fragrant display of more than 4,000 colorful blooms, and a small lake with a tranquil lily pond. Although Jacob Loose's widow, Ella, who commissioned the park in 1927, had requested athletic fields, we're secretly glad someone dropped the ball, so to speak. Without shouts of fouls and scores, Loose Park provides a restful, peaceful retreat.

OVERLAND PARK ARBORETUM & BOTANICAL GARDENS
179th and Antioch
Overland Park, KS
(913) 685-3604
www.opkansas.org

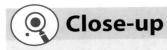

Close-up

Welcome to Paradise

Set among gently rolling hills, **Powell Gardens** (816-697-2600; www.powellgardens.org) is one of the Midwest's most treasured places, offering 915 acres of vivid plants bursting with color, winding pathways along brooks and waterfalls, windswept meadows, and some of the region's most striking architecture. Luckily, this scene of serenity is a mere 40 miles away.

Your tour begins at the visitor center, a handsome stacked-limestone building that houses a conservatory, classrooms, gift shop, and Cafe Thyme, where upscale buffet food is served for lunch, Sunday brunch, and dinner during special events.

When you're ready to explore the grounds, you can take a free trolley ride to the different areas or cross the bridge on foot to the Island Garden set in a 12-acre lake. This is a showplace for native and exotic water plants, rock gardens, and ornamental trees—nearly 800 varieties of plants in all. A three-pooled cascading water garden acts as the focal point. The island's north side allows for an uninterrupted view of the stunning Marjorie Powell Allen Chapel, a wood, glass, and stone triangle in the sky designed by famed Arkansas architect Fay Jones.

After leaving the water garden, head to your right past the Wildflower Meadow. There you'll enter the cool and serene Rock and Waterfall Garden, dressed in every shade of green imaginable in delicate ferns and nearly 50 varieties of hostas. Sweet pinks and whites appear in flowering trees in spring, and in summer raspberry-colored azaleas provide a burst of color. Hidden among these enchanted woods are picturesque decks and secluded benches for cuddling or taking time to reflect.

Just over a bridge is the 3½-acre Perennial Garden, the largest in the Midwest, with more than 5,000 plantings, including many chosen specifically as come-hithers to butterflies. In summer the place nearly pops with orange, deep reds, and brilliant yellows as 250 varieties of daylilies lift their trumpets to the skies. The curving walkways take you through twists and turns to a peaceful pavilion overlooking the lake.

The latest expansion, the Heartland Harvest Garden, boasts a 12-acre edible landscape.

Back at the visitor center you can enjoy a crisp salad or tasty sandwich or buy a book or garden tool in the gift shop. Here's also where you may take part in a class on growing orchids, constructing a birdhouse, or making holiday wreaths from natural elements. Outdoor festivals and events include the popular Booms and Blooms over Fourth of July weekend, with live music and an impressive fireworks display, and several times a year members of the Astronomical Society of Kansas City present stargazing demonstrations.

This hidden, 300-acre gem in south Overland Park is most definitely growing, with new ecosystems, 13 gardens, four conservatories, and a handsome learning center. Five miles of wood chip–covered hiking trails meander through the area and across two 75-foot bridges spanning Wolf Creek. The trails become slightly more challenging along limestone bluffs rising above the southern banks of the creek. Views from here are marvelous, and if you linger long enough you might see a crane or other waterfowl silently land.

Eight natural ecosystems, from prairie grassland and dense woods to a wildflower meadow, provide a surprise at every turn. The highlight is the Erickson Water Garden, with four waterfalls and a bog with more than 100 natural plantings that attract birds, butterflies (more than 500 varieties have been identified here!), and two-footed nature lovers. Benches scattered around the area invite you to rest and listen to the relaxing sounds of cascading water and laughing children.

The Marder Woodland Garden has massive stone pillars supporting wooden arbors at its entrance and overlook. It's a romantic spot with the sound of falling water resonating through towering trees. And your little nature boy or girl will have fun following a spiraling walkway or watching frogs frolic in a pond in the Children's Discovery Garden. Plants and trees are identified here, as they are throughout the garden. An easy, half-mile asphalt trail provides a nice stroll.

The visitor center hosts programs and social events and contains a small gift shop and concession stand. Enjoy your refreshment on the sunny patio.

SHAWNEE MISSION PARK
7900 Renner Rd.
Shawnee, KS
www.jcpard.com/parks
More than three million visitors enjoy this 1,250-acre park every year, more than any other park in the state of Kansas, making the district wonder why it doesn't open a tollbooth. Lucky for us, it's a public park and anyone can enjoy its many natural wonders along with a few treasures where Mother Nature got some human help.

Facilities include a 150-acre lake for boating, fishing, and sailboarding, 12 shelters and numerous picnic areas, horseback and nature trails, an archery range, and a marina. A sandy beach with a concession and bathhouse appeals to sun-lovers. The fee for adult Johnson County residents is $5 and $5.50 for non-residents, $3 and $3.50 for children. Shelters range in size from Shelter No. 3 with a lake view and seating for 32 to No. 10 in the Walnut Grove area with three grills, 20 tables, and seating for 160. Please invite us to that party. In fall this park has a splashy show of colorful foliage that rivals New England. Colorful trees line the main road that circles the park; take one and head to the south side of the park where a 5-story observation tower provides a breathtaking view of the jewel-tone leaves.

Shawnee Mission Park is also home to Theatre in the Park, a popular summer theater venue (see The Arts for more information), and the John Barkley Visitor Center, which has an exhibit on the history of parks in Johnson County. Pet owners, however, make a mad dash to the dog park, a 53-acre fenced area that is leash-free. With access to the lake, it's a favorite with labs, who gleefully swim out to retrieve sticks. Leashes are required everywhere else.

SWOPE PARK
Swope Pkwy. and Meyer Blvd.
(816) 513-7500
www.kcmo.org/parks
Topping out at 1,769 acres, Swope Park is the largest city park in Kansas City and one of the most expansive in the country. The land was donated by millionaire Thomas H. Swope and dedicated on June 25, 1898. It contains two golf courses; areas for softball, soccer, rugby, and Frisbee; horseback trails; and a day camp for kids. And, yes, you can rough it in the middle of a city: Hiking enthusiasts can take a guided scenic tour along the hill south of the Lake of the Woods.

The Lakeside Nature Center (4701 East Gregory Blvd., 816-513-8960, www.lakesidenaturecenter.org) within Swope Park is Missouri's largest wildlife rehabilitation center, caring for more than 3,300 native animals and birds. The center also has a 1,000-gallon aquarium and offers educational programs for all ages, including bird-watching, animal tracking, streamside hikes, and nature photography. The nature center is open 9 a.m. to 5 p.m. Tues through Sat and noon to 4 p.m. Sun. Admission is free, and the center is open year-round, closed Mon. Swope Park is also home to the 8,000-seat Starlight Theatre as well as the Kansas City Zoo and Sprint IMAX Theatre.

TRAILS

Drive around this suburban area and you might dismiss it as row after row of housing developments, shopping centers, and office buildings. But thanks to city fathers with vision, Johnson County, Kansas, is a place of green spaces, meandering streams, and pocket parks, with about 140 miles of trails for walking, hiking, and biking. You just need to know where to look. The following will give you a good head start, but to really get a lay of the land, the Johnson County Park and Recreation District (913-438-7275, www.jcprd.com) offers maps and descriptions. And if you plan to take a phone, park rangers are available through the dispatcher by calling (913) 782-0720.

The Indian Creek Trail and Tomahawk Creek Trail system in Overland Park provides more than 30 miles of hiking and biking leisure. The Indian Creek portion joins Quivira Park at 119th and Quivira and extends to Leawood City Park, where it dips under I-435 and through commercial, residential, and office areas. The areas are shaded, a few park benches are scattered around, and you'll see a charming little waterfall along the way. You can also access the trail at several points, including Corporate Woods office park, where a drinking fountain and picnic shelter mark the entrance to a partially hidden bridge.

i **When exploring our many walking and biking trails, remember it's "Yield to the right and pass on the left." When approaching walkers from behind on a bike or in-line skates, it's courteous, not to mention safer, to announce "To your left" to allow them time to move over.**

Tomahawk Creek Trail runs behind Blue Valley Recreation Fields near 138th Street and Antioch Road, and from Nieman Road and 135th Street around St. Andrew's Golf Course to the Deanna Rose Children's Farmstead, which makes a great stop along the way (see Kidstuff for information about this delightful place). The trail connects with a trail at Miller's Woods.

Mill Creek Streamway Park crosses four counties as it travels along Mill Creek from Woodland Road north to Kansas Highway 10 in Olathe and then continues north through Lenexa, Shawnee (where it dips into Shawnee Mission Park), and Merriam to the Kansas River. If you made it all the way, celebrate with a little dance on 12-acre Nelson Island, the only public-accessible island in the Kansas River, where the trail ends. Mill Creek includes wheelchair-accessible parking, drinking fountains, and shaded picnic areas.

GARDENING ORGANIZATIONS AND RESOURCES

THE LOOSE PARK GARDEN CENTER
5200 Pennsylvania Ave.
(816) 784-5399
www.gardencenterassociation.org
This is the headquarters for several garden clubs, where meetings, shows, and workshops take place. The horticultural reference library has about 1,500 books on every bloomin' thing. It's open 8 a.m. to 4 p.m. weekdays. The Garden Center Association of Greater Kansas City, an umbrella group with about 1,000 members, meets here. Its newsletter, *Garden Bulletin*, is published bimonthly and includes a calendar of events. Membership costs $15 a year. For information call the number above.

MASTER GARDENERS' HOTLINES
These are the experts to call when your dahlia's drooping or your tomatoes are toast. Armed with state horticultural training courses and scads of experience, the volunteers can answer your questions or direct you to other resources. The **Johnson County Master Gardeners** work at the Deanna Rose Farmstead, 137th and Switzer in Overland Park. The hotline (913-764-6306) is staffed 9 a.m. to 4 p.m. weekdays. The **Master Gardeners of Greater Kansas City's** hotline (816-833-8733) is open 9 a.m. to 3 p.m. weekdays, from Mar 1 through Oct 31. Or visit www.mggkc.org

SPORTS

Ballgames! Getcher red-hot ballgames here! In Kansas City we love our sports. Always have, always will, whether our teams are winning or not. And our sports town status began long before the Royals and Chiefs suited up. It started in 1884 when the Kansas City Unions baseball team first took the field.

But it was the Kansas City Monarchs, those champs of the Negro Leagues, that really put us on the map. Satchel Paige, Jackie Robinson, and Buck O'Neil were so important to the sport and this city that we built the country's only Negro Leagues Baseball Museum (www.nlbm.com). You can read more about this terrific memorial in the Attractions chapter.

And no other city in America can rival our history of college tournament basketball. A tournament—Big Six, Big Seven, Big Eight, Big Twelve—has been played in Kansas City every year, sometimes twice a year, since 1946. But it started long before that. In 1937 what is now known as the NAIA tournament, the nation's oldest, began at downtown Municipal Auditorium. By the time the NCAA Tournament final came here in 1940, 10,000 fans packed the stands and March Madness became an official affliction. The NCAA returned in 2005 after a short stint in Texas. And after an eight-year absence, the NAIA returned to Kansas City in 2002. We remain the undisputed Tournament Town.

We're not always watching sports . . . sometimes we're participating in them. You'll find plenty of athletic activities to keep you in liniment, including golf, cycling, hiking, and running. We're also big on joining clubs so that we can talk about our sports when we're not watching or playing; for instance, for a city without a single snowcapped mountain, we have one of the country's largest ski clubs. You'll get contact information in this chapter. But first, let's hit one out of the ballpark.

The listings in this chapter are grouped by spectator, participation, and family sports. The facilities are located in Kansas City, Missouri, unless otherwise noted.

SPECTATOR SPORTS

KANSAS CITY EXPLORERS
(816) 513-5630
www.kcexplorers.com

With 15 years as members of World Team Tennis under their white belts, the Explorers pack 'em in at what must be the prettiest venue in the league. Their court is at Barney Allis Plaza, in the heart of our downtown. Evening games when the lights come on in the art deco skyscrapers, the famous Bartle Hall Pylons stand tall against the night sky—well, it's breathtaking. Add the *ka-pop, ka-pop* of that tennis ball and it's all the night music you need. You can imagine that with only 2,600 seats total, tickets tend to go fast.

KANSAS CITY ROYALS
Kauffman Stadium
Truman Sports Complex
(816) 921-8000, (800) 676-9257
www.kcroyals.com

Here's a trivia question for you, sports buffs: What local team name in the late 1880s sounded a lot like the Red Sox? Give up? It was the Kansas City Blue Stockings. Honest. More than a century later we're still on that side of the color wheel, but you can bet there are more people cheering at the Kauffman than at the old Muehlebach or Municipal Stadiums. For one thing, The K, as we affectionately call it, seats 40,625 fans.

The stadium was named for Ewing Kauffman, who purchased the Kansas City Royals in 1968 and turned the team into one of the most successful franchises in baseball. They won six division championships and two American League pennants. We showed our appreciation by building a fancy new Royals Stadium in 1973, and they proceeded to fill it with two million fans a year more than 11 times. Now that's a lot of beer and peanuts. The stadium is one of the fan-friendliest arenas in pro sports. Behind the fence in right field is a 322-foot-wide fountain, the largest privately owned water display in the world, that puts on a dazzling show between innings and when one of our boys hits a home run. In left field is a 30-by-40-foot Sony JumboTron video display board that was the largest in the country when installed in 1990. Water jets and fireworks filled the sky on October 27, 1985, when Kansas City won the World Series title with an 11–0 victory over the St. Louis Cardinals.

i "I could do that," you mutter after listening to someone warble the National Anthem at the ballpark. Here's your chance, buster. The Kansas City Royals invites choirs, bands, and super stars to sing a capella before "Play ball!," or to lead the crowd in "Take Me Out to the Ballgame" after the seventh inning stretch. Visit www.royals.com to audition.

We said thanks to Mr. K on July 2, 1993, when the 21-year-old Royals Stadium was renamed in his honor, and there wasn't a dry eye in the dugout or stands. A month later tears came again as the only owner the team had ever had died at the age of 76. But George Brett gave us something to cheer about in 1999 when he became the first member of the Royals to be inducted into the Major League Baseball Hall of Fame.

Kansas City ushered in a new era when David Glass took over ownership in 2000. And although we haven't returned to the glory days of 1985—yet—there's always this season. Tickets range from $7.50 to $30. And until we have a championship team, our renovated stadium

gives us plenty to cheer about. With a $250 million price tag, some of the improvements include an additional 39,000 seats, an exciting Walk of Fame area, an eye-popping high-def scoreboard, a kid-friendly Outfield Experience area complete with a carousel, a wide concourse that spans the stadium, and a number of new restrooms that have female fans wanting to kiss David Glass and his son Dan. New restaurants feature fare from local eateries, although we've always thought the ballpark franks and Frosty Malts ("Git yer Frosssty Mallllts!") hit a home run. Fans with money to burn can show off in fancy new home-plate suites.

KANSAS CITY CHIEFS
Arrowhead Stadium
(816) 920-9300
www.kcchiefs.com
Other teams hate to play at Arrowhead Stadium, and it has less to do with the opposition than the fans. Kansas City boosters are known as the loudest and most enthusiastic in the National Football League. Crowd noises have been known to challenge even the most seasoned veteran's concentration; even squinting up at that sea of blood-red jackets, hats, and sweatshirts can be intimidating.

Fans have had plenty of practice chanting in unison; of the nearly 80,000 seats, most are occupied by season ticket holders. The rest are usually snapped up when single-game tickets go on sale in late July. Purchase these through **Ticketmaster,** (800) 676-5488 or www.ticketmaster.com. Whatever your ticket stub says, you'll pay dearly for parking; right now it's $22. The gates open 3½ hours before kickoff to allow for the second sport at Arrowhead: tailgating. And nobody does it better than the KC fans.

Around here, pro football isn't a game, it's a lifestyle. Entire sections of department stores are devoted to Chiefs apparel. Every fall Chiefs flags fly from cars and front porches. Then there are the tailgate parties, when the parking lot takes on a blue haze from row after row of grills sizzling up hot dogs and burgers. The competition is nearly as fierce as what's to come, with groups trying to outdo one another and TV cameras recording the action. You'll see everything from barbecue ribs, baked beans, and cold beer to chilled baby lobster with fine wine. We'll stick with brats, please, with plenty of mustard and kraut.

Kansas City football, too, has had a long history. It started in 1924 with the Blues (that color again!), an NFL team that changed its name to the Cowboys a year later. In 1963 Lamar Hunt moved his Dallas Texans to Kansas City and named them for the city's mayor, H. Roe Bartle, whose nickname was "Chief." The team won the American Football League championship in 1967 and 1970. On January 11, 1970, the Chiefs won the Super Bowl, and in 1972 they moved into their new stadium in the Harry S. Truman Sports Complex. Todd Haley took over coaching duties in 2009—the 11th head coach in the Chiefs history. Here's hoping he takes the 50-year-old franchise all the way to the Super Bowl.

KANSAS CITY ROLLER WARRIORS
Hale Arena at Kemper and other venues
(816) 809-8496
www.kcrollerwarriors.com
Like watching fast women? Wearing knee pads and game faces? Then the KC Roller Warriors— our local dames on roller skates—can offer just your kind of evening. Considering the team names, such as the Knockouts and Victory Vixens, you can expect some outrageous bouts. The grunts and yelps are enhanced with the sounds of local bands that rock out during the games.

The Warriors team, the story goes, is "the angry mutant love child" of skaters Dirty Britches and Princess Anna Conda (Brooke Leavitt and Mandy Durham), who founded the league in 2004. The Web site itself is hilarious, with bios and photos of each player, complete with a cigarette hanging from red lips, a baby on a hip, or a hapless opponent being shoved headfirst into a locker. The brawling broads (and they love it when you call 'em that) play six at-home games; tickets are $13 in advance and $16 at the door. Kids get in for half-price. Games are usually sold out and, frankly, so is the beer.

KANSAS CITY T-BONES
CommunityAmerica Ballpark
1800 Village West Pkwy.
Kansas City, KS
(913) 328-5618
www.tbonesbaseball.com
What do you call a baseball team from the land of sizzling steaks? The T-Bones, of course, and the action can be as hot as a platter of beef. Members of the Northern League, which was founded in 1993 as a way for talented players to continue careers after leaving Major League life, these guys really put on a show. Part of the fun is the stadium itself, the CommunityAmerica Ballpark, built in 2003 with a retro feel that includes plenty of attention to fan comfort and fun. For instance, there are 6,365 fixed seats, and not a one has a bad view. The farthest from the field is a mere 50 feet, so everyone can hear the crack of the bat and the hum of a fastball. A wide concourse allows you to watch the game even while catching a snack at the concession stand. Parents love the children's play area, where they can keep an eye on the kiddies and the on-field action. Little fans will want to spend time with Sizzle the Bull, the entertaining mascot (his sign is Taurus, if you must know).

Tickets are retro as well, starting at just $6 for general admission up to $16. Check out season-ticket plans that get you into all 24 home games. Or bring 19 of your buddies and score the suite, which includes plenty of snacks and grub like pulled-pork sandwiches, for $500. Did we mention parking is free?

KANSAS CITY WIZARDS
(816) 920-9300
www.kcwizards.com
When it was announced that the new major league soccer team in Kansas City would be known as The Whiz, the management got what they wanted: plenty of attention. When the jokes threatened to overcome the players' potential, the name was changed to the Wizards in 1996. Ahhhh, that's better.

For the time being, the Wizards play their home games at CommunityAmerica Ballpark in

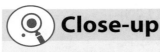

Close-up

Sprint Center

1407 Grand Ave.
(816) 283-7300
www.sprintcenter.com

Is it a spaceship? A giant, glowing pillbox hat? No, it's the Sprint Center, the 18,500-seat arena that helped launch the revitalization of Kansas City's downtown. Opened in fall 2007, the $276 million project hosts sports and concert events. Beyond that, the arena is home to the College Basketball Experience and the National Collegiate Basketball Hall of Fame, sponsored by the Kansas City–based National Association of Basketball Coaches. It houses memorabilia and exhibits and provide a wonderful venue for events and induction ceremonies. This shrine to hoops alone is expected to bring over 150,000 visitors to the center its first year.

And speaking of hang time, the arena's construction involved some pretty precarious moments as 12-foot-by-5-foot glass panels—2,204 in all if you're counting—were carefully installed into the exterior of the 130,000-square-foot structure. The result is a stunning sight that changes with the light of the day, from golden to pink, then glows green at night as a beacon to fans of sports and music.

As a long-needed downtown arena, the Sprint Center anchors the exciting Power & Light District, a 24-hour-a-day entertainment and retail neighborhood.

Kansas City, Kansas; the season runs from Apr through Sept. Tickets cost $12 to $19 for adults and $8 to $13 for youths.

KANSAS SPEEDWAY
1333 Meadowlark Lane
Kansas City, KS
(913) 328-RACE
www.kansasspeedway.com
See the Close-up in this chapter for more on NASCAR racing.

PARTICIPATION SPORTS

Bike or run along our many trails, swing a golf club, bowl a few strings, or take to the ice. We figure you've got to stay active just to burn off all that barbecue. No matter what your pleasure or passion, you'll have an opportunity to play it here. And if you're into fishing or sailing, check out our extraordinary array of lakes in the Parks, Lakes, and Recreation chapter.

Biking

Kansas City has its share of biking enthusiasts, who enjoy our wide streets and miles of trails. The only thing missing is designated bicycle lanes throughout the metro. This may change in the next few years; the MetroGreen plan aims to encourage more two-wheeled transportation with hundreds of miles of trails linking urban to suburban areas. Until that happens, if you do venture out on your Schwinn, do so with caution. Wearing a helmet goes without saying, but also follow all motor traffic rules, be alert, and, above all, make yourself known to drivers. For companionship on the open road, plus information about scenic bike rides and annual charity rides, contact one of the clubs below.

Favored paved trails include the Blue River Parkway, which starts in Minor Park at Red Bridge Road in Kansas City; the Mill Creek Streamway Park, which extends more than 17 miles from the Kansas River to downtown Olathe; and the Indian Creek and Tomahawk Biking and Hiking Trails in Overland Park, which run about 10 miles along the northern edge of I-435. Access points include Corporate Woods and Leawood Park.

i Of the nearly two million people living in the KC metro area, an estimated 270,000 are golfers. No wonder, then, that we've raised some winners. Pros from our town include Tom Watson, Matt Gogel, Bruce Lietzke, and Tom Pernice Jr. (PGA Tour) and Amy Alcott (LPGA Tour).

JOHNSON COUNTY BICYCLE CLUB
www.jcbikeclub.org

This group started in the late 1960s as part of the local parks and rec department and went solo in 1973 with about 30 members. Today more than 400 riders are involved, which means you can find a buddy or group strapping on a helmet to hit the road nearly every day. It sponsors three annual rides of up to 100 miles and holds monthly meetings to demonstrate new equipment and discuss how gel-padded bike shorts are the best garments ever invented. Throughout the year, volunteers host free rides that vary in speed, distance, and starting location but frequently begin or end at a restaurant to further the club's unofficial motto, "Ride to eat, eat to ride!" Membership dues are around $20 a year and many of the events are open to nonmembers for a fee. Find more information on the Web site, or write to 9513 Booth Ave., Kansas City, MO 64134.

THE KANSAS CITY BICYCLE CLUB
(816) 436-5641

www.kcbc.com

This club, established in 1963, sponsors everything from beginner rides to all-day marathons for those who have to see what's over the next hill. The KCBC also has a United States Cycling Federation–sanctioned racing team and hosts the Tour of Kansas City race every fall. Quarterly meetings are held at a different location each time and always include an interesting ride and a picnic. A monthly newsletter keeps members current on upcoming events, newly discovered tours, and training techniques. Annual dues vary.

Fencing

KANSAS CITY FENCING CENTER
9900 Antioch

Overland Park, KS

(913) 579-9535

www.kcfencing.org

Fencing helps develop agility, strength, speed, and discipline. If not, what's the point? This program is taught by some of the country's finest, including head coach Kelly Williams, the top-ranked female saber fencer in the United States. Now she's training others to succeed: Her students have placed in the top eight in United States Fencing Association competition in every age group. Classes are available for beginning, intermediate, advanced, and expert level fencers in three categories: saber, foil, and épée. Intro classes, which include two one-hour classes per week, range from $65 to $85 per month and provide equipment. Open sessions using your own equipment are also available.

Golf

Kansas City has been in love with golf since 1894, when two Scottish duffers created the town's first course in what is now the Hyde Park neighborhood. Did we say "course"? It was actually nothing more than a deserted cow pasture near 36th and Gillham Road. Two years later, in 1896, a group of the original players started the elite Kansas City Country Club

By the early 1900s courses began to dot the landscape, and the increased interest attracted some of the finest golf course designers of the day, including A. W. Tillinghast and James Dalgleish. Kansas City was becoming known as a golfing town. More courses, both private and public, sprang up, and the city played host to a PGA event for more than a decade. All that practicing paid off. Kansas City native Tom Watson has won the PGA Tour Player of the Year six times and eight Majors and has been considered one of the top all-time players since turning pro in 1971. In 2009, Kansas City held its collective breath as Tom came *this* close to winning the Open Championship at age 60. Another native, Matt Gogel, is also making a name for himself.

As interest in golf grew, spurred by Tom Watson's success, Kansas City began to see a need for more public courses, and dozens of city and county greens were developed during the 1980s and 1990s. Today more than one million rounds of golf are played annually on 72 courses (46 public and 26 private) in the Greater Kansas City area. And new courses are added every year to keep up with the demand. You can bet that prime home lots next to new golf courses go fast. Our private courses are superb, and we hope you'll have a chance to play on at least one during your visit; many of them have reciprocal privileges for members of other clubs. In this chapter we'll concentrate on our beautiful public courses. Please note that this list is not inclusive.

Get an overview and list of events at **www .kansascitygolfguide.com** or **www.kcmetro golf.com,** where you can even book tee times. We've listed courses with a wide range of fees.

i **Shave some dollars off your golf game by opting for early-bird savings or twilight hours.**

DEER CREEK GOLF CLUB
7000 W. 133rd St.
Overland Park, KS
(913) 681-3100
www.deercreekgc.com
With its 162 acres of rolling terrain and plenty of mature trees, sand, and water, well-traveled golfers may immediately identify this as a Robert Trent Jones Jr. course. It's certainly one of his most beautiful. Jones has crafted not one but two signature holes into this masterpiece. The No. 3 hole is a 422-yard hole that plays between a creek on the left and a bunker on the right. To make it you'll have to drive it dead-on. And if you didn't care for that water hazard the first time around, you won't care for the second signature shot. It comes at No. 15, a 22-yard par 3.

HERITAGE PARK GOLF COURSE
16455 Lackman Rd.
Olathe, KS
(813) 829-GOLF (4653)
www.jcprd.com
This popular course isn't a walk in the park, although it is in one. The course has proven its level of difficulty by being used for U.S. Open qualifying rounds. The 16th hole is the one that can trip you up on this Don Sechrest–designed course. The 215-yard, par-3 hole requires 190 yards of carry over a body of water. We'd like to have a take in that used golf-ball concession.

IRONHORSE GOLF CLUB
15400 Mission Rd.
Leawood, KS
(913) 685-GOLF
www.ironhorsegolf.com
This 189-acre course has quickly become an area favorite, winning top honors from readers of *Ingram*'s magazine and accolades from *Golf Digest*. It was designed by Dr. Michael Hurdzan, and every effort was made to maintain the natural landscape, which gives the course a mature look that will only improve with time. The par-72 championship 18-hole layout offers a distinct challenge on every hole, and the creek that meanders through the course affects play on no fewer than 15 holes. Ironhorse features bent grass greens, zoysia fairways, and bluegrass and fescue roughs. Golfers can choose from five tee complexes per hole. Total yardage varies from 6,900 yards from the back tees to 4,783 from the forward tees. The upscale homes that surround the course are as magnificent as the grounds.

LONGVIEW LAKE GOLF COURSE
11100 View High Dr.
(816) 761-9445
Near one of the area's most picturesque lakes, this course features varying elevations, elevated tee boxes, and a little longer play. The Scottish-style links offer something for every skill level. Signature holes both include water. No. 8 is particularly challenging because of the pond running along the left side. And one of the pret-

tiest views on the course provides its biggest trouble spot on No. 12, which is played next to Longview Lake.

OVERLAND PARK GOLF CLUB
125th and Quivira
Overland Park, KS
(913) 897-3809
www.opkansas.org
The biggest hazard here is finding a place to park at 5 p.m. Keep driving, though, because playing here is a pleasure. Around 125,000 rounds of golf are played at OPGC per year, a tribute to its beauty, location, and value. With 42 sand bunkers on 13 holes and two lakes affecting 5 holes, you might as well say each hole is a challenge. The course is sited high on a hill in Overland Park with extraordinary views. As you can imagine, tee times go fast, so it's best to call several days in advance. This course also offers a popular par-3, nine-hole ladies' league, and for a community course has a decent pro shop, instructors, and snack bar.

SWOPE PARK MEMORIAL GOLF COURSE
I-435 and Gregory
Swope Park
(816) 513-8910
www.swopememorialgolfcourse.com
This course is carved out of Swope Park, at 1,769 acres one of the country's largest metropolitan parks. The area is also home to Starlight Theatre, the Kansas City Zoo, a hiking trail, and a nature conservatory. But with land this vast you'll feel completely insulated from the world in this natural beauty.

A. W. Tillinghast built the course in 1913, and although it's a shorter course than many more contemporary ones in Kansas City, it has many excellent features. That is, if you're ready for a challenging game. Two of Kansas City's toughest holes are here. No. 17 is slightly uphill, and adding to the tension is a bunker in the middle of the fairway. And on the 14th hole, bunkers to the left of a right turn 250 yards out can make you wonder why you ever took up the sport. Perhaps the reasonable fees will cool you off.

Running and Walking

By the time spring shows her pretty head, plenty of us are hitting the streets to gear up for road races. You'll have lots of chances to get your race-day T-shirts here; there seems to be a fund-raising run or walk every weekend. Following are three of the largest. If you'd like a few pointers before you sign up, we've included information about a local running club.

AIDS WALK
(816) 931-0959
www.aidswalkkansascity.org
The region's largest AIDS fund-raising event brings together around 3,500 people to raise money and awareness for the men, women, and children living with HIV/AIDS in the Kansas City area. The 2009 event alone raised nearly $500,000 for research and programs. The run is usually in April, and past sites have included Mill Creek Park on the Country Club Plaza.

GROUNDHOG RUN
(816) 746-1414
www.childrenstlc.org
This race takes place in the Hunt Midwest Underground Facility Subtropolis, a huge, underground labyrinth big enough to handle an 18-wheeler. The runners aren't too hep on the course's twists and turns, but they dig the 58 degree temperature in the middle of winter. The race is held every February. Get there early; this one attracts 3,000 or so runners, and the space, naturally, is limited.

KANSAS CITY TRACK CLUB
(816) 333-RACE (7223)
www.kctrack.org
Run a few miles, get a free beer. Sounds like a plan. This track club devotes its time to teaching people how to run, keeping them motivated and safe and then rewarding them with some of the best parties around. A 30-year tradition is the 4- to 12-mile Wednesday night fun run that ends at some member's house for potluck dinner. It usually draws 40 to 70 members, and visiting runners are always welcome. Other outings include Sunday-morning long runs and Thursday-night speed sessions.

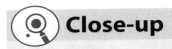 **Close-up**

Kansas City, Start Your Engines

To visualize just how big the Kansas Speedway is, consider that both Kauffman and Arrowhead Stadiums—including their parking lots—would fit into its infield, with room left over for one particular race driver's ego.

The $260 million International Speedway Corporation–owned facility opened in June 2001 and gave Wyandotte County a sound that drowns out even the rumble of racing motors: *ka-ching!* Season tickets went flying out the door, with 40 percent of total ticket sales going to Kansas residents. Fans from 46 states and four Canadian provinces grabbed up the rest. Individual seat prices range from $165 to $330.

Those lucky enough to get seats are not disappointed. The 82,000-seat (which can actually expand to seat 150,000), 1.5-mile tri-oval NASCAR track was designed for the comfort and convenience of the racing teams and the fans. Thanks to a beautifully planned low infield and elevated backstretch, every seat from rows 1 to 65 has an unimpeded view of all four turns and the backstretch. And although the seats are great (especially those personalized with the owners' names), the Fan Walk is even better. Guests access the infield via a tunnel located south of the grandstand. Within the infield fans get an intimate look at the garages, inspection stations, and Victory Lane. An opening in the fence provides a chance to obtain autographs. The Fan Walk adds $15 to your ticket price.

Fans might have to wait to get a driver's scribbled name, but they won't have to wait for much else. ISC and its designers did their homework and found out that racing fans hate to stand in line, so the Kansas Speedway has 16 ticket windows, 18 concession stands (including those selling barbecue), 50 portable food kiosks, and 12 restrooms. That last statistic is very good news for fans who consume 26,203 gallons of beer during a NASCAR Sprint Cup series. Put another way, it's enough liquid refreshment (including beer from our city's own Boulevard Brewing Company) to fill a stock car's gas tank 1,191 times.

To really get in the driver's seat, attend one of the five driving schools that take place at the speedway, including the Richard Petty Driving Experience and the Mario Andretti and Jeff Gordon racing schools. The thrilling experience costs less than you may think. For instance, three laps with professional drivers at the Racing Experience starts at just $125; you can floor it all the way to $4,300 for 80 laps including your own fire suit and helmet. Just the thought of why one would need a "fire suit" is enough to keep us on the other side of the fence. Toll-free numbers for these racing companies are found on the Kansas Speedway Web site.

An even better view, along with a wet bar and private bathrooms, is available in one of the luxury suites. The privilege costs plenty; after a one-time administrative fee of $7,000, the rooms go from $29,000 to $70,000 a year with a four-year minimum commitment. *Ka-ching* indeed.

Drivers appreciate the design as well. Veteran driver Bill Elliott said it may be the best ever built. Creature comforts include garages that measure 5 to 10 feet larger than those at most tracks, increased amperage for trailer hookups, and a terrific family center and playground for their children.

Contact **Kansas Speedway** (913-328-RACE, www.kansasspeedway.com), 1333 Meadowlark Lane, Kansas City, KS to find out more about tickets and events.

The club also puts on 17 or so races a year, including the St. Pat's Run; the Dog-N-Jog Run-Fur-Fun, featuring 980 dogs and their masters; and the Brew to Brew, a 42-mile killer that starts at the Boulevard Brewing Company in Kansas City and ends at the Free State Brewing Company in Lawrence. Certainly the most scenic course is the annual Cliffhanger 5K walk/run held at the historic Cliff Drive in the Gladstone Boulevard area. Although the limestone cliffs provide some challenge, seeing the waterfall fountain is worth it. A $15 membership ($20 for families) gets you discounts and newsletter updates.

TROLLEY RUN
(888) 543-7223, ext. 4
www.trolleyrun.org
Following along Kansas City's long-gone urban trolley track, this is Kansas City's largest run and the fourth largest 4-mile run in the United States. It's actually just a festive street party, because the course is so flat and scenic you won't feel like you've worked at all. Starting in the Waldo area at 75th and Wornall, the run takes you through some of our loveliest old neighborhoods, where dogs and kids line the streets to cheer you on. Keep going: The final reward is a view of the lushly landscaped Brush Creek, a below–street level, 0.75-mile concrete ribbon that has a tiered waterfall at the west end.

The race ends on the Country Club Plaza with music, lots of food, and high-fives all around. On top of that the race, now sponsored by Sabates Eye Center, is held in April, one of our best months weatherwise. If all that doesn't convince you, perhaps this will: Money raised goes to help the Children's Center for the Visually Impaired, an organization that provides training and help to blind and visually impaired infants and children.

Sailboat Racing
JACOMO SAILING CLUB
Lake Jacomo
Blue Springs, MO
(913) 707-8818
www.jacomosailingclub.org

This club has been promoting the sport of sailboat racing since 1958, before the lake was even completed. And you've got to love any organization that calls a meeting in the middle of a crystal-blue lake on a Sunday afternoon. Although the majority of its members like nothing better than a good competitive regatta, some members just come out to watch, cheer, and enjoy the day on the club's nicely equipped pontoon boat. The club offers training sessions for new members, and each June they hold an Open Sail, sort of like an open house but with boats. It's a great opportunity to learn more about the sport, see the different types of fleet boats, and get wet. If you decide to join, an associate membership costs $40 a year and includes all privileges except competing for trophies. A $95 per year membership entitles sailors to skipper their own boat and compete for trophies.

FAMILY SPORTS

Bowling

Interest in this sport seems to ebb and flow depending on how people feel about the shoes. It's popular once again, not only with long-term leagues and little kids but also with teens seeking a fun Friday out with friends. Several bowling alleys in Kansas City cater to the young crowd with laser light shows and booming music.

AMF COLLEGE LANES
10201 College Blvd.
Overland Park, KS
(913) 451-6400
www.amf.com
A real plus for people staying at the Doubletree Hotel across the street, this center offers 32 lanes, seven billiards tables, and a lounge along with a small arcade. They crank up the music for X-treme Bowling, when black lights make the pins and balls glow, dude. And for groups of four, a Fun Pack is the way to go: $10 each will get you shoe rentals, two hours of bowling, a pitcher of soda, popcorn, and a one-topping pizza.

INCRED-A-BOWL
8500 W. 151st St.
Overland Park, KS
(913) 851-1700
www.incredabowl.com

This 65,000-square-foot, state-of-the-art center includes a 40-lane computerized bowling alley, an arcade filled with a hundred of the latest interactive and virtual reality games, and a three-story set of play tubes for the tykes. Teens in particular really go for the Cosmic Bowling every Fri and Sat night, when black lights, fog, glow-in-the-dark balls and pins, and upbeat music take the pain out of a gutter ball. The fun continues until long past midnight. Incred-A-Bowl also has a pro shop, gift store, and snack bar.

Fishing

With all our lakes and parks, you're sure to reel in the largest walleye, crappie, channel catfish, or largemouth bass you've ever seen. Since the region covers two states and nearly a dozen counties, fishing permits vary. But for the most part, Missouri requires a $3 per day nonresident permit, and Kansas charges $3.50 per day. You'll find information about our major lakes, including Jacomo, Blue Springs, and Wyandotte County, in the Lakes, Parks, and Recreation chapter. Following are some additional fishing spots.

LAKE OLATHE
625 Lakeshore Dr.
Olathe, KS
(913) 971-8521
www.kdwp.state.ks.us

You're sure to find a place to capture a competition-size catfish, bass, or even trout somewhere in these 170 acres. There's even an assist from Old Saint Nick; each year the parks and recreation division tosses retired Christmas trees into the area around the fishing piers to create nesting places for fish.

SHAWNEE MISSION PARK
7900 Renner Rd.
Shawnee Mission, KS
(913) 831-3355
www.jcprd.com

Anglers seeking bluegill, carp, and bass show up at this 150-acre lake, one of the most popular in the region. Boat rentals are available, but you'd better reserve yours early; each spring and fall the lake is stocked with rainbow trout. Now that's good eating.

SMITHVILLE LAKE
DD Hwy.
Smithville, MO
(816) 532-4217
www.smithvillemo.org

When people around here say they're "gone fishin'," chances are this is their destination. Just 20 miles north of downtown Kansas City, Smithville's 7,200 acres provide plenty of reeling action. The lake is stocked with tiger musky, walleye, bass, crappie, and several species of catfish for an afternoon of fishing and a fine fillet that night. Boats are available for rent at the two full-service marinas, and five multilane boat launch ramps ensure easy accessibility to the water. And you're in luck: Smithville has 777 campsites, one-third with electrical hookups. Call (816) 532-0803 for reservations.

Skateboarding and Roller Hockey
ROLLER HOCKEY RINK
116th and Knox
Overland Park, KS
www.opkansas.org

Kids love this regulation, 120-by-65-foot rink at Indian Valley Park. The surface is coated for safety (well, at least it's safer), and a 5-foot-tall sideboard surrounds the playing area. Player benches are on each side. Rules and safety suggestions are posted, but there are no supervisors on-site. The rink is maintained by the Johnson County Parks and Recreation Division, and there are no fees for use.

SKATEBOARD PARK
138th and Switzer
Overland Park, KS
(913) 893-6354
www.opkansas.org

After the popularity of iceboarding competitions in the Winter Olympics, this sport skyrocketed. This small park was created thanks to a grassroots effort that began with an Overland Park resource officer. $240,000 later, the community got its center in 1997, complete with ramps, jumps, and rails for all skill levels. It's popular with skateboarders and in-line skaters.

Snow Skiing

KANSAS CITY SKI CLUB
(913) 383-9006
www.kcskiclub.org

Go figure. Here we are, miles away from a mountain, and we have one of the largest ski clubs in the country. And it's active without a flake in sight. With 3,000 members, there's always a group getting together to play volleyball or golf, socialize at an area bar, or take canoe trips in the summer. Oh, yes, and ski. The 50-year-old club sponsors about 31 ski trips each year with destinations as diverse as Colorado, New Mexico, Canada, and Spain. The membership more than pays for itself in what you'll save on each trip. Besides that, it's one of the best ways to meet singles in the area.

SNOW CREEK SKI LODGE
Missouri Hwy. 45
5 miles north of Weston, MO
(816) 640-2200
www.skisnowcreek.com

When ski buffs aren't in a car or van heading to Breckinridge or Vail, you might find them at this ski lodge that opened in 1985. People who expect the Midwest to be flat as a flapjack will be surprised to see a 300-foot vertical drop and enough varied terrain to give beginners and experts plenty of action. Nine intermediate trails are served by two triple chairlifts and one double chairlift, and rope tows get you to the beginner area. The snow base usually ranges from 24 to 60 inches, thanks to 50 snowmaking machines.

A lodge features a cafeteria, bar, and lounge and also houses the ski school and gift shop. The rental shop offers shaped skis with plenty of junior sizes, plus snowboards and ski boards. Jason's Run has enough jumps, bumps, mounds, pipes, and tabletops to keep expert boarders happy. The park opens in mid-Dec and stays open through mid-Mar if the weather cooperates. It's open seven days a week, offers night skiing beginning in late Dec, and stays open until 3 a.m. for special events.

DAY TRIPS AND WEEKEND GETAWAYS

Why anyone would want to leave the pleasant confines of Kansas City is beyond us. But the three small towns in this chapter have enough appeal to pull anyone away from a plate of our famous ribs. Each one has a unique personality and enough attractions to make it well worth the short drive.

But instead of jumping on the highway after dinner, why not slide under a down-filled duvet at a bed-and-breakfast? Each town offers irresistible options, from an antiques-filled estate to a rustic but romantic working ranch. Besides a sumptuous breakfast the next morning, staying overnight gives you one more day to explore a museum, scout out another art gallery, or stop by that pretty park you passed on the way.

There you have it: three destinations that feel like a century away. Best of all, you'll hardly need to top off your gas tank. You can be checking out that cute little antiques shop or sinking your teeth into a square of homemade fudge in less than an hour.

And now, let's get started by doing what so many travelers did in the late 1800s: heading west.

LAWRENCE, KANSAS

Lawrence is a marvelous mix of quirkiness and cosmopolitan flair that can be found only in a college town. Toss in a couple of award-winning restaurants, great music venues, and . . . well, we won't expect you back tonight. In fact, for some tourists a weekend became a week that turned into forever. The town is booming thanks to graduates who stay on and visitors who fall in love with the laid-back pace, vibrant arts scene, and parks and lakes just a short walk or bike ride away. Its historical buildings also rate points: The National Trust for Historic Preservation has named Lawrence one of the dozen most distinctive and unique destinations in the country.

The varied collection of downtown shops is also a draw. At the heart of the 5-block district is Massachusetts Street, which you'll soon call "Mass" like everyone else. The tree-lined avenue is an outdoor art gallery thanks to a successive series of one-year exhibitions of sculptures by national artists. Thirty more outdoor artworks and murals serve as a nice introduction to the galler-

ies and museums around town. Check Web sites **www.visitlawrence.com** and **www.downtown lawrence.com** for a complete listing of shops, galleries, and boutiques. A sampling includes Phoenix Gallery, specializing in custom stained glass, ceramics, textiles, and prints; Borderline Gallery (6 blocks east of Mass on 9th), with unique artwork like copper clocks and raku ceramics; and Silver Works, a gallery of exquisite handcrafted jewelry and crafts Waxman Candles has been creating hand-poured wicked wonders in a variety of shapes and scents for over 30 years. Most shops are located between 6th and 11th Streets on Mass, but don't overlook some gems on adjacent side streets. The apex of arts activities is the **Lawrence Arts Center** (785-843-ARTS [2787], www.lawrenceartscenter.com), in the 900 block of New Hampshire. The center features exhibitions by area and nationally known artists and is home to professional theater and other performances.

Antiques abound as well: you'll hit the jackpot at the **Lawrence Antique Mall** (830 Mass), where more than 70 dealers are ready to help you fill that empty car trunk or suitcase for the trip home. Hungry yet? No doubt you've been tempted by the sight of a dozen or more sidewalk cafes all along Mass. From coffee shops to authentic Mexican food, there's a table or counter with your name on it. If you prefer a more upscale choice—although still friendly—save your appetite for one of Larry Town's superb restaurants. We give 10 points out of 10 for Ten, the restaurant in the Eldridge Hotel (see details later in this section). Start the evening with the locals at the Jayhawker bar right next door, where the martini list is as lively as the conversation. Or have your vodka in the spicy red sauce over pasta at Ten while your date digs into the coriander spiced rack of lamb. At **Pachamama's** (785-841-0990, 800 New Hampshire, www.pachamamas.com) chef Ken Baker turns fresh, local ingredients into memorable meals. Witness his peppered smoked pork tenderloin with souffléd garlic-cheese grits, or wood-fired breast of duckling on smoky greens. And his vanilla bean crème brûlée? Oh, mama. More casual fare, like soups and sandwiches, is found at the **Free State Brewing Company** (636 Mass, 785-843-4555, www.freestatebrewing.com), the first legal brewery in Kansas since pioneer days.

Before or after dinner, consider catching a performance at the **Lied Center of Kansas** (15th and Iowa, 785-864-ARTS [2787]), a dazzling $14.3 million multipurpose facility that's home to KU's concert series, Swarthout Chamber Music, and Broadway and Beyond performances. **The University Theatre** (15th and Naismith Drive on the KU campus, 785-864-3982, www.kutheatre.com) presents a wide array of plays and musical performances, including the popular Kansas Summer Theatre.

Perhaps other nightlife is calling you. Lawrence offers lively music venues, like the Bottleneck at 737 New Hampshire and the Granada on Mass, offering heart-thumpingly loud music from rock to alternative. Liberty Hall on Mass is a restored opera house that provides a beautiful setting for live entertainment as well as cinematic releases.

When you're ready to turn in, Lawrence has several dreamy options. **The Oread** (1200 Oread Ave., 785-843-1200, www.theoread.com), a luxury hotel that opened in 2009, pampers guests with 99 guest rooms and suites, a lavish spa, and exciting dining choices. Five 21 presents classic American cuisine paired with an impressive wine list, while Be Sweet satisfies that hunger for ice cream and desserts. Night owls will want to check out the Cave, a dance club that gives this college town plenty of class thanks to laser lights and a smoke machine. **The Eldridge Hotel** (7th and Mass, 785-749-5011, 800-527-0909, www.eldridgehotel.com) is the only Lawrence business in the same spot it occupied during Kansas Territorial Days and throughout the Civil War. A new hotel was built on the site in 1924, and it's now an all-suite hotel with 48 luxury suites. A honeymoon suite has a shower built for two. **The Halcyon House Bed and Breakfast** (1000 Ohio St., 888-441-0314, www.thehalcyonhouse.com) is a charming European-style inn whose structure was built in 1885. Nine rooms are filled with antiques and flourishes and range from the Nooks and Crannies with a shared bath for $55 to the private Carriage House with its own luxurious bath and fireplace for $149. After breakfast at your hotel or bed-and-breakfast, you can return to downtown to catch all the shops and galleries you missed, or head to one of the area lakes and parks. Anyone who thinks the Kansas prairie is a dull patch of green is in for a pleasant surprise. The Prairie Park Nature Center is a 71-acre park adjacent to seven acres of virgin prairie with 180 species of wildflowers and native grasses that flow like shimmering satin with the wind. You can explore more than a mile of trails that pass through prairie and wetlands and end at a seven-acre urban lake. Interpretive signs along the path point out habitat elements and identify wildlife.

A visitor center is located in a historic train depot at North 2nd and Locust Streets. For more information call (785) 865-4499, (888) LAWKANS (529-5267), or visit **www.visitlawrence.com.**

WESTON, MISSOURI

Blink twice when you reach Weston and you'll wonder where you left the time machine. Antiques shops, a clothing store like none other, more than its share of historic homes, and two fine-dining restaurants should keep you busy for a day or a weekend. Lucky for you Weston has some appealing bed-and-breakfast options and one historic downtown hotel. The hamlet's official tagline might be "the town that time forgot," but you never will.

If it hadn't been for a Missouri River flood in 1881 that shifted the river 2 miles away into Kansas, Weston could have been a major metropolis instead of a side trip. Most of us send a silent thank-you to that watery presence every time we visit this town that's magically stuck in the mid-1880s.

i Most small towns tend to "roll up the sidewalk" early. That's certainly true in Atchison, Kansas, and Weston, Missouri, where restaurants tend to close at 9 p.m. and there are few nightspots. If you're after relaxation and romance, these towns are fine choices. But if you like variety, from art to music to theater, Lawrence is your kind of getaway.

Weston was the first city founded in the six-county Platte Purchase of 1837, and today it remains a hamlet of 1,700 residents—all, it would seem, living or working in a pre–Civil War building or antebellum home. In all, 22 blocks of buildings are listed on the National Register of Historic Places, including the **Price-Loyles Home** (718 Spring St., 816-640-2383), an 1857 three-story Federal-style home that was occupied by four generations of Daniel Boone's descendants. The home, filled with original family furnishings and toys, is open for tours. See more of the town's past at the Weston Historical Museum, which features artifacts depicting life here from prehistoric times to World War II.

Main Street has antiques as well, but these are the kind you can buy. In fact, Weston is a magnet for antiques shoppers from surrounding states. With nearly a dozen Old World emporiums lined up side by side, shoppers look like human rickrack as they go from door to door seeking peeling-paint cabinets and sponged bowls.

Several stores mix old with new, such as the Acorn, where you'll find vintage furniture and linens along with new garden art. And not only will you find that perfect silk pillow at Nelson & Taylor Interiors, but the in-store decorating team will help you coordinate an entire room to go around it. Renditions offers an extensive array of handcrafted Arts & Crafts furniture and accessories with such well-known names as Hile Furniture, Porteous tiles, and gorgeous mica lamps. If you need a pine table to display that new lamp, Youngblood Gallery most likely has it, along with other antiques and giftware. After all, they've been a Main Street beacon for more than 24 years.

One of the most remarkable shops in the region is a few miles out of town. **Locust Grove Antiques** (25180 Hwy. JJ, 816-640-3203) carries a collection of antique and new furniture and accessories arranged in small habitats that make it easy to say, "I'll take the whole room!"

When you're finished sprucing up your home, consider a new outfit at Missouri Bluffs Boutique and Gallery. This is truly the Bermuda Triangle of the Midwest; it's a fact that women who walk in here are never seen again. The store is wall-to-wall with clothing that marries rustic with romance: embroidered and bejeweled vests, sweeping velvet skirts, suede jackets with 6-inch fringe, and hats festooned with fabric roses and netting. Red-and-black cowgirl boots to go with your new getup? Size 7, coming up.

By now you're starving, and Weston can oblige. **The Vineyards** (505 Spring St., 816-640-5588, www.thevineyardsrestaurant.com) serves lunch, dinner, and Sunday brunch in an 1845 antebellum home that is delightful during the day and turns intimate with candleglow at night. The extensive wine list includes selections from Weston's own award-winning **Pirtle Winery.** Save enough time to visit the winery (502 Spring, 816-640-5728, www.pirtlewinery.com) across the street. Housed in a historic church with a wine garden and tasting room, Pirtle's is known for its honey mead, a slightly sweet wine that gives *honeymoon* its name. The shop is open daily from 10 a.m. (it's cocktail hour somewhere in the world!) to 6 p.m.

Another favorite dining choice is **Avalon Cafe** (608 Main St., 816-640-2835, www.avalon-cafeweston.com). This 150-year-old home makes an appealing backdrop for the chef's masterpieces, especially wild game such as elk and duck. The Weston Trio takes the guesswork out of ordering; it usually features a wild-game dish plus a fish and steak with a selection of marvelous sauces. For lunch the baked brie is a gimme. Add a salad and it's plenty to share with a friend for lunch. Avalon is open for lunch and dinner Tues through Sat with a Sunday brunch. Reservations are a must.

If you'd prefer frivolity to fine dining, take a trip to Ireland at **O'Malley's 1842 Pub** (Short and Welt Streets, 816-640-5325, www.westonirish.com), carved out of three limestone brewery cellars built 55 feet belowground. Sean O'Malleys's pub hosts several big events a year (see Annual Events). Weston also has places for pampering. **The Inn at Weston Landing** (500 Welt St., 816-640-5788, 877-249-5788, www.innatwestonlanding.com), is a Celtic-style hideaway that is part of the original Weston Brewing Company built in 1842. The inn's four spacious rooms (all with private baths) have distinct personalities. The Andrew O'Malley room, for instance, reconstructs a delightful cottage on the southern tip of Ireland's Clew Bay with a fireplace, hand-blown windowpanes, and spinning wheel. **The Benner House Bed and Breakfast** (645 Main St., 816-640-2616, www.bennerhouse.com) is a fine example of steamboat gothic architecture. It was built in 1898 for George Shawhan, who owned what is now known as the McCormick Distillery. Strolling from the shops and restaurants, you'll notice the house right away with its wraparound porch, quaint gingerbread details, and large windows overlooking the veranda. Breakfast will be waiting after a night's rest in one of the four upstairs guest rooms, each with private bath.

Other amenities include a hot tub set in the backyard garden, a parlor for socializing, and a sitting room where you can curl up in a rocking chair with a book.

The **Hatchery House Bed and Breakfast** (618 Short St., 816-640-5700, www.hatcherybb.com) is a handsome Federal-style home built in 1845 that got its name for the number of children "hatched" here throughout the years. Present-day innkeepers Bill and Anne Lane have hatched some pretty swell ideas themselves, such as filling the four guest rooms with lovely antiques and keeping the original wood-burning fireplaces intact. We feel a winter trip coming on. If you prefer a "downtown" stay, then the **Saint George Hotel** (500 Main St., 816-640-9902, www.thesaintgeorge.com) has a suite waiting for you. Built in 1845 and recently renovated, the 26–guest room hotel has amenities the steamboat captains it once served could never fathom.

Weston tempts you with festivals and special events throughout the year, including antiques shows in March and April and a July 4 festival with a parade, street fair, and fireworks.

The annual Applefest, held in October, brings together folk artists, a garden market, live music, and everything you could possibly make apples into, including apple butter, fritters, cider, and dumplings. You can also celebrate the harvest at the source; two nearby orchards offer such fall treats as pumpkin patches, hayrides, caramel apples, and free cider. Call **Vaughn Orchard and Country Store** (816-386-2900) and **Weston Red Barn Farm** (816-386-5437) for details.

Before the first frost, townspeople begin planning the annual Candlelight Homes Tour in December, when five historic homes are dressed for the season. Street activities feature carolers, carriage rides, and a chance to whisper wishes to Father Christmas.

For information visit **www.westonmo.com**. A visitor center at 502 Main St. has brochures on shops, lodging, and restaurants. Please be aware that many of the shops and restaurants are closed on Monday.

ATCHISON, KANSAS

A trolley ride past grand Victorian mansions on brick-paved streets, sweeping views of the Missouri River valley from a tree-shaded park bench, and a hot fudge sundae at an old-fashioned soda fountain downtown: If this sounds like an idyllic afternoon, then this lovely riverfront town is for you.

When you come to Atchison you'll be following in the footsteps of the Kansa Indians, who gave the state its name, and Lewis and Clark, who passed through on July 4, 1804. Fifty years later Atchison became one of the first settlements in the Kansas Territory. The town was named for David R. Atchison, then president of the Missouri Senate, who became president for a day when Zachary Taylor refused to take office on a Sunday.

Its location at the westernmost bend of the Missouri River turned the town into a leading commercial center, a role that was expanded when the Atchison, Topeka & Santa Fe Railroad was founded in 1860. Soon bankers and railroad magnates were building impressive mansions and minicastles, many of which still line 3rd, 4th, and 5th Streets.

i Sometimes tiny shops and 10-table restaurants keep strange hours, so to keep from driving 40 minutes only to see a display of closed signs on doors, call to check on open days. In Weston, for instance, it seems the whole place shuts down on Monday.

Other settlers were building grand stone structures as well; the Benedictine monks established **St. Benedict's Abbey** (1020 North 2nd St., 913-367-7853, www.kansasmonks.org) in 1858. It's easy to tell the church didn't come until a century later. A student of Frank Lloyd Wright, Barry Byrne, designed this handsome limestone structure with a 44-foot-high nave ceiling. His wife created many of the interior frescoes. Self-guided tours are available, and if you wish to spend more time in this spiritual setting, weekend retreats can be arranged. Call (913) 367-7853 for details.

In 1863 the Benedictine Sisters established **Mount St. Scholastica College** for women, and in 1938 their beautiful **chapel** (801 South 8th St.) was dedicated. The interior is rich with beautiful marble, including pillars that contain many fossils. A large rose window, stained-glass windows, and a magnificent Romanesque vaulted ceiling make this worth a look. Tours can be arranged by calling (913) 367-6110. The chapel overlooks the river, and a park bench under an ancient tree provides a pleasant stop.

Enough reflection—now it's time to shop! Atchison's claim to fame, of course, is as the birthplace of Amelia Earhart. But these days another woman is putting the town on the map. Mary Carol Garrity's famous home interiors store, **Nell Hill's** (501 Commercial, 913-367-1086, www.nell-hills.com), is a phenomenon that's been covered in *Victoria* magazine, *Kansas City Home Design*, and even the *Wall Street Journal*. Customers from Topeka, Omaha, and of course Kansas City make regular road trips to stock up on European antiques, home furnishings, accessories, and gifts at jaw-dropping prices. Don't worry about getting it all home; Mary Carol ships. And be sure to ask about her books on interior design and gracious entertaining while you're there.

Other antiques shops on Commercial Street are worth checking out as well. This outdoor pedestrian plaza is landscaped with brick walls, seasonal plantings, and fountains. Hungry? Pop into **Marigold Bakery and Cafe** (913-367-3858), a cozy place for crisp salads, sandwiches on focaccia, and homemade pies. Take an extra cookie to go. Most downtown locations are open every day except Sunday. Fashionistas will adore the clothes and accessories at **Amelia's,** 121 North 5th St., and the home furnishing store above it. This emporium is **Garrity's** (913-367-1523), Mary Carol's "new" place for "old" items—as in antiques—as well as her exciting furniture line. Does this woman never sleep?

Now that you've experienced the town's sanctuaries (both religious and 400-count Egyptian cotton) it's time to discover its history. The **visitor center** (913-367-2427, 800-234-1854; www.atchisonkansas.net) is historical itself, housed in the restored Santa Fe Depot at 200 South 10th St. Open every day except major holidays, the center provides maps, a brochure, and a gift shop for souvenirs of your visit. The same address is home to the **County Historical Society Museum,** which has artifacts from steamboats and wagon trains, and the **Atchison Rail Museum,** owned by a voluntary group of railroad enthusiasts who operate a miniature railroad during the summer.

The depot is also where you can catch the Atchison Trolley for a 45-minute narrated tour past 18 sites on the National Register of Historic Places. As you clack, clack, clack over brick streets you'll see some of the most impressive Victorian homes in the Midwest as well as the Romanesque-style post office that was completed in 1894. You may want to hop off at one of the following stops to explore.

i **If you're planning to stay at a bed-and-breakfast, the host can become your new best friend even before you sign the register. Call before your visit, if possible, to request information about upcoming events, what not to miss, and restaurant recommendations. That way you can get the most from your visit.**

The **Evah C. Cray Historical Home Museum** (815 North 5th St., 913-367-3046) is a 25-room mansion that offers a look at the opulence of the Victorian era. Built in 1882, it is distinguished by a three-story fairy-tale tower, ornate fireplaces, and original chandeliers. The carriage house has a video viewing room, country store, and exhibits. A minimal fee is charged. The museum is open daily May through Aug, closed Nov through Feb, and open Fri through Mon all other months. Got that?

The **Muchnic Art Gallery** (704 North 4th St., 913-367-4278) is in a spectacular Queen Anne mansion that was built in 1885 for lumber merchant George W. Howell. His profession dictated the home's lavish use of carved woods, such as the intricate parquet floors of walnut, mahogany, and oak and faces carved on the ornate newel

posts in the lower hall; the eight faces are said to represent the Howell family. Cast-bronze hardware and stained glass in the conservatory are other masterful touches. The home is open on weekends and Wednesday afternoons from Mar through Dec; there is a small fee.

The **Amelia Earhart Birthplace Museum** (223 North Terrace St., 913-367-4217, www.ameliaearhartmuseum.org), also on the trolley route, is a pretty Gothic Revival cottage built in 1861 by the famous flyer's grandfather, Judge Alfred G. Otis. The Ninety-Nines, a women's pilot organization Earhart helped found in 1929, now operates the museum, which features period furnishings. Open daily, but hours vary throughout the year. Donations are appreciated.

It's time to land somewhere for lunch. **Jerry's Again** (121 North 5th, 913-367-0577) tempts you with salads, soups, and sandwiches. In fact, a shopping trip to Garrity's Encore upstairs usually ends right here with a slice of one of Virginia's legendary pies. **Paolucci's** (113 South 3rd, 913-367-6105) is a family establishment that provides a taste of Italy in this small town. A vast take-out menu includes meatball sandwiches, but we'd prefer dining in to dig into a platter of shrimp scampi or pasta with sausage. Ready for bed? Part of the allure of tiny towns is that lodging choices always seem to include a bed-and-breakfast. Atchison has two delightful options. St. Martin's Bed and Breakfast is perched on a stone wall and provides a glorious view of the river from the back patio. You may never want to leave the luxury of the spacious Gold Suite, with its grand king-size bed, claw-footed bathtub, and shower for two. Four other rooms are available, including the ultraromantic Anna's Room in shades of taupe and mauve with a dreamy view.

Owners John and Janet Settich are well known for their breakfasts, which often include one of John's famous omelets along with a delightful platter of fresh fruit and gourmet cheeses. **St. Martin's** is at 324 Santa Fe St. Call (913) 367-4964 or (877) 367-4924. You may view the rooms online at www.stmartinsbandb.com.

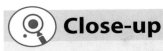

Close-up

Downtown Parkville, MO

(816) 505-2227
www.parkvillemo.com

This riverfront village is a charming little getaway for a day of shopping, yet is close enough to drop in for lunch. The real pull is its mix of two dozen one-of-a-kind shops and galleries filled with gifts, decor, and fine art. **River's Bend Gallery** (201 Main St., 816-587-8070), will delight you with gorgeous etched-glass vases, ceramics, and photographs; vivid pastel landscapes you'll want to get lost in; and silver and pewter jewelry at terrific prices. **Wines by Jennifer** (405 Main St., 816-505-9463) is part wine bar, part classroom as you learn about vintages while imbibing. It's a popular place for girlfriends to plan a night out.

Just a short walk away are shops along English Landing Drive. Discover your inner child at H.M.S. Beagle, a science store with telescopes (come back at night for a lesson), toys, and gifts. Or discover your creative side at Florilegium, a shop filled with antiques along with needle art. Ready to drop? You'll have your choice of restaurants to recharge your energy level. **Cafe des Amis** (816-587-6767) serves country French fare on a lovely treetop deck. The pizzas at **Stone Canyon** (816-746-8686), especially the roasted potato and chicken version, are legendary. Café Cedar serves Mediterranean and Greek fare; live music entertains patrons on the weekend. Feel free to dance when you hear your song. Or work off your meal with a stroll along the groomed trails that meander through 115 acres of river valley woods and wetlands, complete with a romantic waterfall. Read more about this nature sanctuary in the Parks, Lakes, and Recreation chapter.

It's a lovely time to visit any month, but Atchison sparkles during its special events. In July a celebration on the 4th serves up food, music, and fireworks at the Amelia Earhart Stadium, and two weeks later the Annual Amelia Earhart Festival treats residents and guests to outdoor concerts, arts and crafts, food, a carnival and street dance, and a spectacular fireworks display on the Missouri River. In October the Atchison Homes Tour lets us peek into some of the fabulous old homes. The Oktoberfest Arts and Crafts Festival is a downtown event with more than 100 arts and crafts vendors plus German food and music. And count us in for the Haunted Homes Tour, which extends through Halloween. This narrated trolley tour takes you around "the most haunted town in Kansas." The trolleys are rolled out again for the annual Tour of Lights each December, an hour's round-trip of festive holiday lights and decorations all around Atchison. For more information on all these events, call the **Atchison Area Chamber of Commerce** at (913) 367-2427 or (800) 234-1854, or visit www.atchisonkansas.net.

Appendix

LIVING HERE

In this section we feature specific information for residents or those planning to relocate here. Topics include real estate, education, health care, and much more.

RELOCATION

All right already, we've convinced you to move here. Congratulations, neighbor. You're going to love living in the heartland. We've helped you pick your neighborhood, line up some festivals, locate parks and lakes, and find where to get a great meal. Now let's move you in.

To smooth your move we've divided this chapter into topics of major interest to those planning—or just contemplating—a move to Kansas City: Neighborhoods and Real Estate will help you decide where you want to live. Once you've settled on a location, Getting Started will help you get hooked up to utilities. Getting Legal provides basic information about licenses you'll need, and Getting to Know You introduces those little nice-to-know services in town.

Whatever your reasons for making the move, welcome to Kansas City! The listings are in Kansas City, Missouri, unless otherwise noted.

NEIGHBORHOODS AND REAL ESTATE

Kansas City real estate agents fight over who gets to take the couple from California on a tour of available homes. Once the visitors get a gander at the five-bedroom beauty on two acres for the same price as a two-bedroom bungalow in San Jose, they'll practically wrench the contract out of the agent's hand.

A recent survey conducted by the National Association of Homebuilders ranked Kansas City No. 1 in housing affordability among metropolitan areas with populations over one million. Let's compare apples to apples, or in this case a four-bedroom, two-and-a-half-bath home in a neighborhood that would appeal to a middle-manager transferee. According to Sperling's Best Places 2009 Home Price Comparison Index, that exec would pay double to live in Deerfield, Illinois or Spokane, Washington. Moving from La Jolla, California? See how far your $1.87 million will go in the heartland, as in a mansion in Mission Hills, an equestrian estate, or a three-story chateau on one of our pristine lakes. No wonder one California transplant thought an ad for a $130,000 home here was for the down payment alone.

Is it any wonder *Money* magazine named Overland Park, Kansas, No. 6 in its Top 100 Places to Live? This pretty suburb excelled in such categories as low crime rate, short commute distance, job growth, green spaces (there are seven public golf courses here), and median home prices around $20,000 less than the Best Places average. Tiny Parkville, Missouri, got a pat on the back from *Men's Journal* in 2007; it was the only Midwest community to be named one of the 50 Best Places to Live.

Families will be happy to know they're welcome here; we rank No. 3 among large metropolitan areas for relocating, according to Worldwide ERC. But singles—bring it on! We moved up eight spots to No. 30 in *Forbes* magazine's Best Cities for Singles, based on our nightlife, culture, job growth, and "coolness" factor. Dig it. Both of those rankings were helped by what *American-Style* magazine found when it named us one of its annual Top 25 Arts Destinations.

Factor in our low tax burden and the picture gets even better. According to the Tax Foundation, homeowners in Missouri pay 10.49 percent of their income in local and state taxes, and Kansas homeowners pay 10.88 percent. Both numbers are well below the national average of 11.33 percent.

In fact Kansas City ranks well below the national average in cost of living and costs for housing, utilities, and grocery items. According to the American Chamber of Commerce Researchers, we are one of the nation's best bargains. Our residents average about 28 percent above the national median in real income, which combines "affordable" with "cost-effective." That means we have more disposable money for shopping, dining out, and recreation. No wonder big retailers like Nordstrom and Crate and Barrel can't get here fast enough. Let me at those Johnson County shoppers!

Kansas City also offers solid business opportunities for both corporations and employees. *Expansion* magazine rated Kansas City No. 3 on its 50 Hottest Cities in the U.S., based on our central location and low cost of living. *Fortune* has referred to our town as one of the best places for doing business. Perhaps more important in terms of lifestyle, the same magazine listed Kansas City as most beloved by its own resident executives.

Perhaps one reason the execs are so happy is that they're not behind the wheel. Kansas City is second only to San Antonio for freeway miles per capita, which means our workforce has a faster and easier commute than other cities our size. On average, most commuters get to the office before the cup of coffee gets cold, in about 20 minutes. One executive who left behind a 90-minute commute each way in Chicago said living 10 minutes from his office has meant a true lifestyle change. He has more time to spend with his family, can easily make a 5 p.m. tee time, and has far less stress.

Giant corporations are proud to call Kansas City home. Sprint Nextel's 3.9 million–square-foot world headquarters is in Leawood, Kansas. Hallmark Cards, one of the world's best-known brands, with sales of $4.2 billion, is based here. So is H&R Block, the nation's largest tax preparation firm, which was founded in 1955. American Century Investment Inc., the mutual fund giant, was begun in Kansas City in 1958, and here it stays. And other large corporations are locating here to reap the rewards of our central location and wealth of educated, friendly work-

ers. *Management* magazine rates us among the top 25 "Hottest Real Estate Markets." Once transferred employees get a chance to experience the Midwest lifestyle and buying power, they're thrilled to call Kansas City home.

Although these corporate giants have helped grow our economy and attract a top-notch work force, Kansas City remains a hotbed of entrepreneurial and small business activities. In fact, 99 percent of local companies employ 250 or fewer workers, accounting for 64 percent of total employment. They find plenty of support through training and specialized programs. *Entrepreneur* magazine rates Kansas City as one of the best three cities for supporting small business, and *Inc.* magazine has called us "an entrepreneur's dream." Our diversity—a healthy mix of big corporations and small companies—is one reason we tend to weather a recession better than most other cities do.

Our job force is consistently ranked among the most educated and productive in the United States, but we realize there's more to life than just work. We are, above all, a city of balance.

We tend to take our city's riches for granted, but newcomers are often surprised at our varied and vibrant arts culture. The Nelson-Atkins Museum of Art features one of the world's finest collections of Asian art and has more Henry Moore sculptures than any place this side of the Atlantic. The museum has completed its dramatic expansion—the Bloch Building—which elevated its standing even more. Down the street, the Kemper Museum of Contemporary Art showcases works by Dale Chihuly and Louise Bourgeois.

Music lovers have the Kansas City Symphony, Lyric Opera, Chamber Music series, and jazz concerts at the Folly Theatre. Art galleries abound here, especially in our revitalized inner-city Crossroads Arts District that's home to dozens of small showrooms and artist studios. And just on the horizon—due to open in the fall of 2011 during the biggest party this town has ever seen—is the $340 million Kauffman Center for the Performing Arts, which will make a monumental addition to our city's skyline and way of life. Yet with all our highbrow offerings, one of our most appealing aspects is our mix of cultures. You can enjoy an evening of Beethoven on Saturday night and spend Sunday afternoon at a blues jam.

And we like to exercise our bodies as well as our minds. Long known as a major league sports town, we offer more recreational amenities than most cities our size. With hundreds of parks, lakes, golf courses, recreation centers, and public pools in every community, we offer ample opportunities for family entertainment and a healthy lifestyle. In fact, *Men's Health* magazine ranks Kansas City second in cardiovascular fitness and fourth for running and jogging.

You'll find all four seasons beautifully represented here. Outdoors, in fact, is where Kansas City really shines. Real estate agents tell stories of newcomers who expect to find dusty streets with tumbleweeds scuffing the car door and instead are enchanted by our lush green spaces and acres of forests.

The City of Fountains is also a wellspring of education. We boast a network of highly rated public schools, private and parochial schools, top-notch technical and vocational programs, and private and state-affiliated colleges and universities. Parents are involved in their students' school programs through parent-student-teacher programs and are quick to vote "yes" when it comes to updating existing schools, building new ones, and improving services.

Many of our public schools and their educators have received state and even national recognition, including Teacher of the Year honorees, Triple A–rated schools, and Blue Ribbon awards from the U.S. Department of Education. Graduating students find a wide variety of choices, whether they seek the small student-teacher ratio of a private college like William Jewell or the excitement of the University of Missouri–Kansas City, with 13,000 students. Graduate degree programs abound, offering working adults a chance to take classes part time while maintaining their careers.

With our great schools, friendly neighborhoods, and abundance of recreational opportunities, Kansas City is a great place to raise a family. In fact, Overland Park, Kansas, is the "kid-friendliest" suburban area in the country (among those with populations over 100,000) according to the Washington-based group Zero Population Growth. The group looked at factors like education, environment, health, public safety, and community life.

Wellness is also an element that puts Kansas City ahead. It's significant that people come here from all over the country to obtain premium health care. More than 60 hospitals and specialized clinics stand ready to meet any medical need, from the birth of a baby to the rarest forms of cancer. Greater Kansas City is also home to award-winning medical research based at the University of Missouri School of Medicine, the University of Health Sciences, and the University of Kansas Hospital, which was recently ranked 30th in the nation for its heart program by *U.S. News & World Report*, and that was before the judging panel witnessed the new state-of-the-art Center for Advanced Heart Care, which opened in October 2006.

In 2000 they were joined by the Stowers Institute for Medical Research, a $195 million, 600,000-square-foot facility funded by James Stowers Jr., founder of American Century Investments. With its current endowment of $1 billion, the center is devoted to studying gene-based afflictions such as cancer, Alzheimer's disease, and rheumatoid arthritis. Largely due to the Stowers project, eight primary research institutions are collaborating through the Kansas City Area Life Sciences Institute, with a goal of making our city one of the nation's top 10 centers for life sciences and biotechnology research in the years ahead.

Add to the mix our Midwestern friendliness and small-town values, and it's easy to see why people who have grown up here wouldn't want to live anywhere else. And people who move here realize they've stumbled upon the nation's best-kept secret.

You'll have your pick of neighborhoods and homes here, and chances are for far less money than you'd ever imagine possible. And you'll be amazed at how quickly you'll be welcomed into the neighborhood. No matter what your interests, you'll soon find a garden club or singles' group to join, an invitation to a Chiefs' tailgating party, or another soccer mom who's happy to let you take Tuesday. Let's take a drive around the neighborhoods. Notice all the people waving? Yes, we really are that friendly in Kansas City.

Ready for the grand tour? We divide this section into states, then counties, then by city. Each community, whether it's populated by 334 or 134,000, is governed by a mayor and city council. Granted, this gets a little confusing when a dividing street has a different speed limit depending on whether you're heading north or south. But on the plus side, having so many communities with their own histories and sense of pride means more festivals and Fourth of July fireworks displays for the rest of us.

i Just moved into town and miss your old friends? You can make new ones through the New Neighbors League. Whether you're interested in gardening, travel, antiquing, wine tastings, golf, bowling, or canasta, you'll find a group to join. Check out www.kcnnl.com.

Missouri
Cass County
www.casscounty.com

If you prefer the quiet, scenic countryside to a metropolitan environment, you may want to explore some of the many advantages Cass County's cities provide. From its rural beginnings, Cass is becoming a hot ticket in terms of new business and residential development thanks to a low cost of living, efficient transportation, and room for expansion. Its diverse economic base includes biotech firms and manufacturers, and new, attractive industrial parks are popping up throughout the region.

Cass County students receive a superb education in 10 school districts that do an excellent job balancing studies with healthy recreational programs. Parents will also like the fact that their dollars go far here in terms of quality housing.

Well-kept older homes, bright new subdivisions, or a custom-built estate: You'll find it all in Cass.

And where new homes are built, retail and services are sure to follow. The county has exciting new shopping districts to take care of its residents. Families can also "take it outside" at any number of nearby parks, lakes, and golf courses. Some of the most popular fishing and boating lakes are nearby, including Lake Winnebago, RainTree Lake, and the natural paradise known as Lake Jacomo. Take your pick from the following Cass County cities.

BELTON
www.belton.org

A sleepy little town that has seen remarkable growth lately as families move south to get nice homes for far less than in town, Belton has its own school district and a population of around 24,000. It's a bit of a drive to the airport (about 45 minutes), but you can be on the Plaza in about 20 minutes. Homes tend to be traditional and cost from $60,000 to more than $1 million for mansions sitting on enormous estates.

LAKE WINNEBAGO

Ah, this is the life! Although some people simply maintain a vacation home here, most choose the resort-type amenities every day. Yet even with its Lake of the Ozarks feel, it's just 30 minutes from downtown.

Housing options are attractive, diverse, and amazingly affordable when compared with resort-caliber cities across the nation. Students attend the highly rated Lee's Summit school district, and health care and shopping options are all within easy reach. About 900 lucky folks live here, and there's always room on the lake for one more boat. Homes range from $90,000 to more than $350,000.

i You can check out hundreds of homes during the Home Builders Association of Greater Kansas City's Parade of Homes. These tours are held for two weeks each spring and fall, and the homes are typically professionally decorated. Contact the association for dates at (816) 942-8800, or check www.kchba.org.

RAYMORE

www.raymore.com

Known as a small rural farm community years ago, recently Raymore has had the greatest percentage of population increase of any Kansas City suburb. The population numbers around 8,000 right now, but the growth will continue. Close to Belton, you can expect the same 20-minute drive to the Plaza. Or you can stay home and have a cookout with your neighbors; this is a friendly place. Home prices range from $60,000 to $500,000.

Clay County

www.claycogov.com

Surrounded by the natural beauty of rural landscapes, yet with the convenience of urban living, Clay County offers the best of both worlds. In fact, 20 percent of Kansas City, Missouri, extends into Clay. Its residents are proud of the eclectic mix of neighborhoods, its colorful history, and exciting growth.

Clay County is the fourth largest county in the metroplex, ranking third in both total retail sales and total effective buying income. Just 15 minutes from downtown Kansas City, it has attracted giant companies like Citicorp and Union Pacific to its 400-square-mile confines. In fact, the small community of North Kansas City is home to more than 30 of the Fortune 500. Liberty boasts such highly visible names as Ferrellgas and the Hallmark Cards Distribution Center.

Education is a priority as well. Students are served by the respected North Kansas City and Liberty school districts. Also found in Liberty is William Jewell College, a four-year private residential college that is highly regarded nationwide. Newcomers to Clay County enjoy the balance of small-town living and metropolitan attractions. Lakes and parks await, and there's excitement to be had as well at two riverboat casinos. And you can bet little ones will love living near Oceans of Fun and Worlds of Fun.

Sound good? When you're ready to move here, you'll have a variety of housing choices, from Tara-like estates on acreage to historic older homes. And if a friendly neighborhood is your style, Clay also offers lots of new subdivisions.

GLADSTONE

www.gladstone.mo.us

Sometimes referred to as Happy Rock, this community of some 27,200 is about 10 square miles in area and is completely surrounded by Kansas City North. It's a great place for families, thanks to its proximity to Smithville Lake, Worlds of Fun, and Oceans of Fun. The airport is just 20 minutes away. Homes tend to be ranch or traditional and cost $60,000 to $400,000.

LIBERTY

www.ci.liberty.mo.us

Historic charm, small-town spirit, and recreational amenities galore appeal to families living in this 27-square-mile city. Its population is on a steady incline (an 18 percent increase each decade since 1940), yet Liberty has a friendly, country town appeal.

As one of Missouri's oldest settlements, Liberty is home to a number of well-preserved original structures like the Jesse James Bank. But families won't need to rob a bank to live here; home prices are favorable. You can choose anything from renovated older homes in quiet neighborhoods for $100,000 to country estates on sprawling acreage for $1 million or more.

NORTH KANSAS CITY

www.nkc.org

Boasting a large and diverse economic base, North Kansas City is home to more than a thousand businesses that include some of the world's leading corporations. Yet neighborhoods offer the peace and relaxation of well-kept homes set on tree-lined streets.

A highly developed park system offers ball fields, playgrounds, swimming, tennis, and walking trails. And its 5,000 residents can find a full calendar of professional sports events, plus entertainment and shopping at the nearby River Market and Country Club Plaza.

Housing options run the gamut from small starter homes to nice-size family homes ranging from $75,000 to well over $1 million.

Jackson County

www.jacksongov.org

Named for General Andrew Jackson at the height of his popularity, this county is blessed with beautiful rolling hills, wooded sites, and mature greenery. It's the population center of the metroplex, so within its nearly 605-square-mile area are densely populated urban centers as well as growing cities like Lee's Summit and a variety of small towns.

It offers the region's most diversified and exciting cultural avenues, yet affordable and attractive housing options still abound. You'll have your choice of lovingly restored historic homes, sleek renovated lofts, cottages in tree-lined neighborhoods, lakeside estates, and affordable reverse ranch-style homes in new subdivisions.

An excellent network of educational opportunities are here, including two highly rated two-year community colleges, plus the University of Missouri at Kansas City, Kansas City Art Institute, Avila College, Rockhurst College, and DeVry Institute. When it's time to put down the books, Jackson County provides the area's most vibrant entertainment districts. The River Market, Country Club Plaza, and Westport are all here, providing four-star restaurants, charming bistros, and world-class shopping.

Jackson County is also at the heart of our cultural center with its showpiece, the Nelson-Atkins Museum of Art, as well as the stellar collections of the Kemper Museum of Contemporary Art. Art galleries and studios are here as well, too many to count, because a new one seems to pop up every week.

For more recreational activities (although a day shopping on the Plaza can get your heart racing), the county has the 1,800-acre Swope Park, home to the Kansas City Zoo, a wonderful nature center with educational facilities and hiking trails, and a golf course. Swope Park also has the exciting Starlight Theatre, one of the most successful professional outdoor theaters in the country.

Yet with all its many delights, Jackson County real estate is surprisingly affordable. Homeowners have a wide array of choices in charming older neighborhoods, downtown high-rises, new subdivisions, and luxurious lakeside locations. Here, too, is where many young professionals and empty nesters find the city's most exciting apartments and condominiums, including those on the Plaza or Crown Center that provide "city" living at its best.

i Make friends fast through New Friends of Kansas City, a social organization where women can meet other women who share the same interests, whether it's antiquing, playing cards, attending sports events, or trying new restaurants. Though the membership is limited to women only, there are plenty of activities that include spouses. Membership is $20 a year. Visit www.newfriendsofkc.com.

BLUE SPRINGS

www.bluespringsgov.com

The original pioneers found this area to be the ideal stopover due to the abundance of clear, clean water from a nearby spring at the mouth of the Little Blue River. Water is still quite a draw for this community. Lake Jacomo and Longview Lake are nearby, and you'll have your choice of 14 city parks. Three golf courses mean there's no waiting for tee times. About 50,000 lucky people make their homes here and send their children to AAA-rated Blue Springs schools.

Home prices can still be a bargain, beginning at $80,000, but can easily escalate to $1 million or more for estates on spectacular lands. Bring your horses.

GRANDVIEW

www.grandview.org

Situated on the southern edge of Jackson County, Grandview's residents value a stable neighborhood environment yet enjoy the convenience of major interstates a few miles north. A major intersection, the Grandview Triangle, has been redesigned to make commuting a piece of cake. About 25,000 people live in Grandview, and houses range from $45,000 to around $200,000.

INDEPENDENCE

www.ci.independence.mo.us

One of our most vibrant historical areas, this is a great place to visit and an even better place to live. After all, it was good enough for Harry S. Truman. About 111,000 people can proudly say the buck stops here, and it can for you, too, for $50,000 to $300,000.

Besides offering a wealth of historical sites, Independence is close to downtown, the Plaza, and the airport. Travel to each is around 15 to 20 minutes.

KANSAS CITY

www.kcmo.org

Over half a million people live in Kansas City, and who could blame them? You could write an entire book about its lifestyle, fountains, food, and friendliness . . . hey! We did!

The city is made up of three distinct major areas: midtown, where homes cost $20,000 to $400,000; Country Club Plaza, where you would pay between $50,000 and $2 million; and south Kansas City, where homes range from $80,000 to $750,000. Kansas City is also where to find exciting lofts and condominiums in the River Market, downtown, and the West Bottoms. Prices range from $100,000 to well over $1 million.

Although it takes a bit of a drive to get to the airport (from 30 to 60 minutes), look what's nearby: the Plaza, the zoo, Crown Center, the River Market, Nelson-Atkins Museum of Art, and the stay-and-play Power & Light District downtown.

LAKE LOTAWANA

www.lakelotawana.org

Ideally situated just 20 miles from downtown Kansas City, this lake community offers both summer and year-round homes centered on a sparkling 600-acre lake. It's the perfect backdrop for magnificent waterfront estates. Its 2,200 residents enjoy a vacation-like lifestyle and needn't spend a million dollars to achieve it. Small bungalows and lake cabins are still available for less than $100,000, but there are also showplaces that cost $1 million or more.

LAKE TAPAWINGO

Just west of Blue Springs and close to the urban amenities of Lee's Summit and Kansas City, this small lake community provides a tranquil setting. The lake itself is small, which is how the 890 or so residents like it: no loud motorboats to break the peaceful sound of children playing Red Rover at dusk. Although you'll still see small cottages dotting the rolling wooded landscape, homeowners with real buying power have discovered this beauty and have built magnificent lakeside estates worth well over $1 million.

LEE'S SUMMIT

www.cityofls.net

Located in eastern Jackson County, Lee's Summit is the third largest city in Missouri based on geographic size. With more than 90 subdivisions, it's also the fastest growing community in the Kansas City area.

Families love it here thanks to an award-winning school district and plenty of recreational opportunities at nearby Longview Lake and Lake Jacomo. Arrowhead Stadium is a 15-minute drive. You'll see a wide variety of architectural styles in the neighborhoods, from traditional to contemporary. Expect to pay from $80,000 to $1 million, which would get you a palatial home on a golf course.

RAYTOWN

www.raytown.mo.us

When Raytown was incorporated in the 1950s, it had a population of 850 in a 2-mile-square land area. Today it has grown to 12 square miles and a population of 31,850. It's close to some of the area's most beautiful lakes, including Blue Springs, Longview, and Lake Jacomo.

Home prices are very reasonable here. You'll see bungalows, ranches, Victorians, and traditionals ranging from $60,000 to more than $250,000.

Platte County

www.co.platte.mo.us

Overlooking the point where the Missouri and Kansas Rivers meet, Platte offers the rolling hills, dramatic limestone overlooks, and lush woods that appeal to so many homeowners. It's home to one of the country's most fetching river towns yet is just minutes away from the vibrancy of downtown Kansas City; in fact, Platte County offers some of the most stunning views of the city's skyline.

Executives who travel on business find this region ideal, with the airport just minutes away. Or you can work close to home at one of dozens of new office and industrial parks that have sprung up here.

The nearly 12,000 students enrolled in four public schools get a quality education thanks to excellent schools and a strong student-teacher-parent system. Undergraduate and graduate programs are also available from Park University and Webster University.

As for lifestyle, many Kansas Citians enjoy visiting towns in Platte for their "day trip" amenities, including antiques shops, galleries, and unique restaurant choices. Lucky for the county's population of nearly 69,000, all that fun is in their own backyards. So are beautiful riverfront parks, lakes, and acres of wetlands that make fishing a joy.

PARKVILLE
www.parkvillemo.com
Nestled in the natural beauty of wooded hills and the limestone bluffs of the Missouri River, this is a highly desirable area. It's home to Park University, and its historic downtown area is filled with antiques shops, restaurants, and art galleries. A nature center and riverside park add to its charm.

Parkville affords an extraordinary view of the Kansas City, Missouri, skyline. To get there takes only 15 minutes, and the airport is a pleasant 15-minute drive. About 5,500 people live here, and the architecture varies from traditional to historic.

RIVERSIDE
www.riversidemo.com
As a Northland suburb of Kansas City, Riverside is known for its pleasing small neighborhoods, large industrial parks, and extensive business district. With a population of fewer than 3,000, it offers a small-town spirit with easy access to the region's finest cultural, educational, and social amenities. Home styles and prices vary greatly, from $75,000 to $250,000.

> **i** To shop for a home in your pajamas, simply click on www.realtor.com/kansascity and you can scan about 8,000 homes. You can select your potential abode by region, zip code, price range, or other criteria, such as number of bedrooms and whether you want treed acreage or lakefront living.

WEATHERBY LAKE
Only 57 years old, this delightful community is centered on a man-made lake set in panoramic rolling hills and lush woods. The community originally was developed as an enclave of summer homes, but people found it too hard to leave at the end of the season. Now Weatherby supports neighborhoods ranging from lake cabins to gorgeous estates. City leaders were smart enough to put strict zoning laws into place early to maintain the area's rural and rustic feeling, which its 1,700 residents find so appealing. Homes range from less than $80,000 to more than $1 million, including one real-life castle with a price tag over $8 million. Sold!

Kansas
Johnson County
www.jocoks.com
We've always known Johnson County was in a class all its own in terms of beautiful parks and lakes, lovely neighborhoods, and excellent schools. But the rest of the nation has caught on: *Fortune* magazine calls it one of the premier counties in the nation in terms of business climate and exceptional quality of life. Its many attributes have attracted such corporations as Sprint Nextel, Applebee's International, Black and Veatch, Yellow Corporation, Universal Underwriters, Farmers Insurance, and FedEx.

Nationally recognized for its superb public schools, Johnson County offers many choices for private education and parochial schools. The area is also home to excellent opportunities for higher education, including the award-winning Johnson County Community College, and satellite campuses of Baker University, St. Mary College, MidAmerica Nazarene University, Ottawa University, and the Edwards Campus of the University of Kansas. These programs allow working adults to obtain bachelor's or master's degrees while remaining close to home and work. Excellent health care choices are within the county's boundaries as well.

The living is easy in Johnson County, thanks to the first-rate recreational opportunities at its many lakes, parks, and recreational centers. Golfers can choose from some of the most challenging and luxurious public and private courses in the metro. And if shopping is your sport, look no further. Overland Park alone offers more than 40 open-air plazas as well as enclosed modern complexes with hundreds of shops, department stores (can you say Nordstrom?), restaurants, and theaters. Historic sites and museums, even ones kids will love, are within JoCo's boundaries.

Its many attributes have made it one of the fastest growing counties in the Kansas City area and state. In fact, Johnson County accounts for 71 percent of the total population growth in Kansas, adding approximately 10,000 new residents each year. And yet with all its natural beauty, tremendous growth, and clean, attractive cities, Johnson County's home prices are among the lowest of any area.

COUNTRYSIDE

How about holding a block party where the entire city shows up? That's a real possibility in this delightful little community of just 312 citizens and 133 homes. It's bound by Nall and Lamar Streets, 61st Street to the north, and Shawnee Mission Parkway to the south, creating a square-mile garden. You just have to love a neighborhood whose city tree is the red cedar and city bird is the house wren.

Homes are so choice here that people stand in yards and ask residents, "Are you leaving soon?" as if you're in a prime parking space. The answer is no, usually. Who would want to leave paradise?

Houses in Countryside, for the most part, are cute bungalows, some ranch style, and prices can go from $100,000 to $200,000 or so. Good luck. Countryside recently became part of the City of Mission but retains its own homes association.

DESOTO

This has long been a sleepy little town of just over 3,200 residents, but that's all been changing in the past few years. DeSoto's location between Lenexa and Lawrence on Kansas Highway 10 makes it a prime place for residential, retail, and commercial growth. And with ready access to the desirable lifestyles of both Lawrence and Kansas City, you might say DeSoto is the best of both worlds. Its progressive school system, which also serves residents of western Shawnee, is another plus. The Plaza is still only 25 minutes away, the airport, 40.

Right now home prices are relatively low, considering that so many of the homes include acreage, but that will start to change. Prices range from $90,000 for a simple ranch to $400,000 plus for an estate set way back on vast acreage. Got horses?

FAIRWAY
www.fairwaykansas.org

This is one of the most desirable addresses, thanks to a storybook setting of pretty ranch homes and stone cottages with small but beautifully landscaped yards. The landmass is only about 1 square mile, but it packs in around 3,900 people, and they love the small town in a big-city atmosphere. And the location? Let's just say it got its name from the three panoramic golf courses nearby.

Its proximity to the Plaza (just 5 to 10 minutes away) plus parks and the excellent Shawnee Mission School District make this area ideal for singles and for couples with young children. Look for prices from $200,000 for a tiny ranch to well over $1 million.

LAKE QUIVIRA

Located in both Johnson and Wyandotte Counties, Lake Quivira affords residents a lakeside lifestyle that is still conveniently located in town. Distinctive homes and tranquil neighborhoods are found in this gated community of around 1,900. Swimming, boating, and sailing are all part of the allure, plus a jogging track around the area's 1.3 square miles. Home styles vary greatly from small older bungalows to stunning contemporary showhomes. Prices range from $100,000 to well over $2 million.

LEAWOOD
www.leawood.org

Answer "Leawood" to a question of where you live and you instantly get more respect. Pure snobbism? Not really. Leawood just happens to be one of the prettiest places around, with lovely homes with nice-size yards and a convenient location (10 minutes to the Plaza, 20 to downtown) that still feels like it's out in the country. Perhaps that's because it used to be. Leawood dates back to territorial days and was built on farmland acquired by early settlers. Over 29,000 live in this area that primarily sits between State Line and Mission Roads and extends from 83rd Street south to 202nd Street.

The city was named for the original landowner, Oscar G. Lee. The spelling was changed slightly by the developer. Leawood offers a pleasing mix of older, well-kept neighborhoods along tree-lined streets and vibrant new subdivisions. And with its "halfway mark" between the Country Club Plaza and Town Center Plaza, shopping doesn't get much better. Expect handsome traditional homes from $250,000 to upward of $5 million. You heard us.

LENEXA
www.lenexa.org

Ah, suburbia. Lenexa sits in west-central Johnson County, south of Shawnee, and is home to more than 40,000 people. You can see the city's roots as a town along the Santa Fe and Oregon Trails in late-19th-century buildings that still stand in Old Town Lenexa.

Residents are family oriented; during summer there's a festival or celebration every week, including a barbecue contest in June, the Spin-

ach Festival in September (perhaps you shouldn't mention that one to your kids), and the Chili Challenge in October. Maybe it's a good thing Lenexa offers so many recreational opportunities to work off all those calories. Shawnee Mission Park, Sar-Ko-Par Trails Park, Ernie Miller Nature Park, and the Johnson County Arboretum are close by.

The Plaza is about a 20-minute drive, and it's 40 minutes to the airport. Look for generally traditional architecture in the price range of $100,000 to more than $500,000.

MERRIAM
www.merriam.org

Welcome to Worlds of Fun . . . in Merriam? In 1880 famed architectural designer George Kessler turned 40 acres of wooded hills into a lovely park area, complete with a lake, tennis courts, and boating. And at the turn of the 20th century, Kansas Citians were coming to the Hocker Grove Amusement Park's dancing pavilion, skating rink, and rides. The amusement parks have closed, but Merriam still offers a wonderful lifestyle for its 12,000 residents. With the city's ready access to the highway system, the Plaza is just 12 minutes away, the airport about 25.

Home prices in Merriam vary dramatically depending on whether the house is a two-bedroom bungalow or a five-bedroom reverse ranch on a landscaped lot. Expect to find homes between $80,000 and more than $300,000.

MISSION
www.mission-ks.org

A charming 'burb in the northern section of Johnson County, Mission offers neighborhood shopping centers, excellent schools, and tree-lined streets. And location? You can practically be on the Plaza before you find your charge card. The airport is 30 minutes away. Homes here are typically traditional or ranch style, with a few fairy-tale Tudors tossed in for looks.

The excellent Shawnee Mission School District is a draw for families, but first-time homebuyers often shop here first for homes in the $80,000 range. Larger homes can run higher than $300,000.

MISSION HILLS

www.missionhills-ks.gov

The Beverly Hills of Kansas City, Mission Hills is status plus. Exclusively fine homes—there are no shopping centers to ruin the line of expansive lawn after lawn. And it may be the most impressive art gallery in town: Sculptures and fountains are dotted within its 2.5-mile radius, gifts from developer J. C. Nichols.

The city also contains three of the area's finest golf clubs. This is the only city of its size in the country that can claim this distinction. There are 1,327 homes and villas here in a delightful range of styles that makes rubbernecking fun. You'll see colonial, Tudor, Spanish, traditional, and a handful of contemporary homes. Prices range from around $400,000 (a bargain if you can find one) up to $6 million. Pull your Mercedes or Beemer out of the garage and you can be at the Plaza within 5 to 10 minutes, to the airport in 30.

MISSION WOODS

www.missionwoodskansas.com

Exclusive, exquisite, and in demand. Occupying 20 acres of land, yet with only 165 or so residents, Mission Woods has the distinction of having the lowest population of any of the incorporated cities of Johnson County. Homes here quietly go on the market (you'll never see a yard sign) and are quickly sold.

Amenities include a nearby golf country club, tennis club, several parks, and both private and parochial schools. Thanks to its location at the intersection of State Line Road and Shawnee Mission Parkway, the Plaza is at its doorstep.

This is truly one of the most beautiful little cities in the country, and the privilege of living here will cost between $500,000 and $2 million, but we know of a recent $5.2 million sale. All things considered, that may well be a bargain.

OLATHE

www.olatheks.org

From the Indian word for "beautiful" (pronounced *Oh-LAY-thuh*), this city covers 50 square miles. Its size holds many advantages, including two airports, Johnson County Executive and the Indus-

trial Airport, and its own award-winning school district.

It's also home to Hillsdale Lake, a gigantic recreational area, and Olathe Medical Center. Homes here range from $75,000 for a modest starter home (ideal for singles, young couples, and retirees) to more than $3 million for a gorgeous estate overlooking the lake at Cedar Creek. Its diversity means you'll see architecture in a variety of designs, from traditional to Spanish, California contemporary to prairie style.

OVERLAND PARK

www.opkansas.org

Overland Park has shaken off its roots as a bedroom community to become a vibrant city with its own personality. Today it's home to 166,700 (no, make that 166,701!) with a population growth that's one of the fastest in the metro. Families in particular love it here, and it's been rated among the best places in the country to rear children. Schools are excellent, and it's blessed with nearby parks, lakes, and mile after mile of hiking and biking trails. Other pluses are the Johnson County Arboretum and Deanna Rose Children's Farmstead.

And you'll have just the place to buy all those cute kids' clothes, as well as your own fashions. Overland Park is home to Oak Park Mall, one of the largest malls in the state and the only one with Nordstom as its anchor. The Plaza is just a 20-minute drive, and the airport another 10 minutes or so.

Look for two-story traditional homes for the most part, for mortgages from $100,000 to $1 million.

PRAIRIE VILLAGE

www.pvkansas.com

"Charming" is the word that most comes to mind to describe this hamlet of established neighborhoods with an abundance of trees and 10 parks. Located just west of State Line and south of Mission Hills, this is a real draw for affluent singles and families who enjoy a small-town atmosphere that's close to everything. Prairie Village is home to two delightful open-air shopping centers,

Corinth Square and the Prairie Village Shops, which means a grocery store, a gift shop, and an ice-cream parlor are just a stroll or bike ride away. No wonder people who grew up here tend to stay in the neighborhood.

Big-time shopping and entertainment venues on the Plaza are a short 10 minutes away; although the airport is a 30- to 40-minute drive, you won't want to leave home very often. The typical Prairie Village home is traditional, Cape Cod, or ranch, costing from $120,000 for a two-bedroom start-up home to around $850,000.

ROELAND PARK
www.roelandpark.net
This is a quaint, older neighborhood in the northeast corner of Johnson County with plenty of pluses. It's 10 minutes away from the Plaza and 10 to 15 minutes from downtown and is within the desirable Shawnee Mission School District. The population is around 7,000, and home styles tend toward traditional, ranch, and bungalow. Prices generally run from $100,000 to $250,000.

SHAWNEE
www.cityofshawnee.org
Shawnee Mission Park alone is enough reason to want to live in this Johnson County community. It offers the Theatre in the Park, a fabulous lake, and a 450-foot-tall observation tower. Hey! I can see my house from here! There are 21 other parks to explore as well. Other recreational opportunities, at least for teenagers, can be found at the nearby malls, including Oak Park Mall and the Great Mall of the Great Plains. And the Plaza is a quick 10-minute drive away.

Shawnee has nearly 50,000 residents and is one of the fastest growing cities in the state. Look for traditional-style homes in the $80,000 to $800,000-plus range.

SPRING HILL
www.springhillks.org
Located in northeast Kansas, Spring Hill straddles the Johnson and Miami County lines, giving residents amenities of a big city in a rural setting. Incorporated in 1885, Spring Hill has recorded

strong residential and commercial growth in the past few years and expects that to continue.

It has about 2,500 residents, and an additional 6,000 people live outside its boundaries but within the school district. And like the good neighbors they are, they work together to address community needs. This city is about 20 to 30 minutes from I-435, the main artery. Houses tend to be on large-acreage lots, many with separate garages. The house prices are as varied as the style of homes available, from $50,000 to well over $500,000.

STANLEY
Early settlers in this area purchased their home lots for about $10 an acre, and although you can add some zeroes to that now, the lifestyle is worth every penny. Stanley was annexed by Overland Park in 1985 but feels like its own little world with rolling, wooded acres. Many of the homes take advantage of the landmass, with homes set half an acre away from the road down a curving path. Several estates have horse pastures.

Stanley is at the heart of the top-rated Blue Valley School District and is close to Town Center Plaza and fine restaurants. Architectural styles vary greatly, from Colorado lodge to traditional. Prices range from $140,000 to more than $500,000. There are a few multimillion-dollar estates in this ZIP code.

WESTWOOD
www.westwoodkansas.com
Looking like a picture postcard of everything you could want in a neighborhood, Westwood offers well-manicured lawns, beautiful older homes, and picturesque neighborhoods. Its tidy size, just 1 square mile, gives it a small-town feeling. Parks and walking trails make Westwood great for families, and a health club with tennis courts and swimming pool are pluses. Ideally situated close to the Plaza and Overland Park, Westwood provides its 1,800 residents with the best of the metroplex.

Home styles range from darling bungalows to handsome Spanish-style structures. Expect to pay from $150,000 for a modest home to $1 million or more.

WESTWOOD HILLS
www.westwoodhills.org

Although at just three-quarters of a square mile, Westwood Hills is one of the smaller cities, it is one of the loveliest residential choices. It is filled with charming neighborhoods, serene streets lined with mature shade trees, and a showcase of eclectic architectural styles. Many are storybook Tudor-style with stone or brick set amid lush landscaping.

The award-winning Shawnee Mission School District makes this an ideal community for families as well as young professionals. A very desirable address; expect home prices from $240,000 to $2 million.

Wyandotte County

www.wycokck.org

Named for the Wyandot Indians who once made this area their home, Wyandotte County, or WyCo, is steeped in the history of the Old West yet offers a progressive lifestyle. With its central location along river bluffs overlooking the confluence of the Missouri and Kansas Rivers, it offers easy access to the entire region. The airport is just 10 to 15 minutes away, and downtown Kansas City, Missouri, from 5 to 10 minutes.

This county offers something even more appealing to homebuyers: Some of the lowest home prices in the Greater Kansas City area. Triple-A school districts also rank high on the plus side; the New Stanley School, for instance, was singled out for the state's "Next Century" program of excellence. Health care is also tops here thanks to the University of Kansas Hospital's well-respected programs.

Within the county are exceptional recreational opportunities, including the Agricultural Hall of Fame, an outdoor music theater, and the 1,500-acre natural wonder known as Wyandotte County Lake Park. Among its many amenities are playgrounds, tennis courts, horse paths, and a 400-acre lake for fishing and boating.

If sports are your game, there is spectacular Kansas Speedway, a $250 million NASCAR facility with state-of-the-art features. Homebuyers, start your engines!

BONNER SPRINGS
www.bonnersprings.org

On the western edge of Wyandotte County, Bonner has easy access to many areas of interest, such as Verizon Amphitheater, where headline musical acts appear, and the Renaissance Festival takes place in the fall. The Kansas Speedway is nearby as well.

With a population of around 6,750, the city has its own school district. Homes generally go for $60,000 to more than $500,000.

KANSAS CITY
www.wycokck.org

The Wyandot Indians first settled here in 1840, and the oldest home is the Grinter House, whose owner operated a ferry across the Kansas River (which we call the Kaw) in 1857. Today KCK is home to several ethnic groups. Strawberry Hill has a strong Slavic community, and the Rosedale and Argentine areas have Mexican American settlements. Both groups celebrate their heritage with several festivals during the year.

The city provides excellent access to the other Kansas City's downtown district. It's about 5 minutes across the Lewis and Clark Viaduct, the Plaza is a 10-minute drive, and it's just 20 minutes to the airport. With a strong government in place, KCK is coming into its own. Home prices cover quite a spread, from starter homes in the $40,000 range to grand new estates with large lots for $400,000. The city also has a hidden gem in its historic Westheights Manor neighborhood, where homes average $250,000.

Real Estate Companies

Kansas City is home to hundreds of real estate companies and thousands of agents, most of whom are licensed on both sides of the state line. Although some of these professionals specialize in certain areas of the region or in specific categories such as historic homes, sleek condos, or estates with surrounding acreage, most will be happy to locate whatever home you seek.

Some neighborhoods and subdivisions are so desirable they have their own real estate offices, such as Hallbrook in Leawood and Cedar Creek in Olathe. However, any Realtor can take you on a tour of the area.

It's often tricky to find a Realtor in a new city. We suggest you ask friends and family for references; if they've had a good experience with an agent, they'll be thrilled to tell you about it. And if you're being transferred for business, often your company's human resources department can make recommendations.

If in doubt, call the Kansas City Regional Association of Realtors (913-498-1100, www.kcrar .com). The Web site includes links to related organizations such as the National Association of Homebuilders and area home inspectors. You'll also find a link to a list of available homes in the area that are shown by Realtor members, or go to www.heartlandmls.com. You can find homes by location, price range, or categories such as maintenance provided or acreage. The Better Business Bureau of Greater Kansas City (816-421-7800) is another resource to make sure you're working with a professional firm you can trust.

GETTING STARTED

Naturally you'll want to get the lights, water, and gas turned on and the telephone hooked up, so we'll start with the basics. Sounds easy, until you remember that the Kansas City metro area comprises more than 150 cities in a 19-county area (more or less, depending on who's counting). To make it more confusing, some counties use two or more utility companies. This creates a new version of the old joke: How many newcomers does it take to turn on the lights? Two: one to find out whom to call and the other to bang his head on the wall. If you can get through this maze of numbers, more power to you.

Utilities

If you have questions about what service provider serves your area, check with your Realtor, landlord, homeowners association, or city or county clerk. When you call the utility customer service representative, be prepared to make a security deposit to establish service. Requirements for ser-

vice deposits vary and are usually based on an amount totaling two months' worth of bills.

Most deposits are refunded after one year or when service is terminated. Water deposits range from about $20 to $75 or more, but rural dwellings can have a much heftier fee—as much as $1,500— if a meter must be installed. Just one more thing to ask your Realtor before you sign on the dotted line. Following are the basics. And honestly, once you make it past the conundrum of our utility providers, you're home free. With the lights on.

i To get underground utility lines marked before digging, call (800) 344-7483 in Missouri and (800) 344-7233 in Kansas.

Electricity
MISSOURI

INDEPENDENCE
(816) 325-5000
www.ci.independence.mo.us/pl

KANSAS CITY POWER & LIGHT
(Western Cass and Jackson, southern Clay and Platte, and most of Johnson Counties)
(816) 471-5275
www.kcpl.com

PLATTE-CLAY ELECTRIC COOPERATIVE
(Northern Platte, northern Clay, and Ray Counties)
(800) 431-2131

KANSAS

BOARD OF PUBLIC UTILITIES
(Kansas City, KS)
(913) 573-9190
www.bpu.com

WESTAR
(Olathe, Bonner Springs, Leavenworth, Lawrence, DeSoto)
(800) 794-4780
www.westarenergy.com

Gas

MISSOURI

MISSOURI GAS ENERGY
(Jackson, Platte, Clay, Ray, and Cass Counties)
(816) 756-5252
www.missourigasenergy.com

KANSAS

ATMOS ENERGY
(Portions of Johnson, Wyandotte,
Leavenworth, and Douglas Counties)
(800) 621-1867
www.atmosenergy.com

KANSAS GAS SERVICE
(Parts of Johnson, Wyandotte, Franklin,
Miami, Douglas, Anderson, Osage, and
Leavenworth Counties)
(800) 794-4780
www.oneokkansasgas.com

Water

MISSOURI

MISSOURI WATER DEPARTMENT
(Kansas City)
(816) 221-6505
www.kcmo.org

KANSAS

BOARD OF PUBLIC UTILITIES
(Kansas City, Kansas)
(913) 573-9000
www.bpu.com

WATER ONE
(Johnson County)
(913) 895-1800
www.waterone.org

Telephone

AT&T
Residential customers
(800) 464-7928
www.att.com

EVEREST
(913) 825-3000
www.everestkc.com

SPRINT NEXTEL
(800) SPRINT1
www.sprint.com

TIME WARNER CABLE
(816) 222-5776
www.timewarnercable.com

Cellular Phone Service

SOUTHWESTERN BELL MOBILE
(800) 331-0500

SPRINT NEXTEL
(800) SPRINT1
www.sprint.com

VERIZON
(800) 922-0204
www.verizonwireless.com

Cable

COMCAST
(888) 266-2278

DIRECTV
(816) 421-4004
www.directv.com

TIME WARNER CABLE
(816) 222-5776
www.timewarnercable.com

Trash

Many homeowners associations provide curbside trash pickup as part of their dues. And many cities in the metropolis offer a curbside recycling program or have developed convenient drop-off centers at churches and shopping areas. Check with your Realtor or your homeowners association contact. For more information on recycling, call the Mid-America Regional Council's recycling hotline at (816) 474-TEAM.

The following companies cover the greater Kansas City area; you may also contact them for information regarding items for recycling.

DEFFENBAUGH DISPOSAL SERVICE
(913) 631-3300

HICKMAN DISPOSAL SERVICE
(913) 831-2072

REB TRASH SERVICE
(913) 779-6592

Post Offices

To locate a post office near you, visit www.usps .gov. Get a handy online guide at http://movers guide.usps.com.

GETTING LEGAL

Motor Vehicle Registration

In Kansas City we rely on our vehicles to get us around, and we have the highway miles to prove it. With three interstates, four interstate linkages, and 10 federal highways, you can get just about anywhere you want in 20 minutes or less.

Now let's get you legal and on the road. In both Kansas and Missouri, license plates are issued upon vehicle registration. Each state has different rules and procedures. Find out specifics on current requirements, and necessary inspections, fees, and locations at the following Web sites:

MISSOURI
www.dor.mo.gov.

KANSAS
www.ksrevenue.org/dmv

Voter Registration

Generally registration for voting must be completed at least 20 days prior to primary or general elections. However, in Jackson, Cass, Clay, and Platte Counties, residents must wait 28 days after registration to be eligible to vote. In Johnson County it's 14 days. You must reregister each time you change your residency or name.

Application information includes your name, birthplace, birth date, mailing address, telephone number, place of previous registration, and usually your Social Security number. An oath or signature is required to verify that all information is true.

To register in either Kansas or Missouri, you must submit information with a current address and meet the following requirements: You must be a U.S. citizen or have a naturalization number if you were born outside of the country, be at least 18 years of age, and meet the residency requirements for your voting precinct.

Registration centers are located throughout the metroplex, and any of the centers below can direct you to the one most convenient to you. Kansas residents have the option of mail-in registration. In Missouri, that option is restricted to those who are unable to travel to a registration center in person.

Good Phone Numbers to Know

Emergency: 911
Child abuse: (800) 392-3738
Missouri Poison Control Center: (816) 234-3430
Kansas Poison Control Center: (913) 588-6633
Directory assistance (local): 1411
Local from pay phones: 411
Weather forecast: (913) 831-4141
Road condition information (Kansas Highway Patrol): (913) 782-8100
Legal Aid of Western Missouri: (816) 474-6750
Legal Aid for Wyandotte and Leavenworth Counties: (913) 621-0200

JOHNSON COUNTY BOARD OF ELECTION
(913) 782-3441
www.jocoelection.org

**KANSAS CITY, MISSOURI, BOARD
OF ELECTION**
(816) 842-4820

WYANDOTTE COUNTY BOARD OF ELECTION
(913) 334-1414

Driver's License and Permit

To receive a driver's license with full privileges in either Kansas or Missouri, you must be at least 16 years of age. New Kansas residents must pass only a vision test if your out-of-state license is current.

In Missouri, if your out-of-state license is valid, you are required to take a vision and road sign recognition test. If your current license has been expired for more than 90 days, you will be required to take the driving and written test as well.

Kansas offers a special restricted license for young adults at least 14 years old for the purpose of going to or from school or work; this license requires the written permission of a parent or guardian.

Missouri

Licenses are issued on a six-year basis (every three years for those older than 69), and new residents are required to apply immediately. Bring a valid out-of-state license. You'll be required to pass a vision and road sign recognition test. If your license has expired you'll need to take a written test and will be sitting in a car with a Missouri State Highway Patrol officer. Contact the following office for examination and testing; there may also be an area office closer to you:

KANSAS CITY
(816) 889-2461
www.dor.mo.gov

Kansas

Licenses are issued every four years, and new residents are required to apply immediately. Bring your valid out-of-state driver's license with you. New residents must pass only a vision test, unless your current license has been expired for more than 90 days. Then a driving and written test is required. (We were serious when we said to apply immediately.) For examination and testing, contact one of the following offices:

JOHNSON COUNTY
(913) 826-1800

WYANDOTTE COUNTY
(913) 573-2821

Hunting and Fishing Licenses

Licenses are required in both states for fishing as well as hunting small and large game. In Kansas the waiting time after registration is 60 days. In Missouri new residents are eligible for a license after 30 days. And just wait till you see the bass in Lake Jacomo!

The cost for licenses varies depending on your age (seniors and youth get reduced rates), residency status, and the duration of the license. Nonresident licenses carry significantly higher price tags. Fishing licenses can be purchased for as long as one year or a mere 24 hours. They're available for purchase at local sporting good stores and most public lake marinas. For current rates or questions on specific game stamps or licenses, contact the respective state offices:

MISSOURI DEPARTMENT OF CONSERVATION
(816) 356-2280
www.mdc.mo.gov

**KANSAS DEPARTMENT OF WILDLIFE &
PARKS**
(913) 894-9113
www.kdwp.state.ks.us

EDUCATION AND CHILD CARE

Our city's commitment to education shows up in one of the first questions parents ask when shopping for a home: "How are the schools around here?" The answer, particularly in our suburban areas, is "excellent." Here in the heartland, Junior isn't the only one bringing home a bright-red A on his report card; many of the institutions in our 36 school districts have achieved the highest distinctions awarded by their states.

That's not to say they all make the grade. Our largest district, Kansas City, Missouri, with 32,000 students in 70 schools, is plagued by the same problems most other urban cities have: poor attendance, below-average test scores, and low graduation rates. And these troubles remain despite spending $2 billion to create impressive magnet schools with themes like science, foreign languages, performing arts, and college preparation.

Yet families with inner-city addresses still have excellent options such as Montessori, private schools (both religious and nonreligious), and 20 charter schools, which are independent public schools designed and operated by educators, parents, community leaders, and others.

These institutions, along with our top-notch suburban public schools, have elevated our overall educational rankings to some of the highest in the nation. Banners boasting A-plus rankings are posted next to glass cases crowded with 3-foot-tall basketball trophies. Elementary schools proudly show off Blue Ribbon certificates at parent-teacher meetings. And quality schools help produce students who are eager to continue their education: Greater Kansas City's 82 percent high school graduation rate beats the national average by at least seven points. In three Johnson County districts, more than 90 percent of the graduates are college bound.

We take a look at some of the elementary and secondary education choices available, both public and private, as well as list resources for day care programs within the metroplex. In the following section we graduate to our many fine colleges and universities as well as other learning options for adults and seniors.

PUBLIC SCHOOLS

Following is an overview of area public schools that have achieved impressive state and national honors. The accolades are shared by administrators, teachers, and students, as well as the parents who stay involved in school activities and tend to vote "yes" on school bonds. The schools are listed alphabetically by state.

Missouri

BLUE SPRINGS
www.bluespring-schools.net
Jackson County's second largest district has two high schools, four middle schools, and 12 elementary schools; yet despite escalating enrollment, it has garnered state and national recognition. Thanks to a $30 million bond election, which received an 85 percent approval, a districtwide technology program will make computers accessible to each staff member and student. *Expansion Management* magazine consistently bestows its highest Gold Medal award on the district, and the *Wall Street Journal* named it one of the top 10 in the nation.

GRANDVIEW
Students who live in south Kansas City don't have a problem finding their lockers; they go to one school from kindergarten through eighth grade.

And the kids aren't the only ones singing this one-school system's praises: The state named it one of the best small schools in language arts and science. The district's high schools also receive high marks from the state in journalism, art, music, and business, and 75 percent of its students participate in extracurricular activities.

INDEPENDENCE
www.indep.k12.mo.us

For a district that's more than 135 years old, Independence looks remarkably fit. It has been accredited with distinction by the Missouri Department of Education, making it the largest district in the state to be so honored. Two of its high schools have received A-plus ratings, and three elementary schools are national Blue Ribbon winners. Its 21st-century early childhood education program is a model for the nation.

NORTH KANSAS CITY
www.nkcsd.k12.mo.us

Parents, businesses, and community members work together in this district through projects such as YouthFriends, Partners in Education, the Community Committee, and educational foundations. The results are schools that consistently earn A-plus rankings and students who score above state and national averages. The district also features the GED Online series, a pilot program for the state, as well as all-day kindergarten, summer enrichment classes, and before- and after-school child care. High school graduates who meet academic requirements are eligible to receive free books, tuition, and fees for two years at a community college or vocational school in Missouri.

PARK HILL
www.parkhill.k12.mo.us

In southern Platte County parents, educators, and students work together through programs like Parents as Teachers and Community Education. This commitment has helped earn the district Accredited with Distinction status from Missouri as well as a Gold Medal from *Expansion Management* magazine. Students in the district have earned perfect SAT scores and the state Heisman trophy for athletics.

Kansas

BLUE VALLEY
www.bluevalleyk12.org

Serving more than 42,500 students in 42 schools, this southern Johnson County district has earned a reputation for high academic performance. Fourteen schools have received the prestigious Blue Ribbon Award. The district has also implemented successful community outreach programs, including SHARE (Seniors Helping and Refining Education), which places senior citizens in the schools to share time and talents, and YouthFriends, which pairs adults with children who benefit from individualized attention.

DESOTO
www.usd232.org

Administrators in the fastest growing school district in Kansas planned for growth by building 11 new facilities in the late 1990s. And not just any square box will do: The elementary school design has won international acclaim as a "Kid Friendly School." Technology plays a big part in learning, with computers in each classroom and additional computer labs for students that include CAD (computer-aided drafting) units.

KANSAS CITY
www.kckps.org

With more than 20,000 students speaking 16 languages, this district is making a concerted effort to expand special programs for students with limited English proficiency. Stanley Elementary is the district's only year-round elementary school.

OLATHE
www.olatheschools.com

An expanding student population makes this southwest Kansas district the fourth largest in Kansas, but it may be the teachers who put it on top. Among their honors are 12 Presidential Awards for Excellence in math and science teaching and 14 National Blue Ribbon Awards from the Department of Education.

SHAWNEE MISSION
www.smsd.org

This school district challenges students to do their best through such initiatives as the International Baccalaureate Program, an advanced system of studies that earns students college credit, and the Center for International Studies, which gives students in grades 9 through 12 an opportunity to develop skills in Arabic, Chinese, Japanese, Russian, and geopolitics. National Merit Scholarships are well represented here; recently 44 district students took home honors.

PRIVATE SCHOOLS

The Kansas City area offers a variety of choices for private education at the elementary and secondary levels. The **Missouri Council for American Private Education** publishes a directory of the state's private schools for around $10. For more information write to the organization at 334 Nantucket Dr., Ballwin, MO 63011 or call (314) 214-8255.

The Kansas State Board of Education publishes the annual **Kansas Educational Directory** listing private schools in the state. The directory is available at libraries, online at www.ksde.org, or by calling (785) 296-4961.

Nearly every Catholic Church in Kansas City has an affiliated school where children receive an outstanding education along with lessons in religion. For information about schools call the specific church directly or the area's diocese. In Missouri contact the **Roman Catholic Diocese of Kansas City–St. Joseph** at (816) 756-1850 or www.diocese-kcsj.org/schools. In Johnson and Wyandotte Counties in Kansas, contact the **Archdiocese of Kansas City** in Kansas at (913) 721-2082 or www.archkckcs.org.

For information on schools affiliated with the Lutheran Church in Kansas and Missouri, contact the **Director of Lutheran Schools** in Missouri (314-268-1508) or Kansas (785-357-4441).

Many of our prestigious private schools teach children from tots to teens, so students don school colors from the morning they arrive in a stroller until the afternoon they drive away in their SUV or Mom's BMW. Combining as many as five grade levels is a practice that instills a sense of family and school spirit that extends far beyond the campus gates. A diploma from one of these schools, coupled with a diploma from a top university, can almost guarantee an interview with Kansas City's best companies; alumni tend to look after their own.

The schools listed here are arranged alphabetically by state.

Missouri

BARSTOW
11511 State Line Rd.
(816) 942-3255
www.barstowschool.org

In 1884 two Wellesley College grads, Mary Barstow and Ada Brann, came to Kansas City to establish a local school comparable to the independent schools in the East. With the financial backing of several notable city leaders, including William Rockhill Nelson and August Meyer, their School for Girls was officially opened. Although lofty in goal—Brann's motto was "to educate a woman is to educate a nation"—the school had humble beginnings. The first class consisted of five girls sitting in a sparsely furnished parlor at 1204 Broadway. The school moved frequently, all within the posh Quality Hill area, and by 1897 began accepting a few boys in its college preparatory program. That same year Brann returned to her home in New England, which left the dynamic redhead, Barstow, to continue the school. It thrived after moving to a four-story schoolhouse in an apple orchard at 15 Westport Rd.—what is now a CVS drugstore parking lot at Westport and Main. Parents of 93 students paid $62.50 per term.

In 1909 boys were admitted to the lower school only, and by 1923 Barstow had a new home at 50th and Cherry in the flourishing Rockhill section of town. By 1954 the school's enrollment of 170 was expected to quickly double after the board voted to allow coeducation. This created a need to move to 40 acres "in the country" at 115th and State Line Road. The new school was dedicated on May 5, 1962, where it stands today surrounded by lovely neighborhoods and massive estates. More than 600 students, from preschool through 12th grade, share the campus, providing a sense of family in the communal lunchroom and extra cheering power during varsity pep rallies.

PEMBROKE HILL SCHOOL
5121 State Line
(816) 936-1200
www.pembrokehill.org
Alumni still call their alma mater Pem-Day from when this private school was known as Pembroke–Country Day, an all-boy school founded in 1910. Some of Kansas City's most prominent families sent their sons to Pem-Day and their daughters to Sunset Hill, which opened in 1913. The two schools had many similarities: Both were highly regarded and independent; teachers often taught at both institutions; and several activities, especially theatrical programs, involved students from both campuses. When the two schools merged in July 1984, the newly named Pembroke Hill School adopted traditions from both facilities. For example, students voted to keep Pem-Day's colors of red and blue on the school's banner; the motto "Freedom with Responsibility" came from Sunset Hill. Another beloved tradition remains from the girls' school days: May Day, complete with music, poetry, and dancing around the Maypole, is observed each spring.

PHS is located on two campuses less than a mile apart near the Country Club Plaza; it's quite a stirring sight to see a football game in play while driving past the field on your way to dinner on fall evenings. Make sure to lower your car window to get the full effect. The school offers an extended day program until 6 p.m. for children through fifth grade, a service that continues during winter and spring breaks. And its students learn the importance of giving back to the town that has provided so much: All upper school students must complete 60 hours of community service before graduation; many easily surpass this requirement. Currently 1,200 students are enrolled from age two through 12th grade. Of

these, nearly 240 are receiving more than $2 million in financial assistance.

ST. TERESA'S ACADEMY
5600 Main St.
(816) 501-0011
www.stteresasacademy.com
The oldest school in Kansas City remains one of its best. This Catholic, independent college-preparatory school for young women was founded in 1866 and is sponsored by the Sisters of St. Joseph of Carondelet. Students are treated to a 20-acre collegelike campus in one of the most elegant residential areas of Kansas City, Missouri, near Loose Park. A renovated quadrangle draws students from more than 70 elementary schools and various ethnic, social, and economic backgrounds. The school emphasizes a well-rounded experience by encouraging involvement in sports (it has one of the most respected athletic programs in the area) and community service. Volunteering a minimum of 90 hours is a prerequisite to graduation. The academy enrolls just over 500 students.

Kansas

CHRISTOTS COUNTRY DAY SCHOOL
21403 Midland Dr., Shawnee
(913) 422-5684
www.christots.com
With activities that include gardening, music, and visiting the school's rabbit and baby goats, it's enough to make you want to revert to childhood. Students from 18 months to third grade also learn phonics, geography, math, science, and computer skills through a Montessori-based teaching discipline. The school is set in wooded acreage, and the children spend plenty of time outdoors participating in games and watching for the deer that live just beyond the facility's fence. The school has been in operation since 1986; all classes are led by certified teachers.

HYMAN BRAND HEBREW ACADEMY
5801 W. 115th St., Overland Park
(913) 327-8180
www.hbha.edu

In 1966 parents who wanted to provide a Jewish day school for their children rented space at Ohev Shalom Synagogue and began with 33 students. In 1973 a high school department was added. Over the years the academy has moved several times to adjust to its growing enrollment needs; in fall 1988 it found its permanent home when the architecturally stunning Jewish Community Campus opened in south Overland Park. Since then space has been added to support a biology lab, fine arts center, Judaic studies rooms, two computer labs, and a foreign language classroom. Speaking of language skills, the admissions form states that new applicants entering grades 4 through 12 must be able to read and write Hebrew. The children come from a variety of racial, national, and economic backgrounds (over 50 percent receive financial assistance), yet all are being raised in the Jewish faith. Currently around 300 students are enrolled from kindergarten to grade 12.

KANSAS CITY CHRISTIAN SCHOOL
4801 W. 79th St., Prairie Village
(913) 648-5227
www.kcchristianschool.org
The hallmarks of this 50-year-old institution are its Biblical integration, character training, and parental involvement. In fact, parents don't just bake cookies for the booster club; they sign a form promising to be active in their child's academic and spiritual upbringing. Advanced placement classes in English and math provide college credit. The 14:1 student-to-teacher ratio helps turn out quality students, and the Discover Program caters to students with learning disabilities. The emphasis is on academic competence as well as compassion.

CHILD CARE

Kansas City is a family-oriented community with hundreds of day care options for working parents. Churches offer programs ranging from daily child care to weekly "mom's day out" relief, and the phone book is filled with Montessori and other organizations that accept children from several weeks of age through kindergarten and beyond. National companies such as Kindercare and La Petite Academy are well represented.

Several agencies provide resources and referrals to help you find a competent center, including the **Johnson County Child Care Association** (913-341-6200), **Heart of America Resource and Referral** (800-753-9981), and **Day Care Connection** (913-962-2020).

The two state organizations that oversee day care licensing and registration are the **Missouri Department of Health's Bureau of Child Care Safety and Licensure** (816-325-5860) and the **Kansas Department of Health's Johnson County Branch of Health and Human Services Child Care Programs** (913-894-2525).

HIGHER EDUCATION

Kansas City, it should be noted, is a university town. Never mind that the homecoming parade is an hour or so away. In fact the traffic you hear on crisp fall evenings is alumni driving to the University of Kansas in Lawrence, the University of Missouri–Columbia, or Kansas State University in Manhattan to cheer at ballgames before heading to favorite beer joints from school days. But woe is the couple with mixed allegiances; the ride home from a game between dueling schools can be pretty chilly. After all, one team has to lose.

Yet despite the lure of these Big Twelve schools, degree seekers can choose in-town options without sacrificing prestige. Several of our colleges are nationally recognized for excellence yet offer students smaller class sizes for more personal attention. And don't worry that the little darlings will be denied interaction with other cultures by staying close to home; we draw students from around the world.

High school grads can select from an array of universities, community colleges, and trade schools. Several out-of-town entities maintain classrooms within our geographical area, an ideal way for working adults to obtain a four-year or advanced degree.

In addition, to help fuel our reputation as the life sciences center of the country, we have a number of respected schools in the health care field training medical doctors and researchers. Other professional schools offer degrees in chiropractic, dentistry, and osteopathy. See the Health Care and Wellness chapter for these options.

We cover some of Kansas City's classiest institutions and then take a look at other learning choices for adults and seniors, including dance and cooking classes. There could be tap shoes or a sauté pan in your future.

The listings are arranged in alphabetical order by type of institution and are located in Kansas City, Missouri, unless otherwise noted.

Two-Year Institutions

JOHNSON COUNTY COMMUNITY COLLEGE
12345 College Blvd.
Overland Park, KS
(913) 469-8500
www.jccc.edu

Hear the deep, grinding sound of a bulldozer? Must be another building going up at Johnson County Community College. In the sleepy suburb of Overland Park sits a community college with the sheer size and academic power to rival many four-year universities. JCCC's 18 redbrick buildings are linked by walkways and gardens dotted with outdoor sculptures and rimmed by 13 parking lots. No wonder first-timers need a map to get around the 234-acre campus.

The campus has to be immense to support its enrollment: With more than 38,000 students each semester, JCCC is the third largest institution of higher education in the state. It offers a full range of undergraduate credit courses that form the first two years of most college curricula as well as more than 50 one- and two-year career certificate programs that prepare students to enter the job market.

Its Center for Professional Education is the largest continuing education program in the region, enrolling more than 12,000 students in more than 600 certification workshops and seminars each year.

But it's the three-year Chef Apprenticeship program that's brought the school national acclaim. Here's where some of the country's best chefs have trained; in fact the school has placed extremely well in international cooking exhibitions, usually bringing home gold and silver medals.

METROPOLITAN COMMUNITY COLLEGES
3200 Broadway (administrative center)
(816) 795-1000
www.mcckc.edu

Metropolitan Community Colleges is actually a system of five colleges—Blue River, Longview, Maple Woods, Penn Valley, and the Business & Technology Center—in nine locations throughout the Kansas City area. More than 40,000 students choose these schools every year for more than just economic reasons.

Four-Year Colleges and Universities

AVILA COLLEGE
11901 Wornall Rd.
(816) 501-2400
www.avila.edu

The Catholic college was the first college in Kansas City to offer programs in nursing, gerontology, and social work. It is also the first (and currently only) four-year college in the city to offer a paralegal program approved by the American Bar Association and one of only 23 colleges in the country to offer a four-year degree in radiological technology.

PARK UNIVERSITY
8700 Northwest River Park Dr.
Parkville, MO
(816) 741-2000
www.park.edu

The campus is arguably the most beautiful in the Midwest, thanks to its picturesque site overlooking the bend of the river, the quaint town of Parkville, and the skyline of downtown Kansas City, Missouri. Opened in 1875, the buildings were constructed of native limestone; in fact the campus is a geologist's dream, with fossils from the Paleozoic period visible in building blocks and stone stairways. The boulder at the entrance of Copley Hall is a glacial deposit. Poets might find inspiration in walking the 800 acres of woodlands, waterfalls, and wildflowers.

The student body (of around 1000) represents 30 states and more than 50 foreign countries. And more than 85 percent of undergraduate students receive some form of financial aid in the form of grants, loans, and work-study positions.

Perhaps the university's most inspiring site is the Black History Wall located near the 6th Street entrance. The landmark is inscribed with the names of four African-American employees who contributed to Park's rich history, including Spencer Cave, head groundskeeper from 1875 until his death in 1946 and who, one alumnus said, "taught us more than our professors."

ROCKHURST UNIVERSITY
1100 Rockhurst Rd.
(816) 501-4000
www.rockhurst.edu
The university serves approximately 3,000 students (about 72 percent Catholic) at the main campus in Kansas City's cultural district and the Ignatius Center of Rockhurst University/Saint Louis University, located in suburban Kansas City.

Older students also choose Rockhurst for a superior education. Its Continuing Education Center, through subsidiary National Seminars, is the nation's largest provider of adult continuing education. And Rockhurst's Executive Fellows MBA program boasts an alumni list that includes more than 400 top leaders in major organizations throughout the Kansas City area and the nation.

UNIVERSITY OF MISSOURI–KANSAS CITY
5100 Rockhill Rd.
(816) 235-1111
www.umkc.edu
In the heart of Kansas City's cultural and entertainment zone stand the red tile–roofed buildings of the University of Missouri–Kansas City. The campus was established in 1933 and soon other colleges were merging with the school to form an arts and sciences focus. The Kansas City School of Law joined in 1938, followed by dental, pharmacy, medical, and nursing schools. Today 13 schools

and colleges offer more than 125 degree options to more than 14,000 students. In 1963 the University of Kansas City became part of the University of Missouri system, joining three other campuses located in Columbia, Rolla, and St. Louis.

UMKC is also home to the Henry W. Bloch School of Business and Public Administration; the Conservatory of Music; Kansas City Repertory Theatre, the premier resident theater company of the Midwest (read more about this in The Arts chapter); National Public Radio's local affiliate, KCUR–FM (see Media); and a Gallery of Art.

WILLIAM JEWELL COLLEGE
500 College Hwy.
Liberty, MO
(816) 781-7700
www.jewell.edu
The college adheres to the principles of a century and a half ago: Provide a superior quality education while retaining its Missouri Baptist heritage.

One of the college's strengths is its incoming freshman program that links new students with five mentors, including two faculty members and three students. Newbies get acquainted fast thanks to team-building exercises held at the new Tucker Leadership Lab. This same facility, including rock climbing walls and towers, challenging rope and bridge courses, and the "Sweet Chariot" 250-foot swing ride, is also popular with corporate teams and not-for-profit groups.

Graduate and Master's Programs

Adults who want to further their careers have plenty of options through universities that offer MBAs, including schools that have primary campuses in Kansas City and off-site universities that have developed a satellite presence in town.

BAKER UNIVERSITY SCHOOL OF PROFESSIONAL AND GRADUATE STUDIES
6600 College Blvd.
Overland Park, KS
(913) 491-4432
www.bakerspgs.edu
Working adults can complete a degree almost as fast as they can say the name of this program.

Well, almost. Students can obtain an under-graduate degree in just three years of intense work. Baker's SPGS offers accelerated MBA and MSM degrees as well. It's quite a commitment; students typically attend one three-hour class a week with interim group study assignments. With a main campus in Baldwin City, Kansas, the uni-versity maintains satellite locations in Overland Park, Kansas, and Lee's Summit, Missouri.

HENRY W. BLOCH SCHOOL OF BUSINESS AND PUBLIC ADMINISTRATION
5100 Rockhill Rd.
(816) 235-1111
www.umkc.edu
This school, located at the University of Missouri–Kansas City campus, offers both an MBA, which can be completed as a part-time student, and an Executive MBA, which is a 21-month, intensive program with classes that meet every other Fri and Sat. One of the school's strongest points is its connections with and support from area busi-nesses that can lead to job placement.

MIDAMERICA NAZARENE UNIVERSITY
2030 E. College Way
Olathe, KS
(913) 782-3750
www.mnu.edu
Busy professionals can complete an MBA degree within two years at MidAmerica with the help of other students, caring instructors, and a personal laptop computer that's part of tuition. Here, courses are laid out in a structured manner in which each class builds upon the last to provide a feeling of integrated knowledge. This system is one reason the university has such a successful completion rate for its program.

UNIVERSITY OF KANSAS EDWARDS CAMPUS
12600 Quivira Rd.
Overland Park, KS
(913) 897-8400
www.edwardscampus.ku.edu
Now adults in Kansas City can chant "rock chalk Jayhawk" while driving just a few miles to cam-pus. The master's program is designed to meet the needs of a typical student, who is 33 years old, works full-time, and has a family; most classes meet one night a week, and computer labs are open days, evenings, and weekends.

i At Kansas City Art Institute's annual Student Ceramic Sale, held on campus a few weeks before Christmas, you can snag great artwork at remarkable prices. Call KCAI at (816) 474-5224, or visit www.kcai.edu for details.

OTHER LEARNING EXPERIENCES

With so many credit and noncredit classes avail-able around town, adults can expand their minds or their waistlines. You'll find classes for sports enthusiasts (think sailing and ice-skating) in the Parks, Lakes, and Recreation chapter.

COMMUNIVERSITY
5327 Holmes
(816) 235-1448
www.umkc.edu/commu
Called the university without walls, this is a mixed bag of adult education classes taught by volun-teer instructors at various homes, gardens, and classrooms throughout the city. Want to learn how to buy a house, and then decorate it the feng shui way? Learn breathing techniques from a "recovering lawyer"? Here's where to find these and dozens of other classes in categories like Arts and Crafts, Inner and Outer Paths (yoga to read-ing auras), Food (tamales and paella to dim sum), and Business and Legal Issues that tackle reading an investment prospectus or writing a news story. There's even a class on chain mail—as in armor. Other teachers, called conveners, include professional chefs, financial planners, and artists.

THE CULINARY CENTER OF KANSAS CITY
7917 Foster
Overland Park, KS
(913) 341-4455
www.kcculinary.com

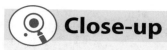

Close-up

Kansas City Art Institute

If you could point to one reason our town is so flush with art galleries and artist studios, it's the Kansas City Art Institute. Young creative minds come here from 45 states and five foreign countries to study with some of the best instructors in the world. And if at first they grumble about being stuck in a cowtown, they soon fall in love with our exciting, urban city, and many of them stay after graduation.

Yet as a frontier town in the mid-1880s, Kansas City was an unlikely place for the founding of an art school. It began in 1885 when a small group of art enthusiasts organized a Sketch Club to "talk over art matters in general and to judge pictures." The club moved into quarters in the Deardorf Building at 11th and Main Streets and held its first public exhibition in the spring of 1887. The Kansas City Art Association and School of Design was incorporated in July of that year.

As the rowdy town's first cultural institution, KCAI has enjoyed support from prominent business and civic leaders, starting with Howard Vanderslice, who in the 1920s purchased a stone mansion and surrounding eight acres at 44th and Warwick for the school. Four years later the Art Institute renamed the residence "Vanderslice Hall." Today the school shares its neighborhood with the Nelson-Atkins Museum of Art and the Kemper Museum of Contemporary Art.

The college recently expanded its campus within the Southmoreland Neighborhood by purchasing two properties at 43rd and Walnut and opening the H&R Block Art Space, a gallery for contemporary work by students and other artists. The new Jannes Library, situated in a stately old mansion known as the Cunningham Estate, recently opened.

The private four-year college awards bachelor of fine arts degrees in ceramics, design/illustration, fiber, painting and printmaking, photo and new media, sculpture, and art history or creative writing with a studio art emphasis. The 600 students join an impressive roster that includes Walt Disney, painters Jackson Pollock and Keith Jacobshagen, ceramicists Richard Notkin and Akio Takamori, sculptor Robert Morris, and photographer Thomas Barrow.

For more than three decades KCAI has hosted a lecture series, open to students and the public, starring some of the world's most respected artists and scholars.

KCAI also offers many outreach programs, including evening and weekend continuing education courses for credit and noncredit, family studio workshops, and a high school summer residency program. Student exhibits are held twice a year on campus, providing an opportunity for the public to experience and buy the work on display.

For more information contact the Kansas City Art Institute at 4415 Warwick Blvd., Kansas City, MO 64111; (816) 474-5224; www.kcai.edu.

Follow your nose to Old Overland Park and join fellow culinarians, both skilled and novice, in hands-on cooking classes and demonstrations. The classes are fun and educational, and the best part is you get to taste the results afterward. Instructors are chefs from some of Kansas City's top restaurants as well as other talented area cooks. CCKC has four to eight classes per week, and many of the favorites sell out as soon as the 20-page newsletter hits the mailboxes. Popular offerings include a Wine Country Dinner, with comice pear and Stilton salad, crispy crusted salmon with thyme-infused zucchini broth, and black bottom coconut cream pie; and a Bistro Dinner Under the Tuscan Sun, with penne puttanesca, honey-glazed pork tenderloin with fennel, and winter pears in wine served with Gorgonzola and walnuts. Are you drooling on the page yet? Classes are matched to the season, so you'll learn barbecuing techniques in summer and holiday entertaining tips in winter. There are plenty of basic cooking classes as well, covering topics such as choosing a knife or stocking the pantry.

Classes are held in a lovely space, a cross between a Tuscan country house and villa in the south of France, that's also available for private parties, weddings, and corporate team-building events. Join the Frequent Fryers Club and get a discount on your fifth class.

NEW WRITER'S WORKSHOP
6000 Lamar
Mission, KS
(816) 630-7063
www.kansascitywriters.com
If you long to unleash your writing potential or want to find out how to get your work published, this is the course for you. New writers will find a relaxed, supportive atmosphere and an instructor (always a published writer) who will help develop creativity, writing skills, and marketing techniques. Classes are held mornings for eight consecutive sessions each fall and cover fiction, nonfiction, and poetry. Fees range around $50, and there are classes made just for young writers.

THEATRE FOR YOUNG AMERICA ACTING CLASSES
Mission, KS
(816) 460-2083
www.tya.org

Some students at this theater and education center are seeking acting careers; others simply want to improve their voices, body movements, creativity, and self-esteem. Classes for ages 3 through 18 are taught by professional actors and experienced theater craftspeople. The center also provides work/study programs to give students a chance to learn scene crafts, lighting, directing, and other behind-the-scenes skills. The classes are affiliated with the not-for-profit Theatre for Young America; for more information on performances see the Kidstuff chapter.

THE WRITER'S PLACE
3607 Pennsylvania
(816) 753-1090
www.writersplace.org
Newcomers to the craft of writing as well as frequently published sages come together in this grand stone mansion in Kansas City's elegant Valentine Neighborhood. Before its rebirth as classroom, library, and literary community center for readers and writers, the handsome building—complete with turret—spent time as a private home, brothel, and church. It could even serve as inspiration for one genre of fiction—the ghost story: Some say it's haunted.

The Writers Place also hosts ongoing events, open to the public, that include book discussions, poetry readings, and dramatic presentations. Fund-raising events are always a lively soiree. The organization currently has 1,000 members; dues are $40 per year for individuals, $60 for families, and $20 for students.

HEALTH CARE AND WELLNESS

When moving to a new city, even more important than locating the nearest ice-cream parlor is finding the closest hospital. In Kansas City, chances are you'll have one practically in your backyard.

Even more good news is that many of our hospitals are nationally known for specialties like cardiac care, cancer diagnostics and treatment, and even kidney transplants. Chalk it up to the fact that Kansas City is home to three medical schools: the University of Kansas Hospital, known for its outstanding research programs; the University of Missouri–Kansas City, offering a unique six-year program combining B.A. and M.D. degrees; and the University of Health Sciences, with a focus on osteopathy. Practitioners of chiropractic have the highly respected Cleveland Chiropractic College. While we're busy training the best physicians and health care workers in the world, they're busy falling in love with this town. After graduation they tend to plant their comfortable white shoes right here.

We're also making medical breakthroughs that can help eliminate disease, speed the recovery process, and improve the patient's quality of life. For instance, our neurosurgeons were the first in the region to operate on tumors and lesions near the brainstem that were once thought to be inoperable. Heart surgeons performed the first endoscopic vein removal from the leg in the Midwest.

And our KU Hospital was one of the first hospitals to perform deep-brain stimulation surgery to help control tremors associated with Parkinson's disease. It has performed more of these surgeries than any other hospital in the world.

Kansas City is fast becoming a world leader in the exciting field of life sciences with the opening of the Stowers Institute for Medical Research. This $200 million facility is devoted to finding cures to gene-related diseases like cancer and Alzheimer's. Find out more about this biomedical research center in this chapter's Close-up.

As for immediate care, we'll start our rounds by covering the area's three largest health care organizations with multiple facilities and then follow up with individual medical centers and other health care providers. And we promise, no "cutting-edge" jokes.

All institutions are located in Kansas City, Missouri, unless otherwise noted.

SAINT LUKE'S HEALTH SYSTEM

www.saintlukeshealthsystem.org

This organization consists of three hospitals, a home health and wellness agency, fifteen physician practices, and thousands of affiliated physicians in the Kansas City metropolitan and surrounding regions. Following is a look at each hospital in the immediate area.

Saint Luke's Hospitals

SAINT LUKE'S HOSPITAL OF KANSAS CITY
4401 Wornall Rd.
(816) 932-2000

For more than a century, Saint Luke's has been serving the health care needs of a growing city. Founded in 1882 as a 50-bed institution at 10th and Campbell Streets, the hospital moved to its present location near the Country Club Plaza in

1923, when a six-story, 150-bed facility was dedicated. Today the hospital campus covers more than 8 square blocks and includes more than a dozen major facilities. The 623-bed tertiary-care hospital offers more than 56 medical specialties through its network of 484 physicians.

One of its primary focuses is on cardiac health. The Mid America Heart Institute, located at the Wornall Road campus, is the No. 1 preferred heart care facility in the region. The institute performed the world's first coronary angioplasty for an acute heart attack in 1980, revolutionizing heart attack treatment worldwide. This 210-bed specialty heart center is complemented by six groups of doctors who specialize in cardiac and pulmonary research and care.

St. Luke's Hospital is also highly regarded for its cancer prevention, diagnosis, and treatment centers. Its Centers for Breast Care of the Cancer Institute provides the latest in imaging and diagnostic techniques, including stereotactic core biopsy.

i Most of the larger hospitals and health care groups provide community outreach programs including nutritional counseling, fitness programs, CPR training, and even babysitting classes. Many of these programs are free or inexpensive. Call around; often the hospitals publish schedules in a newsletter or on their Web sites.

SAINT LUKE'S NORTHLAND HOSPITAL
5830 Northwest Barry Rd.
(816) 891-6000

Smithville Campus
601 S. U.S. Hwy. 169
(816) 532-3700
www.saintlukeshealthsystem.org
One medical staff of more than 247 active physicians serves the two campuses. The Barry Road facility is an 80-bed general acute-care hospital including a special-care nursery. The Smithville location opened in 1938 as the first Northland hospital. Today it encompasses 92 beds.

SAINT LUKE'S SOUTH
12300 Metcalf Ave.
Overland Park, KS
(913) 317-7000
This 75-bed facility offers a range of health care services including emergency, physical and occupational therapies, happy-mom-happy-baby birthing suites, prenatal services and a Level II nursery, cardiac diagnostic testing and rehabilitation, sleep disorder center, pain management clinic, and radiology services, along with surgery center.

Saint Luke's South was designed to be exceedingly patient friendly, with new technology such as wireless communication, electronic patient records, and bedside registration. Now that's a brilliant idea! It also offers a 90,000-square-foot medical office building on its campus.

Additional Services from Saint Luke's
SHAWNEE MISSION MEDICAL CENTER
9100 W. 74th St.
Overland Park, KS
(913) 676-2000
www.shawneemission.org
Back in the days of $4 house calls, residents of northeast Johnson County had few choices when it came to health care. Eight doctors practiced in the county, and the nearest hospital was a four-bed facility in Gardner, Kansas. Thanks to two doctors, Al Armbruster and Donald Smith, Shawnee Mission Hospital opened in 1962. Its 15-acre campus was donated by J. C. Nichols, a gift that was appraised at nearly $6.5 million at the time. Dr. Smith delivered the first two babies born at the 102-bed hospital.

Today the campus has expanded to 54 acres, which includes a 383-bed acute care hospital, a freestanding outpatient surgery facility, a community health education building, five medical office buildings, an employee child care center, and a community fitness course.

A member of the Adventist Health System, it has 640 physicians on staff and employs 2,500 associates. Its primary medical services are cardiovascular, women's care, surgery, and outpatient programs.

Other programs associated with Saint Luke's follow.

ASK-A-NURSE
(816) 932-6220, (800) 932-6220
www.saint-lukes.org
Stubbed toe? Chest pain? Is it a cold or the flu . . . or perhaps that potato salad that sat out all day? You can get immediate answers to your medical questions 24 hours a day, seven days a week through this free service. It's also a handy way to find out about upcoming community education classes and register at the same time. And if you're new in town, you can find a physician (within the Saint Luke's family, of course) who meets your specific needs.

THE CANCER INSTITUTE
(913) 676-8156
This oncology partnership, affiliated with Saint Luke's Health System, provides the community with a wide variety of services from a single source.

The institute collaborates with Kansas City's academic and research communities to provide research, therapies, and ongoing care. Specific services include inpatient oncology treatment, radiation therapy, breast centers at Menorah Medical Center and Saint Luke's Hospital, the Blood and Marrow Transplant program, a gynecologic oncology practice, and Gamma Knife services at Research Medical Center.

CRITTENTON BEHAVIORAL HEALTH
10918 Elm Ave.
(816) 767-4101
Located on a picturesque 156-acre site near Longview Lake in southeast Kansas City, Crittenton is Kansas City's premier provider of psychiatric care for children and their families.

Founded in 1896, the center has evolved into a comprehensive system of care that includes acute inpatient hospitalization, partial hospitalization, community-based services, and prevention services. On any given day, more than 100 children and young people receive treatment in one of the therapeutic programs. Additional behavioral health programs, for children and adults, are available at several locations through the system. These include addictions services and assessment centers.

HOME CARE AND HOSPICE
(816) 756-1160
As the largest full-service home care organization in Kansas City, this organization provides home health services to help patients remain independent and decrease the time they need to spend in the hospital; hospice services, which provide caring medical and emotional support to patients and their families during the last days of life; plus home pharmacy infusion, medical equipment, and private-duty services.

CARONDELET HEALTH

This national network of hospitals is operated by the Sisters of St. Joseph Health System. In Kansas City they operate the two hospitals described below, as well as other facilities and services, including St. Mary's Manor, Carondelet Manor, and Villa Saint Joseph long-term care facilities; and home care services, a hospice, a pharmacy, and eight physician offices under the Carondelet name.

SAINT JOSEPH HEALTH CENTER
1000 Carondelet Dr.
(816) 942-4400
www.carondelethealth.org
Established in 1874 as the first private hospital in Kansas City, today this facility has 300 beds and is served by more than 720 staff physicians. With its handsome central atrium and architecture, it looks more like a hotel than a hospital. Patients also like the smaller waiting rooms spread throughout the place rather than having one huge Grand Central Station with screaming kids and four television sets, all tuned to different stations. The attached Medical Mall has a nice food court that beats most cafeteria choices hands down.

Saint Joseph's specialized services include Level II trauma care, a chest pain center, cardiac

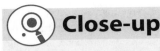

Close-up

The Stowers Institute—Hope for Life

In 1994 Jim and Virginia Stowers decided they wanted to give back something "more valuable than money" to the millions of investors in American Century mutual funds who made their success possible. As cancer survivors, they decided to put their fortune to work to find the causes of cancer and other gene-based diseases.

Starting with an initial gift of $50 million, they created the Stowers Institute as a nonprofit medical research organization. They purchased the 10-acre site formerly occupied by Menorah Hospital in the heart of the city and began construction of the 600,000-square-foot complex in 1998. Since then the Stowers have followed their initial gift with stock and cash that raised the institute's endowment above $2 billion.

The center is well on its way to turning Kansas City into "Biomed Valley," attracting top researchers and scientists from around the world. And although experts tried to convince the Stowers that the best-of-the-best would never transfer to Kansas City, they were soon proved wrong. Dr. Bill Neaves, the institute's CEO, and Dr. Robb Krumlauf, its scientific director, are beginning to staff the facility with the world's top minds. They've been joined by Dr. David Chao as president.

They tend to be impressed with the city, but they are overwhelmed by the institute. Its laboratory and research support space is unsurpassed. And the buildings and grounds at 1000 East 50th St. are simply magnificent. The general architect is the Kansas City firm of Peckham Guyton Alvers & Viets, but MBT Architecture of San Francisco, one of the few firms in the country specializing in research facilities, designed the laboratory and research spaces.

The landscaped grounds include waterfalls and walking trails, and the building's entrance is defined by a 31-foot double helix sculpture. The sculpture and the glass panels in the library's fireplace contain the institute's slogan, "Hope for Life."

At its opening, the center was staffed with four laboratories headed by independent scientists. Since then it has recruited additional scientists and highly ranked experts in bioinformatics and transgenic technology. When fully operational, the institute will house at least 50 independent research programs focused on understanding the genes and proteins that control how cells in our bodies divide, differentiate, migrate, and die. By studying these fundamental processes in cells, scientists hope to discover how genes cause many diseases, particularly cancer. For more information about the Stowers Institute, log on to **www.stowers-institute .org** or call (816) 926-4000.

The Stowers center served as a catalyst for the Kansas City Area Life Sciences Initiative, a coalition of businesses, hospitals, and universities with a common goal: to improve the quality of life.

and pulmonary rehabilitation center, Lifeflight Eagle air medical services, and family-centered maternity care including neonatal intensive care.

Also on-site are an asthma center, a pain management center, a sleep lab, and programs for wellness, sports medicine, and nutrition.

i The Web site of Leawood's American Academy of Family Physicians, www .familydoctor.org, has health information fact sheets in both Spanish and English, self-care flowcharts, drug data, and more. By the way, Kansas City is home to the international headquarters of the American Academy of Family Physicians.

ST. MARY'S HOSPITAL OF BLUE SPRINGS

201 W. R. D. Mize Rd.
Blue Springs, MO
(816) 228-5900
www.carondelethealth.org

This 111-bed acute care hospital opened the first Birthing Center in Missouri, providing a homelike environment for families. The hospital also has a 24-hour emergency room, Lifeline, hospice care, pain clinic, mobile CT scanner, and physical therapy unit.

Ongoing community wellness programs include coping with diabetes, prenatal and postnatal education, and CPR classes. St. Mary's Manor, a skilled nursing and residential care facility, is located adjacent to the hospital campus.

HCA MIDWEST

(816) 508-4000
www.hcamidwest.com

Through this network of 12 state-of-the-art hospitals and multiple treatment facilities, HCA offers superb care in the Greater Kansas City area. Whether you need a heart transplant or just a doctor with a heart, HCA can handle it. In fact, HCA offers seven Chest Pain Centers, each accredited by the nationally recognized Society of Chest Pain Centers.

Thanks to a recent $450 million capital investment, this health care system can pull from some of the nation's leading medical and nursing schools. More than 3,000 physicians serve patients through primary care, inpatient and outpatient services, employer health programs, home health and hospice care, and wellness programs. Hospitals within the HCA umbrella include Baptist-Lutheran Medical Center, Overland Park Regional Medical Center, Independence Regional Health Center, Medical Center of Independence, Research Medical Center, and Menorah Medical Center (see separate listings for most of these).

MENORAH MEDICAL CENTER

5721 W. 119th St.
Overland Park, KS
(913) 498-6000
www.menorahmedicalcenter.com

Menorah first opened its doors on Rockhill Road in Kansas City in 1931 and moved to its new location in 1996. The new campus includes a 158-bed acute care hospital, doctors building, and outpatient clinics. It may be the most beautiful facility in the city with its handsome architecture, fountains, and gardens that can be viewed from patient rooms and waiting areas. An appendectomy in 15 minutes? Sure, doc, but did you see the daffodils in bloom?

Within the 110,000-square-foot center is a sophisticated cardiology center including open-heart surgery, angioplasty, pacemakers, diagnostics, and a full range of modern cardiac care. The Family Birthing Center has 12 luxurious birthing suites that cater to new parents by providing private baths and showers with a jetted tub, sleeping facilities for Dad or a support person, and in-room private dining. We'd like to make a reservation for Friday, please.

Other patient-care touches include a pre-op pediatric party where younger patients get a first-hand look at the operating room to help ease any fears. They can also try out the kid-size electronic jeep they'll be driving into surgery. A kosher kitchen takes care of the special needs of Jewish patients, and the arboretum is a tranquil garden with a walking trail that beckons caregivers and patients to relax.

OVERLAND PARK REGIONAL MEDICAL CENTER

10500 Quivira Rd.
Overland Park, KS
(913) 541-5000
www.oprmc.com

This center was among the first health care facilities to bring quality patient care to southern Johnson County. Opened in 1978, today it encompasses a 249-bed acute care hospital, three medical office buildings, three pharmacies, and offices for more than 385 physicians.

Overland Park Regional offers several services that set it apart from other centers in the area. For instance, it has the only nationally verified Level II Trauma Program in Johnson County, including 24-hour emergency services. It also offers a Stroke

Prevention and Recovery Program through its emergency department.

The hospital's Diabetes Wellness center is recognized for excellence by the American Diabetes Association. Its Burn and Wound Care Program is known as one of the region's most comprehensive. And the Geropsychiatry Program offers special care for the elderly, including crisis stabilization in the 24-bed unit; comprehensive psychiatric, medical, and neurological evaluations; individualized, ongoing treatment programs; and free follow-up visits.

Overland Park Regional is also home to a Sleep Disorders Center that evaluates, diagnoses, and treats patients with sleep problems. There's no question that new parents have a hard time sleeping, but they'll have a nice time with delivery thanks to the center's Pre-Delivery Program that includes "Birth Day Beepers" for the dad or birthing coach and 20 luxurious suites that pamper the new family. And if problems should arise, the center has Johnson County's only Level III Neonatal Intensive Care Unit, providing the highest level of care for premature or sick infants.

RESEARCH PSYCHIATRIC CENTER
2323 E. 63rd St.
(816) 444-8161

This center offers a full continuum of behavioral health services, including inpatient and partial hospitalization programs, as well as a CareNet Clinic that provides crisis intervention, outpatient counseling, and community support groups. The 40-member medical staff and 100-member allied staff provide services available to the Greater Kansas City area.

The center's Senior Adult Inpatient Treatment is known regionally and nationally for its quality and longevity. Patients are treated based on their needs, either as high-functioning seniors or those who suffer from organic or chronic mental illness. Separate treatment programs are available through the Child and Adolescent Program, which includes a tutorial system that helps patients from ages 13 to 18 keep up with schoolwork.

BAPTIST-LUTHERAN MEDICAL CENTER
6601 Rockhill Rd.
(816) 276-7000
www.babtist-lutheranmedicalcenter.com

When Baptist Medical Center and Trinity Lutheran Hospital merged in 2000, they created a new entity to serve the south Kansas City community better. Licensed for 354 beds, the medical center is located on a 37-acre campus that includes outpatient facilities, medial office buildings, and a Pavilion Health Club that's dedicated to the rehabilitation and prevention of illness and disease. Baptist-Lutheran has approximately 1,000 employees and more than 700 physicians on its medical staff.

In addition to the traditional hospital services such as emergency, critical care, surgery, and other offerings, the center maintains the Center for Radiation Therapy; the Goppert Family Care Center, an extended-hour program that treats all aspects of the community's health needs; and the Center for Eye Surgery, which provides glaucoma and cataract surgery and features two suites specifically for laser procedures. The Pain Management department (816-276-7094) provides services relating to acute and chronic inpatient and outpatient situations. Patients can be referred by their physicians or self-admitted.

The medical center is involved with several community activities. It teams with the Yellow Cab Company to provide free rides home to people who can't (or shouldn't) drive from restaurants, parties, or bars during the holidays. Since its inception, Holiday Cab has provided more than 23,000 rides. Baptist-Lutheran is the exclusive local provider of the Lifeline 24-hour emergency response system. Subscribers keep a small pager with them at all times, so help is just a push-button away.

INDEPENDENTLY OPERATED HOSPITALS

CHILDREN'S MERCY HOSPITAL
2401 Gillham Rd.
(816) 234-3000
www.childrens-mercy.org

Numbers for Health-Related Questions or Emergencies

Look to these organizations for help. Crisis lines are answered 24 hours a day.

Life-Threatening, Police, and Fire Emergencies: 911
AIDS Counseling & Information Hotline: (800) 590-2437
AIDS Testing Council of Greater Kansas City: (816) 751-5166
Al-Anon, Alateen: (816) 373-8566
Alcoholics Anonymous: (816) 471-7229
Alzheimer's Disease & Related Disorders Help Line: (913) 831-0003
American Cancer Society of Wyandotte & Johnson Counties: (913) 432-3277
American Diabetes Association: (816) 361-3361
American Heart Association: (913) 648-6727
American Lung Association: (816) 842-5242
American Red Cross: (816) 931-8400
ANSWER Network Teen Suicide Hotline: (800) 784-2433, www.teenanswer.org
Arthritis Foundation: (816) 753-2220
Battered Women's Hotline & Shelter: (816) 861-6100
Domestic Violence Network: (816) 995-1000
Kidney Foundation: (913) 262-1551
Mental Health Crisis Hotline: (888) 279-8188; TDD (800) 955-8339
Narcotics Anonymous: (816) 531-2250
Poison Control Center, Kansas: (913) 588-6633, (800) 332-6633
Poison Control Center, Missouri: (800) 366-8888
Rape Crisis Hotline: (816) 531-0223
Safehome Sexual Assault Hotline & Shelter: (913) 262-7273
Substance Abuse Center: (913) 362-0045
Sudden Infant Death Syndrome Resources: (913) 649-6996
Suicide Prevention Hotline: (913) 831-1773

PHYSICIAN REFERRALS
The following are referral centers that are not tied to any particular hospital or health care group.
Cass County Referral: (816) 884-3291
Jackson/Clay/Platte County Referrals: (816) 531-8432
Kansas Medical Society (serving Johnson and Wyandotte Counties): (913) 432-9444, www.msjwc.org
West Central Missouri Medical Society: (816) 679-4135

You and your child will immediately know this is a special place when you see the lobby filled with bright colors, children's artwork on the walls, and physicians who often wear Hawaiian shirts instead of white jackets.

The hospital's history can be traced to 1897 when two sisters, Dr. Alice Berry Graham, a dentist, and Dr. Katharine Berry Richardson, established the Free Bed Fund Association to treat "sick, crippled, deformed, and ruptured" children from families that couldn't afford health care. Today the Children's Mercy health care system includes the state-of-the-art, 194-bed hospital in Kansas City, busy outpatient clinics in midtown, and a hospital in suburban Johnson County (described separately).

The hospital serves children from birth to age 18 and provides outpatient care in 35 pediatric subspecialties. Children's Mercy has the region's only Level I pediatric trauma center and emergency department as well as a Level IV neonatal intensive care nursery.

Along with providing the very best care possible, the hospital caters to young patients' emotional needs. Little ones are encouraged to bring a favorite stuffed animal or doll along with them, which promptly receives a bracelet that matches the child's. Kids can get an online tour of the hospital with Mercy Bear, with helpful tips for parents along the way.

The hospital continues to expand its services, thanks to several generous gifts from Kansas City citizens and annual fund-raising efforts. It is involved in a 10-year, $129 million expansion that will increase services at the two locations and continue its ongoing research programs in genetics, cancer, neonatal, immunology, and nursing. The sisters who began this service with one child more than a century ago would be proud to see that their work continues: Children's Mercy provides more than $20 million in charity care per year.

CHILDREN'S MERCY SOUTH
5808 W. 110th St.
Overland Park, KS
(913) 696-8000

This facility brings the nationally recognized pediatric expertise closer to families in the south metropolitan area. It offers convenient access to outpatient pediatric surgery, 16 pediatric specialty clinics, a short-term-stay inpatient unit, after-hours clinic, and radiology services. More important, it continues the central hospital's renowned kid-glove treatment for little patients that takes much of the fear out of surgery and medical procedures.

UNIVERSITY OF KANSAS HOSPITAL
3901 Rainbow
Kansas City, KS
(913) 588-5000

KU MED WEST
7405 Renner Rd.
Shawnee, KS
(913) 588-1227
www.kumed.com

For nearly a century the University of Kansas Hospital has been providing leading-edge medicine and care to the people of the region. The hospital was separated from the University of Kansas system and placed under its own authority in 1998.

At the region's only true academic medical center, the physicians at KU Hospital are dedicated researchers, scientists, and educators. Their achievements are many. Neurosurgeons were the first in the region to operate on tumors and lesions near the brain stem that were once thought inoperable. Heart surgeons performed the first endoscopic vein harvesting in the Midwest.

KU Hospital was one of the first hospitals in the world to perform deep-brain stimulation surgery, which significantly controls tremors associated with Parkinson's disease and other brain disorders; it has performed more of these surgeries than any other hospital in the world. The hospital also performed the first kidney transplant in the state and has the first and only liver and pancreas transplant program in the area. A heart transplant program opened in 2002. Its Kidney Institute is one of the top programs in the world in fighting polycystic kidney disease. Its award-winning 110-bed Center for Advanced Heart Care facility, across the street from the main hospital, opened in October 2006. Honestly, the architecture and art displayed throughout are so beautiful the staff is having a hard time getting patients to leave after they are healed. The amenities are pretty artful as well with private rooms, overnight accommodations for visitors, and a decentralized nursing setup that means a caring health care provider is just steps away.

The facility also has the region's only burn center certified by the American College of Surgeons and the American Burn Association. And its new heart-lung program features the most advanced diagnostic and treatment technology in the region. A $23 million investment added two state-of-the-art catheterization labs, operating suites, and therapeutic procedures. Its PET (positron emission tomography) scanner is the most accurate imaging technology available for tracking cancer and heart disease, allowing doctors to view a patient's internal organs at the cellular level.

Along with treating more than 200,000 inpatients and outpatients a year, KU Hospital provides health and wellness programs to another 10,000 people. For instance, about 3,700 people line up in their vehicles for a flu shot every fall. "I'd like fries with that" is not an option.

NORTH KANSAS CITY HOSPITAL
2800 Clay Edwards Dr.
North Kansas City, MO
(816) 691-2000
www.nkch.org

For more than 40 years this hospital has expanded to meet the growing needs of its community north of the river. Today it's a fully equipped 350-bed regional medical center with more than 550 physicians representing 45 medical specialties.

It's perhaps known best for its superb maternity unit, which treats the birthing process as the magical time it is. For example, the private labor, delivery, recovery, and postpartum rooms are designed to pamper Mom and baby with all the comforts of home, including a specially designed birthing bed, private bath with jetted tub, television, and VCR. Dad can rest on a foldout sleeper chair and enjoy meals at the dining table. To celebrate the big moment, parents receive a decorative birth announcement and a diaper bag filled with gifts, including a logo T-shirt. No wonder more than 1,800 births take place here every year. Extraordinary medical care is close by if needed: The Level II neonatal intensive care nursery is on the same floor.

Cardiac care is also a specialty. North Kansas City Hospital was the first health care provider in Kansas City to use minimally invasive techniques for open-heart surgery. This advanced surgery offers less discomfort and a quicker return to home and everyday activities. To diagnose and treat heart problems before surgery is necessary, the hospital offers one of the area's most advanced cardiac catheterization labs.

North Kansas City Hospital has also made strides in its cancer treatment program. It was the area's first medical facility to eliminate the need to remove the prostate when cancer is confined to the area. And new gastrointestinal procedures take advantage of fiber-optic technology to allow the detection of polyps in the colon and remove them without major surgery. The center also offers the Northland's only hospital-based radiation therapy services.

Its new Health Services Pavilion is just what the patients ordered. This $94.8 million facility consists of six levels and offers expanded outpatient services in one easily accessible location. Along with plenty of covered parking, the center has large, visitor-friendly waiting areas; Tiny Town, a section designed just for kids; and a health and wellness center for fitness and rehabilitation programs.

OLATHE MEDICAL CENTER
20333 W. 151st St.
Olathe, KS
(913) 791-4200
www.olathehealth.org

Founded in 1953 as the Olathe Health Foundation, the hospital established new facilities at its present location in 1987. When it built the expansive campus it was truly out in the boondocks. Today it's surrounded by homes, shopping centers, and office parks.

The 150-bed center's comprehensive patient services include anesthesiology, dermatology, diabetic, education, cardiac care and rehabilitation, community service, emergency medicine, general surgery, laser surgery, and MRI. Also on-site are facilities for pain management, oncology treatment, speech and audiology, support groups, and wellness programs. Many of Olathe Medical Center's more than 300 active staff physicians have offices located on the center's health campus and at health care facilities of Olathe

Medical Services, Inc. The new Miami County Medical Center in Paola, Kansas, is a subsidiary.

PROVIDENCE MEDICAL CENTER
8929 Parallel Pkwy.
Kansas City, KS
(913) 596-4000
www.providence-health.org
The Sisters of Charity opened Providence Hospital in 1920, and in 1976 the center relocated to a new building on a spacious campus in western Kansas City, Kansas. In 1994, Saint John Hospital in Leavenworth, Kansas, became an affiliate of Providence to further expand regional health care delivery.

The mission continues to focus on Providence's special identity as a Catholic hospital while expanding its services. Some of these programs include a radiation oncology center, a cardiac center offering open-heart surgery and rehabilitation; geropsych services, and a broad range of general and specialized surgical services including neurosurgery and ophthalmology.

Along with the 400-bed hospital, the campus maintains Providence Place, a 90-bed nursing facility that provides diverse health education and screening programs.

i Finding the right doctor in the Yellow Pages is nearly impossible. To save time, and to make sure the doc matches your particular needs—including coverage by your insurance—call the referral centers shown in this chapter. Most hospitals and groups also provide referrals, but be aware that the list will come from their own rosters.

ADDITIONAL SERVICES

KANSAS CITY HOSPICE
Main Office: 9221 Ward Pkwy., Suite 100
(816) 363-2600
www.kansascityhospice.org
For more than 20 years, Kansas City Hospice has provided medical, emotional, and spiritual support to area residents approaching the last stage of life. More than 130 professional staff in three Kansas City Hospice offices serve more than 2,000 Kansas and Missouri families each year, regardless of their ability to pay.

These families receive individually tailored care from a team that can include nurses, medical social workers, home health aides, art and music therapists, bereavement counselors, chaplains, and specially trained volunteers. Together they manage pain and provide caring, gentle support.

The Carousel Program (913-894-8228), Kansas City's only pediatric hospice in the region, cares for newborns through teenagers.

The organization's new resale shop, Top Drawer, offers great bargains on gently used clothing and estate items. People who donate their goods have excellent taste: Offerings include designer duds, furs, and antiques. It's located at 3826 West 95th St., Leawood, Kansas, in the Ranch Mart Shopping Center. Call (913) 642-2292 for hours.

THE REHABILITATION INSTITUTE OF KANSAS CITY
3011 Baltimore
(816) 751-7700
www.rehabkc.org
The institute is a not-for-profit Heart of America United Way agency that helps children and adults with disabilities realize their highest physical, social, and vocational potential. Programs include community integration, day treatment, and outpatient medical services. It is also one of the largest vocational rehabilitation centers in the state of Missouri, with extensive work evaluation, counseling, and placement programs. The institute has a team of more than a hundred full-time staff who help those disabled by stroke and spinal cord injury along with those affected by birth, childhood, or adult-onset diseases.

More than 1,700 people come to the institute each year to increase their functional capacity through medical rehabilitation; another 1,800 patients receive vocational rehabilitation to enhance their employment opportunities. Programs are available at six locations throughout Kansas City and outlying areas.

VISITING NURSE SERVICES OF HEALTH MIDWEST
(816) 531-1200
www.vnakc.com

Established in 1891, this not-for-profit home health care agency offers the area's most comprehensive range of in-home services. As a United Way agency, it cares for adults throughout metropolitan Kansas City and surrounding rural areas regardless of the patient's ability to pay.

Home care can be as simple as providing skilled services that allow an older adult to live independently, such as physical therapy and nutritional counseling, or as complex as administering chemotherapy. Nursing visits, personal care assistance, and antibiotic treatments can all be handled in the comfort of the patient's home.

MENTAL HEALTH

JOHNSON COUNTY MENTAL HEALTH CENTER
Northeast: 6000 Lamar, Suite 130
Mission, KS
(913) 831-2550

Southwest: 1125 W. Spruce
Olathe, KS
(913) 782-2100
www.jocogov.org/mentalhealth

This community mental health center provides professional assistance to service the emotional and mental health needs of Johnson County residents. Programs include individual, family, and group counseling and treatment. Fees are based on the client's ability to pay. A 24-hour crisis service is available for situations requiring immediate attention; the after-hours emergency number is (913) 384-3535.

MENTAL HEALTH ASSOCIATION OF THE HEARTLAND
739 Minnesota Ave.
Kansas City, KS
(913) 281-2221
www.mhah.org

This center is dedicated to promoting the mental health of the community and improving the quality of life of persons with mental illness through advocacy, education, and support. A new service for people diagnosed with a mental disorder who just want to talk can be reached at (913) 281-2251. The Teen Help Line is (913) 281-2299.

TWO RIVERS PSYCHIATRIC HOSPITAL
5121 Raytown Rd.
(816) 356-5688
www.tworivershospital.com

Set in a serene, parklike environment, this 80-bed facility provides short-term treatments for adults, children, and adolescents suffering with mental illness or chemical dependency. Some of the services offered are a Masters and Johnson Trauma and Dissociative Disorders program, eating disorders treatment, on-site accredited school program, and free assessments.

Underlining its treatment is a commitment to safety and confidentiality. The center is CHAMPUS approved and has received accreditation with commendation from JCAHO. Diagnosis and treatment are available 24 hours a day, seven days a week.

WESTERN MISSOURI MENTAL HEALTH CENTER
1000 E. 24th St.
(816) 512-7000
www.med.umkc.edu

This academic training and research center provides acute care to the seriously mentally ill in its role as the regional inpatient and emergency psychiatric hospital for the state of Missouri and the University of Missouri–Kansas City School of Medicine. The center also operates supervised housing, prevocational services, and outpatient substance abuse treatment.

RETIREMENT

We'll be the first to admit that Kansas City hasn't made its reputation as the retirement center of the universe. Maybe we should. After all, the wonderful attributes that make this town great for families—low cost of living, a wealth of recreational choices, vibrant arts and culture environment, friendly people, and excellent health care options—make it a terrific place to retire. And if you're leaving one career and thinking about starting another, our network of college courses and entrepreneurial programs will help you get started, you young whippersnapper, you.

Best of all, we treat older Americans as the gems they are. Want proof? The Shepherds Centers of America started right here in Kansas City. This seniors-helping-seniors program helps participants maintain independent and productive lifestyles while they enjoy newfound creative outlets. Activities range from meal delivery, to legal counseling, to classes in art, to writing, to travel. Today the concept has been copied at more than a hundred centers nationwide, with new sites opening every year.

Kansas City is also home to one of the country's most respected retirement communities, John Knox Village, which has been instrumental in developing programs and excellent living options for seniors for more than 30 years. In fact, our senior communities are so stellar, Mom and Dad might have to fight off their kids wanting to move in with them. Again.

You'll find the right living arrangement to fit your lifestyle, including luxurious villas with a health club, salon, and garden outside your door; assisted care facilities; and even services that care for patients with Alzheimer's.

Let's take a look at all the services and programs available for our mature residents. You might find yourself fudging on your birth certificate just to be able to participate.

Opportunities are listed in alphabetical order by category, followed by a Retirement Communities section. Organizations are located in Kansas City, Missouri, unless otherwise noted.

EDUCATION

It's never too late to learn. Teachers and professors adore having mature students in the classroom to provide a unique view on a subject and serve as role models for the younger generation. Many of our universities and colleges offer discounts to seniors; check out "Colleges and Universities" in this chapter's Higher Education section. In addition, our parks and recreation departments offer educational programs in everything from art to tap dancing. You'll find individual listings in the Parks, Lakes, and Recreation chapter.

And if you live in Johnson County, you're really in luck; there's a club just for you at JCCC. Read on.

BROWN & GOLD CLUB
Johnson County Community College
12345 College Blvd.
Overland Park, KS
(913) 469-8500, ext. 4305
www.jccc.edu/brownandgold
If you're a Johnson County resident age 55 and older, this is your ticket to ride. For a mere $10 a year you can take credit classes free (some restrictions apply), get discounted fees for continuing education courses, and attend parties, special lectures, and events throughout the year. Since the club began in 1972, more than 5,000 members have joined. Programs include travel, from trips as close as Overland Park's New Theatre Restaurant

to a 10-day Caribbean cruise; social events such as a dance for St. Valentine's Day; special lectures; and discounted or free tickets to entertainment at the college's Carlsen Center. It's enough to make you lie about your age.

SENIORNET
Johnson County Community College
(913) 469-2323
www.seniornet.org
Keep in touch with friends around the world, learn more about health issues, or sell your rocking chair on eBay. Older Americans are jumping onto the computer with help from programs like SeniorNet. This nonprofit organization provides computer instruction and access to an online network in an easy-to-learn and fun environment.

SeniorNet has more than 22,000 members in the Western Hemisphere and more than 125 sites across the country. In the Kansas City area, classes are taught at several locations, including KCPT, the public television station, and the Johnson County Community College campus in Overland Park. Membership is $35 a year. For information or to join, contact the area coordinator, John Duff, at the number shown above.

RECREATION

In Kansas City, seniors can keep active and healthy, thanks to a plentitude of programs through organizations like banks and savings and loans. Check with yours to see if they host travel groups and special events. Several area hospitals also offer programs specifically geared toward older citizens. These include free or reduced-cost health screenings and classes for CPR, fitness, and nutrition. For more information see the Health Care and Wellness chapter.

Our parks and recreation departments provide dozens of programs for seniors. Each county has its own parks and rec department; you'll find them listed in Parks, Lakes, and Recreation.

CLASSIC SENIOR GAMES
Jackson County Parks and Recreation
(816) 795-8200, ext. 1278

Each September, this Olympic-style event brings out the competitive nature in men and women who don't feel 50 years old. But that's the minimum age for these games; you'll also see plenty of participants pushing 80. Sports include swimming, tennis, track and field, and horseshoes. Medals are awarded for a variety of categories. This four-day event is recognized by the United States National Senior Sports Organization.

i One of the best ways to make friends in Kansas City is through volunteering, and perhaps there's no better place to lend a hand than at your friendly neighborhood hospital. You can serve as an escort for patients or even as a rocker in the nursery!

50 PLUS PROGRAM
Johnson County Park and Recreation District
(913) 831-3355
www.jcprd.com, www.50plusprogram.com
Arts and crafts classes, group travel, cards and games, gardening . . . do these folks ever slow down? Johnson County's 50 Plus Program offers so many classes and events there's no time to grow old and creaky. A recent list of springtime activities included West Coast Swing, Latin Rhythm Workout, Working with Digital Photography, Hands-On Investing, Basic Spanish, and a rather curious class, New Spouse Checklist. Travel opportunities have included trips to China and the Yangtze River, Spain and Portugal, and Branson, Missouri.

Other programs include regular health screenings at reduced or no cost, CPR training, yoga, and joining friends for regular nature walks. What are you waiting for?

SENIOR ARTS COUNCIL
(913) 897-4165
www.kckpl.lib.ks.us
This group began in 1977 as a way for senior arts and crafters to showcase their talent and continue to learn new creative skills. Each meeting, held the last Monday of each month at 1 p.m., includes a guest artist or speaker. The fee is $10.

SENIOR PEERS ACTIVELY RENEWING KNOWLEDGE (SPARK)
4825 Troost
(816) 235-2870
www.umkc.edu/spark

You've got to love this acronym, eh, Sparky? This program, hosted by the University of Missouri–Kansas City and affiliated with Elderhostel Institute for Learning in Retirement, provides courses each summer at the school's campus. Noncredit courses touch on such topics as computers, the Internet, Spanish, music, and Kansas City history.

Most classes meet once a week for four, six, or eight periods. An annual SPARK membership costs $51 and includes three classes and admission to various social activities throughout the year. There is a fee, usually around $10, for each additional class. Call the number above for more information. Persons with speech or hearing impairment may call Relay Missouri at (800) 735-2966 (TT), or (800) 735-2466 (voice).

SHEPHERD'S CENTER OF KANSAS CITY CENTRAL
5200 Oak (and other locations)
(816) 444-1121
www.shepherdcenters.org

The Shepherd's Center movement was started in 1972 by 25 Catholic, Jewish, and Protestant congregations in one area of Kansas City. The goal was to create programs that would enrich the lives of seniors, help them to remain independent, and to celebrate life.

The first center was a smashing success from the start. Each Friday, 400 to 500 men and women took classes on everything from painting and journaling to learning to play bridge. Soon the center was helping 4,000 people stay active and engaged in life. The genius of the program is that it is an interfaith ministry by and with older adults rather than a ministry to them. Many of the programs are taught by senior volunteers.

Shepherd's Center soon became a model for other programs throughout the country, and an ad hoc committee was formed in 1973 to respond to requests from other communities. The Shepherd's Centers of America was incorporated a year later. Today this organization coordinates nearly 100 independent Shepherd's Centers throughout the country. Centers in the Kansas City area provide classes in foreign language, computers, tai chi, and creative writing; there are dozens of classes and groups.

In addition, senior volunteers go into the community to help their neighbors. A few of the 25 services are Meals on Wheels to deliver a hot noontime meal to those who can't leave their homes; Wheels That Care, providing free transportation to doctor's visits, pharmacies, and grocery stores; Respite Care to offer short-term relief for caregivers of homebound loved ones; and Care Home Contacts, to visit nursing home residents who don't have family or friends. There are other Shepherd's Centers throughout the city. Contact the number above or go online to learn more.

SERVICES

AMERICAN ASSOCIATION OF RETIRED PERSONS
700 W. 47th St., Suite 110
(866) 389-5627
www.aarp.org

It's a rite of passage: Turn 50 and get a big packet of information from AARP. Frankly, we can't imagine anyone who would say no to this collection of benefits for $12.50 a year. A sampling includes discounts on everything from lodging and car rentals to cruises and information and resources on health, fitness, and insurance, as well as legal and consumer issues. And with more than 30 million members, AARP is the largest advocacy group for older adults in the United States.

Joining the local chapter will net you invitations to social events, provide opportunities to volunteer your time and expertise, give you access to the organization's home-delivery prescription drug service, and much more. Plus, your spouse gets in free whether he or she is 50 or not. Membership also includes subscriptions to the monthly *AARP Bulletin* and the bimonthly *Modern Maturity*.

AARP'S 55 ALIVE/MATURE DRIVING PROGRAM
700 W. 47th St., Suite 110
(866) 389-5627
www.aarp.org

This program is just what is says: teaching older Americans how to drive defensively. The comprehensive, eight-hour course covers topics such as age-related changes that can affect vision, hearing, and physical strength. Check with your auto insurance carrier; some agencies provide discounts to seniors who have completed the course.

AREA AGENCY ON AGING–JOHNSON COUNTY
11875 S. Sunset, Suite 200
Olathe, KS
(913) 894-8811 (press "1" for Aging Information)
www.jocoks.com/humanservices-aging

The goal of the AAA is to help older adults in Johnson County maintain independence and dignity in their own homes and in the community. A few of the programs include in-home services such as minor repairs and preparing for winter; noon meals and fellowship at senior centers and through home-delivered meals for homebound seniors; legal services and insurance counseling; and client assessment referral and evaluation (CARE), which provides preadmission assessments for persons considering nursing facilities or long-term care services. In addition, the Catch-a-Ride program (913-477-8105) provides older adults and persons with disabilities with a free ride to grocery stores, senior centers, and health care appointments.

AREA AGENCY ON AGING–KANSAS CITY
600 Broadway, 300 Rivergate Center
(816) 474-4240
www.marc.org

This initiative of the Mid-America Regional Council serves older residents in Cass, Clay, Jackson, Platte, and Ray Counties in Missouri. Some of the programs and services include providing hot meals and activities at senior centers; delivering meals to residents who are unable to leave their homes; offering adult day care services and homemaker and personal care services such as grocery shopping; providing transportation to medical appointments, and offering advocacy in legal and consumer situations.

Generally, the MARC adult programs are available to those age 60 and over, regardless of income. There are no predetermined fee scales, but participants are encouraged to make voluntary contributions to offset the cost of the services they receive. In addition, a limited number of programs are available to those between the ages of 18 and 59 with significant disabilities.

VOLUNTEERING

That friendly face who shows you to your seat at the ballet? That's a volunteer, and not only does she get to meet new people and contribute to the community, she gets a free seat for the *Nutcracker*. Pretty sweet, indeed. Kansas City provides thousands of opportunities for seniors to donate time, talent, and expertise. You've read about some of them here, such as the seniors-helping-seniors programs through the Shepherd's Centers. In addition mature adults can mentor at-risk youth, read to little kids, teach English to immigrants, and yes, serve as ushers or guides at one of our many cultural centers. Call your favorite venue found in The Arts chapter; chances are they're holding a nifty uniform in just your size.

Following are other worthwhile volunteer opportunities.

CATHOLIC CHARITIES
(913) 621-1504
2220 Central Ave.
Kansas City, KS
www.catholiccharitiesks.org

The volunteer opportunities at this organization are as big as your heart. This nondenominational group is always grateful for people who serve at community kitchens, read to small children, mentor youths in need, set up households for immigrants, and serve as hospice caregivers. Catholic Charities helps more than 75,000 people every year; you can make it 75,001.

HEART OF AMERICA UNITED WAY

(816) 235-6675

www.hauw.org

The umbrella organization services hundreds of not-for-profit groups throughout the greater Kansas City area and serves as a resource center for volunteer opportunities. Give them a call to match your talents with a need, or show up at their annual Day of Caring, held every June. This communitywide service event mobilizes volunteers from over 126 companies, federal agencies, and labor unions.

i One of the best ways to stay active is to volunteer. Share your expertise as a SCORE volunteer, serve as an usher, serve at a soup kitchen, or pull weeds at a community garden. You'll find opportunities in this section, or contact the Heart of America United Way (816-235-6675), which can match your interests with an organization that needs you.

RETIRED & SENIOR VOLUNTEER PROGRAM (RSVP)

www.hauw.org/rsvp

This program gives seniors a chance to learn new skills and share their expertise with others while making new friends through volunteering. Opportunities include serving as ambassador at the airport, becoming a resource guide at Union Station, or mentoring students at area schools. Contact the United Way at Jackson, Clay, and Platt Counties at (816) 474-5111, ext. 245; in Wyandotte County it's (913) 371-3674. Or call the Johnson County Volunteer Center, (913) 341-1792.

THE SERVICE CORPS OF RETIRED EXECUTIVES (SCORE)

4747 Troost

(816) 235-6675

www.scorekc.org

If you've ever run a company, managed a department, or written a brochure, someone in the business world needs your talents. This organization pairs retired executives with small business owners in need of advice. Sponsored by the Small Business Administration, the program has experts in virtually every area of free enterprise, including management, finance, marketing, and human resources.

The Kansas City chapter's volunteers join more than 11,500 nationwide who donate their time and talent to help nearly 300,000 entrepreneurs every year. The satisfaction that you helped should be enough, but sometimes there are more immediate bonuses, like the one a businessman in Johnson County who provided advice to a young woman starting a candy company got. He has enough chocolate to last another lifetime.

RETIREMENT COMMUNITIES

JOHN KNOX VILLAGE

400 Northwest Murray Rd.

Lee's Summit, MO

(816) 524-8400, (800) 892-5669

www.johnknoxvillage.org

This 40-acre retirement community is practically its own town. Residents find everything they could need or want for the best years of their lives, including a variety of housing options, a maintenance-free lifestyle, plenty of activities, and a full continuum of health care services.

There are nearly 15,000 homes at John Knox, providing more than 70 floor plans including apartments, cottages, duplexes, town houses, and single-family homes. All maintenance and utilities (except telephone) are included in a monthly fee. No shoveling snow or cutting the lawn, but many of the residents enjoy tending the garden. And with all those chores done for you, you'll have more time to enjoy the fitness center, two swimming pools, fishing lake, nine-hole golf course, bowling alley, and 2,000-seat pavilion for dances and shows.

The Village also offers plenty of choices when it comes to dining. The Villager Restaurant has sit-down table service and a Sunday Family Brunch once a month. A more casual choice is the cafeteria-style dining room with a spectacular view of the golf course and lake. And for date night, take your sweetie to the Fireside Dining Room, with dishes that range from soup and sandwiches to grilled tuna steak.

Part of the real joy of living here are the ongoing activities like craft lessons, musical groups, a variety of clubs to join, and trips to take as a group. Security is another benefit; the campus has its own security force with officers patrolling the area 24 hours a day, 365 days a year. Residents also have access to health and wellness programs and services, including nutritional and rehabilitation services. And because John Knox Village is a continuing care retirement community, it also offers access to 24-hour nursing care, an assisted living facility, a fully accredited, 430-bed skilled nursing center complete with an Alzheimer's unit, a physician's clinic, and the adjacent 102-bed acute care Lee's Summit Hospital, all on the campus.

Residents may choose to pay an annual rental fee or enter into an entry fee agreement that's available in four different levels of care.

i One of the best things about turning 60 in Johnson County is getting a free subscription to *Best Times*. This monthly publication of Aging International Action of Johnson County provides information about services and events for seniors. Call (913) 477-8242 for subscriptions.

TOWN VILLAGE LEAWOOD
4400 W. 115th St.
Leawood, KS
(913) 491-3681
www.townvillage.com
You've got a lot of living to do, and Town Village is just the place to enjoy it. It's close to entertainment, outdoor activities like parks and golf courses, and some of the best shopping and restaurants in the region, so you'll have plenty to keep you busy. But you might find yourself spending most of your time at this campus,

especially once you taste the four-star quality food served in the light-filled dining room. No mush here; how about Cornish game hens, trout amandine, chicken stir-fry, or another one of the delicious entrees that rotate on a four-week cycle, so diners are never bored.

Other amenities include arts and crafts, an indoor pool, resident gardening area, fitness center, and a Cultural Guild, which brings in artists, musicians, and actors to entertain the residents. Spacious apartments are available, from studios through two-bedroom, two-bath homes.

VILLAGE SHALOM
5500 W. 123rd St.
Overland Park, KS
(913) 317-2600
www.villageshalom.org
A retirement village with its own award-winning art gallery? This beautiful campus in south Johnson County was designed as a nurturing—even exciting—environment for seniors. Near the Jewish Community Campus, Menorah Medical Center, and a number of activities, it provides fellowship for those who value Jewish traditions. The villas, apartments, and suites are beautifully designed for comfort and luxury, and the grounds are landscaped with lovely gardens and walking paths. Community-oriented services include Rachel's Cafe, a kosher dining room; a day spa; and the ElderSpa Wellness Center. The Epsten Gallery is a two-story, museum-quality art showroom that features exhibits from around the world. In addition, within the community are a full-service bank, children's outdoor playground for visiting family members, and a social hall and synagogue.

Village Shalom offers maintenance-free villas, apartments, and Shalom Suites, which provide assisted living or skilled nursing services. The Weinberg Health Center has additional facilities to meet the special needs of those residents with Alzheimer's and other diseases.

MEDIA

Perhaps Kansas Citians have so many media choices because more than half of us live in the Show-Me State. Our need-to-know mentality can be appeased through a breathtaking variety of ways, including a daily newspaper, a handful of weeklies, 10 television stations, 20 FM and 23 AM radio stations, and a growing list of public interest Web sites. And whatever your livelihood or hobby, from golf to computers, fine dining to fitness, chances are there's a special-interest publication to help you do it better, find out where to enjoy it, or at least commune with others who share your passion.

Following are some of our more interesting means of communicating, listed by category.

DAILIES

THE EXAMINER
410 S. Liberty
Independence, MO
(816) 254-8600
www.examiner.net
This newspaper serves the towns of Independence, Blue Springs, and Grain Valley. Published Tues through Sat.

THE KANSAS CITY STAR
1729 Grand
(816) 234-7827
www.kansascity.com, www.kcstar.com
Although the *Star* is the only daily newspaper that serves the entire metroplex, it has never used its "only game in town" status to deliver less-than-stellar reporting. It mirrors our town's tragedies and triumphs with insight and depth. The Thursday Preview provides a week's worth of entertainment and arts coverage throughout the region. The *Sunday Star Magazine* brings us profiles of people, places, and events in our area worth a closer look.

THE OLATHE DAILY NEWS
514 S. Kansas
Olathe, KS
(913) 764-2211
www.olathedailynews.com

This community paper is the place to find news about local schools, business, and social events in the booming southwest region of the metroplex. It's published on Wed and Sat.

i Along with the *Kansas City Star*, the Nelson-Atkins Museum of Art, and our city's many boulevards, parks, and gardens, William Rockhill Nelson left another, more furry legacy. He imported squirrels from neighboring states and let them loose in Kansas City's new green spaces. So some fall, as you're watching the long-tailed creatures leap around in search of acorns, you can say, "Nuts to you, Mr. Nelson."

WEEKLIES

THE BUSINESS JOURNAL
1100 Main St., Suite 210
(816) 421-5900
www.bizjournals.com/kansascity
Kansas City's edition of American City Business Journals Inc. is delivered to nearly 11,000 offices each Friday. Its editorial focus—banking, sales and marketing, business owner profiles, growth strategies—is geared to decision makers in companies with fewer than 100 employees.

THE CALL
1715 E. 18th St.
(816) 842-3804
www.kccall.com

"We call it like it is" was the motto of Chester A. Franklin, an ambitious businessman and community activist who founded one of the nation's most respected African-American papers in 1919. The paper quickly developed a reputation as an advocate for social justice, with articles about lynchings, police brutality, segregation, and discrimination in housing and employment.

THE INDEPENDENT
4233 Roanoke Rd.
(816) 471-2800
www.kcindependent.com

If you're anyone in Kansas City society, your engagement, wedding, and birth announcements will have been covered by the city's oldest magazine; if your last name appears on a street sign, building, or museum anywhere in town, chances are your photo accompanied the write-up. Since 1899 the city's crème de la crème have turned these oversized black-and-white pages to see who wore what designer's gown to the latest ball or to muse about gentle gossip in "Over My Shoulder." The readership represents Kansas City's most influential, active, and civic-minded citizens . . . and certainly some of its most affluent. The *Independent* arrives in polished brass mailboxes on Saturday morning 45 times a year and is available at a select number of newsstands.

THE LEAVEN
12615 Parallel Pkwy.
Kansas City, KS
(913) 721-1570
www.theleaven.com

The weekly newspaper of the Archdiocese of Kansas City in Kansas is distributed free to families who belong to Catholic parishes throughout Wyandotte, Johnson, and Leavenworth Counties. Each issue covers national and local news, book reviews, and a calendar that lists upcoming social and educational events, retreats, and meetings.

THE PITCH
1701 Main St.
(816) 561-6061
www.pitch.com

This free weekly with an 80,000 circulation is the city's most recognized alternative tabloid. The editor boasts that the paper is dedicated to "hard-hitting journalism, smart criticism, lively features, and good old-fashioned muckraking," but the real reason folks pick it up is to see what band is playing at Knuckleheads or what food critic Charles Ferruzza thinks of the new restaurant in town. Its calendar offers the area's most complete coverage of live music, dance, and theater (including some in Lawrence, Kansas, a college town about half an hour away). Even the ads are pretty entertaining; here's where to find outlets for any vice from martinis to water pipes, sexy lingerie to sex partners.

The annual Best of Kansas City issue—usually in mid-October—has the typical "best brunch" categories along with a few fresh options such as best guilty pleasure. Just thinking about those answers gives us goosebumps. The paper's online incarnation provides a repeat of the printed page with added links to other sites, Web-exclusive features, essays, and blogs that will make you blush. The writing style is not for the timid.

MAGAZINES

INGRAM'S
2049 Wyandotte St.
(816) 842-9994
www.ingramsonline.com

For more than a century this monthly, and its predecessor, *Corporate Report*, has been a staple among area business leaders. The magazine does a fine job at promoting Kansas City's strengths by profiling a geographical portion of the city including schools, economic growth, and real estate options. There's stiff competition to make the magazine's annual Corporate Report 100, a list of Kansas City's fastest-growing companies, and perhaps even tougher competition for the annual best-of survey published each August.

KC BUSINESS
7101 College Blvd.
(913) 894-6923
www.midwestceo.com

Here's where to find the city's movers and shakers, the leaders who shape the metro. The editorial delves into the "why" beyond just the "who." Along with covering the business side of our town, this monthly publication takes a look at why we all work so hard; it features lifestyle elements such as fashion, cars, and entertaining. Annual must-reads include the list of Influential Women and KC Business Rising Stars.

KC MAGAZINE
7101 College Blvd.
Overland Park, KS
(913) 894-6923
www.kcmag.com

Every city has one: a glossy magazine that celebrates the region's most interesting people and places. Published monthly, each issue offers late-breaking takes on around-town happenings, profiles of hometown celebrities, tips on making your space more livable, and handy guides to restaurants and events. Naturally it showcases the most glittering parties in town, giving readers a "who-wore-what" replay. Once a year the magazine publishes the Best of Kansas City survey in which community readers provide their own favorites along with readers' top picks.

KANSAS CITY HOMES AND GARDENS
4121 W. 83rd St.
Prairie Village, KS
(913) 648-5757
www.kchomesandgardens.com

The fact that Kansas City can support two home and garden magazines is testament to our appreciation for graceful living, lovely gardens, and gracious entertaining. This magazine also has a lake living section to appease the hundreds of residents who spend summer weekends at the Lake of the Ozarks, four hours south of Kansas City.

SPECIAL INTEREST PERIODICALS

CAMP
1600 Genessee, Suite 525
www.campkc.com

A print and online resource for the local (and growing) lesbian, gay, bisexual, and transgender community, *Camp* covers arts and entertainment, previews upcoming events such as the Gay Pride Parade, and touches on health and social issues. The publication also offers a roster of businesses that cater to and support this thriving group. Reporters also sign in on travel destinations that are gay friendly. The tabloid is available at bookstands and musical venues throughout the city.

DOS MUNDOS
902-A Southwest Blvd.
(816) 221-4747
www.dosmundos.com

Dos Mundos, or *Two Worlds*, has provided a bilingual forum for Kansas City's vibrant and growing Hispanic population since 1981; 80 to 90 percent of the information is translated. The readership is diverse: Of the more than 125,000 Hispanics living in the Kansas City metropolitan area, only about 60 percent are of Mexican origin. The remainder are mostly Puerto Ricans and Cubans. Along with national news, *Dos Mundos* covers local news, sports, and entertainment and provides a much-needed focus on Hispanic heritage.

JAM (JAZZ AMBASSADORS MAGAZINE)
P.O. Box 36181
Kansas City, MO 64171
(913) 967-6767
www.kcjam.org

One of the finest regional jazz magazines in the country, *JAM* has covered the Kansas City jazz scene since 1986. It is distributed free to 500-plus Kansas City Jazz Ambassador members (one more great reason to join this organization), and available free at local jazz venues, record stores, bookstores, and libraries. Whether your musical taste runs to jazz, Dixieland, or bebop, *JAM* is the

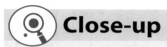

Close-up

William Rockhill Nelson

Many of us read all about it in the *Kansas City Star*, the venerable newspaper founded by William Rockhill Nelson on September 18, 1880. In Kansas City this newspaperman from Indiana saw a town where he could make both money and a difference—and he eventually did both. His other legacies include our park and boulevard systems and the art gallery that bears his name.

Nelson quickly showed his business acumen by charging 2 cents for his paper instead of the nickel that the other three dailies already in print did. The last of his competitors, the *Kansas City Journal*, held on until 1942. As Nelson's fame and legend grew—thanks in great part to his unconventional tastes and famed battles with the establishment—he was often interviewed by national magazines like the *Saturday Evening Post*. Theodore Roosevelt became a personal friend who often came to Kansas City to seek his advice.

Nelson's paper's reach expanded along with his waistline when in 1891 he delivered the *Weekly Kansas City Star* to country towns throughout Kansas, Missouri, Nebraska, Colorado, and Oklahoma. For 25 cents a year subscribers were treated to reprints from the daily *Star* and the editor's political views.

By 1901 he had purchased the *Kansas City Times*, a morning daily, and began calling his empire "the twenty-four-hour *Star*." The *Star*'s afternoon edition ceased in 1990. In 1911 the paper moved to its current location, a redbrick Italian Renaissance–style building at 18th and Grand where there were no private offices. Nelson said the layout was designed so that everyone could feel equal; employees knew it was so the boss could keep his eyes on them.

By the time he died on April 13, 1915, Nelson's fortune was estimated at between $5 million and $10 million and the Star's circulation was more than 200,000. His will stipulated that after the death of his heirs the entire fortune would be converted to cash and given to the arts. His majestic home, Oak Hall, is now the site of the Nelson-Atkins Gallery of Art. He had already made our city a work of art; he used his paper to campaign for paved roads and streets, sidewalks, and streetlights. And he was instrumental in creating the city's parks system in 1881 when he hired landscaper George E. Kessler to design a boulevard and park system that is still considered one of the finest in the world.

As for the *Star*, Nelson thought it couldn't continue without him. But survive it has, and has thrived under the helm of talented and forward-thinking managers and through the pens of award-winning journalists. Its reporters and editors have won eight Pulitzer Prizes and four Polk Awards. Yet its most famous reporter wasn't around long enough to earn more than a paycheck: Ernest Hemingway joined the staff in October 1917 but left the next April to drive ambulances in the war. Hemingway credited a *Star* editor, C. G. "Pete" Wellington, with teaching him to write clearly and provocatively. The paper's style sheet at the time admonished, "Use short sentences. Use short first paragraphs. Use vigorous English." Okay.

When Nelson's daughter, Laura Nelson Kirkwood, died in 1926, the paper was sold in accordance with his will. With financial help from her husband, Irwin, thirty *Star* employees purchased the paper for $11 million. In 1977 it was sold to Capital Cities Communications Inc. for $125 million; it later became part of the Knight-Ridder chain, and today it is part of the McClatchy family.

place to find where musicians are jamming at nightclubs and festivals, learn more about our town's musical heritage, and read where to board the bus for the next pub crawl. *JAM* is produced in even-numbered months.

KANSAS CITY SMALL BUSINESS MONTHLY
P.O. Box 754
Shawnee Mission, KS 66201
(913) 432-6690
www.kcsmallbiz.com

Small and emerging businesses in the area have a friend in publisher/editor Kelly Scanlon. Her monthly tabloid covers need-to-know topics such as how to keep employees happy, cope with rising health care costs, decide whether to incorporate, measure trade show results, market globally, and write a sales script. And that was just October. Each issue also profiles a successful business, provides strategies for home offices, and includes a comprehensive calendar of seminars and events. The annual "Entrepreneur's Guide" is a keeper, covering legal, marketing, e-commerce, taxes, real estate, education, and training subjects. *Small Business Monthly* is distributed free to qualified readers and is available by subscription.

TELEVISION

Along with cable programming, Kansas City supports nine local stations, including network affili-ates and one independent station. The stations are listed along with their non-cable channels. Kansas City also has two cable companies, Time Warner and Comcast.

WDAF Channel 4 (Fox)
KCTV Channel 5 (CBS)
KMBC Channel 9 (ABC)
KCPT Channel 19 (PBS)
KCWE Channel 29 (CW)
KSHB Channel 41 (NBC)
KPXE Channel 50 (ION)
KSMO Channel 62 (MyNetworkTV)

RADIO

A few stations offer jazz programming at various times throughout the week, and KCIY–FM 106.5 provides what it calls "smooth jazz" from a variety of contemporary artists like Diana Krall and David Sanborn. Classical music lovers also go wanting in Kansas City, since its only all-classical station, KXTR, left its FM status in 2000. It now has far less reach on its new home at KXTR, 1660 AM.

Drive-time listeners hoping to get away from the in-your-face ramblings of radio personalities can tune to KCUR–FM 89.3, a noncommercial station that broadcasts National Public Radio locally produced programs.

INDEX